JOHN
TASKER
HOWARD

WITH THE ASSISTANCE OF
ARTHUR MENDEL

Our Contemporary Composers

AMERICAN MUSIC IN THE
TWENTIETH CENTURY

1941

THOMAS Y. CROWELL COMPANY

NEW YORK

COPYRIGHT 1941
by John Tasker Howard

MANUFACTURED IN THE UNITED STATES OF AMERICA
BY THE VAIL-BALLOU PRESS, BINGHAMTON, NEW YORK

*All rights reserved. No part of this book may
be reproduced in any form except by a reviewer
who may quote brief passages in a review to be
printed in a magazine or newspaper*

To R. H. H.

PREFACE

TEN years have passed since the appearance of the author's first book, *Our American Music*. That volume dealt with our historical development through three centuries, and after treating of the background and the lives and works of our earliest and nineteenth-century composers, discussed the music of our contemporaries, to 1930.

In the single decade since that time, so much of significance has taken place, so many new composers have appeared, viewpoints and conditions have changed so materially, that the need for a supplementary and companion volume has already become apparent; for a book dealing exclusively with recent and present-day American music and its composers—in short, with OUR CONTEMPORARY COMPOSERS.

Anticipating this need, the author started work on such a volume several years ago, intending that it be ready for publication in 1938 or 1939. Illness delayed his progress, however, and although recovery is now complete, this incapacity was of such duration that it was thought wiser to seek aid in finishing the book, rather than to delay its completion and publication for too long a period.

For this purpose the author sought the assistance of his friend and colleague, Mr. Arthur Mendel, who has borne a considerable share of the writing in the last four chapters, mostly from notes and material which the author himself had previously assembled. Through long association and through frequent consultation, Mr. Mendel is thoroughly acquainted with the author's viewpoints and opinions, and has been willing to present them rather than his own. For this, as well as for his labors, the author extends his sincere thanks.

In the matter of opinion, however, while the personal viewpoint of the author is of course essential to any work that aims at discussion of trends and idiomatic tendencies, he has felt in many cases that his personal opinions should be supplemented by, and even subordinated to, the best critical attitude of the present day towards its own music. Hence, quotations from reviewers of the daily press are frequently inserted, particularly those following première performances of important works. The research worker of the future may have rare sport from learning how we have overpraised our then-forgotten composers, and derided and belittled our Mozarts and Wagners.

As for the content of this book: an earnest attempt has been made to render it as comprehensive as possible, to include all those who have made themselves known for works in the larger forms. With the exception of Charles T. Griffes, who was so in advance of his time that he belongs to the present day, it has seemed superfluous to include lengthy discussion of composers who had passed from the scene before *Our American Music* was written, and whose lives and works are fully treated in that volume. Consequently, such men as Edward MacDowell, Horatio Parker, and others, are mentioned only for their influence on more recent musicians. In the field of light music, the same is true with Victor Herbert and John Philip Sousa.

It has also seemed unwise to lengthen these pages with detailed discussion of composers who are known exclusively or principally for shorter works—songs, teaching pieces, etc. The American song and its composers are treated fully in such books as William Treat Upton's *Art Song in America*. Hence, such estimable writers as Oley Speaks, Geoffrey O'Hara, Wintter Watts, and others, are not represented here. Some of the Broadway songsmiths are included, it is true, but in most cases for the effect their work is having on the nationalist expression of our symphonists rather than for their actual songs.

PREFACE

There are many whom we should like to thank for helpful co-operation in preparing the material for this volume. Our gratitude goes particularly to the composers who have answered the detailed and rather impertinent questionnaires which were sent them. These have been most helpful in gaining the composers' own viewpoints towards their work, and for showing what they are seeking to accomplish.

JOHN TASKER HOWARD

Glen Ridge, N.J.,
January, 1941

CONTENTS

1. From Yesterday to Today 3
2. Bridges to the Past. 10
3. Safe and Sound 23
    Henry Kimball Hadley 23
    Deems Taylor 27
    John Alden Carpenter 35
    Daniel Gregory Mason 40
    David Stanley Smith 45
    Charles Wakefield Cadman 47
    Sons of Harvard 53
    Ernest Schelling 62
    Richard Hageman 64
    From West of the Alleghenies 65
    Women Composers 72
    Howard Hanson 74
    Leo Sowerby 80
    Albert Stoessel 82
    Douglas Moore 85
    Seth Bingham 90
    Abram Chasins 91
    Samuel Barlow 92
    Werner Janssen 94
    Bernard Rogers 97
    Horace Johnson 98

CONTENTS

    Harold Morris 99
    Randall Thompson 109
    Composer Performers 111

4. UNFAMILIAR IDIOMS 114
    Pioneer Free-Thinkers 115
    Roy Harris 132
    Aaron Copland 145
    Louis Gruenberg 150
    Emerson Whithorne 155
    Walter Piston 159
    Quincy Porter 161
    Richard Donovan 162
    Richard Hammond 163
    Lazare Saminsky 164
    Frederick Jacobi 167
    Roger Sessions 169
    Philip James 171
    Bernard Wagenaar 174
    Werner Josten 176
    John Duke 178
    Harl McDonald 179
    Arthur Shepherd 181
    Some Other Middle-Westerners 183
    Nicolai Berezowsky 184
    Otto Luening 186
    Ernst Bacon 187
    Exotics by Birth or Choice 188
    Marion Bauer 192

5. NEWCOMERS 207
    Juilliard Alumni 208
    The Eastman Group 214

CONTENTS

	From the Curtis Institute	. 220
	From Other Schools and Teachers	. 224
	Dante Fiorillo	. 228

6. EXPERIMENTERS 237
    Scientific Innovators 238
    Unicorn and Lion 241
    Atonalists 248
    "New Music" 250
    From France 252
    The Clever Ones 256

7. FOLK-SONG AND RACIAL EXPRESSIONS 267
    From Indian Sources 268
    The Anglo-Saxon Heritage 270
    Negro Composers 277

8. BROADWAY AND ITS ECHOES 284
    Jazz 286
    "Swing" and its Performers 290
    Broadway Composers 296
    Jazz in the Concert Hall 304
    Further Echoes of Broadway 313

9. TODAY AND TOMORROW 321
    Philanthropic Foundations 324
    Composers' Organizations 326
    Music During the Depression 329
    The Federal Music Project 330
    Other Institutions in the 1930's 332
    Radio and Sound Films 334
    ASCAP and Payment for Performing Rights . . 335
    Grand Rights 340
    The NAACC 342

CONTENTS

Performances by Major Orchestras 343
Recent Recruits 345

APPENDIX:
1. A Selected List of Books Relating to Contemporary American Music 349
2. Recorded Works by American Composers . . 351
3. List of Composers by States in Which They Were Born 372
4. Orchestral Works Which Have Received the Eastman School Publication Award 376
5. Orchestral Works Which Have Received the Juilliard Publication Award 377
6. National Broadcasting Company Commissions and Prizes 378
7. Columbia Broadcasting System Commissions . . 379
8. Composers Who Have Received Guggenheim Fellowship 381
9. Composers Who Have Been Fellows of the American Academy in Rome 382
10. Pulitzer Traveling Scholars in Music . . . 382
11. Works Issued by Society for the Publication of American Music 383
12. Works Commissioned by the League of Composers 385
13. Works Honored by the National Federation of Music Clubs 388
14. American Works Performed at the Festivals of the International Society for Contemporary Music . . 389

INDEX 393

ILLUSTRATIONS

Howard Hanson	*Frontispiece*
George W. Chadwick	12
Deems Taylor	28
John Alden Carpenter	36
Randall Thompson	110
Roy Harris	132
Aaron Copland	146
Vittorio Giannini	208
Samuel Barber	220
Charles E. Ives	244
John Powell	270
William Grant Still	280
Jerome Kern	300
George Gershwin	308

Our Contemporary Composers

AMERICAN MUSIC IN THE
TWENTIETH CENTURY

I

FROM YESTERDAY TO TODAY

AMERICAN music is coming of age. To the quantity of music our composers have produced, particularly in recent years, the following pages are ample testimony. But it is not alone in size and bulk that these works are noteworthy; a large number of them are marked by the distinction and the individuality of their composers, and many of them seem to voice the spirit and temperament of America.

The time for an apologetic attitude towards our music has passed; we may as well be rid of our inferiority complex altogether, for we have arrived at a stage in our development where a judicious recognition of our limitations does not require, or even tolerate, any admission that our composers are inferior to their foreign colleagues. To admit that we have produced no Beethoven or Wagner is not to belittle our musical product; as a nation we were in our musical infancy (perhaps we should call it our prenatal stage) when these giants were active, and since their time Europe itself has not produced their equal. Now that the world is eagerly awaiting a new musical Messiah, America is as likely to produce him as any nation of the Old World.

Nor is it a confession of present-day mediocrity to admit that in past years American composers leaned heavily on European models. That they should have looked across the Atlantic is thoroughly understandable; our nineteenth-century composers studied abroad, principally in Germany, at a time when Continental Europe was acknowledged to be the wellspring from which all musical tradition and progress flowed. Moreover, our racial roots were not in the soil of the American continent, but in various nations of Europe.

The history of American music has been sufficiently treated elsewhere [1] not to need recounting here. This volume is to be concerned with American composers of the present day, and the degree of success with which they have interpreted their native—or in some cases, adopted—country. Suffice it to say that periodically over the past three centuries, native elements in our music have been overwhelmed by wholesale immigrations of foreigners and foreign ideas—principally after the American Revolution in the late eighteenth century; in the years around 1848, when German refugees fled the Central European revolutions; and, in our own century, after the World War.

For many years Americans were content to tolerate such a state of affairs. The fact that a native or resident composer could write music that was "correct," and sounded well, was in itself sufficiently remarkable to constitute a creditable achievement. So the last quarter of the nineteenth century saw America producing a number of serious composers, writing in the large as well as the smaller forms, but almost without exception having little that was individual to say for themselves. There was a notion, too, that music-making must be a formal and polished affair.

We had *John Knowles Paine* (1839–1906) and *Dudley Buck* (1839–1909), and the various members of the Boston group who followed them, and who are discussed in the first chapter of this volume. There had, it is true, been individualists during the nineteenth century: *Louis Moreau Gottschalk* (1829–1869); *Stephen Foster* (1826–1864), who contented himself with simple folk-songs; *Ethelbert Nevin* (1862–1901); and finally, *Edward MacDowell* (1861–1908), who was unique in being the first American composer to win recognition abroad for his works in the larger forms. But these men were indeed exceptions, and for that reason their names stand out in bold relief.

---

[1] J. T. Howard, *Our American Music* (New York: Thomas Y. Crowell Company, 1931).

So we arrived at the beginning of the twentieth century with little if any national feeling in our native music, but with an extremely vocal demand that we become nationalists overnight. With the Spanish War, the national consciousness that had been smoldering for several decades burst into flame, and there was a hue and cry that something drastic be done about our shortcomings in music as well as in the other arts. We were becoming increasingly aware that our music to date had proved little more than German, French, or Italian music composed by Americans.

With this realization the pendulum swung sharply in the opposite direction. We overlooked the fact that a composer like Stephen Foster had achieved national expression wholly unconsciously, that he had turned naturally and simply to the things he knew best without any thought of what significance his product might possess. We were confident that the situation could be immediately corrected by drastic methods.

In consequence, anything that derived from the North American continent was seized upon as fair game for adaptation. The Russian composers, the Norwegians, the Spaniards, had achieved nationalism by using their native folk-songs. All Americans needed to do—so ran the argument—was to seize upon the folk-songs of their own people. Soon there arose a group that appropriated songs of the American Indian, while others turned to the "spirituals" of the Negro, little realizing that the Indians and the Negroes are peoples with temperamental characteristics often quite different from those of the composers who used the material, and thus Indian and Negro melodies were almost as exotic as Chinese or Moroccan. Nothing in the composer of European antecedents gave him any racial sympathy for these melodies; he was bound to approach them objectively and self-consciously, except in those few instances where they had formed part of his childhood environment.

It was a Bohemian who most forcibly turned our thoughts to the treasures on our own continent. Antonin Dvořák came here as a teacher during the 1890's, and while he was with us he composed his *New World Symphony* and *American Quartet*, largely as examples of what a composer might do with native material. The fact that by using Negro- and Indian-like themes he achieved nothing more than a Bohemian's impressions of our country, and a poignant expression of his own homesickness, might have shown our composers that only a Negro or an Indian may write Negro or Indian music. Few were as analytical as that, however; the majority saw merely that Dvořák had composed truly great works on material he found here. To be American they needed only to do likewise.

The reaction, of course, was bound to come in a few decades, and with it the realization that nationalism is a deep-lying characteristic and that its expression must be spontaneous; that a pair of blunt shears is not enough to cut the tough cord that has tied us to our European cousins for several centuries. Some persons have been so conservative as to feel that the cord should not be altogether severed.

In more recent years, jazz has come into our midst, and once again some of the nationalists thought they had found in it a panacea for all our ills. It is true that jazz, and its latest offspring "swing," reflect a number of traits in our national temperament which we have accepted as being American. There is a restlessness in this music that betokens our craving to be always on the move, as well as a monotony of underlying rhythms which is nothing if not standardized. Even though most of the jazz written today is the product of the sophisticated East, produced under commercialized conditions, it nevertheless has its roots in the American soil. Originating with the Negroes, it has come to Broadway and Tin Pan Alley, and in a very real sense it has become a Jewish interpretation of the Negro. And what could be more American than such a combination, even though it does ignore those of us who have Puritan ancestors? The Mayflower must look elsewhere for a spokesman. Again, remember, jazz successfully caters to the widest American public, which unconsciously but inevitably shapes its development.

FROM YESTERDAY TO TODAY

Regardless of the geographical or even racial sources of the material our composers use, it may be well to examine what it is they must express if they are to prove the musical mouthpieces of America. In spite of its cosmopolitan character, the American people has developed a number of traits that are individual and definitely to be recognized. How successfully they can be expressed through a medium so abstract as music is another matter, but the temperamental characteristics are nevertheless present and waiting to be translated. In fact, some of our contemporary composers do seem to be definitely affected by one or several of them.

First comes our buoyancy. There is in the American disposition a carefree, jaunty attitude altogether distinct from the light-hearted moments of other nationals. It may be argued that this phase of our temperament represents the Irish in our blood, just as some feel that our thrifty countrymen show Scotch extraction. But it cannot be denied that the American, when he snaps his fingers at the Universe, shows an impertinence beyond the temerity of his foreign relatives, a daring that has come from the tradition of pioneers—bold men in a land blessed beyond most by nature and geography.

Those who profess the ability to reduce jokes to classification and formulae hold that there is a definite American humor; that just as British wit is based largely on understatement, the typical American humor rests largely on exaggeration, on the absurdity and ridiculousness of overstatement. Hence the comic strip, a thoroughly American institution.

As for our idealism, our conception of what expansive living should be in a land where every man is free to determine his own destiny, we have that too. Though each of us may have a different vision of how his ideals may be achieved, we do have ideals, whether they be material or spiritual. In the nineteenth century our idealism was expressed through sentiment; today that sentiment is tempered, but not destroyed, by twentieth-century realism.

By reputation Americans are always in a hurry. We like to call such haste a spirit of enterprise, but whatever we term it, it was probably developed by the need our ancestors felt for combating the elements and fighting for their existence in a land where the first necessity was to provide a living. Now that the material resources of the Continent are largely harnessed, we have so acquired the habit of hurry that we must still make haste to get all we can from what life offers us.

Our inventive genius has come from the enterprise of our forefathers, and America has made remarkable contributions to the mechanical and scientific progress of the world. We have created skyscrapers, subways, and machines for doing almost everything that man found drudgery. Perhaps such machines have come near to destroying us. But we have made them, and even though we are as yet unable to use them with complete wisdom, they constitute a factor that has had a definite influence in shaping the American temperament.

Our desire for standardization is another trait that seems part of the native character, one that is apparent, as has been remarked, in jazz. Our eagerness to join something, whether it be the local Rotary Club or the Daughters of the American Revolution, arises not only from a love of sociability but also from a desire to be like other Americans. It may be this craving which is at the bottom of the demand that American art be truly American, even though it is apparent that too much standardization might altogether destroy anything so incorrigibly individualistic as artistic expression.

And now that the three centuries of our occupation of the North American Continent have developed these and other traits for our literature and art to express, creative American music stands at the threshold. Exactly where the door may lead is not so easily determined. There are a number of composers and critics who can tell exactly what the American music of the future will be but unfortunately no two of them make the same prophecy.

The only recourse the student has is to open the door and look inside for himself. From what has already been accomplished, and from the aims and ideals of our individual composers, we may learn something of present and future trends. But whatever we do or do not learn about the future, we will most assuredly find that the first forty years of the twentieth century have produced a vast accumulation of native works of which Americans may well be proud.

2

BRIDGES TO THE PAST

THE years since 1930 have brought about epochal changes in American music. True, the World War and its aftermaths had an immediate effect, and our music began to show their influence during the 1920's; but it was not until the fourth decade that the younger group of composers began to feel sure of themselves, or that any but their intimates began to take them seriously and to recognize their vitality.

Particularly significant is the gradual disappearance from concert programs of works by those composers who link us with our nineteenth-century background, and who date from the time, not long distant, when the American composer was a rare specimen whose very existence was something to talk about. Throughout the post-War decade these men were our leading composers, and it was their music that set the standard of respectability and eminence. Today, however, performances of Chadwick, Parker, Foote, Mrs. Beach, and others of the "New England Group" are infrequent, and even MacDowell is suffering a neglect which in his case seems undeserved. Among his major works the Second Piano Concerto is heard occasionally, but the other orchestral works, even the noble *Indian Suite*, have passed into obscurity. MacDowell has sunk, or risen, to the level of a symbol, as the first serious American composer of definite individuality.

It is in these years, too, that a number of the older composers have died. In 1930 most of them were still living, though MacDowell and Horatio Parker, of course, had been gone for some years. The great bulk of MacDowell's work had been done before 1900. Parker lived until 1919. One of his two outstanding works, the oratorio *Hora Novissima*, was composed during 1891 and 1892, and the opera, *Mona*, was produced at New York's Metropolitan in 1912. Both are still considered highlights in American music by musicians and students, but they are seldom heard nowadays.

After 1930 *George W. Chadwick* was the first of the older group to pass on, in 1931, in his seventy-seventh year. He had been unique in blending the academic tradition with flashes of Yankee humor. Historically, he is important because he carried the banner of John Knowles Paine, the trail-blazer for all our symphonic composers. Chadwick had the craftsmanship of Paine, and beyond that a genuine spark of inspiration; in his music one hears now a sly chuckle, now the voice of real emotional warmth. Philip Hale described him as having "a certain jaunty irreverence"; there were remarks in his music that only a Yankee could have made with impunity.

He composed twenty major works for orchestra, eleven of them published during his lifetime. Of these, the *Symphonic Sketches*—with their care-free *Vagrom Ballad*—and the *Sinfonietta* are the best. There are also five string quartets, a piano quintet, an opera, *Judith*, which was produced in concert form, several operettas, considerable choral music, and over a hundred songs, of which the setting to Sidney Lanier's *Ballad of Trees and the Master* is the most notable.

Chadwick was born in Lowell, Massachusetts, on November 13, 1854. He was educated in the New England Conservatory in Boston, where he had harmony lessons with Stephen A. Emery, and then went to Berlin to study with Jadassohn. After two years he decided that he wanted more than Jadassohn could give him, and he debated whether to go to Paris and César Franck or to Munich and Rheinberger. He chose Rheinberger and from him learned what Carl Engel has termed "an orderly idea of strict composition." It is interesting to speculate on what might have happened to Chadwick and his pupils if his Yankee spirit had come into contact with the mysticism of Franck.

He returned from his studies in 1880, and started his career as a teacher. Among his early pupils were Horatio Parker, Sidney Homer, and Arthur Whiting. In 1882 he became an instructor at the New England Conservatory, and fifteen years later he was made its director. He held this position until his death, April 4, 1931.

Arthur Foote outlived Chadwick by six years. He too was definitely of New England, and during his eighty-four years of life he observed many changes and fashions in music. In his time he welcomed innovations; as a member of the program committee of the Harvard Musical Association, he fought the conservatives in demanding new works—a new symphony by Raff, perhaps, or Rubinstein, men who were modernists in their day. When he attended the first Bayreuth performances in 1876, he was entranced by the new and strangely beautiful harmonic structure of Wagner.

As he came to old age he was still sympathetic to change, but frank to admit that some of the radical methods were a little too much for him. A few months before his death he wrote: [1]

> As one of the older generation, I should hardly be expected to feel in the same way about the happenings in the past twenty-five years—about polytonality, "linear" counterpoint, etc.
>
> Dissonance and consonance seem to me to be complementary: while music entirely consonant soon becomes monotonous, that which is constantly dissonant is not only tiresome, but, worse than this, unpleasant. Dissonance is not undesirable in itself, but often becomes so because of the unskillful way in which it is used. It is rather "old hat" to bring logic into the question, but after all this does exist in music from Bach to Sibelius.

To which he added, significantly, "All in all, ours has been a great time in which to be living and to watch the development of music."

[1] "A Bostonian Remembers." *Musical Quarterly*, January, 1937.

By Pirie MacDonald

George W. Chadwick

BRIDGES TO THE PAST

His artistic integrity is proved by his steadfastness of purpose in his own music. Whatever it possessed or lacked, its style did not change with each new fashion; he knew what he wanted to say and how he wanted to say it. Thus his music was distinguished by clarity and directness, good taste and craftsmanship. To say that it is not great music is not to belittle its importance in its day.

Unlike his colleagues, Foote had not gone abroad for training. Born in Salem on March 5, 1853, he entered Harvard and became a music pupil of John Knowles Paine. Later he studied with B. J. Lang, who started him on his career as organist. Among his eight major works for orchestra, the most ambitious were the symphonic prologue, *Francesca da Rimini*, and the *Four Character Pieces after Omar Khayyam*. His choral works include *The Wreck of the Hesperus*, *The Farewell of Hiawatha*, and *The Skeleton in Armor*. Of his eight chamber music works, the rather Brahmsian Quintet is probably the most distinguished.

Recent performances of Foote's major works have been almost exclusively confined to his *Night-Piece* for flute and orchestra, originally composed sometime between 1911 and 1914, and a still earlier work, his Suite in E for strings, dating from 1909. When this was performed by the Boston Symphony Orchestra, in December of 1936, Foote was himself present, to step out on the platform with firm, unfaltering step and receive a heart-warming ovation. It was hardly four months later, on April 9, 1937, that he died.

Rubin Goldmark was not one of the Boston—or New England—Group, but his creative work belongs to the opening years of the twentieth century, and he had much in common with his neighbors to the east. A nephew of the Austrian Carl Goldmark, he was born in New York in 1872. After he had gained his academic education in New York, he studied music at the Vienna Conservatory. Then he returned to his native city to study piano with Joseffy and composition with Dvořák, who was then teaching at the National Conservatory in New York.

Aside from his creative work, most of his career was devoted to teaching composers, and from 1924 until his death, March 6, 1936, he was head of the composition department at the Juilliard Graduate School in New York. It is a tribute to the educative character of his teaching that in spite of the conservative nature of his own music, he numbered among his pupils such widely divergent types as Frederick Jacobi, Aaron Copland, Nicolai Berezowsky, Bernard Wagenaar, Vittorio Giannini, Paul Nordoff, and the late George Gershwin.

Goldmark drew on the native scene for the subjects of his most important works. His *Requiem* for orchestra was suggested by Lincoln's Gettysburg Address, and its austere grandeur and directness of purpose make it faithful to its theme. In *The Call of the Plains* for orchestra (and also for violin and piano), Goldmark caught something of the vastness of our prairies. He also tried using Negro material in his *Negro Rhapsody*, for orchestra.

Another figure who has passed away in recent years is *Mortimer Wilson*, who died January 27, 1932. Wilson, too, was important as a teacher of composition. Technically he was one of the best-equipped composers of his time. Himself a pupil of the German Max Reger, he could toss involved counterpoint from his pen as easily as he could talk to his friends. His dislike of the obvious was so great that it became a severe limitation rather than a virtue. Where he thought another composer might have extended and developed a theme, Wilson would snatch the tune away and tell the listener he could have no more of it.

He was born in Iowa, in 1876, and in his fifty-six years achieved an imposing list of published works: a suite for trio, *From My Youth*, later scored for full orchestra; two Sonatas for violin and piano; three Suites for piano; a Trio; an *Overture "1849"*; a "scenic fantasy" for orchestra, *My Country;* and many shorter pieces. He also had five symphonies in manuscript.

The opening of the fifth decade found several of the veterans still living and active. *Edgar Stillman Kelley* achieved his eightieth birthday April 14, 1937, and the following months were marked by performances of his works in celebration of the event. One of the tributes was the formation of the Edgar Stillman Kelley Society, a non-profit organization for publication of the works of younger American composers in "study-score" form. Quite appropriately, one of the "younger" composers chosen by the committee for publication was Dr. Stillman Kelley himself. The work selected was one which, though it had been intended as his first symphony, had lain unfinished for many years. He had composed the first movement and sketched the others, but it was not until his seventy-eighth year that he brought *Gulliver* to completion.

The first movement tells of Gulliver's voyage and shipwreck. Then "Gulliver Sleeps and Dreams." In the third section the Lilliputians appear, heralded by the national anthem, "Glibdrib," which is turned into a double fugue as the diminutive natives enmesh the "Man Mountain." In the finale a hornpipe announces that Gulliver is rescued and homeward bound. The music is orthodox in form and idiom, and far from profound. But the subject is not profound either, nor exotic, so why should we expect the color of *Scheherazade* or the intensity of *Tristan?* Orchestrally the score is far more than competent, and the humor is youthful without becoming second-childish.

Stillman Kelley was born in Sparta, Wisconsin, in 1857. He first studied in Chicago and then went to the conservatory in Stuttgart. When he returned to America he settled first in San Francisco. In 1890 he came East, and for a number of years conducted comic opera companies. After eight years in Berlin, teaching piano and composition, he was awarded a Fellowship in Musical Composition by the Western College at Oxford, Ohio, and was invited to make his home and pursue his career as a composer on its campus.

He has many major works to his credit: for orchestra, the Chinese suite, *Aladdin;* a *New England Symphony;* a symphonic poem, *The Pit and the Pendulum;* and a symphonic suite, *Alice in Wonderland*. His chamber music includes a String Quartet and a Quintet, and his oratorio, *The Pilgrim's Progress*, has had many performances.

Mrs. H. H. A. Beach, the younger sister of the Boston Group, has passed the age of seventy, and may look back on the past half-century as a period in which she played a prominent part in the development of American music. Known to the layman best, perhaps, for several songs—*Ah, Love, but a Day*, and *The Year's at the Spring*—she numbers among her published works a *Gaelic Symphony*, a Concerto for piano and orchestra, a Quintet, a *Theme and Variations* for flute and string quartet, and a Sonata for violin and piano. In 1893 she was commissioned to write a work for the dedication of the Woman's Building at the Chicago World's Fair, and she composed a *Festival Jubilate*. In 1898 she wrote a *Song of Welcome* for the Trans-Mississippi Exposition at Omaha, and in 1915 a *Panama Hymn* for the Panama-Pacific Exposition in San Francisco. More recent is the *Canticle of the Sun*, which was performed at the Worcester Festival in 1934.

Mrs. Beach's maiden name was Amy Marcy Cheney, and she was born September 5, 1867, in Henniker, New Hampshire. She was musical from childhood, so sensitive to melody that any sad or sentimental music upset her completely. The story has already been told of how her mother punished her childish misdeeds by playing Gottschalk's *Last Hope* instead of giving her a New England spanking.

Like Arthur Foote, the young Miss Cheney received her musical education in America, principally in Boston. She was married before she was twenty, and it was not until her husband's death in 1910 that she resumed her musical activities seriously, particularly concert performance. Then she went to Germany, where she stayed for four years, playing her Piano Concerto with orchestras in Hamburg, Leipzig, and Berlin.

Since then Mrs. Beach has lived mostly in this country, busy at composing and on the concert platform. Her activities have naturally lessened during recent years, but throughout her career her energy has seemed almost inexhaustible. In her works she has made liberal use of folk-songs, but she has never felt that by doing so she was writing nationalistic music. She has merely adapted for her own purpose melodies she thought would be useful. In her opinion, nationalism is too subtle a quality to be acquired merely by thinking about it. She has used Negro and Indian themes, but she has also used bird-calls, Eskimo songs, Balkan themes, in fact anything she has happened to like.

There was a considerable period during which *Walter Damrosch* abandoned the idea of adding the laurels of a composer to his many achievements as conductor and musical ambassador and missionary. He had come to the conclusion that the rival conductor who had dubbed his first opera "the *Nibelungen* of New England" was probably right. This work was *The Scarlet Letter*, produced in Boston in 1896. He composed another opera, *Cyrano de Bergerac*, which was performed at the Metropolitan in New York in 1913, but after that he stopped writing for over twenty years. He had plenty to do in other directions.

In 1936, when the principal activity of his eighth decade, the Friday broadcasts of orchestral concerts for school children, had become more or less a routine matter for his ageless energy, he turned once more to his desk and produced an *Abraham Lincoln Song*, for baritone solo, chorus, and orchestra, which was performed at the Metropolitan Opera House on April 3, and broadcast to the nation over an NBC network. The text was taken from Walt Whitman's "O Captain, My Captain."

One more taste of writing music was not enough, for in the following year he gave us nothing less than another full-length opera, a version of Edward Everett Hale's *The Man Without a Country*, with a libretto prepared by Arthur Guiterman. This was first produced during the spring season of the Metropolitan on May 2, 1937, and was retained in the repertoire for the following regular season.

However much Dr. Damrosch may have enjoyed his return to composing, his latest works add little to his honorable record of achievement. For the opera, Mr. Guiterman supplied the composer with a version of Hale's classic which may have been traditional grand-opera material, but which certainly did not enhance the power that lies in the stark simplicity of the original. Perhaps the added love story was necessary as the occasion for a duet, but the swashbuckling heroics of the Guiterman climax came dangerously close to the ridiculous. All the accepted formulae were present in both libretto and music, but the breath of life was absent from both of them. The music was expertly wrought and competent, at times pleasant, but it was thoroughly undistinguished and lacking in any real vitality.

Damrosch will assuredly leave his name in history as one of our great men in music, but not as a composer. That branch of his work has been a diversion for his youth and his latter years, and no one begrudges him the enjoyment it has afforded, so long as he does not ask us to remember him by it instead of by his truly great achievements.

And they have been monumental. Born in Breslau, Germany, on January 30, 1862, he came to New York with his family when he was nine years old. His father, Leopold Damrosch, had first come to America to conduct the New York Männergesangverein, a male chorus. In 1874 he organized the New York Oratorio Society, and in 1878, after a season with the Philharmonic, he was made conductor of the newly formed Symphony Society of New York.

Leopold Damrosch died suddenly in 1885, and his son, not yet twenty-three, stepped immediately into his shoes as conductor of both the Oratorio and Symphony Societies. He had been his father's assistant as conductor of German opera at the Metropolitan, and in 1894 he organized his own company, which for five years gave German operas in New York and other cities. After 1900 he was for two years conductor of German operas at the Metropolitan.

During his conductorship of the Symphony Society of New York he introduced many new works which have since proved to be masterpieces—among them Tschaikowsky's Fifth and Sixth Symphonies, and Brahms' Fourth. He also directed the first American performances of several operas: Saint-Saëns' *Samson and Delilah*, Tschaikowsky's *Eugene Onegin*, and Wagner's *Parsifal*. He was a pioneer in welcoming the works of American composers to his programs, and it was he who commissioned George Gershwin to compose his Piano Concerto.

In 1928 the Symphony Society was merged with the New York Philharmonic and, aside from a few guest appearances as conductor, Dr. Damrosch had planned to retire. But a year later he found himself an important factor in an infant field—the radio. He was started on his series of broadcasts during school hours, and since then millions of children throughout the country have listened each week to his benevolently paternal "Good morning, my dear children," and have learned much about good music.

So Walter Damrosch does not need the role of composer for immortality, and it is not necessary that one admire him as a creative artist in order to do him high honor. His name will go on the roll with that of Theodore Thomas, as belonging to one who has done more than his share in helping to make America musical.

Among the older composers of Teutonic background and style, two more must be mentioned here. *Louis Victor Saar,* who died on November 23, 1937, came of a family that was distantly related to Franz Schubert. He was a native of Rotterdam, Holland, born December 10, 1868, and a graduate of the University of Strasbourg. He had studied at the Royal Academy of Music in Munich, and had been a pupil of Rheinberger and Brahms. He came to America in 1894, as an accompanist at the Metropolitan Opera House, and taught at the National Conservatory and at the Institute of Musical Art. From 1906 to 1917, he headed the theory and composition department of the Cincinnati College of Music, and later occupied a similar post at the Chicago Musical College.

Saar wrote a considerable number of chamber music works and

a good deal of choral music, and edited old music for several American publishers. His orchestral works included a *Rococo Suite* (1915), a suite, *From the Mountain Kingdom of the Great North West* (1922), and another, *Along the Columbia River* (1924).

Henry Holden Huss also comes of a family to which a famous man in history belonged—John Huss, the Bohemian patriot-martyr. But Henry Huss was born here, in Newark, New Jersey, on June 21, 1862. He studied in Munich with Boise and Rheinberger, and later returned to New York, where he has spent most of his long life teaching, lecturing, composing, and giving joint recitals with his wife, the former Hildegarde Hoffman. His String Quartet in B minor, which won a National Federation of Music Clubs prize, is published by the Society for the Publication of American Music. He has played his Rhapsody and his Concerto for piano and orchestra with many orchestras both in this country and in Europe. He is also the author of a *Nocturne*, for orchestra and mixed voices, and of *The Ride of Paul Revere*, for soprano, women's chorus, and orchestra.

There are other composers who belong chronologically to this chapter, but whose music and idioms place them elsewhere. Some of them, like Charles Martin Loeffler, were indeed contemporaneous with the musicians we have been discussing, but, like Loeffler, they were ahead of their time, artistically, and their musical speech connected them with a younger generation. We shall meet them later in these pages. A few more, however, should be discussed here; composers who belong to the older order, but who bridge the gap from the early years of the twentieth century to the present day.

James Philip Dunn (1884–1936) was a composer who possessed a facile talent, prolific almost to a fault. He was born in New York City, received a bachelor's degree from City College, and then studied music at Columbia, first with MacDowell and later with Cornelius Rybner. For many years he was an organist, first at St. Patrick's in Jersey City and later at St. Henry's in Bayonne, New Jersey.

Dunn was the perpetrator of many rather trivial songs and lyric ballads, but he was also the composer of many works in the larger dimensions. An *Overture on Negro Themes* was published first for organ, and in 1925 in full score for orchestra. In manuscript Dunn had two String Quartets; a Piano Quintet; a Violin Sonata; an opera, *The Galleon*; a Symphony; a Symphonic Poem; and a Passacaglia and Fugue for orchestra, *The Barber's Sixth Brother*, based on tales from the Arabian Nights.

On one occasion Dunn was most timely in his choice of subject. When Lindbergh landed in Paris, in May of 1927, all Tin Pan Alley rushed to its pens and pencils to turn out *Lucky Lindy* and dozens of other songs about the hero. Dunn thought that the symphonists should be represented, too, so he started to work on Decoration Day and in three weeks completed his tone-poem, *We*. It was a vivid bit of program music, describing the flight, its start and finish. It was first performed at the Stadium Concerts, August 27, and later enjoyed a number of performances from various orchestras.

George Templeton Strong has chosen the life of an expatriate, and for almost a half-century has lived permanently in Europe. He was born May 26, 1856, and has a long list of works to his credit. A few years ago, in 1935, the Philadelphia Orchestra played his *Chorale on a Theme by Hassler*, beautifully textured music, exquisitely scored for strings. On October 21, 1939, Strong, at the age of eighty-three, had the pleasure of sitting by the radio in Geneva, Switzerland, and hearing his *Die Nacht* played by the NBC Symphony Orchestra under Toscanini.

Templeton Strong was born in New York. His father was an amateur organist, and for four years president of the Philharmonic Society. In 1879 Strong went to Leipzig, where he studied with Jadassohn. He came to know MacDowell at Wiesbaden, and finally settled in Switzerland. When MacDowell returned to America he persuaded Strong to try living here too, but after a year in Boston (1891–92), as a teacher at the New England Conservatory, Strong was so discouraged by the failure of American composers to find recognition in their own country that he went back to Europe for good.

His works include three symphonies; two *American Sketches* for violin and orchestra; a suite for orchestra; a symphonic poem, *Le Roi Arthur*; and miscellaneous choral works, instrumental pieces, and songs.

Blair Fairchild (1877–1933) was another expatriate. He had gone abroad as an attaché in the diplomatic service, at Constantinople and later at Teheran, and in 1903 had settled in Paris as a music teacher. There he remained until his death. In 1938 a distinguished group presented a memorial concert of Fairchild's works at New York's Town Hall, with a program which included his Sonata for violin and piano, his Trio, and a group of solo songs, and his four Psalms for soli and chorus, sung by the Schola Cantorum.

Others of Fairchild's works are Three Symphonic Tableaux for orchestra, *East and West*; three symphonic poems; a ballet, *Dame Libellule*, which is in the repertory of the Paris Opéra Comique; considerable chamber music; and a number of choral works, songs, and smaller pieces.

3

SAFE AND SOUND

IN SOME respects *Henry Kimball Hadley* belongs in the preceding chapter, for it was not only his New England birth and his studying with Chadwick that made him an heir to the mantle of the Boston Group. His work bears the stamp of its tradition. Yet, even though he died in September of 1937, he still belongs to the present. His works, some of them new, have been performed consistently throughout the last decade, and not until the time of his last illness did he cease his intense activity as composer and conductor, and as founder and moving spirit of the National Association for American Composers and Conductors. It was through this organization that he felt he could best do something practical for his fellow composers, whose interests were always close to his heart.

Hadley was undoubtedly the most prolific of all American composers to date; in fact he was once dubbed the Henry Ford of our composers. This, as I have remarked elsewhere, is not an altogether fair characterization unless we remember that Mr. Ford really makes a very good car, which almost invariably achieves its destination. Hadley's music is neither experimental nor radical; it is thoroughly traditional and not concerned with new tonal devices; it is seldom deeply reflective or profound; but it is always effective, aimed directly and accurately at its goal.

His training and experience made him one of the best equipped of our native musicians; he was one of the first Americans to gain routine training as an orchestral conductor. He was born in Somerville, Massachusetts, December 20, 1871, the son of the director of music in the public schools of that Boston suburb. The father gave his son piano lessons and helped him to compose little pieces. Then the boy went to the New England Conservatory and studied composition with Stephen A. Emery and with Chadwick. When he was twenty his overture, *Hector and Andromache,* was performed by the Manuscript Society of New York, with Walter Damrosch conducting. Two years later he was made conductor of the Laura Schirmer-Mapleson Opera Company, and toured the country. Then he went abroad to study with Mandyczewski in Vienna.

When he returned, he became music director of St. Paul's School in Garden City, Long Island. But in 1904 he was abroad again, this time for five years, the last of them spent in Mainz as conductor of the Stadttheater where he produced his one-act opera, *Safie.* In 1909 he went to the Pacific Coast, to be conductor of the Seattle Symphony Orchestra. For five seasons, from 1911, he conducted the San Francisco Orchestra, and later he was for six years an associate conductor of the New York Philharmonic. In 1929 he organized the Manhattan Symphony Orchestra in New York, which he conducted for three seasons. In addition to these positions he appeared frequently as guest conductor at festivals, and with orchestras and opera companies, in America, in Europe, and in the Orient.

He had five operas to his credit. After *Safie* came *Azora,* produced by the Chicago Opera Company in 1917. In 1918 his third opera, *Bianca,* won a thousand-dollar prize and production by the Society of American Singers. Then came a work produced by the Metropolitan in New York, in 1920, and retained in the repertoire for a second season. This was *Cleopatra's Night,* which several critics hailed as the most colorful American opera that had been produced up to that time. Hadley's last operatic work was *A Night in Old Paris,* a one-act affair produced over the radio by the National Broadcasting Company, February 22, 1933.

As a symphonic composer Hadley was extremely facile. His imposing list of performed and published scores almost betray themselves by the very ease with which he handled his material. Yet they are so playable, so agreeable, that these qualities do actually atone for whatever the works may lack in philosophic contemplation. Before Hadley had attained the age of sixty, in 1931, he had written four symphonies—all frequently performed and two of them published. The first, *Youth and Life,* was heard originally in 1897, in New York. The second, *The Four Seasons,* won the Paderewski prize in 1901, and another award from the New England Conservatory. The Third Symphony, untitled, was first played in Berlin in 1907, and in America in 1908 by the Boston Symphony. The fourth, *North, East, South, and West,* was written for the Norfolk Festival in 1911, and was later played by the Boston Symphony Orchestra and at Queen's Hall, London.

He also composed many overtures and tone-poems. *In Bohemia* was the first of the concert overtures to be published. It was first played in 1902, in Pittsburgh. *Salome,* another overture first heard in Boston in 1907, was one of Hadley's own favorites among his orchestral works. In 1909 the rhapsody for orchestra, *The Culprit Fay,* was awarded the thousand-dollar prize offered by the National Federation of Music Clubs. Another tone-poem, *Lucifer,* was written for the 1915 Norfolk Festival. There were also the *Symphonic Fantasia;* an *Othello* overture; a tone-poem, *The Ocean;* three ballet suites; and a cello concerto. A visit to the Orient had inspired a suite, *The Streets of Pekin,* which was performed by seventeen orchestras during the season 1930–31.

After 1931 Hadley continued composing works which had immediate and repeated performances. One of them was a cantata, *Belshazzar,* which was first performed in the Robin Hood Dell, Philadelphia, in the summer of 1932. The next year he composed the music for the annual midsummer festival of the Bohemian Club in San Francisco. He had been given this task once before, in 1912, when *The Atonement of Pan* was produced by the Bohemians, with David Bispham in the leading role. The 1933 work was called *The Legend of Hani,* and John Charles Thomas sang the principal part.

In 1935 Hadley produced his *Scherzo Diabolique,* which attempted the portrayal of "the hazards of fast driving, the onrushing myriad headlights of approaching autos, the whirring and whizzing of cars as they pass." It is perhaps an American counterpart of Dukas' *Sorcerer's Apprentice;* the listener expects to hear the car dashed to pieces on its wild midnight ride, and he joins the bassoon in its delicious sigh of relief at the safe ending of the journey.

It was in the same year that Hadley composed his fifth symphony—*Connecticut-Tercentenary,* commissioned by Mrs. Carl Stoeckel for performance in the Music Shed at Norfolk, Connecticut. This, too, is program music. It has three movements: 1635, 1735, and 1935. The first, depicting the perils and hardships of the early settlers, is interspersed with Indian themes. The second movement shows a rural contentment, and the last gives an impression of present-day life in Connecticut. The following November Hadley conducted the work in New York, at a concert of the American Academy of Arts and Letters. There was also a Concertino for piano and orchestra, played for the first time by Eunice Howard with the Brooklyn Symphony Orchestra under the composer's direction in March of 1936. In addition to his major works Hadley published some two hundred songs and many shorter instrumental pieces.

During his career he was accorded many honors: Tufts College made him a Doctor of Music in 1925; he was elected a member of the American Academy of Arts and Letters; and the French Government awarded him the Order of Merit. He was a well-known figure at musical gatherings in New York, and to his many friends he was a genial, witty companion. Although he took his work seriously, he was never the egoist, and he was as much interested in gaining hearings for his colleagues as for himself. It was this spirit that led to his founding the National Association for American Composers and Conductors. During his three seasons with the Manhattan Symphony he conducted thirty-six

American works, of which only eight were his own. He was a crusader as well as a composer.

DEEMS TAYLOR

In many musical circles the mere mention of *Deems Taylor* is certain to start a lively argument, particularly among the radicals. To the modernist cult his name is anathema; he is scorned by many of them as a reactionary, one who deals exclusively in borrowed ideas and idioms. Some of this feeling is undeniably justified; Mr. Taylor has on occasion served us old wine in bottles that are none too new, but the detached observer cannot escape the impression that to some of his colleagues his principal crime has been the achievement of a material success traditionally denied the serious creative musician.

Except for George Gershwin, who may be eliminated from comparison because he came to the concert hall by way of Broadway, Taylor's name is undoubtedly the most widely known among laymen of any of our serious composers. Much of his fame has of course come from his radio talks, as commentator on the Sunday afternoon broadcasts of the New York Philharmonic-Symphony Society, and on various commercially sponsored programs; but most of the news that has been printed about him, much of it on the front page of newspapers, has related to the music he has written.

Now that his first successful major work, the orchestral suite *Through the Looking Glass,* is some twenty years old and has become a standard item in the repertoire, and a good dozen years have passed since the première of his first opera, *The King's Henchman,* it is possible to gain a degree of perspective on Taylor's work and to examine some of the elements that have brought it wide acceptance. There are a number of them.

In the first place, he has one of the keenest minds ever granted to a musician. If he is an opportunist, he knows which opportunity to seize and how to make the most of it. Everything he has done has been well timed. He is so inordinately clever that his career is a complete denial of the theory that a man may be jack of all trades but master of none. Among those he has mastered are: newspaper-man, music critic, artist with brush and pen, linguist, translator of prose and verse, and radio commentator. To these we should add carpentry, which may or may not be altogether removed from his talent as composer.

Because of Taylor's varied gifts and his ability to accomplish an outstanding job in so many fields, the problem is one of determining how far his composing is truly creative, and how far it is manufactured by an intellect which can imitate anything it chooses. In other words, does he speak his own musical thoughts, expressing them in a manner peculiarly his, or does he manufacture his music with skill and craftsmanship from materials created by his predecessors?

There are those who charge him with using the latter process. In reviewing *Peter Ibbetson*, Lawrence Gilman wrote, in part: [1]

Mr. Taylor is not, of course, the first composer to reflect the idioms of his predecessors. The mighty Richard himself paid his respects to Beethoven, Weber, Chopin. Debussy flattered Moussorgsky, Wagner, even Massenet. Listening to "Tristan," to "Pelléas," we realize the derivation of certain passages, the source of a harmonic progression or a melodic phrase.

But these men assimilated that upon which their imaginations fed, made it a part of themselves. . . . And the same sort of esthetic metabolism goes on in the case of every creative artist who speaks to us out of his own imaginative experience. That which has entered into him becomes transformed, is turned into living tissue. Whatever he says to us, regardless of its derivation, has become his by virtue of his creative way of saying it, acquires a vital unity and authenticity.

Mr. Taylor has not yet shown us that he can accomplish this sort of creative imaginative transmutation. The material that passes through his mind acquires a depressant quality, amorphous and uncharactered; the Wagnerisms, the Debussyisms, are watered down, thinned, and we get something that is neither of the pleasure of recognition nor the emo-

[1] *New York Herald Tribune*, February 8, 1931.

ASCAP

Deems Taylor

tion of surprise. We realize only that something has happened to the masters, without benefit to Mr. Taylor or to us. . . .

This view represents the extreme indictment, and there are others who feel the charge unjust. Walter Damrosch protested against Gilman's review: [2]

The article seems to me more like the effort of a district attorney who is determined to convict Deems Taylor at all cost as a criminal for having composed an opera. It takes so little cognizance of its many beauties, and presents such a terrible arraignment of the defendant's faults and past sins of omission and commission. And it offers apparent and abundant proof that the composition of the opera "Peter Ibbetson" was a premeditated crime which carries with it no recommendation for mercy.

As a colleague and voluntary witness for the defendant, I should like to offer not only heartfelt testimony as to the defendant's high musical ability as a composer, his remarkable knowledge of the stage, his emotional appreciation of the beautiful story of Du Maurier's, but many "extenuating circumstances," such as—a truly exquisite orchestration, a flow of melody which is often of great tenderness, a delicious sense of humor, and altogether a music which envelops the drama with moments of such beauty that the effects of this combination left the huge audience of Saturday afternoon bathed in tears of sympathy and appreciation. . . .

These two viewpoints embody the opposing opinions which are generally held regarding Taylor's music. Each is extreme, and probably the middle ground would hold that his works are obviously derived, as a rule even labeled, but that nevertheless he has composed music which at times is gripping, and often makes little chills run up and down the listener's spine. And to the layman who is not over-analytical, that is the real test of music.

He was born in New York, December 22, 1885. After attending the Ethical Culture School, he entered New York University, where he wrote the music for four comic operas as part of his undergraduate activities. In 1910, four years after Taylor's

[2] Letter published in *New York Herald Tribune*, February 15, 1931.

graduation, Charles Dillingham produced one of these musical comedies, *The Echo,* as a starring vehicle for Bessie McCoy.

From 1908 until 1911 Taylor studied harmony and counterpoint with an obscure musician named Oscar Coon. In his book of collected essays, *Of Men and Music,*[3] the composer has drawn a sympathetic word-picture of this unusual man, "who had ventured to consider Wagner a genius in an era when it took courage and independence to do so." Taylor apparently learned much from Coon, who was his only teacher; beyond these lessons the composer of *The King's Henchman* and *Peter Ibbetson* is entirely self-taught.

His various occupations, aside from composing, fill a good part of his half-column in *Who's Who.* In the years immediately following graduation from college he was a member of the editorial staffs of encyclopedias, *Nelson's* and the *Britannica.* From 1912 to 1916 he was assistant editor of an industrial house-organ, *Western Electric News.* The following year he was assistant Sunday editor of the *New York Tribune,* and in 1916–17 the *Tribune* correspondent in France. From 1917 to 1919 he was associate editor of *Collier's Weekly.* By this time he had won such recognition as a composer, largely because of the *Looking Glass* suite, that he was appointed music critic of the *New York World,* a position he held until 1925. In that year the Metropolitan Opera Company gave him a commission for an opera, and he resigned from the *World* so that he could devote all his time to writing it. After the production of *The King's Henchman,* he was editor of *Musical America* from 1927 to 1929. Then followed the composition and production of *Peter Ibbetson,* in 1931, and various free-lance assignments and engagements which have not demanded all of his time, but which have no doubt proved exceedingly profitable. As this book goes to press his latest opera, *Ramuntcho,* has been completed and is awaiting production.

He has been awarded the honorary degrees of Doctor of Music (New York University, 1927) and Doctor of Letters (Juniata

[3] New York: Simon and Schuster, 1937.

College, 1931), and election to membership in the American Academy of Arts and Letters (1935). He is a director of the American Society of Composers, Authors and Publishers, and a trustee of the American Academy in Rome.

Apart from his collegiate musical comedies, his early works were an orchestral score, *The Siren Song*, which won first prize in the National Federation of Music Clubs competition in 1913; *The Chambered Nautilus*, a cantata for mixed chorus and orchestra; and *The Highwayman*, a cantata for women's voices, composed for the MacDowell Festival at Peterborough in 1914.

Through the Looking Glass was first composed in the years 1917–19 as a work for chamber orchestra, and was introduced by Carolyn Beebe and the New York Chamber Music Society. Then Taylor rescored it for full orchestra, and since 1922 it has been given repeated performances by almost every orchestra in America, and by many in Europe. It is an extremely successful handling of Lewis Carroll's gentle humor, half tender and half mocking. Taylor kept this balance in his music. He caresses his theme affectionately and then chuckles as the ridiculous but rather touching White Knight falls off in front when his horse stops, and backwards when it goes forward. The whole piece has an irresistible sparkle and brilliance. *The Portrait of a Lady* was composed shortly after *Through the Looking Glass* and revised in 1924, though it was not published until late in the 1930's.

The King's Henchman held the Metropolitan boards for three seasons, at that time a record of performances for an American opera. When Taylor was commissioned by the board of directors in the winter of 1925 to write an opera for which they promised a production, he asked Edna St. Vincent Millay for a libretto. She responded with the story of Aethelwold, sent by King Aedgar of England to fetch Aelfrida for his queen. The subject of *Tristan*, doubtless, but of John Alden and Priscilla, too.

The première on February 17, 1927 was a gala event. It had been heralded by tremendous advance publicity. All of New York that could buy tickets at a premium turned out to hear the opera with which the Metropolitan, by commissioning an American composer to write it, had broken tradition. It met with stirring success, and the critics were as enthusiastic as the public. Lawrence Gilman, who four years later was to deplore the borrowings of *Peter Ibbetson,* was one of the leaders in bestowing laurels. In the *Herald Tribune* he called *The King's Henchman* "the best American opera we have ever heard." He wrote of the music as "richly textured, mellifluous," and praised its "grace and movement and flexibility." "It is," he remarked, "the writing of an expert craftsman, an artist of sensibility and warm responsiveness."

Strangely enough, the score was just as clearly derived from Wagner as was the later *Peter Ibbetson,* perhaps more so because of its subject. Taylor himself remarked, before the *Henchman* production, "I can only hope that its spiritual grandfather may turn out to be Wagner rather than Puccini." In his music he used leit-motives for his principal characters and for some of their thoughts and emotions, and he altered these motives to match their moods and their deeds. But whatever its derivations, this was music of warmth and richness. It was also good theatre.

It may be that the critical fraternity felt that a composer might be forgiven for his derivations in his first opera, but that in his second he must stand on his own feet. At any rate, *Peter Ibbetson* did not meet with the almost unanimous acclaim that greeted its predecessor. With the public, however, it became more popular than even *The King's Henchman* had been, and in its third season at the Metropolitan it was accorded the honor of performance on the opening night. It remained in the repertoire for still another season.

For his libretto Taylor himself worked with Constance Collier on the play she had made from Du Maurier's novel, which had been produced some years before with herself and the Barrymore brothers in the leading roles. It is an appealing dream story, which spins a fancy all men would like to believe: that our dreams are more real than our bodily existence, and that if we "dream true" we can take ourselves wherever we wish to be. The plot tells of the orphaned Peter Ibbetson, who had been adopted by a wicked old uncle. As a young man, Peter meets his childhood playmate, Mimsie, now Mary, Duchess of Towers. He remembers her childish instructions for dreaming true: "You lie on your back with your feet crossed, and your arms above your head. . . . When it is rightly done, your dream will take you anywhere you please." Peter tries it, and finds himself with Mimsie, his father and mother, and the old major who took them walking and told them wonderful stories along the way.

Peter is desperately unhappy with his bullying uncle, and when the old rake throws doubt on the young man's parentage by hinting that he himself is his father, finally asking how Peter can tell whether it is true or not, Peter kills him. He is condemned to die, but Mary pleads successfully that his sentence be commuted to life imprisonment. Then she sends him a message bidding him to "dream true." Every night for thirty years they meet in their dream world, and watch themselves as children playing together, listening to the songs and stories of the old major. Then one night Mary does not come, and Peter knows she is dead. He is dying himself, and in the closing scene Mary comes and takes him away with her.

No one can deny that Taylor accomplished a thoroughly musicianly job in this opera. The music, even when it seems derived from Wagner, Debussy, or Puccini, is always appropriate. The orchestration is rich and resourceful. The score is consistent and, in the symphonic interludes between scenes, eloquent. As incidental music to the drama it would have been almost perfect. The folk-like songs of the chorus which accompany the dream scenes breathe a fanciful fragrance and mysticism. Yet I, for one, had a feeling that as a complete show the opera did not quite come off.

It seemed to me that the music often halted the action, that it made the characters seem stilted and stagey. It may be, too, that opera cannot deal effectively with such lines as "The death sentence has been commuted," or "Dear Colonel, will you take me in to see the dancing?"

The production, first presented on February 7, 1931, was magnificent. Edward Johnson sang Peter, Lawrence Tibbett the Uncle, and Lucrezia Bori, Mimsie. The work became tremendously popular and provided the Metropolitan with sold-out houses. In the summer of 1931 it was produced at Ravinia, near Chicago.

Others of Taylor's works for orchestra are a rhapsody for strings, wind, and piano. *The Portrait of a Lady; Jurgen,* a symphonic poem originally commissioned by Walter Damrosch and the New York Symphony Society; and *Circus Days,* composed and scored for jazz orchestra a number of years ago, then rescored for symphony orchestra with added saxophones, and published in its final version in 1934. In this fantasy-suite Taylor uses his memory of childhood to recall familiar scenes. The thrill of "Street Parade" opens the proceedings, and after an excited introduction we hear the band in its pompous march. "The Big Top" comes next, and beneath its canvas we hear of its many wonders, all timed to schedule like clockwork. Then we hear the "Bareback Riders" as they defy danger for our amazement.

The fourth piece has three sub-divisons: *The Lion Cage* (and how the King of Beasts can roar!), *The Dog and the Monkey,* and the ponderous *Waltzing Elephants.* After this comes the "Tight-Rope Walker," way up high in the wood-winds; then "Jugglers," recklessly bandying the themes about. "The Clowns" come next, and perform their antics to the tune of saxophones and wah-wah mutes on the trumpets and trombones. The Finale is unnamed; Taylor gives us no indication of what he meant it to represent. Perhaps it pictures the tired but radiantly happy trip home.

Taylor has been much in demand for providing incidental music for the theatre. Two scores were for New York Theatre Guild productions: *Liliom* and *The Adding Machine.* Others have been for *Beggar on Horseback*, *Will Shakespeare*, *Humoresque*, *Rita Coventry*, Gilbert Miller's production of *Casanova*, and Katharine Cornell's appearance in *Lucrece*. Out of the music for the last two Taylor subsequently fashioned concert suites: the *Casanova* ballet music for orchestra, and the *Lucrece* suite for string quartet. He acted as musical advisor and commentator for the Walt Disney film *Fantasia*, and in November, 1940, Disney announced that Taylor would compose a new score for the film *Alice in Wonderland*.

JOHN ALDEN CARPENTER

By heritage and tradition, *John Alden Carpenter* might easily have been a conservative, if not a reactionary. Surely the New England ancestry implied in his name, and his training at Harvard under the academic John Knowles Paine, would in themselves have been sufficient to lead him into well-trod paths. To this background he has added a thoroughly respectable career as a business executive; until his retirement in 1936 he was vice-president of the family firm of George B. Carpenter and Company, Chicago merchants in mill, railway, and vessel supplies. Instead of allowing this vocation to make him prosaic or even cautious in his music, he used it to gain an economic independence which has enabled him to compose the kind of music he wanted to write, regardless of its commercial value.

He was born February 28, 1876, in Park Ridge, Illinois. His mother was a talented amateur singer, and she gave him his first music lessons. When he went to Harvard, he studied with Paine and took all the music courses the college offered. Then he studied for a short time in England, with Edward Elgar, and later with Bernhard Ziehn in Chicago.

Carpenter's progress from his early compositions—particularly the Violin Sonata of 1911—to the *Skyscrapers* of 1923-4 and his still more recent works, shows an interesting evolution. Regardless of how truly creative he may be, it denotes an artist who attempts his own thinking. Even before the Sonata, in such songs as *The Green River* (1909), we find whole-tone progressions and an apparent desire to exploit the upper reaches of the overtone series; and these things were written by a man who at that time had not yet heard one note of Debussy.

The Sonata commands attention for several reasons. It is Franckian in spirit, but it is not a mere echo of César Franck. It adds to the Belgian's contemplativeness a rugged vigor that sweeps it along to its close. The work stamps its composer as one who is not afraid of showing influences, yet who is not content to be an imitator.

Soon after the Sonata, Carpenter turned to program music and wrote the orchestral score that first brought him to the attention of music-lovers generally—*Adventures in a Perambulator*. This was in 1914. Within its own prescribed limits this suite accomplishes exactly what it was intended to do; it furnishes a bit of whimsy and musical description that evokes a chuckle rather than a hearty laugh. The baby, wheeled along the sidewalks by his nurse, sees "The Policeman," "The Lake," and the "Dogs," and hears the "Hurdy-Gurdy." The effects are skillfully gained, more by impressionistic methods than by realism. This is by no means a work in the grand manner, but then, infants do not generally think in the grand manner.

Following the Suite, Carpenter wrote his Concertino for piano and orchestra (1915). Again he did not reach out for lofty heights, but contented himself with what he termed an intimate conversation between two friends—the piano and the orchestra. In this work he shows a firmer grip on his tools, a more certain touch in his handling of them. The work also shows some innovations: shifting accents that point to the jazz rhythms of later works, quadruple figures imposed on a triple pattern, and vice versa. There is also present a Spanish flavor which is often found in Carpenter's later writings, particularly in his first experiment with the ballet, *The Birthday of the Infanta*, composed in 1917–18, and produced by the Chicago Opera Company in 1919.

Greystone

John Alden Carpenter

In this ballet Carpenter is dexterous in presenting the colorful scenes of the action—the dance of the dwarf, the jugglers, the gypsy dancers, the mock bull-fight—even though he may not have been emotionally capable of the tragic heights demanded by Pedro's death. Nor is *The Birthday of the Infanta* as important in itself as it is in showing a logical step in Carpenter's progress as a creative artist. It forms a bridge between the Sonata and the Concertino on the one hand, and on the other the subsequent ballets, *Krazy Kat* and *Skyscrapers*. Jazz made its first appearance in Carpenter's music in *Krazy Kat*, and he first used cacophony in *Skyscrapers*; both works marked him immediately as one who consciously seeks out something alien to his own nature for the solution of specific problems.

Krazy Kat, composed in 1921, was of course based on the George Herriman cartoons. Superficially the humor is nothing but slapstick—Ignatz Mouse hurling bricks at the head of Krazy Kat, and the spectator varying the intensity of his guffaws according to the force of the blow. But Carpenter has not written purely slapstick music. Krazy is an intensely human figure, his weaknesses and his vanity common to all men, and Ignatz Mouse, cruelly deriding him, is life bringing us to earth from our dreams.

The score sharpens the elemental nature of these conflicting passions, and intensifies the fundamentally American quality of exaggeration in symbolism. Jazz rhythms, fox trots, quasi-Broadway tunes, and even the Spanish atmosphere of Krazy's dance, are highly appropriate; but it is a more subtle, intangible quality that gives this music its authentic American flavor.

Skyscrapers followed *Krazy Kat*, and was first produced as a ballet at the Metropolitan Opera House, New York, in 1926. It was composed in 1923–24. To recite its program, and then to say that its music brings the noise of rivets and emphasizes the monotony of labor and the fever of relaxation, would indicate that the composer had turned to wholly obvious devices in an attempt to write music of today. The work could easily have been altogether objective, if nothing beyond description had been attempted.

The condensed scenario, as printed in the published score, affords a description of the action:

Skyscrapers is a ballet which seeks to reflect some of the many rhythmic movements and sounds of modern American life. It has no story, in the usually accepted sense, but proceeds on the simple fact that American life reduces itself to violent alternations of work and play, each with its own peculiar and distinctive character. The action of the ballet is merely a series of moving decorations reflecting some of the obvious external features of this life.

There is nothing strikingly novel in all of this; it presents a form of symbolism suggested to a number of artists by the machine age. There was accordingly every opportunity for Carpenter to be thoroughly commonplace; it is not difficult for even an experienced composer to write music that is merely noisy, and to consider it reflective of city streets and amusement parks. But Carpenter uses a fine restraint: he goes the limit only at climactic moments, and thereby saves for himself the effectiveness of contrasts. Under the surface there is an irony and a human pity for the futility of all the hurly-burly. There is also present a musical element which to many contemporary composers is either a lost or a shunned art—the development of ideas and material. In *Skyscrapers*, ideas do not crowd upon each other in such rapid succession that they lack room to show their full contours, to attain their natural growth.

For a number of years after *Skyscrapers*, Carpenter's only major work was the String Quartet, performed at the Library of Congress Festival in 1928. In this absolute music, the composer used the complex rhythms he had been employing in his recent program-music. The Quartet was an interesting mixture of charm and whimsicality, with, at times, uncompromising severity.

In 1931 the United States George Washington Bicentennial Commission invited Carpenter to compose an ode for the forthcoming bicentennial celebration in 1932. For this occasion he wrote the *Song of Faith*, for chorus and orchestra, using a text of his own. The music embodied an idealism that was fitting to its subject; a warmth of melodic line seasoned by vital and stimulating rhythms.

The next major work was *Patterns*, first performed by the Boston Symphony Orchestra in the autumn of 1932, scored for orchestra and piano obbligato, and composed in one movement. There is no literary significance in the title; its implications are wholly musical. Some passages in the score are distinctly sentimental, and at other times the atmosphere alternates between a Spanish flavor and jazz. Several of the critics at the première felt that the work lacked continuity, but they admitted that the composer may have anticipated such a criticism by his title.

A year after *Patterns* Carpenter produced *Sea Drift*, inspired (like Delius' work of the same title and the *Sea Symphony* of Vaughan Williams) by the sea poems of Walt Whitman. This was first performed in November of 1934 by the New York Philharmonic-Symphony under Werner Janssen. On this occasion Lawrence Gilman wrote: [4]

> This music is charged with . . . the sensibility of those dreamers and visionaries who have watched the fading out of the sun from a day that is irrecoverable, and who can tell us of its decrescent loveliness only in music and in words that are charged with a deep nostalgia of the spirit—who, with Whitman, listen "long and long."
> . . . This music of Mr. Carpenter's is richly and beautifully spun. It is the music of a poet. Mr. Carpenter has written nothing more fine-textured than the close of this sea-piece.

Since its first performances *Sea Drift* has been heard elsewhere, at the Eastman Festival in Rochester (1936) and at the Hollywood Bowl (1937).

Carpenter's Quintet for piano and strings was first performed at the Coolidge Festival at the Library of Congress, Washington, in April, 1935. It proved to be music of naturalness and sincerity, even though its appearance in the company of works by Quincy Porter, Werner Janssen, and, the following evening, Stravinsky, may have made it seem a bit tame. Yet the use of the piano for

[4] *New York Herald Tribune*, November 9, 1934.

percussive effects was altogether contemporary in feeling, and the refinement of its idiom lent distinction to the work's rich chromaticism.

January of 1936 marked the first performance of *Danza*, by the Boston Symphony, a piece less important than others of Carpenter's works, but altogether charming, and reflective once more of the Spanish element that often creeps into his music. In the following year his Concerto for violin and orchestra was presented by the Chicago Symphony Orchestra, with Zlatko Balakovic as soloist. A Symphony written for the fiftieth anniversary of that orchestra, in 1940, was described as "airy, bright, urbane, and pleasant" and Carpenter himself was quoted as saying, "it is peaceful music and, in these days, that is something." [5]

DANIEL GREGORY MASON

Daniel Gregory Mason was also a pupil of John Knowles Paine, but he is frank to say he found Paine's classes at Harvard so uninspiring that he virtually dropped his music while he was in college, except for writing the music for the Hasty Pudding Club shows. Mason is also one who would have found it exceedingly easy to travel paths that had been well trod by others. He is a member of the musically famous Mason family; a grandson of Lowell Mason and a nephew of William Mason, the distinguished pianist and teacher of the latter half of the nineteenth century. Daniel Mason's own father was the Henry Mason who was one of the founders of the organ and piano-manufacturing firm of Mason and Hamlin.

He was born in Brookline, Massachusetts, November 20, 1873. Before entering Harvard he had some lessons with Ethelbert Nevin, and after graduation he studied with Chadwick in Boston and Percy Goetschius in New York. Then he went to Paris to work with d'Indy. Since 1900 he has been active, not only as a composer, but also as a lecturer, writer on music, and teacher. For

[5] *New York Herald Tribune*, October 25, 1940.

his books alone Mason would be entitled to a high place in our musical life. In 1909 he joined the music faculty of Columbia University, and in 1929 he was made MacDowell Professor of Music. In April, 1940, he retired from the chairmanship of the music department and was succeeded by Douglas Moore.

It is, however, principally as a composer that he would like to be known, for he takes this phase of his work most seriously. Whatever criticisms may be leveled at his product are no doubt the result of the cerebral industry that he devotes to composing. It may be that some of his works are slightly arid because they are too well thought out.

He has very definite ideas on what American music should be, or perhaps it would be more accurate to say, what it should *not* be. He decries jingoism on the part of American composers and their friends; he feels that nationalism is important, but that it should not be a narrow nationalism, which he thinks would set our music back several decades. He once wrote: [6]

> With our great material power, our wealth, our vast size, we have plenty of temptation to spread-eagleism, to the bumptious variety of patriotism that expresses itself in the chauvinist and the jingo. But "patriotism" of that egotistic, self-seeking sort is not to be confused with the Emersonian self-reliance in which we have been finding the root of originality. True it is, music cannot be vitally international unless it has begun by being sincerely national. Merely eclectic cosmopolitanism . . . is stillborn, never comes alive at all. But on the other hand jingo music, such as we hear in the perorations of patriotic overtures, never grows up. It is to be hoped that our American music, after its timid, repressed childhood, may have first a lusty youth and then a kind, generous, intelligent maturity.

Although Mason on occasion uses folk-songs in his music, and is intensely interested in them, he came to the conclusion a number of years ago that American music is necessarily eclectic and cosmopolitan; that its distinctiveness must be individual, rather than national. Hence he has followed his own taste in his own music. Taking little spontaneous pleasure in the impressionism

[6] Letter to *Musical America*, May 25, 1933.

of Debussy or Scriabin, or in the primitivism of Stravinsky, he turns to the classic-romantic type of beauty worked out by Beethoven, Schumann, Brahms, and Franck. He is willing to risk the reactionary label, but he is at the same time constantly using some of the dissonant devices of his more modern colleagues.

Among his early works, Opus 5 is a Sonata for violin and piano; Opus 7 a Quartet for piano and strings, which was played by Gabrilowitsch with the Kneisel Quartet. His *Country Pictures* for piano, Opus 9, have been played in concert by Josef Hofmann, John Powell, and Percy Grainger. The first work for orchestra was his Symphony No. 1, published abroad and played by Stokowski and the Philadelphia Orchestra. It had later performances by the Detroit, New York Philharmonic, Chicago, and Boston orchestras.

His Sonata for clarinet (or violin) and piano was one of the first works selected by the Society for the Publication of American Music. His song-cycle, *Russians*, was featured by Reinald Werrenrath with several symphony orchestras. His *String Quartet on Negro Themes* was first printed privately, but later withdrawn and revised, and then issued in its new form by the Society for the Publication of American Music. Other works for string quartet are the *Variations on a Theme by John Powell*, and a Folk-Song Fantasy on the English song, *Fanny Blair*. His *Festival Overture*, for orchestra, was published under the sponsorship of the Juilliard Foundation.

In recent years, Mason has continued his intense activity as a creative musician, and has produced a sizable list of major works. His Second Symphony dates from 1930, when it was first played by the Cincinnati Orchestra under Fritz Reiner. 1931 saw the first performance of the *Chanticleer* overture, by Nikolai Sokoloff and the Cleveland Orchestra; since that time the piece has had more than fifty performances. From these years also comes the *Prelude and Fugue*, Opus 20, for piano and orchestra. This work is dedicated to John Powell, who has introduced it in concerts with the Chicago, Boston, Philadelphia, and New York Philharmonic-Symphony orchestras.

The *Prelude* opens dramatically with a foreboding unison motive in the orchestra, answered by a nostalgic, yearning theme in the piano part. The piece is marked throughout by dignity and brilliance, and reaches a powerful climax as it comes to the *Fugue*. Here the subject is announced first by the piano, in mysterious and tragic mood. The development is based largely on chromatic progressions which bring to it moments of lyric, transparent beauty. The culmination is reached in the final maestoso passage, where the themes of *Prelude* and *Fugue* are combined in a triumphant finish.

Another orchestral work, *Suite after English Folk-Songs*, had its première at a festival in Virginia under the baton of Hans Kindler, April 28, 1934. In the following autumn it was performed at the Worcester Festival and in the winter by the New York Philharmonic-Symphony under Bruno Walter. The work is in three movements and uses five English airs: *O No, John; A Brisk Young Sailor; The Two Magicians; Arise, Arise!*, and *The Rambling Sailor*. The treatment of all of the themes is rhapsodic and rises far above mere quotation and arrangement. Some of the critics at the New York performance acknowledged the merits of the piece but felt that it had its limitations. The reviewer of *Musical America* remarked: [7]

> The connecting tissue has been artfully spun and the work has a pleasant savor of old times without being consciously archaic. It palls, however, because of the uniform level on which it moves, as has been true of similar music conceived on the other side of the Atlantic. The tunes are over-spun and, in effect, unduly magnified in their symphonic elaboration.

At the concerts of the New York Philharmonic-Symphony, November 17–19, 1937, John Barbirolli introduced Mason's *A Lincoln Symphony*, the composer's third work in this form. The

---

[7] January 10, 1935.

first movement is "The Candidate from Springfield," based largely on an actual tune from the 1860 period, the *Quaboag Quickstep*. The second part is called "Massa Linkum," the slaves' view of their friend, in which the English horn voices their grief in a quasi-spiritual. Then comes "Old Abe's Yarns," and the listener is asked to "sense . . . the relief he found in his grotesque, irresponsible, half-demoniac humor." The finale is "1865"; Lincoln "lies dead. . . . The quickstep we once marched with him in triumph has turned to a funeral march in our tragic hearts."

Lawrence Gilman praised this work with the adjectives that only he knew how to use. In his review of the concert, he wrote, in part: [8]

> Mr. Mason . . . has demonstrated again and again throughout this work his depth of insight and of feeling, his power of salient and expressive utterance, his incorruptible honesty and dignity as an artist, his tact and sensibility as a poet and humanist in tones.
>
> His music, at its best, has the lofty simplicity, the noble austerity and plainness, that were essential strands in the complex fabric of Lincoln's soul. It is terse, compact, succinct, saying its say with concentration and most skilled economy of means—never excessive, never overwrought; leading by an extraordinary subtlety and interplay of contrasts to the impassioned sorrow of the final movement—that dirge in which a musician of today pays worthy tribute to a deathless spirit.

There were others in the audience, however, more reserved in their commendation. I, for one, thought the *Quaboag Quickstep* an unfortunate choice to represent the period. Surely the mid-nineteenth century gave birth to tunes of more spontaneous vitality. Mason's use of the melody was indeed the acme of craftsmanship, but he was not able to breathe life into something that had no life. In the slow movement, too, the composer's inspiration seemed to flag. Yet even though he may not have achieved the inspirational eminence of genius, Mason succeeded in paying lofty tribute to Abraham Lincoln.

Others of his recent works include a *Divertimento* for sym-

[8] *New York Herald Tribune*, November 18, 1937.

phonic band, *Sentimental Sketches* for violin, cello, and piano, *Serenade* for string quartet, and a *Free and Easy Five-Step* for small orchestra.

DAVID STANLEY SMITH

Some four years Mason's junior is his Yale colleague, *David Stanley Smith*, who was born in Toledo, Ohio, July 6, 1877. Smith, who was Dean of the Yale School of Music, also retired in 1940, although he continues his classes in composition. He had headed the school for twenty years as successor to Horatio Parker, whose pupil he had been. Smith's father was a self-taught organist and composer, a business man who played the organ in Toledo churches as an avocation; his mother was a singer. After graduating from Yale College, Smith attended the School of Music, where he obtained his Mus.B. in 1903. On Parker's advice he went abroad, to travel and broaden his horizon rather than to engage in any specific study. He then returned to Yale as a member of the faculty of the School of Music, and has been there ever since. In New Haven he also conducts the Symphony Orchestra and the Horatio Parker choir.

Smith's approach to music is a serious one. He insists on regarding the art as worthy of a man of serious purpose and intellectual attainments, rather than as an amusement, a joke, or "a vehicle for proclaiming some 'ism'." He is greatly interested in the architecture of music; he considers it no less important than melodic invention and feeling. And he strives to avoid equally sentimentality on the one hand and harsh impersonality on the other. The fact that he states these things openly has combined with his academic position to make it easy for the unthinking and unlistening to dismiss him as a mere professor. But those with ears to hear know that he is a real musician, to whom composition is something more than a mere intellectual pastime.

Many years before Hanson's *Merry Mount* (the title, by the way, has been a popular one), Smith had written a full-length opera by that name. His First Symphony was played by Stock and the Chicago Orchestra in 1912; the Second was first heard at the Norfolk Festival in 1918; a Third dates from 1928; and a Fourth was written in 1937, and first performed by the Boston Orchestra on April 14, 1939. He has also written a *Prince Hal* overture; a suite of *Impressions* (1916); a *Fête Galante* (1920), for flute and orchestra, played several times by Georges Barrère; a *Cathedral Prelude* (1926), for organ and orchestra (Smith is a Fellow of the American Guild of Organists); an *Epic Poem* (1926); and a *Rondo Appassionato* for violin and orchestra. His *1929—A Satire* forms a pair with the overture *Tomorrow;* they were written in 1932 and 1933. Smith has written of the former: [9]

> The satirical element in the score consists not in any rehashing of the popular music of our times; and not in a realistic medley of sounds purporting to represent the turmoil of modern life. The piece is emphatically not a history of the financial breakdown of 1929. It does no more than symbolize in music's vague way the emotions of the people before and after the crisis. Such climaxes as occur in the music are not stock-market crashes, but the shock which the crashes dealt to the prevailing pleasure-worship.

A "long simple cantilena" which in *1929* is "only a calm episode in the midst of confusion, receives its fulfilment" in the companion-piece, *Tomorrow.*

For chamber orchestra, Smith has written a suite of four pieces entitled *Flowers* (1924); a Sinfonietta for string orchestra (1931); and a Sonatina for junior string orchestra (1932). He has also composed two large choral pieces: the *Rhapsody of St. Bernard* (1915), and the *Vision of Isaiah* (1927).

But his most imposing list of works is in the field of chamber music. Two Sonatas, one for oboe and piano (1918) and one for violin and piano (1921), and two String Quartets, both in C major (1921 and 1934), are published by the Society for the Publication of American Music. Thus Smith shares with Mason the honor, accorded no one else, of having had four works pub-

---

[9] Gilman's Sunday column, *New York Herald Tribune*, November 5, 1933.

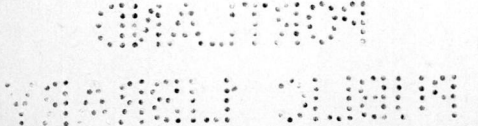

lished by the S.P.A.M. He has written eight string quartets in all. The eighth was heard at the Coolidge Festival in the Library of Congress on April 14, 1940, and although it figured on a program that contained works by Roy Harris and Nicolai Berezowsky, it did not give any impression of belonging to an outmoded style, and it received a welcome that was more than a *succès d'estime*.

In the increased leisure for composition which Smith has secured by retiring from his administrative activities, it is reasonable to expect that many more works will flow from his pen. Perhaps now that he is no longer a professor people will not approach his music with so firm an expectation of hearing an "academic," and will give it a fairer chance.

CHARLES WAKEFIELD CADMAN

Although *Charles Wakefield Cadman* ranks with Deems Taylor in being famous to the general public, he himself is under no illusion as to the greatness of his music. He frankly states that in his opinion the world's greatest music has been written, and all that present-day composers are doing is to reflect in one way or another a little of what is around them. He makes no attempt to be profound in his music, he is content with the satisfaction he gains from expressing himself sincerely and in straightforward fashion.

There was a time when Cadman could fairly be classified as one who specialized in using "American folk-music," particularly the melodies of various Indian tribes, but of late years he has abandoned any thought of achieving nationalism through such methods. Enforced nationalism, he says, "cribs, cabins, and confines." In an interview a few years ago, he was quoted as saying: [10]

I used to think I was writing American music twenty-five years ago when I was at work transcribing and adapting the folk-songs of the American Indian. But I don't now. . . . All these types [Indian,

[10] *Musical Courier*, June 2, 1934; quoted from *Music in New Zealand*.

Negro, cowboy, hillbilly, etc.] are just ingredients. Each one is a basis for American music—but there's no reason to take one type and glorify it above the others. . . . None of these forms represents the real idiom of American music. They are ingredients. . . .

It is not strange that the musical public still looks upon Cadman as one who specializes in folk-melodies, for *From the Land of the Sky Blue Water*, which came to rank with Nevin's *Rosary* in popularity, was admittedly based on an Indian melody. And his opera, *Shanewis*, produced at the Metropolitan in New York in 1918, tells the story of an Indian maiden who came to New York for musical training. A number of Indian melodies appear in the score: the best-known aria, the "Spring Song of the Robin Woman," is based on a Cheyenne melody; the "Intermezzo," uses a song of the Omahas; an Osage ceremonial song appears in the pow-wow scene.

Cadman has passed through a number of distinct phases in his career as composer. In his early days he concerned himself principally with comic operas and operettas. Then he turned his attention largely to writing songs and part-songs. Next came his interest in Indian music. He had already made some settings of Indian themes, and in 1909, when he was twenty-seven years old, he went to the Omaha Reservation with Francis La Flesche, and spent the summer recording on the phonograph some of the tribal songs and flute music. For sixteen years, until 1925, he continued his interest in the subject, and gave many lecture-recitals on Indian customs and music. In recent years he has been interested in composing operas and symphonic works of a more general nature.

He was born in Johnstown, Pennsylvania, December 24, 1881, the son of a metallurgist employed by the Carnegie Steel Corporation. Even though the Cadman home had no piano until Charles was thirteen, the boy was musical from earliest childhood. His teachers were Leo Oehmler of Pittsburgh and Luigi von Kunitz. When he started to compose, he had extreme difficulty in placing his first works with publishers, and in having them performed. For almost two years he walked the sidewalks of New York, trying to interest theatrical agents and managers in an early comic opera. When he was twenty-three he had some song manuscripts accepted by a publisher, but these did not find a ready sale and the copies reposed peacefully, undisturbed, on the publisher's shelves. For a while the same fate was accorded a song published a few years later, in 1906. This was *At Dawning*, which remained practically unknown until John McCormack featured it in his concerts some years afterwards. Then it became a tremendous success, and eventually enjoyed a sale of over a million copies. The publishers showed their fairness by voluntarily offering Cadman a royalty contract, even though they had originally purchased his copyright for a small cash payment.

It is on this song and *From the Land of the Sky Blue Water* that Cadman's fame among the general public rests, but music-lovers know him for many major works in the larger forms. He has composed two Indian operas: *Shanewis*, which has been performed in various other cities, as well as in New York, and *The Sunset Trail*, first heard in Denver and later presented in Rochester, in 1926, by the company which later became known as the American Opera Company. This troupe included the Cadman work in its repertoire on subsequent tours.

Probably Cadman's most successful attempt at grand opera is *The Witch of Salem*. In this, Cadman explicitly states, there is but one Indian character. First performed by the Chicago Civic Opera Company in 1926, it deals with the witch-burning days of the Massachusetts Colony. It is more unified in its structure than *Shanewis*, and shows a better sense of dramatic values. There was also an earlier opera, written in 1916, which did not have its first performance until 1925, at Carnegie Hall, New York. It was called *The Garden of Mystery*, and was based on Hawthorne's story of *Rappaccini's Daughter*.

Cadman has written a great deal of instrumental music. Among his earlier works are a Trio in D Major; a Piano Sonata; a *Thunderbird Suite* for piano, using Omaha themes; an *Oriental*

Rhapsody for orchestra; and a quintet, *To a Vanishing Race*. All of these works seem to embody the composer's out-of-doors spirit, his love of the desert. The Piano Sonata derived its inspiration from Miller's *From Sea to Sea* and *The Ship of the Desert*.

The feeling for the desert is apparent also in the more recent Sonata for violin and piano, in G major. As might be expected, Cadman has not in this work composed music which is self-consciously modern, seeking dissonance for its own sake. He has tried to make the music vital by remaining himself and reacting honestly to his own musical moods. For this reason the Sonata is a quite individual and unified whole.

In July of 1932 the New York Orchestra, at that time conducted by Modest Altschuler, presented Cadman's *Hollywood Suite*, a work consisting of four contrasting tonal sketches: *Mary Pickford*, *Charlie Chaplin*, *To My Mother*, and *Hollywood Bowl*. Dating from the same period is another orchestral work, of a different type and marked by unusual rhythms, *Dance of the Scarlet Sister Mary*.

When the New York Philharmonic-Symphony under Barbirolli performed Cadman's *Dark Dancers of the Mardi Gras* (December 4–5, 1937), it accorded the work its fourteenth performance in America. Its première had occurred four and a half years earlier in the Hollywood Bowl. The composer contributed the following information to the Philharmonic-Symphony program notes:

The work takes its name from the Negro side of the Mardi-Gras, although no Negro themes have been used. It is built on one theme, with extensions. The Negroes of New Orleans have their own Mardi Gras celebration, the same time the white people have theirs. This fantasy is supposed to reflect the fantastic, the grotesque, the bizarre spirit of the carnival. The original theme . . . might represent the romantic feelings of the King and Queen and the Court in Carnival fashion, for they carry out the same traditions as the whites in their Mardi Gras. Dark Dancers you know, not white dancers. The king and court parade along Ranpart Street, which is sometimes called the Negro Main Street of New Orleans. To see the costumes worn and the antics indulged in by colored people is well worth a trip to the Carnival City of America.

The work is scored for orchestra and piano obbligato and in most of the performances the composer himself has played the piano part. In spite of several limitations, the piece is effective in reflecting the grotesque, fantastic and exuberant spirit of the carnival.

Simultaneously with the Sunday afternoon performance of *Dark Dancers* in Carnegie Hall by the Philharmonic-Symphony Orchestra (December 5), the Mozart Sinfonietta played Cadman's *American Suite* for string orchestra in the same building, in the Carnegie Chamber Music Hall. This had already been played the preceding September at the Saratoga Spa festival under F. Charles Adler.

Cadman has added also to his long list of vocal works. Among the new ones are the song-cycle, *White Enchantment*; a cantata, *The Far Horizon*; and a twenty-five-minute opera, *The Willow Tree*, written chiefly for radio and concert performances, with a libretto which sets forth a dramatic situation rather than a full-length plot. The author of this libretto is Nelle Richmond Eberhart, who supplied the texts for all but one of Cadman's operas, and for many of his songs and choral works. The work was first performed on the radio over an NBC network, October 3, 1932. Francis D. Perkins reviewed the performance for the *New York Herald Tribune* [11] with the following comment:

> Both music and text could be described as rather conventional but yet effective for their purpose. . . . Mr. Cadman's music was notably tuneful, pleasant, while bordering at moments on the sentimental, not particularly distinguished in its musical ideas, setting forth the emotions of the situations with fair success, while by somewhat obvious means.

Well known equally as composer and teacher, *Gustav Strube*, who was born in Ballenstedt, Germany, March 3, 1867, has for

[11] December 4, 1932.

many years made his home in Baltimore, where he teaches at the Peabody Conservatory, and where he founded the Baltimore Symphony Orchestra in 1916, and conducted it until 1930. Strube was educated abroad, but came to America as a very young man. He had studied at the Leipzig Conservatory, and had taught at the Conservatory in Mannheim, a city rich in orchestral tradition. In 1900, he joined the first violin section of the Boston Symphony Orchestra, of which he later became assistant conductor.

He has written a long list of works: for orchestra, a Symphony in G; a Sinfonietta; a *Symphonic Prologue;* two Violin Concertos; a *Sylvan Suite;* and *Americana;* for chamber orchestra, a *Divertimento;* numerous works of chamber music, including trios, quartets, a Quintet for woodwind and horn, etc.; and a three-act opera, *The Captive,* with a libretto by Frederic Arnold Kummer. When this last-named work was produced in Baltimore, on February 28, 1938, George Schaun, writing in the *Baltimore Sun,* found that although it was somewhat more interesting orchestrally than vocally, it offered "many richly expressive melodies for both vocalists and instrumentalists." The "finely constructed score, in which thematic material was often developed in the manner of Wagner, lacked some of Wagner's tremendous gift for delineating character," Schaun wrote, but it "could certainly compare with many operatic scores that have had very much greater attention."

Two well-known musicians who have not been heard from as composers for a decade or more are *Cecil Burleigh* and *Howard A. Brockway*. Burleigh, who was born April 17, 1885, in Wyoming, New York, is a violinist and teacher of the violin, having studied his instrument with Witek, Gruenberg, and Auer. He taught at various Middle Western institutions for some years, and since 1921 has been at the University of Wisconsin. He is the composer of no less than three Concertos for violin and orchestra, which have been widely performed; of *Evangeline*, a tone-poem (1929), and *Mountain Pictures* (1930), for orchestra; and of considerable chamber music. Brockway is best known for the collections of Kentucky Mountain Tunes which he published in collaboration with Loraine Wyman. He was born in Brooklyn, New York, on November 22, 1870, studied for five years in Berlin (composition with Boise, piano with Barth), taught privately in New York from 1895 to 1903, and then joined the faculty of the Peabody Conservatory, in Baltimore. In 1910 he moved back to New York, where he has lived since that time, teaching both privately and at the David Mannes Music School. It is a long time since his compositions have been heard. But back in 1895 he composed a Symphony in D, and he is the author also of several other works for orchestra, as well as some chamber music and numerous piano pieces—mostly written in the early years of the century.

SONS OF HARVARD

When the passing of William J. Henderson and Henry Hadley left two vacancies in the membership of the American Academy of Arts and Letters, their places were filled by the election of Albert Spalding and *Frederick Shepherd Converse*. For Converse this was a tribute to a long and honorable career as composer and teacher. More than a quarter of a century earlier, in 1910, he had enjoyed the distinction of being the first American composer to have an opera produced at the Metropolitan in New York.

This was *The Pipe of Desire*, a tragic little fairy tale, vividly portrayed by the music. It had been produced in Boston a few years earlier. Another opera, *The Sacrifice*, was produced by the Boston Opera Company in 1911. At the time these works were presented, Converse had already established himself as a frequently performed composer. He had had orchestral works performed in Munich—the concert-overture *Youth*, in 1897, and a Symphony in D minor in 1898. His romance, *Festival of Pan*, had its première in 1900 by the Boston Symphony Orchestra, and later performances in other cities of America and of Europe. Another romance, *Endymion's Narrative,* was first presented by Wilhelm Gericke and the Boston Symphony. The orchestral fantasy, *The Mystic Trumpeter,* was introduced by the Philadelphia Orchestra under Fritz Scheel in 1905; the dramatic poem, *Job,* was performed at the Worcester Festival in 1907, with Schumann-Heink singing the leading solo part; and his String Quartet, Opus 18, was in the repertoire of the Kneisel Quartet.

These were followed by other major works: *Ormazd,* an orchestral tone-poem (1912); *Ave atque Vale,* another tone-poem (1917); two further Symphonies, in C minor and E major; and incidental music for plays by Percy MacKaye—*Jeanne d'Arc* and *The Scarecrow.* Then, in 1927, Converse produced the first of a series of works based on the American scene. It was entitled *Flivver Ten Million,* and was a merry bit of fun-making describing the delights inherent in Henry Ford's contribution to American life.

The work opens with "Dawn in Detroit." The toilers march to work and make their din as they build their machines. Then comes "The Birth of the Hero," who emerges from the welter, ready for service. He tries his mettle, and wanders forth into the great world in search of adventure. The next movement, "A May Night by the Roadside," is sub-titled "America's Romance," and similarly, the following "Joy Riders" is "America's Frolic." This inevitably leads to "America's Tragedy," or "The Collision." Then comes a reminiscence of the building motive, and in "Phoenix Americanus" the hero, righted though shaken, continues on his way with redoubled energy. This, remarked the composer as he held his tongue in his cheek, is "typical of the indomitable American spirit."

Naturally the work requires the modern orchestra in all its glory of wind and percussion, plus muted Ford horn, a wind machine, a factory whistle and an anvil. Koussevitzky and the Boston Orchestra gave the piece its first performance in the spring of 1927, and after that it was played by orchestras throughout the country.

In the following year, 1928, Converse was ready with another tone-poem picturing America, this time *California,* and in 1929 he composed a suite, *American Sketches,* which was given its first performance six years later by the Boston Symphony, February 8, 1935. In these sketches Converse acknowledges that the source of his inspiration was *The American Songbag* by Carl Sandburg. The four movements are "Manhattan," "The Father of Waters," "Chicken Reel," and "Bright Angel Trail." The last depicts the Southwest and the Grand Canyon, and contains the most thoughtful writing in the entire score.

After he had written the *American Sketches,* but several years before it was produced, Converse reverted from American subjects to a more general field. He composed a tone-poem for soprano and orchestra called *Prophecy,* founded on a text from Isaiah. In describing it the composer wrote: "I have called the work a tone-poem . . . and arranged the lines in a dramatic sequence to express a certain spiritual idea which I think will be clear to all who read it." When the piece had its first performance by the Boston Symphony Orchestra, December 16, 1932, the critic of *Musical America* wrote: [12]

> It seemed on a first hearing that Mr. Converse had found it a bit difficult to insinuate himself into his work; but once it was under way, there was no mistaking the superb workmanship of the piece, and the climax was as dramatic a thing as had been heard in Symphony Hall for some time.

In recent years Converse also produced a String Quartet in E minor and a Concertino for piano and orchestra.

He was born in Newton, Massachusetts, January 5, 1871. As a student at Harvard he attended Paine's classes in music. Then he entered business, but quit it after six months to study with Chadwick and become a musician. Later he went to Europe and

---

[12] December 25, 1932.

studied with Rheinberger in Germany. It was at this time that his early works were played in Munich. He graduated from the Royal Academy there and returned to Boston in 1899. For two years he taught harmony at the New England Conservatory, and then joined the Harvard faculty, first as instructor in composition and later as assistant professor. In 1907 he resigned so that he might devote himself exclusively to composition, but he subsequently went back to the New England Conservatory as professor of theory and composition, and in 1931 was appointed Dean of the Faculty. He resigned from this position in 1938 and was succeeded by Quincy Porter. His death occurred two years later, on June 8, 1940.

In 1930 Converse felt that he might fairly be characterized as conservatively modernistic in his music. More recently, a year or two before his death, he wrote: "I am through with the extravagant elements of modern music. No more experimentation of that sort for me. It is already old-fashioned. What we need is deeper spiritual and emotional significance in our music. Given that, all the rest will take care of itself."

Edward Burlingame Hill is another of the Harvard group, educated in Cambridge and later a member of the faculty. His grandfather, Thomas Hill, was president of the University from 1862 to 1868. Edward Hill was born in Cambridge, September 9, 1872, and when he graduated from Harvard it was with highest honors in music, which he had studied under John Knowles Paine. After graduation, he went abroad to study with Widor in Paris, and then returned to America to work further with Chadwick. In 1908 he joined the Harvard faculty as an instructor. Later he was made professor, and from 1928 to 1934 he was chairman of the Division of Music. He retired from the James E. Ditson Professorship of Music in 1940.

Until recently, Hill's chief fame rested on several programmatic works for orchestra. The best known were the two *Stevensoniana* suites. The first is still in manuscript, but the second is published and has been widely performed. It consists of four pieces based on poems from Robert Louis Stevenson's *Child's Garden of Verses*. The scoring is rich and colorful, with a leaning toward the French Impressionists, but possessed of a tenderness and simplicity that are altogether personal. Amy Lowell's *Lilacs* was the inspiration for an orchestral poem, and Poe's *The Fall of the House of Usher* provided the basis for a symphonic poem.

In late years, however, descriptive music of any sort has ceased to appeal to Edward Burlingame Hill. He prefers to compose absolute music with no intention beyond the development of musical ideas. He believes that the abandonment of descriptive purpose has rendered his music more personal, and while his work is not altogether free from foreign influences, he feels that it tends to be more the product of his environment. He is perfectly willing to risk and admit the conservative label, for he frankly confesses his inability to write or even think atonally, even though he may show an occasional tendency toward mild polytonality. He is in thorough sympathy with contemporary schools of musical thought, even with the radicals, but he realizes that these things are not for him as a composer.

If concert-goers expect a university professor to be academic in his own music, they are happily disappointed in Hill, for whatever they may possess, his works certainly lack a pedagogic flavor. When one of his three symphonies was performed by the Boston Symphony Orchestra in 1931, the critic of the *Musical Courier* remarked: [13] "His chief concern appears to have been to write workmanlike music which falls pleasantly on the ear, and this he has manifestly accomplished." In 1931 Hill composed a Concertino for piano and orchestra which was first performed by Jesús María Sanromá with the Boston Symphony, April 25, 1932. In this work the composer made his bow to jazz, as he had done some years earlier in his four *Jazz Studies* for two pianos. It was a gentlemanly bow, however, discreetly in keeping with a Harvard background. The piece is a short work in three connected movements, the first and last employing lively, vigorous material

[13] March 14, 1931.

which offsets the charming sentimentality of the middle section. Sanromá played the work again two years later, and it was also heard at the Eastman Festival in 1933.

In the summer of 1932 Serge Koussevitzky suggested to Hill that he write a symphony in one movement. The composer responded with a Sinfonietta, Opus 57, which the Boston Orchestra performed in Cambridge, March 9, 1933, and then in Boston. Again animated rhythms characterized the work, which proved to be altogether stimulating and skillfully written. In the same month, on March 29, the piece was played by the Berlin Philharmonic under the baton of Koussevitzky's nephew, Fabien Sevitzky. Later it was heard in Paris.

Professor Hill has another Sinfonietta on his list, numbered Opus 40A, and representing an orchestral arrangement of his String Quartet, Opus 40. The Quartet was composed in 1935, presented in Boston in February of 1936, and featured at the Harvard Tercentenary concerts the following September. As a Sinfonietta the work was introduced by the Boston Symphony during the season of 1935–36. It is conservative without suggesting a conscious harking back to the past. It has individuality and the personal quality Hill aims to achieve, as well as lyric charm. In August of 1937 the Boston Symphony performed two movements of the work at the Tanglewood Estate in Stockbridge, Massachusetts.

When Hill's Third Symphony had its première at the hands of the Boston Symphony, December 3, 1937, the composer again disclaimed programmatic intentions. In a statement included in the program notes he admitted to "no descriptive background" for his symphony. "It aims," he wrote, "merely to present and develop musical ideas according to traditional forms." The result was thoroughly characteristic. In the words of the *Musical America* reviewer: [14]

The work betokened the hand of a master craftsman, well versed in all the tricks of his trade. It did not sound especially modern, al-

[14] December 10, 1937.

though it nodded to more modern harmonic devices. It had a certain restrained humor such as might have been indicated by George W. Chadwick, had he lived long enough to have absorbed the newer harmonic idioms.

In addition to the Quartet, Opus 40, Hill has to his credit several chamber music works. An earlier Sonata for clarinet (or violin) and piano was published in 1926–27 by the Society for the Publication of American Music. A Sextet for wind instruments and piano, Opus 39, was commissioned by Elizabeth Sprague Coolidge and performed at the Coolidge Festival in Pittsfield, Massachusetts, September 20, 1934. In reviewing its performance on this occasion, by Sanromá and the Laurent Wind Quintet, Francis D. Perkins remarked in the *New York Herald Tribune:*[15]

Mr. Hill . . . exhibited an unprofessorial degree of lightness and humor in his sextet for piano and wind instruments. . . . The four movements of this likable work proved deftly wrought and adroitly scored, with a pronounced melodic appeal and varied color. One or two movements left room for a little condensation, but in general the sextet was a notable example of craftsmanship and instrumental knowledge employed by a musician of notable talent and experience.

The Sextet was later published by the Society for the Publication of American Music.

A more recent Quartet for piano and strings, Opus 42, had its first performance, by Sanromá and the Boston String Quartet, in Boston, January 11, 1938. There are also a Concerto for violin and orchestra, composed in 1933–34, and its first movement revised in October, 1937, which was first played by Ruth Posselt and the Boston Orchestra in November, 1938; and a Concertino for string orchestra, Opus 46, introduced by Koussevitzky in Boston on April 19, 1940.

Two of Hill's colleagues at Harvard have been considerably less active than he as composers during the past few years, but they earned their spurs during the first quarter of the century: *William Clifford Heilman* and *Edward Ballantine*.

[15] September 21, 1934.

Heilman comes originally from Pennsylvania, where he was born in Williamsport, September 27, 1877. He graduated from Harvard in 1900, and for many years taught counterpoint, canon, and fugue there, to the great profit of many of the younger generation, who received from him extraordinarily painstaking and perfection-seeking instruction at a time when standards in general were not at all on the level he strove for. When he retired from teaching, in 1925, Harvard gave him the honorary degree of M.A. He was represented on the Tercentenary programs of Harvard in 1936, and his Trio for violin, piano, and cello is published by the Society for the Publication of American Music. Otherwise his music is little known, largely, no doubt, because his own great modesty has kept it in obscurity. But his works include, in addition to those mentioned, an orchestral tone-poem, *By the Porta Catania;* a Suite for orchestra; and some chamber music, songs, and piano pieces.

Ballantine was born in the musical town of Oberlin, Ohio, on August 8, 1886, studied music at Harvard and later in Berlin, and since 1912 has been a member of the Harvard music faculty, where he now holds the rank of professor. His music, so far as it has been heard, is delicate, sensitive, and impressionistic. He has had a feeling that either he or the majority of his contemporaries were out of step. Stylistic doubts have hampered many of our composers, and in Ballantine's case they seem to have put a stop to his creative activity altogether. But his orchestral pieces have been performed by several of the major orchestras: a Prelude to Hagedorn's *The Delectable Forest* (1914); a symphonic poem, *The Eve of St. Agnes* (1917); and a suite, *From the Garden of Hellas* (1923); a tone-poem, *The Awakening of the Woods;* an *Overture to The Piper;* and he has written numerous songs, piano pieces, and short chamber music works. He is undoubtedly best known for the witty trifle, *Variations on Mary Had a Little Lamb* in the styles of various composers.

Two years Ballantine's junior, *Philip Greeley Clapp* also received his education at Harvard. He came of a musical Boston family, having been born in the "home of the bean and the cod" on August 4, 1888. He graduated from Harvard in 1908, and received his Ph.D. there in 1911, on the basis of work he had done in the meanwhile in Berlin and London, including the study of composition with Max von Schillings and research in the British Museum. For two years he taught at Harvard, and after a few years of work in various schools he became Director of Music at Dartmouth College, from which he was absent on leave for a year or two as bandmaster in the American Army in France. In 1919 he became Professor of Music in the State University of Iowa in Iowa City. His orchestral works include several symphonies, a tone-poem for piano and orchestra, *Norge* (1908); *A Song of Youth* (1911–13); a *Dramatic Poem* for trombone and orchestra; and a prelude, *In Summer*. He has also written choral and chamber music.

Donald Tweedy, who was born in Danbury, Connecticut, April 23, 1890, is another composer who received his training at Harvard, where he took his B.A. and, in 1917, his M.A. He studied for a time in Europe, as well as with Goetschius in New York. He has taught at various institutions, including the Eastman School of Music, Vassar College, Hamilton College, and others. He has written a textbook, the *Manual of Harmonic Technic, Based on the Practice of J. S. Bach*,[16] and is the composer of *L'Allegro*, a symphonic study; three Dances for orchestra, from an unnamed ballet; incidental music for Sidney Howard's *Swords*; a ballet, *Alice in Wonderland*; and some chamber music.

Walter Helfer, born at Lawrence, Massachusetts, September 30, 1896, and educated at Harvard, studied composition with the late Stuart Mason in Boston, and later with Caussade in Paris and Respighi in Rome, during his tenure of a fellowship at the American Academy in Rome. His orchestral works include a *Symphony on Canadian Airs*; a Concert Overture in D Major; a *Water Idyl*; and a Prelude, Intermezzo, and Fugue. He has also written some choral works, chamber music, and pieces for

---

[16] Boston: Oliver Ditson Company, 1928.

chamber orchestra. Since 1929 he has taught at Hunter College in New York City.

One of the younger Harvard talents is *William Ames*, who was born in Cambridge, Massachusetts, March 20, 1901. After graduating from Harvard, in 1924, he went to Paris, where he studied piano, organ, and composition, with Nadia Boulanger for three years. He taught privately and held church organ positions for a year or so, and then went to the Eastman School of Music, where he was instructor in harmony and counterpoint until 1938. He has composed two Symphonies and a Rhapsody for orchestra; Sonatas for violin and piano and for cello and piano; two String Quartets; a Quintet for piano and strings and one for clarinet and strings; a Piano Sonata and numerous shorter pieces for piano; songs, and choral music.

ERNEST SCHELLING

Although no new works came from the pen of *Ernest Schelling* during the years immediately preceding his death on December 8, 1939, he continued his activities in the field of conducting. For many years he led the Young People's Concerts of the New York Philharmonic-Symphony Society and in 1935 he became director of the Baltimore Symphony Orchestra, but illness put an end to his tenure of that post after two seasons.

He had had a brilliant career. When he first appeared before the public, it was in the role of concert pianist. Born in Belvedere, New Jersey, July 26, 1876, he was a musical prodigy from early childhood. When he was only four, he made an appearance at the Academy of Music in Philadelphia. When he was six he was taken to the Paris Conservatoire to study with Mathias. Later he worked with Moszkowski, Pruckner, Leschetizky, Huber, Barth, and finally for four years with Paderewski at his villa in Switzerland. He achieved international rank as a pianist, and played in recital and with orchestras throughout America and in Europe.

When the World War came, Schelling was made a captain and later a major, attached to the Intelligence Service because of his abilities as a linguist. In 1918 he went to Poland with his friend Paderewski, at the time the great Pole became premier of his native country. Then, in the summer of 1919, an automobile accident in Switzerland resulted in his having to give up his career as a pianist, and turn chiefly to conducting and composing.

His most important works are *Impressions from an Artist's Life* and *A Victory Ball*. The first is a set of variations for piano and orchestra, each variation depicting one of the composer's friends. It was first played by the Boston Symphony Orchestra, under Muck, in 1916. *A Victory Ball*, for orchestra, takes its program from the poem by Alfred Noyes. The gaiety of the dancers is halted by the sounds of war, by the spirits of the fallen, the roll of the drum, and taps. It is vivid music, uncompromising in its reminder of the horrors of war. It was first introduced in 1923, by Stokowski in Philadelphia, and for several years was performed repeatedly by leading orchestras. In May of 1936 it was produced as a ballet at the Eastman Festival in Rochester.

Schelling also composed a *Légende Symphonique*, played by the Berlin Philharmonic in 1906; a Symphony in C minor; a *Suite Fantastique*, introduced by Mengelberg in Amsterdam (1905); a Violin Concerto, played by Fritz Kreisler with the Boston Symphony in 1917; a tone-poem, *Morocco*, played in 1927 by the New York Philharmonic, with the composer conducting; and a number of piano pieces and some chamber music.

On May 14, 1940, a benefit concert was given in Carnegie Hall in memory of Ernest Schelling, in which Lily Pons, Robert Casadesus and the New York Philharmonic-Symphony Orchestra under Frederick Stock took part. Schelling's *Légende Symphonique*, his *Suite Variée* (a revised version of a Divertimento for strings and piano first performed in 1925), and *A Victory Ball*, were played. The proceeds were to be devoted to a fund in his name for the benefit of distressed musicians.

RICHARD HAGEMAN

Creatively, *Richard Hageman* had been known chiefly as a composer of striking songs until his grand opera, *Caponsacchi*, was produced at the Metropolitan, February 4, 1937. Although he was born a Hollander, in 1882, Hageman came to this country in 1907 and since that time has made his home with us, active as an opera conductor, accompanist and coach for singers, and most recently as a composer and musical director for motion pictures.

Caponsacchi was produced abroad several years before it was given in America. The première occurred at the Municipal Theatre of Freiburg, Germany, February 19, 1932, and was broadcast to the United States. Three years later, March 19, 1935, it was produced at the Vienna Volksoper. In the German version the opera was entitled *Tragödie in Arezzo*.

The Metropolitan production was gorgeously mounted, with a cast headed by Lawrence Tibbett, Mario Chamlee, and Helen Jepson; but even this imposing array of artists, and the commanding presence of the composer as conductor, could not make the material altogether convincing.

For his libretto, Hageman chose Arthur Goodrich's version of Browning's *The Ring and the Book*, a swashbuckling affair in which villainy is unsubtle and unashamed. The good people are very, very good, and the bad people are as horrid as they come in the story books. Consequently Lawrence Tibbett had a role which must have made him as unhappy as he made his unfortunate victims in the opera. The whole affair reverts to the period of the romantic operas of the early nineteenth century; it is probably no worse than many from those days which occasionally appear in the current repertoire of our opera houses, but it certainly adds little to the sum of American operas which seek to express the age in which they are written.

Probably the fairest criticism of *Caponsacchi* was one written for the *New York Times* by Herbert Peyser, following the première at Freiburg: [17]

Caponsacchi is not a work that will arrest the stars in their courses or menace the underpinnings of the universe. Its dramatic ingredients are those which have formed the stock-in-trade of romantic melodrama for a century—or perhaps for even two or three centuries. Its music is eclectic and unoriginal and occupies itself not at all with innovations, experiments, tortured theories or the deeper consideration of soul states or portentous philosophies.

Like Homer and Rudyard Kipling, Mr. Hageman frankly takes his own where he finds it, whether the source be Richard Wagner or Richard Strauss, Puccini, Massenet, Debussy or the great god Platitude. *Caponsacchi* is nothing for sophisticates, and there is not the slightest reason to imagine that its composer ever designed it as such. But if it was thoroughly stage-worthy, entertaining, effective and warmly melodious opera that he contemplated, he must be credited with a complete achievement of his object.

FROM WEST OF THE ALLEGHENIES

Arthur Nevin is another composer whose opera was produced abroad. He spent the summers of 1903 and 1904 on the Blackfoot Reservation in Montana, and there heard the story of *Poia*, which Randolph Hartley put into a libretto for him. President Theodore Roosevelt invited Nevin to give an illustrated talk on the opera at the White House in 1907, but in spite of this endorsement and interest the opera was performed, not in an American opera house, but in Germany, where it had four performances at the Royal Opera in Berlin, during the summer of 1909. Humperdinck, then at work on *Königskinder*, assisted in the German translation of the libretto of *Poia*.

Nevin was born in Sewickley, Pennsylvania, April 27, 1871, the youngest son of a family that boasted another distinguished musician, Ethelbert Nevin, composer of *The Rosary*. Arthur Nevin was educated at the New England Conservatory in Boston,

[17] March 6, 1932.

and abroad with Klindworth, O. B. Boise, and Humperdinck. For five years he was professor of music at the University of Kansas, and for another five years director of municipal music in Memphis, Tennessee.

In 1911 he wrote another opera, *Twilight*. Rumor has it that this one-act work was actually accepted for performance by the Metropolitan, but that through a misunderstanding with the management it never came to performance there. Under the name of *A Daughter of the Forest* it was produced in Chicago in 1918. Nevin's instrumental works include four major orchestral pieces: *Lorna Doone Suite* (1897); *Miniature Suite* (1902); *Springs of Saratoga* (1911); and a Symphonic Poem (1930). There is also a String Quartet in D minor (1929).

In his most recent orchestral work, *Arizona,* Nevin adopts some of the more advanced tonal devices even though he does not lose the traditional viewpoint. This work was first performed by the New York Civic Orchestra under Armand Balendonck, March 6, 1935. It was described by a reviewer of the *New York World-Telegram:* [18]

Mr. Nevin's "Arizona" is a tone poem, or, rather, an orchestral fantasy based on three melodic and several rhythmic subjects, appearing here and there in the scheme and intertwining at the conclusion against a background of progressive chord figures.

In the matter of development Mr. Nevin proceeds through a cumulative intensification of melodic and rhythmic material. His inventive ability is marked and his harmonization is attractively modern in the non-polytonal sense.

He showed a sense of dramatic values in the use of a crashing chord of the eleventh that twice battered its way through the musical web.

A large audience gave Mr. Nevin an ovation when he appeared.

Rossetter Gleason Cole is a composer who wrote an opera on the subject of the Merry Mount colony several years before Howard Hanson finished his work of that name. Then, when

[18] March 6, 1935.

SAFE AND SOUND

Hanson's opera was produced in 1934, Cole changed the title of his own work, still unproduced, from *Merry Mount* to *The Maypole Lovers*. The libretto of the Cole opera was written by Carty Ranck and the composer finished the music in 1927 and the orchestration in 1931.

On January 9 and 10, 1936, the Chicago Symphony Orchestra under Frederick Stock performed an orchestral suite from *The Maypole Lovers*, which the reviewer of *Musical America* [19] called "post-Wagnerian . . . sonorous, well-organized, and colorful . . . written with the careful and expert craftsmanship which distinguishes the other products of his [Cole's] pen." This is what might be expected of a man whose music may frequently be cacophonous enough to satisfy any modernist, but who still clings more or less to a certain nineteenth-century warmth and clarity of melodic outline.

Cole was born in Michigan, February 5, 1866. He was a pupil of Max Bruch in Germany, and of Middelschulte at home. For over thirty years he has lived in Chicago as a teacher, composer, organist, and lecturer. Since 1908 he has been in charge of music at the Columbia University Summer Session in New York.

His *Symphonic Prelude* for orchestra was first presented by the Chicago Symphony under Stock in 1916, and repeated in 1918. An overture, *Pioneer*, was written in commemoration of the Illinois State Centennial (1918), and dedicated to the memory of Abraham Lincoln. A *Heroic Piece* for orchestra and organ was first played at a special concert of the Chicago Symphony in 1924.

Cole has written three major choral works: *The Passing of Summer*; *The Broken Troth*, a cantata for women's voices; and *The Rock of Liberty*, a *Pilgrim Ode*, composed for the tercentenary of the landing of the Pilgrims. His Sonata for violin and piano was first performed in Germany, in 1892, and then in America, by Theodore Spiering, in 1897. A Ballade for cello and orchestra was introduced in Minneapolis in 1909.

[19] January 25, 1936.

Eric Delamarter has for many years been one of Chicago's leading musicians, organist at the Fourth Presbyterian Church, and until recently assistant conductor of the Chicago Symphony Orchestra. He has also been a professional critic—for the Chicago *Record-Herald* and for the Chicago *Tribune*. He was born in Lansing, Michigan, February 18, 1880, studied in Chicago with Middelschulte, and in Paris with Guilmant and Widor. As a composer he has written for orchestra an overture, *The Faun*, and a Suite of incidental music to *The Betrothal*. Although the latter is by no means a new work, it has had several recent performances at the Eastman School in Rochester. At the 1937 Festival it was given as a ballet. Delamarter is also the composer of a Sonata for violin and piano, in E flat, a work of considerable originality, with an interesting slow movement and an individual finale. There are also many songs, some piano music, and pieces for organ, as well as incidental music for plays.

Felix Borowski is another of the Chicagoans who has been active as a composer. He is perhaps best known for his widely played violin piece, *Adoration*, but he is also the author of a number of works in the larger forms. In 1932 the Chicago Civic Orchestra performed a suite from Borowski's ballet, *Boudoir*. On March 16 and 17, 1933, the Chicago Symphony, under Stock, gave Borowski's First Symphony its première performances. It proved to be graceful and expressive, frankly romantic without seeming too old-fashioned to belong to the present.

Several years later, February 22, 1936, the Federal Music Project in Los Angeles produced Borowski's operatic satire, *Fernando del Nonsensico*, in which the composer lampooned traditional opera. Its plot included some of the most ludicrous scenes from *Lucia*, *Aïda*, *Carmen* and other favorites, and ended with the death of practically all the principals. It was also in Los Angeles, and again under the auspices of the Federal Music Project, that Borowski's Second Symphony had its first hearing, in 1936. This too proved to be a work with romantic leanings, with an almost Oriental richness in its harmonic treatment and instrumentation.

Borowski was born in England, March 10, 1872, of Polish parentage. In 1897 he was invited to come to America, to head the theory and composition department of the Chicago Musical College. He has also been a music critic for Chicago newspapers, and program annotator for the Chicago Symphony Orchestra.

Still another Chicagoan who has been active in recent years is *Arne Oldberg,* born in Youngstown, Ohio, July 12, 1874, trained in Chicago, and also abroad under Leschetizky and Rheinberger, and since 1899 head of the piano department at Northwestern University in Evanston, Illinois. His Second Piano Concerto was awarded a first prize of $1,000 in the 1931 Hollywood Bowl competition. When this work had its première performance in the Bowl under Frederick Stock in the summer of 1932, and subsequent hearings in Chicago on November 3 and 4 of the same year, the critics were not particularly impressed. One Los Angeles reviewer found it "pianistically brilliant" but of "great length" and of "uneven and often debatable . . . worth." [20] In Chicago the *Musical America* correspondent considered it "pianistically effective," but felt that "its musical content . . . can scarcely be called original. Mr. Oldberg's fancy roamed far and wide in this work, and the result is a confusing diversity of styles, and some rather obvious resemblances." [21] Both in Hollywood and in Chicago, the soloist was Oldberg's daughter-in-law, Hilda Edwards.

Five years after the first performance of the Concerto, another work by Oldberg had its initial hearings at the hands of the Chicago Symphony, conducted by Hans Lange (March 11 and 12, 1937). This time the critical reception was more favorable. The new work was a symphonic poem, *The Sea,* and the *Musical America* critic described it as "sound music, romantic in outlook

---

[20] *Musical Courier,* August 27, 1932.
[21] November 25, 1932.

and substance, and flawlessly expert in setting forth its picture." [22]

Oldberg's earlier works include two symphonies; a First Piano Concerto; several overtures and orchestral fantasies; a Concerto for horn; a String Quartet; three Quintets; a Piano Sonata; and many smaller works.

Middle Westerner by adoption and Dane by birth is *Carl Busch*, who settled in Kansas City before many of our contemporaries were born. Busch's native town was Bjerre, Denmark (March 29, 1862), and his early training was in the country of his birth, at the University of Copenhagen, and with Hartmann and Gade. In 1886 he went to Paris to study with Godard, and in the following year he came to America. He has been active in Kansas City ever since, as a composer, teacher, and conductor of various choral and orchestral organizations, many of which he himself founded. Busch's Americanization is more than a matter of form. In the plains and prairies he has found inspiration for much of his music. A piece for military band is entitled *Chant from the Great Plains; Ozarka* is a suite for orchestra; *Minnehaha's Vision* is based on an episode from Longfellow's *Hiawatha*. He has made many settings of actual Indian melodies, for voice, for piano, and for orchestra, *e.g.*, the *Four Indian Tribal Melodies*. He has also written two Symphonies; a symphonic prologue, *The Passing of Arthur;* an *Elegy* for string orchestra; a String Quartet; and many cantatas, anthems, songs, and small pieces. In 1912 he was knighted by the Danish government.

Clarence Loomis came to the attention of a large public when his opera, *Yolanda of Cyprus,* was produced in Chicago, New York, and numerous other cities on tour, by the American Opera Company during the season of 1929–30. In this work Loomis made an obvious attempt to subordinate the music to the text. The voices had little to do musically, and what musical delineation was attempted, was given to the orchestra. It was an interesting experiment, one that has often since been tried; and the results were altogether pleasant, in spite of the obvious derivations ap-

[22] March 25, 1937.

parent in the score. In recent years Loomis has been at work on further operas, one of them from Poe's *The Fall of the House of Usher*, and the other a work based on melodies by Stephen Foster—*Susannah, Don't You Cry*. Both works employ librettos by Ethel Ferguson, and the Foster opera was commissioned by Josiah K. Lilly, founder of Foster Hall in Indianapolis. It was produced in New York in the spring of 1939 by the American Lyric Theater.

Loomis was born in Sioux Falls, North Dakota, December 13, 1888. He studied in Chicago and abroad with Schreker and Godowsky, and then became teacher of theory and piano at the American Conservatory of Chicago. In recent years he has been head of the theory department of the Arthur Jordan Conservatory of Music in Indianapolis. He has a long list of works to his credit, in almost every form, choral works, chamber music, and orchestral pieces.

One of the most strikingly individual talents among our composers is that of *Eastwood Lane*, who unfortunately for himself and for us is terrifically handicapped by lack of training. Consequently his works are cast in the smaller forms and employ a limited palette, but they are so spontaneous and virile, so indigenous to the soil of America, that they are far more important than their unpretentiousness would signify. It may be, too, that Lane's talent is of the sort more formal training would have stifled.

He has composed several suites of piano pieces: *Sleepy Hollow*, *Five American Dances*, *Adirondack Sketches*, *Central Park Suite*, and a children's suite called *Knee-High to a Grasshopper*. Some of his works have been scored by Ferde Grofé for Paul Whiteman's Orchestra—among them *Sea Burial* and *Persimmon Pucker*. Grofé presented Lane's ballet-suite, *Fourth of July*, at his Carnegie Hall concert, January 19, 1937.

Lane was born near Syracuse, New York, in the early 1880's.

He is largely self-educated, academically as well as musically. His own reading has meant more to him than the few months he spent at Syracuse University.

Franz Carl Bornschein is a Baltimorean, born in 1879, and at present a member of the faculty at the institution in which he had his own training, the Peabody Conservatory of Music. He has composed a great deal of choral music, as well as many works for orchestra. His most recent symphonic works are *Cape Cod Impressions* and *The Mission Road*, and *Mystic Trumpeter* for orchestra, chorus and soloists. Earlier pieces include a Violin Concerto, a String Quartet, *Three Persian Poems* for orchestra, and many others.

Harvey Bartlett Gaul, born in New York, April 11, 1881, and since 1910 a resident of Pittsburgh, has become widely known for cantatas, church anthems, operettas, organ pieces and songs. In recent years he has been turning his attention to orchestral music. He has written a tone-poem for full orchestra, *Père Marquette*; a *New England Prelude*; an *Introduction to a Speaker*; for string orchestra a suite called *Fosteriana*, a modern treatment of Stephen Foster melodies; and *Three Palestinian Pastels*. There are also three works for string quartet: *Three Pennsylvania Portraits*; *Tennessee Devil Tunes*; and *From the Great Smokies*.

WOMEN COMPOSERS

Mabel W. Daniels has become more widely known in the past few years through frequent performances of her prelude for small orchestra, *Deep Forest*. She is a native of New England, and has composed many part-songs, as well as works for solo voice. Her *Villa of Dreams* was awarded a prize in the 1911 competition of the National Federation of Music Clubs. *The Song of Jael*, a cantata, received its first performance at the hands of Rose Bampton and the Worcester Festival Chorus, under Albert Stoessel in October, 1940.

Gena Branscombe is best known for her choral works. She was born in Ontario, Canada, November 4, 1881, and studied at the Chicago Musical College, and with Humperdinck in Germany. Her cycle for women's voices and orchestra, *Youth of the World*, has had frequent performances, as has her earlier work, *Pilgrims of Destiny*. For orchestra she has composed a *Festival Prelude*, and a symphonic suite, *Quebec*. She has also a long list of shorter choral works, songs, and some chamber music.

Eleanor Everest Freer, born in Philadelphia, 1864, has been one of the most ardent supporters of American opera, and is the founder of the American Opera Society of Chicago. She herself is the composer of no less than ten operas, as well as many songs and piano pieces.

Mary Carr Moore is one of the prominent composers of California, and has the honor of having a club named for her: The Mary Carr Moore Manuscript Club of Los Angeles. She was born in Memphis, Tennessee, August 6, 1873. Her first opera, *The Oracle*, was produced in San Francisco in 1894. The next, *Narcissa*, had its first hearing in Seattle in 1912, and was later given nine performances in San Francisco, with the composer conducting. This was followed, also in 1912, by *The Leper*, a one-act tragedy. *Los Rubios*, a three-act opera, was produced at the Greek Theatre, Los Angeles, in 1931, and *Davide Rizzio* at the Shrine Civic Auditorium in 1932. Mrs. Moore's works have been awarded numerous prizes, and she has also to her credit many songs, part-songs, and instrumental works.

When *Frances Terry's* Sonata for violin and piano was published by the Society for the Publication of American Music (1931), a reviewer in *Musical America* wrote:[23]

> Let us forestall all controversy as to whether woman can write as good music as her male partners and hasten to say that the "weaker" sex does not often write with the breadth and passion revealed by Frances Terry in this opus 15. Dark, brooding, Brahmsian introspection (though the only reminiscence is the Schumann-like bandying of chords in the piano-part of the trio), strength of architecture, and

[23] December 26, 1931.

sure handling of the material, all are in convincing evidence. In short, "Hats off, Gentlemen!"

Miss Terry was born in Connecticut, studied with Scharwenka, lived for a number of years in New York, and is now a resident of Northampton, Massachusetts. Most of her works have been for piano; three Impromptus, an *Impromptu Appassionato,* a suite, *Idyls of an Inland Sea,* six recital Études, a *Ballade Hongroise,* and others.

Frances McCollin is another of the women composers, one who has achieved distinction in spite of the terrific handicap of blindness. She is the composer of a String Quartet, a Piano Quintet, an *Adagio* and a Scherzo for string orchestra, a Trio for organ (or piano), violin, and cello, as well as many part-songs and choral works. *Spring in Heaven,* for women's voices, was awarded a $500 prize by the National Federation of Music Clubs in 1931. Miss McCollin was born in Philadelphia in 1892.

HOWARD HANSON

A few years ago *Howard Hanson* was recognized as the leader of the younger group of American composers, those who were bringing fresh ideas to our native music. Now that he is in his forties the designation "younger" must be dropped, but the leadership remains. As Director of the Eastman School of Music, and through his inauguration and continuance of the American Composers' Concerts at Rochester, he has done more to encourage his fellow artists and to give new talent a hearing than any other single individual in the country. These concerts have taken place every year since their initiation in the spring of 1925.

In spite of his devoted interest in the development of American music, Hanson is no chauvinist; he is not an advocate of a "nationalist" school. To him American music means music written by Americans. It makes no difference what their backgrounds may be, whether they are descendants of the settlers of Plymouth, Jamestown, or Wilmington, or whether they are sons of immigrants newly arrived. His sole interest is that America contribute its gift of music to the world, that a rich creative musical life may flourish in this country, that some of the glorious ideals that are American may be transmuted into living tone.

Similarly, he is not particularly concerned with conservatism versus radicalism. The radical of today may be the conservative of tomorrow, and the degree of his conservatism or radicalism is apt to have very little to do with the quality of his music.

Hanson also believes that every composer must constantly grow, both technically and creatively, must continually search himself to test the basic qualities of his own aesthetic philosophy, must constantly seek for new beauties, and must turn the microscope of his own analytical mind on each new approach evolved either by himself or by others, for the purpose of finding in that new approach the spirit of life which is the basis of all art. As for his own work, he believes that his Third Symphony comes closer to the realization of the ideals he has set for himself than any other work he has written.

He was born in Wahoo, Nebraska, October 28, 1896, the son of Swedish parents, Hans and Wilma Hanson. He was educated at Luther College, Nebraska, Northwestern University in Illinois, the Institute of Musical Art in New York, and for three years he lived in Europe as a Fellow of the American Academy in Rome. Before going abroad he had already occupied the position of Dean of the music conservatory of the College of the Pacific in California. He was only twenty when he was appointed its Professor of Theory.

Upon his return from Rome in 1924, he accepted the directorship of the Eastman School of Music in Rochester, and has held that position ever since. Besides carrying on his administrative work at the school, and teaching, he has been active as a conductor. He inaugurated the American Composers' Concerts soon after he came to Rochester, and he has appeared as guest conductor of orchestras throughout America and abroad. Under the auspices of the Oberlaender Trust of the Carl Schurz Memorial

Foundation, he went to Germany in 1933, and appeared as guest conductor of the Berlin Philharmonic, and the Leipzig and Stuttgart Symphony Orchestras. The programs consisted entirely of American works, and were broadcast throughout Germany. Two of them were sent to America by short-wave transmission.

In addition to his three symphonies (*Nordic,* 1922; *Romantic,* 1930; and the Third, 1937), Hanson has composed five symphonic poems (*Before the Dawn,* 1920; *Exaltation,* 1920; *North and West,* 1923; *Lux Aeterna,* 1923; and *Pan and the Priest,* 1926); a Symphonic Prelude, 1916; a Symphonic Legend, 1917; a Symphonic Rhapsody, 1919; and a Concerto for organ and orchestra, based on themes of *North and West,* 1926. In the field of chamber music he has composed a Quintet in F minor, for piano and strings (1916); a *Concerto da Camera,* for piano and string quartet (1917); and a String Quartet (1923).

The most widely performed of the orchestral works have been the *Nordic* and *Romantic* symphonies, the latter commissioned by Serge Koussevitzky for the fiftieth anniversary of the Boston Symphony Orchestra, and two of the symphonic poems, *Lux Aeterna* and *Pan and the Priest*. The Third Symphony was commissioned by the Columbia Broadcasting System, and had its first performance on the radio September 19, 1937. On this occasion the work consisted of only three movements, and the composer announced his intention of adding a fourth at some future date. This seemed essential upon first hearing, for the third movement is a brief Scherzo which by no means brings the symphony to a satisfactory conclusion.

As a whole, this Third Symphony is more polyphonic than Hanson's earlier symphonies, and harmonically it is purer. It contains fewer superimposed intervals, and more chords essentially of a triad character. Whatever dissonant elements occur are the result of counterpoint rather than of vertical harmonization. In commissioning the work (together with works from several other composers), the Columbia Broadcasting System aimed at encouraging music peculiarly adapted to radio, but Hanson claimed that experience had taught him that it is not necessary to compose or orchestrate differently for radio than for the concert hall. "If music sounds well on the ordinary concert stage," he said, "then it should sound all right when broadcast. Of course, some instruments are better or worse than others from the 'mike' standpoint, but those inequalities are the problem of the sound-engineer, not that of a composer, who should write as he feels. There is no question that good architectural form, and a broad and naturally antiphonal style, help in solving broadcasting sound problems."

Hanson's first major work for voices was *The Lament for Beowulf*, composed in 1925, and since then performed at the Ann Arbor and Worcester Festivals, and by various organizations throughout the country. The *Heroic Elegy* (1927) is also for chorus, but in this the voices have no words. Another work for mixed chorus and orchestra is the *Three Poems from Walt Whitman*, Songs from *Drum Taps*, composed in 1925.

Probably the most extended and ambitious work that Hanson has yet attempted is the opera *Merry Mount*, produced by the Metropolitan Opera Company, New York, February 10, 1934, and given nine performances during that season. The work had been heard in concert form at the Ann Arbor Festival the preceding May 20.

Several years before the actual production of the opera, the libretto which Richard L. Stokes provided the composer was published as a poem in book form. On that occasion Lewis Gannett reviewed the text for the book column of the *New York Herald Tribune*,[24] and thereby provided a highly readable and terse summary of the plot:

Thomas Morton set up a maypole at Merrymount, in Massachusetts, in 1625, to the scandal of his Puritan neighbors, danced, made merry, and sold liquor to the Indians. The Puritans cut down his maypole and shipped Morton back to England. And ever since that day Thomas Morton of Merrymount, of whom so little is known, has

[24] January 16, 1932.

been a glamorous figure to historians seeking new light on old New England. . . .

A Puritan pastor, stirred by the beauty of women in his dreams, but not at all by the little Puritan girl to whom he becomes engaged, is Mr. Stokes' central character. When Marigold, one of the Mount's company of gay cavaliers, steps into the Puritan settlement, Pastor Bradford loses his head completely. He stops her marriage to a fellow cavalier; he provokes his fellow Puritans to rout the wedding festivities, killing her fiancé; he wrestles for the soul of Marigold, and loses his own. In the night he dreams of selling his soul for Marigold's body, bringing death and destruction upon the young Puritan colony as a penalty; and when he awakes to find drunken Indians sacking the Puritan village, it seems but confirmation of his demented imaginings. He seizes Marigold and marches with her into the flames, while the returning Puritans chant the Lord's Prayer.

Even though Stokes disclaimed any intention of writing factual history in this libretto, he was attacked from all sides for perverting historical events. He replied to his critics on several occasions, but most exasperatedly in a letter to the *Musical Courier:* [25]

Between persons addicted to fact and those given to imagination there appears to be fixed an impassable gulf. Almost any public school child should be able to inform your correspondent that, had I restricted myself to the literal data, there would have been no opera of Merry Mount. Even Hawthorne, in order to compose a symmetrical tale of a few pages concerning Thomas Morton's plantation, found himself under obligation to elaborate upon the record. . . .

I distinguish between the truth of fact and the truth of art. Under the dispensation of the latter, I felt free to telescope certain characteristic phenomena of the colonial period of New England. . . .

I am weary of explaining that Wrestling Bradford is a fictitious character, without relation to William Bradford, Governor of Plymouth Colony. . . . The date of 1625 was intended merely as an approximation. . . .

Our enlightened school child would also be aware that the title of "dramatic poem" or "libretto" implies fiction. Is there an opera book in existence that scrupulously transcribes history? And what, after all, is history? Frederick the Great defined it as "a set of lies agreed upon by pedants." It chances that there are available, in the nearest library,

[25] March 10, 1934.

two narratives of Thomas Morton's adventure which were written by leading actors in that incident, Elder Bradford and Morton himself. Any reader desirous of learning the hard and irrefutable facts may take his choice, for these records are as diametrically opposite as the poles.

At the concert performance in Ann Arbor the leading roles of the opera were sung by John Charles Thomas, Frederick Jagel, Leonora Corona, and Rose Bampton, under the baton of the composer. At the Metropolitan Tullio Serafin conducted, and the singers included Lawrence Tibbett, Edward Johnson, Gladys Swarthout and Goeta Ljungberg.

The Metropolitan première was a tremendously successful affair, and according to reporters, the applause of the audience resulted in fifty curtain calls for composer, librettist, and performers. But in spite of the public approbation at the opening, the critics were somewhat reserved in their praise. Olin Downes expressed the following opinion of the music: [26]

> The music is at times conventional and noisily effective. Otherwise, it displays neither originality nor any special aptitude for the theatre. Its strongest point is the choral writing. That is somewhat inappropriate, in the sense of dramatic verity, because we know that no Puritans sang these elaborate choruses, or anything much like them. Dr. Hanson, it is evident, has taken some old and austere hymn-tunes as a model for his polyphonic developments, which are too extensive for verisimilitude and too ponderous for good drama.

Lawrence Gilman found the choruses the most effective feature of the score. In his extended review he wrote: [27]

> Mr. Hanson has set the book to music which makes full use of its broad and lyric utterance. Mr. Hanson has been especially successful in finding music for the choral texts of the book. The choruses of "Merry Mount" will prove, in all likelihood, to be its most memorable artistic achievement. Mr. Hanson, in conceiving them, has remembered Moussorgsky and his choruses in "Boris." There is no harm in

[26] *New York Times*, February 11, 1934.
[27] *New York Herald Tribune*, February 11, 1934.

that. The model is an unsurpassable one, of course, but Mr. Hanson has imparted to it his own secret, his own color and design. . . .

As a whole, Mr. Hanson's score is impressive in its security and ease of workmanship, its resourcefulness and maturity of technique. It is unequal in musical value. But at its best, as in the more puissant choruses, it is moving and individual and expressive.

But Hanson's importance to American music does not rest on any single work, nor, indeed, on any one phase of his activity. If he has a particular artistic creed, it is a belief in the necessity for absolute freedom of creative expression, each composer writing out of the depths of his own soul that which seems to him to be good. When such a creed is generally held by composers, critics, and music-lovers, academic questions concerning degrees of newness will give way, he says, to the more essential problem of assaying each new work for the precious metal of vital beauty, without which no work can live.

LEO SOWERBY

If being distrusted by both right- and left-wingers indicates that a man is a liberal, *Leo Sowerby* is most certainly entitled to that distinction. As he himself remarks, "I have been accused by right-wingers of being too dissonant and cacophonous, and by the leftists of being old-fashioned and derivative."

The following review of Sowerby's Quintet for flute, oboe, clarinet, horn, and bassoon, shows the viewpoint of the right wing: [28]

A glance at the first page will not sympathetically dispose one towards Mr. Sowerby's use of fifths and ninths in parallel motion, when such chords are merely to try to make more interesting an otherwise trivial melody. . . . The [later] pages reveal no especial depth of feeling or beauty of tone combinations. . . .

And from the other side comes this review of the symphonic poem, *Prairie:* [29]

[28] *Musical Courier*, December 26, 1931.
[29] *Musical America*, April 10, 1933.

Somewhat thick in texture, often Debussian in effect, it has not highly original thematic content to recommend it and will probably suffer thereby. But it was pleasant to hear, and it stirred a substantial ripple of applause.

There was a time when Sowerby termed himself a musical Dr. Jekyll and Mr. Hyde, for he had written church music and works derived from ecclesiastical inspiration, and had also toyed with "classical" jazz and written pieces for Paul Whiteman's orchestra. Of late years he feels that he is less consciously "national" in his music than he used to be, even though he has the satisfaction of knowing that a number of critics have described some of his recent works as being of the sort that could have been written only by an American. He does not believe in tags, or labels, or groups or "schools"; he tries merely to be himself, and as he himself expresses it, "not thinking about my style, or idiom, trying constantly to improve my technic, so that when I shall have something to say, I shall be able to say it clearly and directly, and —God willing—simply."

Sowerby was born May 1, 1895, in Grand Rapids, Michigan. Most of his education was gained in Chicago, and, like Howard Hanson, he was a Fellow at the American Academy in Rome. In fact, Sowerby has the distinction of having been the first composer to hold such a fellowship. Since his return from Italy he has lived in Chicago, where he is organist at St. James (Episcopal) Cathedral and teacher of composition at the American Conservatory of Music.

He has been a prolific composer and his works have been widely performed. Several of them had a number of major performances even before he went to Rome in 1921. The orchestral suite, *A Set of Four*, was played by the Chicago Orchestra in 1918; the overture, *Comes Autumn Time*, in the same year by the New York Symphony. The *Serenade* for string quartet was composed as a birthday gift for Mrs. Elizabeth Sprague Coolidge, and played first by the Berkshire Quartet in 1918. The next year the Trio for flute, viola, and piano, and in 1921 the Suite for violin and piano, were played at the Berkshire Festival. Carolyn Beebe and her New York Chamber Music Society played the Quintet for wind instruments in 1920. Sowerby himself played his First Piano Concerto in 1920, and a Symphony was introduced in Chicago in 1922.

While he was abroad his Ballad for two pianos and orchestra and one of his String Quartets were introduced in Rome. Upon his return to America he presented his Sonata for cello and piano at the 1924 Berkshire Festival. His cantata, *The Vision of Sir Launfal*, was first performed in 1926.

A number of his works are for organ: a Symphony in G and *Pageant of Autumn* for organ solo, the *Medieval Poem* for organ and orchestra, and a Concerto for organ and orchestra which E. Power Biggs played with the Boston Symphony Orchestra in April, 1938. There is also a Second Piano Concerto, composed in 1932 and first performed by the Boston Symphony in 1936; a *Passacaglia, Interlude and Fugue* which had its première with the Chicago Symphony in 1934; a Fourth String Quartet, and a Sinfonietta for string orchestra. An earlier Suite for orchestra, *From the Northland*, is still heard in symphony concerts.

The freshness and vigor of Sowerby's style are shown in some of his folk-song settings, particularly in the orchestral versions of *Money Musk* and *The Irish Washerwoman*. The latter exists also in a piano solo version, and it is altogether racy in its rollicking good humor.

ALBERT STOESSEL

Even though *Albert Stoessel* could scarcely be labeled a conservative, his ventures into contemporary idioms are never so far beyond the acceptance of present-day ears that his work leaves the "safe and sound" area. His earlier works were far from venturesome, particularly the *Suite Antique*, which has been performed on numerous occasions. Of recent years, however, Stoessel has been writing more in the spirit of the twentieth century, and in his *Concerto Grosso* for strings and piano he becomes the neoclassicist, using traditional forms and idioms and achieving a contemporary outlook through modal patterns rather than by self-conscious dissonance.

In this Concerto there is no uniform separation of players into *concertino* and *ripieni*, although there are frequent solo passages for smaller ensemble groups. The first movement is distinctly modal in character, and, consciously or unconsciously, the composer lends an American flavor to his work through constantly shifting rhythms. By false accenting he achieves polyrhythms that have the vigor and snap of Broadway, while adhering always to the classic background of the form.

The second movement is a "Saraband," and here again a modal pattern provides its own dissonance. In the third movement the composer offers a "Pavan" which is the most engaging section of the entire work. A stately rhythmic figure shapes a melodic line that is fluent, graceful, and charming. Its harmonic background is rich and sonorous. The finale is an "Introduction and Gigue." Opening with an *adagio* passage, it passes to the *vivace* section which announces the theme of the *Gigue*, as Irish as Saint Patrick's Day in its rollicking 6/8 rhythm.

The *Concerto Grosso* had its first performance by the orchestra of the Juilliard School of Music, New York, January 17, 1936. The composer conducted and Ernest Hutcheson was the piano soloist.

In the fall of 1936 Stoessel completed an opera in which he collaborated with Robert A. Simon, the librettist. This was *Garrick*, which was produced by the Opera Department of the Juilliard School of Music February 24, 1937. The following June it was performed at Chautauqua, New York, and in October at the Worcester Festival in Massachusetts.

Garrick proved to be a thoroughly pleasant affair, and showed that opera in English may not be as impossible of achievement as some people think, particularly when it is unpretentious and avoids the pompous and the grandiose. The plot deals with a supposed episode in the life of David Garrick; one in which the actor pretends to be a cad and a leering boor in order to discourage the love of a young lady who should have been otherwise engaged. At the end Garrick returns to Peg Woffington, although he is madly in love with the young girl.

Simon gave the composer lines which could be set to music expressively, and Stoessel did not fail to make the most of them. When necessary for dramatic action or emphasis, he left them entirely alone, allowing them to be spoken. Hence the drama is never halted or interrupted by musical gesturing or operatics for their own sake. Occasionally the orchestration seemed a bit too heavy, and at such times the singers had difficulty in making their lines understandable. But such a minor fault may be readily forgiven for the compensation of really expressive and beautiful music, which does not object to being melodious. The little Robin song at the end of the first act is charming in its folk-like quality, and its scoring for soloist and chorus helps it to cast a haunting spell.

Unfortunately, composing is something of a side-issue with Stoessel. As director of the orchestra and opera departments of the Juilliard School he is engaged in activities and duties enough to satisfy almost any musician, but in addition, he has been conductor of the Oratorio Society of New York since 1922, he has conducted the Worcester Festival since 1925, and since 1922 he has been Musical Director of the Chautauqua Institution.

Stoessel was born in St. Louis, Missouri, October 11, 1894, and had his musical training from local teachers and at the Royal *Hochschule* in Berlin. He made his debut in Berlin as a violinist, playing three concertos with orchestra. When he came back to America, in 1915, he appeared as soloist with the St. Louis Orchestra, and toured the country as assisting artist with Enrico Caruso. In 1923 he was appointed head of the music department of New York University, but resigned in 1930 to take up his work at the Juilliard School.

DOUGLAS MOORE

Douglas Moore is probably most accurately classified as a conservative, but such a designation by no means implies that he lacks a contemporary viewpoint, or that he does not admire radical music written by others. He expressed his artistic creed when he was invited by Lawrence Gilman to explain his *Symphony of Autumn* for the readers of the *New York Herald Tribune*.[30] He wrote, in part:

I feel very strongly that we are all of us overconscious today of the problems of idiom and esthetics. Most of us compose under the deadly fear of being either not modern enough or too modern. Too many of us worry about whether our music is properly a reflection of America, or suitably international, in order to please whatever faction impresses us the most. The particular ideal which I have been striving to attain is to write music which will not be self-conscious with regard to idiom, and will reflect the exciting quality of the life, traditions, and country which I feel all about me. We are a very different people from the French, for instance, and I cannot believe that the fashions decreed by such elegant couturiers as the Parisian Stravinsky or Ravel, successful as they are in permitting a post-war Europe to express herself in music, are likely to be appropriate or becoming for us. To begin with, we are incorrigibly sentimental as a race, and our realism in the drama and literature usually turns out to be meltingly romantic in execution. Then again, there are few of our endeavors in which we excel by pure cerebration. The best of what we accomplish is usually achieved by dint of high spirits, soft-heartedness, and a great deal of superfluous energy.

The neo-classic school has no use for those qualities; but must they be denied us in music entirely for that reason? It is idle, of course, to assume that we shall be unaffected by what European composers do. Certain tendencies of this age which they advocate, such as condensation, simplification, and a greater objectivication of music, will naturally appear in our work for the reason that this is 1931, and that these are universal tendencies. But if we happen to feel romantically inclined, if we like a good tune now and then, if we still have a childish love for atmosphere, is it not well for us to admit the fact, and try to produce something which we like ourselves?

[30] May 17, 1931.

Born at Cutchogue, Long Island, August 10, 1893, Moore was educated at Hotchkiss School and at Yale University. At Yale he studied music with Horatio Parker and David Stanley Smith, then, after service in the Navy during the World War, he worked in Paris with d'Indy, in Cleveland with Ernest Bloch, and again in Paris, with Nadia Boulanger.

When he went to Cleveland, in 1921, he was appointed Assistant Music Curator of the Art Museum, becoming Curator in 1922. He held this position until 1925, when he was awarded a Pulitzer Fellowship for study abroad. After his work with Boulanger he returned to America and joined the music faculty of Columbia University. In 1928 he was appointed an associate professor. Six years later he received a Guggenheim Fellowship, which he enjoyed during a sabbatical year. He then returned to Columbia, where in 1940 he succeeded Daniel Gregory Mason as head of the music department.

Moore's first work of importance was a set of *Four Museum Pieces*, originally written for organ, and later scored for orchestra. The first movement is *Fifteenth Century Armor*, a knightly joust of bygone days. The second, *A Madonna of Botticini*, paints the clear-eyed serenity of the Madonna by a suggestion of plain-chant. *The Chinese Lion and the Unhappy Flutist* shows a flutist who awakens a sleeping lion, and is forever silenced with an horrendous roar. The last piece is *A Statue by Rodin*. A theme emerges from chaos; it becomes clearer, and the stark figure of the man of the bronze age wakes to the consciousness of his superb strength and power.

The *Museum Pieces* had their first performance in Cleveland in 1923. The following year the Cleveland Orchestra introduced the work by Moore which up to the present time has achieved the widest vogue, *The Pageant of P. T. Barnum*. This embodies a series of scenes dear to the hearts of all Americans. Here is music that comes from the dance halls, not of today, but of the era of the country fiddle and brass bands, when people were not afraid to be sentimental.

Altogether, the work contains five episodes: first, *Boyhood at Bethel*—country fiddles, brass bands, early Connecticut hymnology, the sort of musical environment that doubtless influenced the youthful Barnum. Next comes *Joice Heth*, the 161-year-old Negress who was Barnum's first exhibit, supposedly the first person to put clothes on George Washington. Here we have a Negro spiritual, the less familiar version of *Nobody Knows the Trouble I've Seen*. The third movement shows *General and Mrs. Tom Thumb*, the midgets. A flourish in the drum leads to the report of a cap pistol, and then the flutes and oboes appear in a military theme with syncopated rhythm. *Jenny Lind* is the fourth to appear. After arpeggios on the harp and a melody in the flute, the wood-winds give a suggestion of coloratura and mid-century sentiment that brings back memories. The finale tells of Barnum's greatest and most permanent triumph, his circus. *Circus Parade* brings animals, wagon wheels, calliope, and the great Barnum himself. The only thing missing is the peanuts to provide the proper accompaniment.

In 1928 Moore produced a symphonic poem, *Moby Dick*, and in 1930 a Violin and Piano Sonata which was presented at a concert by the League of Composers. A year later, April 2, 1931, his *Symphony of Autumn* was played for the first time at the American Composers' Concerts in Rochester. This is a short, three-movement work which follows classic outlines. The first movement is in sonata form, and aims to portray the "majestic and mellow sadness of an Autumn afternoon." The second movement was suggested by the "triumphant song of the katydids." In the words of the composer, "Autumn may be theoretically a sad season, but to listen to the chorus of katydids against an ostinato of treetoads, with very white, cold stars overhead and a streamy earth beneath, is to distrust the idea." The last movement of the Symphony suggests the "irresponsible gayety of an Autumn day at noon when the light on the water is silver and there is always a breeze to offer water surfaces to the light."

In the year following the première of the *Autumn* symphony,

Moore returned to the American locale with an *Overture on an American Tune*, which was originally named after the source of its inspiration—*Babbitt*. This, as the name implied, attempted a tonal portrait of Sinclair Lewis's hero, the sentimental, good-natured "go-getter." The work was introduced by David Mannes and the Manhattan Symphony, December 25, 1932.

A Quartet for strings was first played by the Roth Quartet in 1936, and later, in 1938, by the Gordon Quartet at one of the Coolidge Foundation concerts at Columbia University. This is a short work in four movements. The first is pleasantly lyrical, with a rocking triple rhythm as its basis. The second movement is jaunty, with a brief suggestion of Scotch bagpipes. The third section, *andante cantabile*, places a thoughtful, meditative melodic line over a rich contrapuntal texture; and the finale is a jolly *allegro*.

In recent years Moore has been especially interested in the setting of words to music, either for solo or chorus, or in opera. He has already completed one grand opera, a musical version of Philip Barry's play, *White Wings*, and he hopes to undertake another. A setting of Vachel Lindsay's poem, *Simon Legree*, was first performed by the Princeton Glee Club in 1937.

Moore feels that American composers should devote attention to the needs of amateur and school groups, and as an experiment in this direction he composed an operetta, *The Headless Horseman*, which had its first production in 1937 by the children of the Bronxville, New York, public schools.

In the spring of 1939, Moore's "folk-opera," *The Devil and Daniel Webster*, was produced by the American Lyric Theater, an institution founded with the aims of stimulating the production and composition of opera in English and presenting works at prices within the reach of the general public. The American Lyric Theater unfortunately did not survive its first season, but that was no fault of *The Devil and Daniel Webster*, which was generally conceded to be excellent entertainment. The libretto was by the distinguished poet, Stephen Vincent Benét.

In Lawrence Gilman's Sunday column a few weeks before the production, Moore wrote of his aims: [31]

> Mr. Benét and I have classified *The Devil and Daniel Webster* as a folk-opera because it is legendary in its subject matter and simple in its musical expression. As a matter of fact, this particular legend is a fiction, although related to the authentic powers of Webster as an orator, and the music makes no conscious quotation from folk tunes. The exact category into which it falls finds no convenient label. We have tried to make an opera in which the union of speech, song and instrumental music will communicate the essence of the dramatic story, enhanced but not distorted. . . . There is nothing revolutionary or even original in all this. The German Singspiel and the French Opéra Comique had much the same point of view and were conceived for general entertainment purposes. We hope that *The Devil and Daniel Webster* will be judged in terms of its power to interest and appeal to the average American who likes music and likes the theater, but is not necessarily experienced as an opera-goer. This platform is in no sense an artistic manifesto directed against anybody or anything; it is simply the working plan of this particular opera.

This is a modest statement indeed, and the general feeling after the performance was that Moore had been perhaps too modest in his whole approach to the work, subordinating the music too severely to the text. The story is of a New Hampshire farmer who has sold his soul to the Devil for the material prosperity he needs in order to marry. The Devil, disguised as a Boston attorney, breaks in upon the wedding festivities to claim the bridegroom's soul, but he is thwarted by the legal skill and eloquence of Webster, who wins a verdict in favor of the farmer in a remarkable plea to a jury composed of famous traitors and scoundrels summoned from the infernal regions by the Devil. This plea, incidentally, is based on a speech actually delivered by Webster.

Mr. Moore has set the lyrics smoothly and expressively [wrote Oscar Thompson].[32] The score is not a weighty or complex one, but

---

[31] *New York Herald Tribune*, April 19, 1939.
[32] *Musical America*, May 25, 1939.

is the work of a serious, well-grounded musician, who thinks in terms of melody rather than tune, and whose orchestration is that of a full-fledged opera rather than of the Broadway "musical." . . . Still, the effect is very much that of incidental music, because of the preponderance of spoken dialogue and the casualness of the musical passages. It is to be suspected that Mr. Moore felt called on to subordinate his own talents to those of the poet, with a result that his music, good as it is, is crowded into second place.

SETH BINGHAM

An elder colleague of Moore's in the Music Department at Columbia, *Seth Bingham,* is also a Yale man. In fact, he is the composer of the stirring Eli song, *Mother of Men.* Born in Bloomfield, New Jersey, April 16, 1882, Bingham was home-taught and largely self-taught until he was eighteen years old. At Yale he studied under Horatio Parker; and in the years 1906–07 he worked with Widor, d'Indy, and Guilmant, in Paris. He is particularly known as an organist who has held several church organ positions, and is now organist of the Madison Avenue Presbyterian Church in New York City. His organ works are well known; they include a Suite, otherwise untitled, and two others bearing the names *Harmonies of Florence* and *Pioneer America.* He has an opera, *La Charelzenn* (1917), in manuscript. Among his numerous choral works is the folk-cantata *Wilderness Stone,* which has been performed by the Schola Cantorum of New York, and broadcast over both NBC networks. The piece is based on a love episode from Stephen Vincent Benét's epic poem of the Civil War, *John Brown's Body,* and consists of thirty-nine short numbers, set for narrator, soprano, tenor, bass, chorus, and orchestra. Bingham has written *Tame Animal Tunes* for chamber orchestra; a Suite for wind instruments; a *Wall Street Fantasy* (1912) for symphony orchestra; a Passacaglia (1918); two suites, *Memories of France* and *The Breton Cadence;* and an orchestral version of *Pioneer America.*

According to his own account, Bingham's early music shows

French influence, while his later works are more modal and more Yankee in flavor. He finds abundant sources of inspiration in our folk-music, our jazz and our American scene. He considers that in his Americanism he is pursuing a universal goal, since, as he says, "America is not yet American but is still Anglo-Saxon-Negro-Scandinavian-Russian-Italian-German-Irish-Jewish."

ABRAM CHASINS

Abram Chasins first came into prominence when Josef Hofmann, Benno Moiseivitsch, Josef Lhévinne, and a half-dozen other first-rank pianists played his little Chinese pieces, *Rush Hour in Hong Kong* and *Flirtation in a Chinese Garden*. Shortly after the appearance of these miniatures came a set of twenty-four Preludes for piano, and a Piano Concerto which Chasins played with the Philadelphia Orchestra in 1930.

He was born in New York, August 17, 1903. Musical from babyhood, he was put to work as a little boy with Mrs. Thomas Tapper, that friend of all true talent, who first discovered Leo Ornstein. Then Chasins came to the attention of Ernest Hutcheson. Josef Hofmann took him to Europe, and Rubin Goldmark gave him lessons in composition. For several years he taught composition at the Curtis Institute in Philadelphia, but he resigned in 1933 to devote his time to composing and radio broadcasting. In the latter field he performs in the dual role of commentator and pianist.

In an article entitled "New Blood in American Music," [33] David Ewen characterized the work of Chasins:

> In his piano works, Chasins reveals a style that is fluid; it emerges from his pen uninterruptedly in a smooth and even flow. His ideas are always bright and spontaneous. He has an extraordinary ability to twist and fashion his themes into intriguing forms and shapes. Finally, Chasins can write music of a serene and contemplative beauty, almost rare in our time; if there is music by a modern American composer

[33] *Musical Courier*, September 16, 1933.

more beautiful or more tastefully written than the slow section of Chasins' first piano concerto, I have yet to hear it.

The Second Piano Concerto was performed by the composer and the Philadelphia Orchestra under Stokowski, March 3 and 4, 1933. In this Chasins made a conscious attempt to deviate completely from accepted conventions of structure. In utilizing the idea of a solo instrument with orchestra, he brought into consolidation several of the smaller forms—waltz, fugue, and others. The drawback to this plan was of course its tendency to the episodic and fragmentary, but Chasins managed to overcome this difficulty to a partial degree with his melodic inventiveness. After the première performances he rewrote the Concerto completely; in its revised form he played it in the spring of 1938 with the New York Philharmonic-Symphony Orchestra under Barbirolli.

During the last five or six years Chasins has found little reason to change the ideals he started with. He has maintained a modern concept of tone relationships, but he has continued to pay homage to his musical idols: Bach, Brahms, Wagner, Chopin and Rimsky-Korsakoff. He dislikes all that seems affected and self-conscious in contemporary music, and his own technique gives him the right to be impatient with badly made music where good workmanship is missing.

He is not pursuing a nationalistic goal. He says he knows of no American school of music and he doubts whether one will develop. He feels that nationalism is simply a contemporary phase throughout the world. He insists that the greatest composers in their most inspired moments "defy any nationalistic leanings"; that when they reach the white heat of inspiration they invariably transcend "the inhibiting factor of a national idiom."

SAMUEL BARLOW

Another composer who declines the nationalist label is *Samuel L. M. Barlow*. He explains that neither *Indian Love Lyrics* nor *Swanee River* have penetrated deeply enough into his artistic being to be considered roots. If he has any, he thinks they are more likely to be found in Purcell or the Scotch ballads, straight or via the Kentucky Mountains. And while Barlow's political activities have been markedly to the left, his music seems to stick in a middle path; in his own words, "international, melodious, and (quite unintentionally) of the school of Ravel (if any)." He once remarked, "My method of orchestration is as modern as I can make it, but tunes which wouldn't shock Papa Brahms keep sticking their necks out."

Barlow was born in New York June 1, 1892. He claims that he fell out of his crib to compose, and that he played the piano (badly) at the age of five. The quality of his playing was apparently improved by piano lessons in Boston, and in later years with Isidor Philipp in Paris. At Harvard he took the usual music courses, and he also studied theory with Franklin Robinson in New York, and orchestration with Respighi in Rome.

His activities in addition to composing have covered a wide field. He has been, for short periods: lecturer for the New York Board of Education; First Chairman, New York Community Chorus; Lieutenant, U.S. Army in France; Director of the American Merchant Marine Insurance Company; teacher in various settlement schools; orchestral conductor for the New York Theatre Guild (during the season 1937–38 he composed and conducted the music for the Guild production of *Amphitryon*); newspaper critic; piano soloist with symphony orchestras; executive, National Committee for Defense of Political Prisoners; Treasurer, American Guild for German Political Freedom; speaker for Musicians' Emergency Fund.

Although his music had been heard occasionally since 1913, it was in 1928 that his first truly important work was heard in America, when Fritz Reiner presented the symphonic poem *Alba* at a concert of the Cincinnati Symphony. Three years later, Eugene Goossens, conducting the Rochester Philharmonic, presented Barlow's Piano Concerto, with the composer at the piano. Several of the Rochester critics felt that some of the work's distinction lay in its avoidance of the extremes of pedantry and the academic on the one hand, and the American weakness for jazz on the other.

Early in 1935 (January 11) Barlow enjoyed the distinction of being the first American composer to have a work produced at the Opéra-Comique in Paris. This was *Mon Ami Pierrot,* to a libretto by Sascha Guitry. In composing this one-act opera, Barlow encountered several difficulties. To sustain the spoken word it was necessary to take care not to swamp it under the music. As the libretto was a period story, he must be careful to compose his score in as classic a vein as possible, and to meet the difficult task of writing music of folk character without borrowing. Hence the only liberty he allowed himself was as modern an orchestration as possible.

So far the opera has not been produced in America, but its overture has been heard several times in concerts. Others of Barlow's works include a symphonic work, *Babar,* first performed by the Philadelphia Orchestra under Stokowski; *Biedermeyer Waltzes,* played at the Augusteo, Rome, in 1935; and a piece, *For Strings,* played in the same year by the Monte Carlo Quartet. He has also written two operas besides *Mon Ami Pierrot: Eugénie,* and *Amanda* (one act).

WERNER JANSSEN

Although *Werner Janssen* has achieved his widest fame as a conductor, he has also composed several significant works: *New Year's Eve in New York; Louisiana Suite,* with its *Dixie Fugue;* a *Foster Suite;* two String Quartets; and music for motion pictures.

A few years ago, musicians and music-lovers hailed Janssen as the Messiah we had been awaiting, an American who would take front rank as an orchestral conductor, and who would become the director of one of our major orchestras. This was when he returned from triumphant engagements abroad, hailed by Sibelius as the greatest interpreter of his music, and engaged for the coming 1934–35 season as one of the conductors of the New York Philharmonic-Symphony.

But the talented young man unfortunately became the victim of his friends and his admirers, particularly of those who made the wish father to the thought. No living creature could have lived up to the advance accounts of Janssen's prowess as a conductor. The publicity was tremendous, it even included a two-installment "Profile" by Alva Johnston in *The New Yorker*,[34] which divulged the information that previously contracted engagements had made it necessary for Janssen to decline an offer from Henry Ford of a hundred thousand dollars for ten radio concerts.

The pity of the whole affair was that Janssen did an excellent job with the Philharmonic-Symphony; his performances and interpretations were sensitive and musicianly, far more than competent. Yet he was not the combination of all musical virtues that had been pictured, and people were inevitably disappointed. As a result he lasted for his first season's engagement, and then departed for other fields. He has been conducting and composing in Hollywood, has had profitable radio engagements, and for the 1937–38 season he was called to Baltimore to lead the symphony orchestra in the absence of Ernest Schelling. In March, 1938, he was named regular conductor of the organization, but after one more season he felt that in the three months of the year that the orchestra played together an adequate ensemble could not be developed, and he offered his resignation. He was succeeded by Howard Barlow.

Janssen's career should satisfy the human-interest demands of any biographer. Born in New York, June 1, 1899, he is the son of a restaurant proprietor—August Janssen of the Hofbrau House, originator of the famous slogan, "Janssen wants to see you." The father had a low opinion of musicians and wanted his son to enter the restaurant business. Consequently it was with con-

---

[34] October 20 and 27, 1934.

siderable chagrin that he learned that the boy had been stealing off to Carnegie Hall, and studying symphonic scores in his bedroom. The disagreement between father and son lasted for years, and after college the young man went his own way, through Tin Pan Alley, where he became a writer of popular songs, through playing the piano in numerous dives and studying symphonic scores simultaneously, until finally, after being acclaimed in more than a half-dozen foreign countries, he was awarded an honorary doctor's degree by his alma mater, Dartmouth. As a sign of reconciliation, Janssen *père* consented to sit on the platform when the degree was conferred.

Janssen's own music is expertly devised and possesses a truly American flavor. *New Year's Eve in New York* is vivid program music in its tonal description of revelry, and altogether contemporary in its inclusion of the musical sounds and rhythms of Broadway and Times Square; yet it is considerably more than mere picture music. It contrasts the elements of merry-making and idealism with subtlety and telling effectiveness. The "Dixie Fugue" from the *Louisiana Suite* develops itself through intricate rhythms to a stunning finale, where the theme appears in augmentation. It was while Janssen was a Fellow at the American Academy in Rome that the Rome String Quartet played for the first time his *Miniature Fantasy on Popular American Melodies* (1932). The work seemed to please its Italian listeners, even though the full significance of its four episodes—*North, South, East* and *West*—may have escaped them.

The Second String Quartet was first performed at the Chamber Music Festival at the Library of Congress, April 9, 1935. It was reviewed as follows in the *New York Herald Tribune:* [35]

> The only discernible influence upon his [Janssen's] style is that of Sibelius, and one may have at a first hearing mistaken for an influence what is only a Norse essence.
>
> On the basis of intuition, one would surmise that the first two movements of the quartet are personal expressions, and the last two con-

[35] April 10, 1935.

sciously American in content and treatment. The incisive force and nervous vigor of the "Agitato et Energico," and the veiled humor and sincere sentiment in the "Commodamente Presto-Andante Sostenuto" seem to be attributes of the composer. At least, one is conscious in these sections of a more direct contact with the inspirational impulse.

The melodic line and the harmonic basis of the slow movement, "Largamente Sostenuto," are strongly suggestive of the Negro spiritual. The resemblance does not anywhere amount to imitation, yet the accents, the mode and the rhythm are adumbrations of that lyrical type. It is not the transcript of a racial song, but the etherealization of an idiom. In the last movement, a lively and jocular "ritmico," Mr. Janssen has utilized to admirable effect the spirit but not the maddening ictus of jazz.

BERNARD ROGERS

Bernard Rogers is a native of New York (born February 4, 1893) who studied in America with Ernest Bloch and Percy Goetschius, and abroad with Frank Bridge and Nadia Boulanger. He was awarded the Pulitzer Traveling Scholarship in 1918, and from 1927 to 1929 he was a Guggenheim Fellow. For nine years he was on the staff of *Musical America,* and for the past decade he has been a member of the faculty at the Eastman School of Music in Rochester.

Rogers feels that whatever national idiom we may develop in this country can never be conscious. It must be based on the hope that is in us. If we develop deep and strong personalities, our music will be deep and strong, universal as fine art always is. He also feels that arbitrary classifications of composers are gratuitous; that labels have a tendency to separate composers. Instead of a lot of small star-dotted systems, sublimely oblivious of each other, we need a decent, friendly, and tolerant artistic universe, to which we may all belong, whether we write in a key or out of one.

Rogers' first orchestral work was a tone-poem, *To the Fallen*, composed in memory of those who died in the great war, and first played by the New York Philharmonic. *The Faithful* was written next, and then *Fuji in the Sunset Glow.* These were followed by a *Soliloquy* for flute and string quartet, and a *Pastorale* for eleven instruments. A symphony, *Adonis,* was played by the Rochester Philharmonic, and at Chautauqua, New York. A String Quartet was introduced at one of the League of Composers concerts in New York, and a *Prelude to Hamlet* by the Rochester Philharmonic.

Rogers' recent works include a Second and Third Symphony; a second *Soliloquy,* this time for bassoon and strings; an opera, *The Marriage of Aude,* produced at the Eastman Festival, May 22, 1931; a cantata, *The Raising of Lazarus,* presented under the same auspices the following year; and a number of miscellaneous orchestral works which include *Two American Frescoes, The Supper at Emmaus,* and *Five Fairy Tales* ("Once Upon a Time"). The last was played at the Eastman Festival, April 4, 1935, by the New York Philharmonic-Symphony, February 27, 1936, and by the Chicago Symphony in 1937. It was this work that was accepted by the Juilliard Foundation as the 1936 orchestral work for publication. The subjects of these *Fairy Tales* are drawn from Andrew Lang, and the work proved to be faithful to the moods of its program. At the tenth Festival of American Music in Rochester in 1940, the programs included a new *Dance of Salome* by Rogers, as well as a ballet-piece, *The Colors of War.*

HORACE JOHNSON

A few years ago *Horace Johnson* was known to the public largely through his songs: *The Pirate, When Pierrot Sings, The Three Cherry Trees, Thy Dark Hair,* and others. Recently, however, his orchestral works have enjoyed so many performances that he has come into his rightful place as a symphonist.

Johnson feels that if classifications are necessary, he would belong in the right wing, although he whimsically remarks that "white wing" might be a more accurate term for a composer who is not anxious to pile into his music all the refuse he finds on the streets. He feels that music may be strongly flavored by modern conditions, even if it is not (as he thinks much American music is) orchestrated with, and marked by, a tendency to sacrifice pure tonal color.

He was born in Waltham, Massachusetts, October 5, 1893, and was a pupil of Bainbridge Crist in Boston. For a number of years he was a musical journalist in New York, and then spent several years abroad. Upon his return in 1931, he became managing editor of the *Musical Courier,* and in May, 1939, was appointed New York City Director of the WPA Federal Music Project, succeeding Chalmers Clifton.

Johnson's most successful work for orchestra is *Imagery,* which has almost achieved a record of performances for a native work. In the season of 1937–38 alone, it was played twenty-six times. *Imagery* was composed in 1924–25 and was first performed in 1926. Quotations from Rabindranath Tagore provide programs for the three separate movements. The first is "Procession to Indra," which depicts the slow-moving caravan and the incantations, with wood-winds, brass, tambourine, and tam-tam, establishing an Oriental background. The second movement is a dance, "Aspara," as is the finale, "Urbasi," which grows more and more intense and impassioned. Others of Johnson's orchestral works are a tone-poem, *Astarte;* a suite, *Streets of Florence; Joyance,* for string orchestra; and a sprightly piece, *In the American Manner,* which is published for the piano.

HAROLD MORRIS

When *Harold Morris* played his Piano Concerto with Koussevitzky and the Boston Symphony, October 23 and 24, 1931, H. T. Parker remarked in the *Boston Evening Transcript:* [36]

. . . No thin blood runs in Mr. Morris; none of the hesitating, refuge-seeking temperament that too often dulls American music-

[36] October 24, 1931.

making. He speaks out. Yesterday his audience could not choose but hear. Some of us made bold to fancy we were "sitting in" at an event.

To the program notes Morris contributed the following description of his composition:

The concerto was started several years ago. The beautiful spiritual, "Pilgrim's Song," shows the effect of civilization on the slaves of the Southern States and is in great contrast to the rugged, rhythmic character of the African Negro drumbeat, with which the first movement opens, and is used throughout this movement and momentarily in the last as a binding link between the movements. The other material in the concerto is, I hope, the natural and logical result of growing up with, and studying, folk music as we have it in the South. But I do not mean to imply that I believe in leaning entirely on folk music or that it should in any way limit or hamper our modern musical expression; but rather that it should be the basis, as it was with composers of the past.

In 1932 the Juilliard Foundation selected this Concerto as its work for publication the following season.

Morris was born in San Antonio, Texas, in 1890. He received a B.A. degree at the University of Texas, and then studied at the Cincinnati Conservatory of Music, from which he was graduated with highest honors. He has been a lecturer at the Rice Institute in Houston, Texas, and is now a member of the faculty of the Juilliard School of Music in New York.

Before the Piano Concerto added to his reputation, Morris had achieved distinction with his Piano Sonata, which in its published form is now in its third edition. He has, also, two other Piano Sonatas; a Violin and Piano Sonata; a Quintet for strings and piano; two String Quartets; a Quartet for piano, violin, cello and flute; two Trios; a Symphonic Poem for orchestra after Tagore's *Gitanjali*; a Symphony after Browning's *Prospice*; and a Violin Concerto which won the award of the National Federation of Music Clubs for the best score submitted by an American composer. This latter work had its first performance in May,

1939, at the hands of Philip Frank and the NBC Symphony Orchestra under Dr. Frank Black.

Charles Haubiel, born in Delta, Ohio, in 1894, first came into prominence when his symphonic poem, *Karma,* won first prize in the Schubert Centennial Contest of the Columbia Phonograph Company in 1928, and the piece was recorded. Several years later, in 1935, his *Ritratti* (Portraits) was awarded second prize in the symphonic contest sponsored by Swift & Company, and was performed by the Chicago Symphony Orchestra, December 12 and 13, 1935.

Haubiel is a middle-of-the-roader in his music. His style is a synthesis of romantic-classic-impressionist elements, a sort of combination of Brahms and Debussy. His teachers were Rosario Scalero in composition, and in piano, Rudolph Ganz and the Lhévinnes. In addition to *Karma* and *Ritratti,* he has composed five symphonic works: *Pastoral, Mars Ascending, Vox Cathedralis, Suite Passecaille,* and *Solari;* some chamber music; and many shorter works. His *Passacaglia* in A minor ("The Plane Beyond") shared with the *Little Symphony* in G by Robert L. Sanders the prize awarded in February, 1938, by the New York Philharmonic-Symphony Society, and was played by that organization under the composer's own direction on December 18, 1938.

Beryl Rubinstein has been known for a number of years principally as a pianist and as director of the Cleveland Institute of Music, but his Second Piano Concerto, first performed with the Cleveland Orchestra in 1936 and later published by the Juilliard Foundation, and the Juilliard School's production of his opera, *The Sleeping Beauty,* have focused attention upon him as a composer as well.

Born in Athens, Georgia, October 26, 1898, he started his career as a child pianist. He studied in America with Alexander

Lambert, and in Europe with Busoni. From 1905 to 1911 he toured the country as a child prodigy, and at thirteen made an appearance with the Metropolitan Opera Orchestra in New York.

The Concerto is written in three movements, and while it shows a fondness for certain modern effects, particularly in the polytonal opening of the third movement, in general it adheres rather closely to traditional harmonic formulae. At times Rubinstein's music seems to derive chiefly from the French Impressionists.

Critical attention to the opera, which the Juilliard forces produced January 19, 1938, was largely centered on the libretto by John Erskine, in which the famous author of *Helen of Troy* interpreted anew the traditional fairy-story of *The Sleeping Beauty*. In the *New York Herald Tribune*,[37] Lawrence Gilman devoted two columns to Erskine's part in the proceedings and contented himself with a single paragraph on Rubinstein's music:

> ... Mr. Rubinstein has set it [the libretto] to music that has the right touch of light-handed gayety and sentiment and unpretentiousness. There are charming pages in his score. ... Mr. Rubinstein has had the taste and the esthetic tact to keep his writing in the vein of the words and action of the comedy. ...

Others of Rubinstein's works include a Scherzo and a Suite for orchestra; a *Passepied* for string quartet; and many smaller pieces, mostly for piano. He is the author of an *Outline of Piano Pedagogy* and holds the honorary degree of Doctor of Music from Western Reserve University.

Quinto Maganini has been one of our most industrious and prolific composers, and as conductor of his own Sinfonietta has been able to introduce to the public a number of his colleagues' works, as well as some of his own.

Maganini was born in Fairfield, California, November 30, 1897. He started his professional career as a flutist in the San Francisco Orchestra in 1917. Two years later he became a member of the New York Symphony Orchestra under Walter Dam-

[37] January 20, 1938.

rosch, and remained with that organization until it was merged with the Philharmonic Society in 1928. In 1927 he was awarded the Pulitzer Scholarship in music, and in 1928 and 1929 a Guggenheim Fellowship.

His most ambitious and extended work is one which deals with California history: *The Argonauts,* an opera cycle on which he worked for fourteen years, and which has been published but not yet performed in its entirety. California is also the subject of *Tuolumne,* a rhapsody for orchestra which was first played by the New York Philharmonic in 1924 and the New York Symphony in 1925. *South Wind,* for orchestra, is described by the composer as "decorative music," unconcerned with facts, and seeking merely to picture a sunrise over the Mediterranean. It was originally entitled *Night on an Island of Fantasy.*

Some of Maganini's best work has been written for small orchestra: his *Ornithological Suite* (with cuckoos, hummingbirds, and mockingbirds), the *Sylvan Symphony, Cuban Rhapsody,* and others. He has also made arrangements of early American music.

Like Maganini, *Carl Ernest Bricken* won both the Pulitzer Traveling Scholarship and a Guggenheim Fellowship. He is a native of Shelbyville, Kentucky, where he was born in 1898, and studied at Yale University and with Scalero. While at Yale, he conducted the Yale Symphony Orchestra. From 1925 to 1928 he was on the faculty of the Mannes School, and the following season he taught theory at the New York Institute of Musical Art. In 1931 he became professor of music and chairman of the music department in the University of Chicago, and since 1939 has occupied a similar post at the University of Wisconsin. Bricken has written a Suite, a Symphony, and a Prelude for orchestra, and numerous works of chamber music. In the summer of 1934 he served as guest conductor of the Chicago Symphony Orchestra.

A. Walter Kramer, born in New York City, September 23, 1890, has in recent years been occupied with editorial duties that have almost excluded creative activity. Kramer, trained as a violinist, graduated from the College of the City of New York in 1910, and thereupon joined the staff of *Musical America* under John C. Freund. In 1922 he went to Europe, where he remained for several years. Then he became music critic and editor-in-chief of *Musical America,* until May, 1936, when he resigned to become Managing Director and Vice-President of Galaxy Music Corporation, a New York publishing house. In 1934 he succeeded John Alden Carpenter as president of the Society for the Publication of American Music, of which he was one of the founders. He is a member of the advisory board of the League of Composers, and of the United States Section of the International Society for Contemporary Music. His *Two Symphonic Sketches,* Opus 37A, for violin and orchestra, have been played by the leading orchestras. He has also written a Symphonic Rhapsody for violin and orchestra, and his orchestration of Bach's D minor *Chaconne* has been widely played. But he is best known for his songs: *The Faltering Dusk, The Last Hour,* and many others.

Mana-Zucca is the pen name under which the original Miss Zuckerman (December 25, 1890, New York City) has become famous, chiefly as a composer of songs. She has also written a Piano Concerto, a Sonata for violin and piano, and several other ambitious works. But it is as the composer of *Rachem, The Big Brown Bear, I Love Life,* and similar songs, that she is known.

Mortimer Browning (Baltimore, 1891) has become widely known for his concert songs, but he has also attracted attention for larger works, among them a Sonatina for piano, violin, and cello which was performed at the Westminster Festival in Princeton (1937), a number of choral works, and a *Mary Poppins Suite* for orchestra. For the Children's Theatre of Greenwich House, New York, he has written and prepared the music for a number of plays, and he has also composed incidental music for two Broadway productions—*Gala Night* and *Paging Danger.* His experimentation with new mediums led him to compose a Concerto in F for Theremin and orchestra, of which the first movement was performed at Town Hall, New York, by Lucie Bigelow Rosen, with piano accompaniment.

Samuel Gardner is widely known to the concert public for a racy little violin piece, *From the Canebrake*, but he has composed several works of larger dimensions. His *Broadway* was first played by the Boston Symphony in its 1929-30 season, and before that Gardner himself had played his Violin Concerto with the New York Philharmonic under Mengelberg. His String Quartet won the Pulitzer Scholarship, and a symphonic poem, *New Russia*, was awarded the Loeb Prize, both in 1918. There are also a quintet, *To the Fallen;* a Prelude and Fugue for string quartet; and a set of Variations for string quartet.

Gardner was born in Russia, August 25, 1891, and was brought to this country when he was six years old. He studied with Franz Kneisel and Percy Goetschius, and then started his career as a concert violinist. He was a member of the Kneisel Quartet during the season 1914-15; the following year a member of the Chicago Symphony; and in 1916-17 of the Elshuco Trio.

In spite of a heavy schedule as staff pianist at the National Broadcasting Company in New York, *Robert Braine* continues his activities as composer. His works include three operas and a number of orchestral works which have been heard on the radio: *S.O.S.; The Song of Hiawatha;* a *Concerto in Jazz* (also performed at a Paul Whiteman concert); *The House of Usher;* a Rhapsody in E flat; *Harlequin and Columbine;* and *City of Dreams*, for jazz orchestra.

He was born in Springfield, Ohio, May 27, 1896, and educated at the Cincinnati College of Music. He is a composer who feels that the day of "freak" music is past, and that the idea that we have to invent new scales in order to write something new is ridiculous. Composers, he claims, should realize that they are writing music for people to listen to, to be interested in, and to be thrilled by; they are not writing to astound and confound other composers and teachers of theory and harmony.

Braine's *Choreographic Impressions* were performed in part at the October, 1939, symposium of American orchestral music in Rochester, and his *Theater Sheet* figured in the ballet program at the tenth annual Festival of American Music in Rochester in April, 1940, with Howard Hanson conducting.

James G. Heller is a composer to whom music is an avocation, for he is Rabbi of the Plum Street Temple in Cincinnati. He is also Chairman on Synagogal Music of the Central Conference of American Rabbis, professor of musicology at the Cincinnati Conservatory of Music, and program-annotator for the Cincinnati Symphony Orchestra.

He was born in New Orleans, January 4, 1892, and was educated in music both in his native city and in Cincinnati, where he studied with Edgar Stillman Kelley. In his music he seeks to compromise between the old and the new, to use the discoveries of modern music that seem significant and beautiful, without sacrificing the orderliness and purposefulness of the older music.

Although he had completed a number of works previously, Heller made no attempt to publish any of his music until the Society for the Publication of American Music selected his *Aquatints*, for string quartet, in 1929. Others of his works include *Four Sketches* for orchestra, performed by the Cincinnati Symphony, February 7, 1936; a Sonata for violin and piano; an *Elegy* and *Pastorale*, for voice and string quartet; a Trio; Four Solo Services for Friday Evening; and an oratorio, *Watchman, What of the Night?*

Joseph Waddell Clokey, born in New Albany, Indiana, August 28, 1890, was also a pupil of Stillman Kelley. He is known principally for choral works. He is skillful in using sharp contrasts, sudden changes of tonality, and cannily planned dissonance. Recently a more serious study of the nature of church music, liturgies, medieval music, and plainsong, has made his style more objective, modal rather than chromatic. In this way his dissonance results from free counterpoint rather than from conscious chord construction.

His works include five operas, numerous part-songs, cantatas, sacred choruses, and organ music. He has also made some highly effective choral transcriptions of early American songs: an anthem by Billings, Stephen Foster songs, and two choice examples of gutter-balladry—*Cocaine Lil* and *Frankie and Johnnie*.

Theodore Cella, born in Philadelphia, November 3, 1897, has been harpist of the New York Philharmonic since 1920. Before that he was for six years harpist of the Boston Symphony. A composition pupil of Charles Martin Loeffler, Cella is the composer of several colorful scores which have been performed by the leading orchestras of the East. The New York Philharmonic-Symphony has played *On a Transatlantic Liner* (1931), *Through the Pyrenees* (1932), and *Alpine Impressions* (1937); the Boston Symphony has performed *Carnival* (1932) and *The Lido* (1934). *On a Transatlantic Liner* has also been played by the Philadelphia Orchestra (1933) with the composer conducting. All of these works are melodious and richly scored.

The press of teaching duties has unfortunately prevented *Edwin John Stringham* from adding very much to his list of compositions during recent years. His new works are confined to a *Nocturne* for orchestra, played by the Philharmonic-Symphony January 20, 1935; a *Notturno* for winds and harp; a Quartet for strings; and some choral music. He is working on a Second Nocturne for orchestra, and a set of seven orchestral pieces.

He was born in Kenosha, Wisconsin, July 11, 1890, and spent many years in Colorado. In 1930 he came to New York, where he taught composition at Union Theological Seminary and acoustics at the Institute of Musical Art of the Juilliard School, and was General Musical Editor for the American Book Company, later becoming Chairman of the Music Department of Queens College.

Stringham is a firm believer in rhythmic counterpoint. He is fond of masses of orchestral color, and he frequently uses jazz rhythms. His earlier works include three Symphonic Poems; a Symphony; a *Set of Three Pastels*; a Concert Overture; and various shorter pieces and songs.

Frederick Preston Search is one of the composers who have been honored by having a work accepted by the American Society for the Publication of American Music. This was in 1934, when the Society issued his Sextet in F minor, for strings. A reviewer in *Musical America* [38] characterized the work as representing "an original native talent that has its basis firmly in traditional form and idiom." The writer continued:

> One feels that the composer writes not only with erudition, but with a certain instinct for transformation of his themes by spontaneous and plastic means, and that there is a degree of passion and intensity in the work.

Search belongs among the romanticists rather than the modernists, and he still holds to traditional standards of beauty and melodic line. His works include *The Bridge Builders*, for soloists, chorus, and symphony orchestra; a symphonic poem, *The Dream of McCorkle;* an orchestral Rhapsody; a piece for orchestra entitled *Exhilaration;* and a *Festival Overture*, all of which have been performed in recent years by the Federal Symphony Orchestra in San Francisco. He has also eight String Quartets, two Cello Sonatas and a Cello Concerto; a Piano Quintet; a Piano Septet, and many smaller works.

He was born in Pueblo, Colorado, July 22, 1889. He has studied cello with Adamowski in Boston, and Klengel in Leipzig. He was a conducting pupil of Artur Nikisch and studied composition with Max Reger. In 1913 he made his debut as a cellist in New York. In recent years he has been bandmaster of the Federal Concert Band of the San Francisco Federal Music Project. He lives in San Francisco but spends much of his time on his ranch at Jamesburg, California.

Elliot Griffis is the composer of a String Quartet which won a Pulitzer Scholarship. In 1919 he published an atmospheric Piano Sonata which has had a number of performances. He was born in Boston, January 28, 1893, and studied under Horatio Parker at Yale and Stuart Mason at the New England Conservatory in Boston. He has written a Symphony and two other

---

[38] April 6, 1935.

symphonic works: *A Persian Fable* and *Colossus;* a set of Variations for strings; two String Quartets in addition to the one already mentioned; an operetta; a Sonata for violin and piano; and numerous piano pieces and songs.

Another New Englander is *Carl McKinley,* who was born in Yarmouth, Maine, on October 9, 1895. The quality of his work as an undergraduate at Harvard won him a Naumburg Fellowship, which made it possible for him to study in New York during the winter of 1917-18 under Goldmark, Déthier, and Rothwell. For some years he was a church organist in Hartford, Connecticut, and later played the organ at the Capitol Theater, in New York. The years 1927-29 he spent abroad on a Guggenheim Fellowship and on his return he was appointed to the faculty of the New England Conservatory of Music. His *Masquerade,* the piece by which he is chiefly known, was introduced by Gabrilowitsch with the Philadelphia Orchestra in 1930, and has had some fifty or more performances since then by major orchestras. His *Indian Summer Idyl* was played by the New York Philharmonic in 1919, and he has written a good deal of music for organ, piano, and chorus.

RANDALL THOMPSON

If *Randall Thompson* had composed nothing more than the slow movement of his Second Symphony, he would be entitled by virtue of that work alone to a high place among our contemporary composers. For here is the voice of a true poet, calmly reflective, breathing its yearnings and aspirations through a Negro-like theme suggestive of *Deep River*. The entire symphony is simple and unaffected, and carries out successfully the composer's intention to be "primarily melodious and objective." As Lawrence Gilman wrote: [39]

> He [Thompson] has made use of popular idioms, melodic and rhythmic, and his manipulation of these is civilized and craftsmanlike.

[39] *New York Herald Tribune,* November 3, 1933.

He has not hesitated at times to be obvious; he has not strained, he has not constricted his fancy and his feeling; he has not been afraid to sound quite different from Schoenberg. His music has humor, and warmth, and pleasantness; many will find it agreeable and solacing.

But although Thompson does not scorn the past, he is by no means a thorough conservative. His idiom is personal and forward-looking, and even though he may not din our ears with dissonance, his medium is nevertheless thoroughly contemporary.

The Second Symphony offers an excellent illustration of this point. The work is highly rhythmic, but Thompson has not used the obvious percussion devices in producing and emphasizing his rhythms. The music itself is intrinsically rhythmic, and rather than utilizing a modern battery of percussion, the score contents itself with cymbals and kettle-drums.

Thompson, who since 1939 has been Director of the Curtis Institute in Philadelphia, was born in 1899 in New York City. He graduated from Harvard in 1920 and received a Master's Degree two years later. He studied music under Spalding and Hill at Harvard, and later worked with Ernest Bloch. From 1922 to 1925 he was a Fellow of the American Academy in Rome, and in 1929 and 1930 he was granted a Guggenheim Fellowship. He has been an assistant professor of music at Wellesley College and a lecturer at Harvard, and was for two years professor of music and director of the University Chorus at the University of California. He is the author of a survey, *College Music*,[40] made under the auspices of the Carnegie Foundation.

His orchestral works include two tone-poems, *Pierrot and Cothurnus* (1922) and *The Piper at the Gates of Dawn* (1924); a *Jazz Poem*, with piano solo (1928); and the two Symphonies (1929 and 1930). In addition to these works he has composed considerable choral music. The most extended piece in this form is *The Peaceable Kingdom*, commissioned by the League of Composers and first performed by the Harvard Glee Club and the Radcliffe Choral Society, March 29, 1936, in New York. This is

[40] Macmillan Company, 1935.

Randall Thompson

a work for mixed voices, a cappella, subtitled, "A sequence of sacred choruses—text from Isaiah."

The words are drawn verbatim from the Bible, and given modern treatment in the music. The opposed choirs of the double chorus are used to carry out the dual idea which was suggested to the composer by a painting entitled *The Peaceable Kingdom*, by Edward Hicks, an American painter of the eighteenth century. The picture shows on one side William Penn making peace with the Indians, and on the other, Daniel in the midst of a group of lions. As the composer remarked, "the lions in this part look as though they were trying to make peace with Daniel; they appear to be succeeding."

Satire is often the basis for Thompson's choral music, sometimes gentle and occasionally slapstick, as in *Americana*, which uses as a text excerpts from Henry L. Mencken's department in the old *American Mercury*. Here burlesque oratorio music matches the inanities of the items Mencken chose from the newspapers of the nation. In *Rosemary*, for women's voices, the four divisions are entitled "Chemical Analysis," "A Sad Song," "A Nonsense Song," and "To Rosemary, on the methods by which she might become an angel."

Thompson's varied activities in the last few years have kept him from composing anything but a Suite for clarinet, oboe, and viola. But he feels that his style has continued to develop, particularly as it may have been influenced by the increasing amount and variety of American music that has become accessible in recent years. He might be termed a "reasonable nationalist," pursuing "a nationalistic as a means toward a universal goal."

COMPOSER PERFORMERS

Several of our best known performing artists are also composers, although known only secondarily by their creative activity. Among them, the names of at least a few should be mentioned. *Rudolph Ganz*, born in Zürich, Switzerland, February 24,

1877, and a pupil of Busoni, is prominent as pianist, conductor, and teacher. He is president of the Chicago Musical College, has appeared as guest conductor with many of our major orchestras, and succeeded Ernest Schelling as conductor of the Young People's Concerts of the New York Philharmonic-Symphony Orchestra. He has written a Symphony; a *Konzertstück* for piano and orchestra; a Suite for orchestra on American scenes; a series of *Animal Pictures;* numerous piano pieces; several choruses for male voices; and many songs. *Albert Spalding*, born in Chicago, August 15, 1888, is one of America's best answers, in the field of performing music, to the charge that her native stock does not produce musicians. Of course the charge is not heard nowadays as much as it was, and no doubt Spalding's violin-playing is one of the reasons why it isn't. He is the author of two Violin Concertos; an orchestral Suite; a Violin Sonata; a String Quartet; and numerous smaller pieces and transcriptions. *Efrem Zimbalist*, born in Rostoff-on-the-Don, April 9, 1889, is American by adoption, of course. He is one of the many Russian-Jewish violinists who have enriched our concert life. Composing is an avocation with him, but he has produced major works, including a String Quartet; a Sonata for violin and piano; an opera; and a symphonic poem, *Daphnis and Chloë*, performed in January, 1932, by the Philadelphia Orchestra under Stokowski. Perhaps *Pietro Yon*, born in Settimo Vittone, Italy, August 6, 1886, should not be counted an American composer. His birth, training, and style are all Italian, and his music, which is practically all for the services of the Catholic Church, keeps close to recent Roman traditions. It includes numerous organ works; six masses and many motets; and an oratorio, *The Triumph of St. Patrick*, dedicated to the late Cardinal Hayes, whose seat was at St. Patrick's Cathedral in New York, where Yon is organist.

But the most eminent of our performer-composers was the late *Leopold Godowsky*, who was born in Vilna, in the Lithuanian section of eastern Europe which now belongs to Soviet Russia, on February 13, 1870, and who died November 24, 1938. Godowsky's worldwide fame as a pianist began when he was a child. He toured America as early as 1884, and in 1890 he came here to stay for an extended period, which eventually lasted his whole life through, with interruptions, as when during the first ten years or so of this century he made his headquarters in Berlin. He was generally acknowledged to be one of the greatest masters of the piano, and one of its foremost teachers. But he was at least as much interested in composition as in performance, and his work in this field attracted extravagant praise from such critics as James Gibbons Huneker, among others. For orchestra he wrote three symphonic *Metamorphoses*; for piano, fifty-three studies on the Chopin Etudes, in which the latter were combined and dressed up contrapuntally in ways that made them transcendently difficult to play; *Triakontameron*, a set of thirty pieces each written in a single day, of which "Alt-Wien" has become the most popular; and numerous other works.

Opinions on Godowsky the composer, as on Godowsky the pianist, were divided. But on Godowsky the wit opinions were unanimous in the affirmative. Perhaps we may make room for the most famous of the Godowsky stories. At the debut of Jascha Heifetz, in 1917, Mischa Elman, who was sitting with Godowsky, remarked that the hall was terribly hot. "Not for pianists!" was Godowsky's classic retort.

4

UNFAMILIAR IDIOMS

Once more the arbitrary division into classifications becomes exceedingly difficult, if not misleading. Some of the composers who appeared in the preceding chapter have also tried their hands at the strange and unusual, and many pages from their scores have sounded harsh and dissonant to ears unaccustomed to advanced tonal combinations. John Alden Carpenter is by no means a conservative, particularly in *Skyscrapers*; Howard Hanson is altogether contemporary in his viewpoint; Albert Stoessel does not hesitate to adopt neo-classicism; yet these men are accepted unreservedly by all but the reactionaries among concert-goers. They move in thoroughly respectable company.

In the following pages we shall meet composers who are somewhat to the left of our safe and sound group, men and women who are to a degree pioneers, though not out-and-out experimenters. Some of them may be no more advanced in their harmonic thinking than several of their colleagues in Chapter 3, but they have chosen a more difficult road to acceptance by the public, and most of them have consciously written for a small audience.

It is not possible to classify our "modernist" composers, even the most advanced of them, according to the several European divisions. Some of them may fairly be said to be neo-classicists, but after all, neo-classicism embraces a number of diverse, though sympathetic, elements. We cannot point to any of our countrymen as pure atonalists or polytonalists. Even those who have experi-

UNFAMILIAR IDIOMS

mented with quarter-tones have not done so exclusively. Rather do we find a number of our composers sampling several of these devices, and each striving, consciously or unconsciously, to work them into his own individual speech.

It is also fair to question the inclusion in this chapter of three composers who appear in its early pages: Charles Martin Loeffler, Henry F. Gilbert, and Charles T. Griffes. None of these men is living today, and, moreover, Loeffler has been widely recognized as one of our most brilliant creative talents, Griffes is no longer strange to our ears either as an impressionist or as a mystic, and Gilbert's racy music is not played very often. But all three of them were uncompromising in writing as they wanted to write, with no concessions to what the public might accept. In their time they composed in what were unfamiliar idioms, and they were willing to accept the approval of their own artistic consciences as adequate reward.

PIONEER FREE-THINKERS

Charles Martin Loeffler was not American by birth, nor can we claim his music as being in any way native in character. Yet he represented something that was exceedingly precious at a time when our best-equipped composers, with the exception of MacDowell, were thoroughly academic. Loeffler was an independent thinker, an artistic hermit, and his sparkling and colorful scores were studded with jewels that were all too rare in his contemporary New England.

Some have tried not to be dazzled by the jewels. Paul Rosenfeld has gone so far as to compare Loeffler's music to the dead Queen of Castile, whose remains were swathed in royal robes and hung with gold and precious stones.[1] Rosenfeld thinks that Loeffler's many years in Boston made his work sterile, that with all his brilliance he succumbed to the correct manners and inhibitions of New England.

[1] *An Hour with American Music* (Philadelphia: J. B. Lippincott Company, 1929).

This seems entirely unfair. We can be more objective about Loeffler than was possible even in 1929, when Rosenfeld advanced his opinion, and most of us still not only admire the jewels, but feel the strong pulse of life behind them.

When Loeffler came to us in 1881 he was a young man of twenty who had already gained an unusual background. He was born in Alsace, January 30, 1861, had lived in Russia, and had been one of Joachim's favorite violin pupils. He studied in Paris with Massart (pupil of Kreutzer) and played in the Pasdeloup Orchestra. He was engaged for the private orchestra of Baron Paul von Derweis, who spent his summers at his castle near Lake Lugano and his winters at Nice. Whenever the household moved from summer to winter quarters, three special trains were needed to carry the family, the guests and the tutors for the children, the servants and the horses, the orchestra of seventy and the mixed choir of forty-five. Loeffler became a favorite with the Baron, and he was often asked to help in the performance of chamber music by members of the family.

When he arrived in America he first spent a year in New York, playing in Damrosch's orchestra and sometimes with Theodore Thomas. Then Major Higginson asked him to come to Boston to play in the Boston Sympathy, which had just finished its first season. Loeffler shared the first desk with Listemann, the concert master, and later with Franz Kneisel. He was with the orchestra until 1903, when he resigned, gave up playing the violin in public, and determined to devote the rest of his life to composition and to his farm at Medfield, Massachusetts. He lived there until his death, May 19, 1935.

Spiritually, Loeffler was a mystic, a deep student of medieval thought and culture, profoundly interested in Gregorian plainsong and the church modes of the Middle Ages. Living in the twentieth century, he seemed a wanderer searching for a place where pious mystics spoke his language. Not finding it, he lived in his dreams. There he polished his music until it was refined to a purity that would satisfy his sense of the exquisite.

He published practically nothing until he had finished his career as a violinist. Many of his works had been performed, but he had kept them all in manuscript. In 1891 the Boston Symphony played his suite for violin and orchestra, *Les Veillées de l'Ukraine* (after Gogol); in 1894 his *Fantastic Concerto* for cello and orchestra; and in 1895 his *Divertimento* for violin and orchestra.

His first published orchestral works were the dramatic poem *La Mort de Tintagiles* (after Maeterlinck), and a Symphonic Fantasy based on a poem by Rollinat. These were issued in 1905, though both were written earlier. In 1907 the Boston Symphony Orchestra introduced the work which is still the most played of Loeffler's compositions—the *Pagan Poem*. This had been first composed in 1901, as a work for piano, two flutes, oboe, clarinet, English horn, two horns, three trumpets, viola, and double bass. Then Loeffler arranged the score for two pianos and three trumpets, and it was played at the home of Mrs. Jack Gardner in Boston, in 1903. After that the composer expanded it to symphonic proportions, for piano and large orchestra, and it was finally performed in its permanent form with Heinrich Gebhard playing the piano part.

The *Pagan Poem* is based on the eighth Eclogue of Virgil, in which a Thessalian girl tries to become a sorceress, to draw her truant lover home. The three trumpets (treated *obbligati*) suggest the refrain of the sorceress. First they are heard off-stage, then nearer and nearer until they finally come onto the platform, and the orchestra voices the triumph of the sorceress in an outburst of exultant passion. The dark, brooding music brings the odor of strange incense and magic incantations. It paints a vivid picture of the lovesick sorceress, chanting her passionate songs.

The plain-chant, Gregorian influence on Loeffler's music is most apparent in the *Music for Four String Instruments* (published in 1923), and in the symphony, *Hora Mystica*, written for the festival of 1916 in Norfolk, Connecticut. It is also evident in his setting of the "Canticle of the Sun" by St. Francis, entitled *Canticum Fratris Solis*. This remarkable work was commissioned by the Library of Congress, under the provisions of the Elizabeth Sprague Coolidge Foundation, and was first performed in Washington, at the first chamber music festival of the Library of Congress, in 1925. It was scored for solo voice and chamber orchestra, and it utilized old church modes and sometimes definite liturgical motives.

Besides his songs, to poems of Verlaine, Baudelaire, Rossetti, Poe, Yeats, Loeffler composed and published two Rhapsodies for oboe, viola and piano (*L'Étang* and *La Cornemuse*); a chorus for women's voices, *By the Rivers of Babylon;* an eight-part chorus for mixed voices a cappella, *For One Who Fell in Battle;* a poem for orchestra, *La Bonne Chanson;* another orchestral poem, *Memories of My Childhood* ("Life in a Russian Village"); and *La Villanelle du Diable*.

Although his closing years were those of a recluse, and even though he suffered from failing health, he continued to compose almost until the end. Mrs. Elizabeth Sprague Coolidge commissioned, in addition to the *Canticle*, a *Partita* for flute, violin and piano. In 1931 the Juilliard Foundation published *Evocation*, for orchestra, women's chorus, and speaking voice, which Loeffler had composed for the Cleveland Orchestra. It was first performed in Cleveland, February 5, 1931, and on a subsequent performance by the Boston Orchestra, the reviewer of *Musical America* remarked: [2]

What sets this work apart from other music of the time is the manner in which the composer has used the advanced orchestral technique of the day to build an art form of almost classic purity and one entirely free from the harshness that characterizes much contemporary music. Its luminous clarity, delicate coloring, and fine workmanship are a constant delight.

One of Loeffler's closest friends, and perhaps his most understanding critic, is *Carl Engel*. Although as a composer Engel

[2] April 10, 1933.

is known almost exclusively by a few songs and by his *Triptych*, a sonata for violin and piano, all composed a score of years ago, he cannot be omitted from any discussion of American music. Born in Paris in 1883, and educated abroad, he came to this country in 1905, and was for twenty years associated with the Boston Music Company. In 1922 he succeeded Sonneck as chief of the music division of the Library of Congress. Three years later, the Elizabeth Sprague Coolidge Foundation in the Library of Congress was founded. The administration of the activities of the Foundation, in holding festivals, awarding prizes, and commissioning works, was in the hands of Engel, as chief of the music division, and under his guidance the Library became one of the nerve centers of American musical activity.

At Sonneck's death, in 1928, Engel became editor of *The Musical Quarterly*, and shortly afterwards president and editor-in-chief of the publishing firm of G. Schirmer, Inc. He has been a very influential figure in American musical life, was one of the founders and an early president of the American Musicological Society, and is a member of numerous important bodies, including: the advisory board of the League of Composers, the board of the United States Section of the International Society for Contemporary Music, the American Academy of Arts and Sciences, the International Society of Musicology and the Société française de musicologie.

Is *Ernest Bloch* an American? The motive to claim him as one is strong, for he is one of the most distinguished of living composers; and since he long ago adopted us by becoming an American citizen, and is by no means the only composer discussed in these pages who was born and educated abroad, there seems no reason not to recognize the adoption as a reciprocal one. Born in Geneva, Switzerland, in 1880, he did not come here until 1916. Since then, he has lived most of the time in this country. Some of his most important works were written before he arrived, but it was America that first gave wide recognition to his genius, it was from here that his fame spread across the Atlantic, and it is by American firms that almost all his works are published.

Bloch is an acknowledged master of his craft. Technique, whether of harmony and counterpoint, of form, or of orchestration, is his servant, so that one rarely thinks of the means he has used; it is the music itself, the sum total of effect that carries its message, and causes the listener to feel the primal urge that inspired it. His music-drama, *Macbeth*, has been compared to Moussorgsky's *Boris* in the power of its delineation of character. He is perhaps the most truly Jewish composer there has ever been, a son of ancient Judea, moved by what he himself has termed "the vigor and ingenuousness of the Patriarchs, the violence that finds expression in the books of the prophets, the burning love of justice, the desperation of the preachers of Jerusalem, the sorrow and grandeur of the book of Job, the sensuality of the Song of Songs."

The Jewish spirit was not always apparent in his earliest works —the Symphony (1901–02), *Macbeth* (1910), or the symphonic poems *Hiver* and *Printemps* (1905). But as early as 1913 it inspired the *Trois Poèmes Juifs;* and it has found expression in a whole series of works since then: several *Psalms* for voice and orchestra (1914); the *Schelomo* Rhapsody, for cello and orchestra which Lawrence Gilman called "the finest work yet written by any composer, living or dead, for the cello" (1915); the *Israel* Symphony; *Baal Shem*, for violin and piano (1923); *Méditation hébraïque* and *From Jewish Life*, for cello and piano (1924); *Voice in the Wilderness*, for cello and orchestra (1936); and the *Sacred Service* for the Synagogue (1932).

Bloch did not come from a musical family, but he began early to play the violin, and at the age of eleven he solemnly vowed that he would devote his life to composing music. He studied with Ysaÿe, Jaques-Dalcroze, Rasse, Knorr, and Thuille, in Belgium, France, Germany, and Switzerland. For a time he had to give up his musical career and act as traveling salesman for his father's clock business. But later he became professor of composition and lecturer on aesthetics at the Geneva conservatory. In 1910, his opera, *Macbeth*, was produced in Paris. But despite the considerable impression it made upon musicians there, it was never again heard until 1938, when it was produced in Italy, where Bloch was widely appreciated in the 1930's before the Fascist government became anti-Semitic. In fact, in 1929 he was made an honorary member of the Academy of Santa Cecilia, in Rome.

In 1916 Bloch came to America, as conductor of an orchestra that played for Maud Allen, and in 1917 joined the staff of the David Mannes School, in New York, as teacher of composition. At about this time the Flonzaley Quartet introduced his B minor String Quartet, which made a deep impression, and the late Dr. Karl Muck invited him to conduct his *Trois Poèmes Juifs* with the Boston Symphony Orchestra. In May, 1917, the Friends of Music in New York, under the late Artur Bodanzky, presented an entire program of Bloch's compositions. He was appointed in 1920 to direct the newly founded Cleveland Institute of Music. After six years there, he went to California, where he headed the San Francisco Conservatory.

In 1930 he received a ten-year subsidy to devote himself entirely to composition. Much of the time since then he has spent abroad, where his reputation, particularly in Italy and in England, has grown greatly.

It would be a mistake to think of Bloch only as a national or racial voice. He has spoken the international language of music with commanding authority, and his greatest works, apart from *Schelomo*, include several which have no clearly Jewish character: the Suite for viola and orchestra (1919), the Sonata for violin and piano (1920), the stirring Quintet for piano and strings (1924), the Concerto Grosso for piano and string orchestra (1925). In recent years he has also written a Violin Concerto, introduced by Szigeti and the Cleveland Orchestra under Mitropoulos in December, 1938; a Piano Sonata, published in Italy in 1936; and a symphonic suite, *Evocations* (1937).

In a letter published in the *New York Times* [3] Bloch summed up his aims as follows:

> I did my best—I never bowed to fads or fashions of the day. I never attempted to be "new," but to be "true" and to be human, in a general sense, though faithful to my roots.

He has paid tribute to his two homelands, that of his birth and that of his adoption, in the "symphonic fresco" *Helvetia* (1929), and the "epic rhapsody" *America* (1925)—both symphonic works of large proportions. Throughout all his nationalistic works, whether Jewish, American, or Swiss, Bloch has aimed at portraying the high ideals which animate the best men of all races as well as the special characteristics which in a better world should endear them to each other.

In *America*, he was avowedly concerned with "the future credo of all mankind," "the common purpose of widely diversified races ultimately to become one race, strong and great." The work ends with an anthem—to be sung by a chorus and the audience, with the orchestra—and motives from this anthem are used as the stones out of which the whole structure of the symphony is erected. In the very first bars the motive to which the word "America" is set, at the beginning of the anthem, appears dimly and primitively, and this motive with others is heard constantly throughout the three movements, slowly taking shape, "rising, falling, developing, and finally asserting itself" in the last measures of the finale. The first movement treats of "1620." "The Soil"—"The Indians—"(England)"—"The Mayflower"—"The Landing of the Pilgrims." Indian themes, the trumpet's "Call of America," *Old Hundred*, a sea chanty, all combine to tell of the country before and after the Pilgrims landed in Plymouth. The second movement is "1861–1865— Hours of Joy—Hours of Sorrow." The drama of the North and South; happiness, war, distress, and agony. Negro songs; a bit from Stephen Foster; *Pop Goes the Weasel*; then War songs—

[3] August 11, 1940.

John Brown's Body, The Battle Cry of Freedom, Tramp, Tramp, Tramp. Strife, battle, yet the "America call" is heard above the din, symbolizing the fact that America, though bleeding, is not fatally wounded. The finale is "1926—The Present—The Future." Speed, noise, jazz, the pomp of material prosperity. An inevitable collapse, and a gradual rebuilding that comes at last to the anthem—the promise that our ideals will save us.

The score won the *Musical America* prize of $3,000 during the season of 1927-28, and shortly afterwards was played simultaneously by several of the leading orchestras. It had a mixed reception, least friendly in the most "advanced" circles. For Bloch had frankly sought to reach a mass audience—had written an anthem quite in the "community sing" tradition, and based a whole programmatic work upon it. Let it be admitted that the anthem is not first-class, and that is an important admission, for the anthem is perhaps the one thing that keeps the whole work from being first-class. If enthusiasm for the work must be tempered by that realization, it is also true that the years that have passed since *America* was written have brought artists the world over to a recognition of the importance of putting their highest abilities, so far as possible, at the service of the widest public. *America* is an illustration of the difficulty of the task, the danger of leaning too far to one side or the other. But that very fact is a tribute to Bloch's courage in bringing forward such a work at a time when the general critical public were not aware even of the importance of what he was trying to do. It seems likely that if and when conductors decide to revive *America*, which has been very little played in a decade, they will find both public and critics in a more favorable mood to recognize its noble spirit and high craftsmanship, while not blinking the fact that it meets the man in the street (perhaps we should say the "man in the concert hall") rather more than half-way.

If official recognition of Bloch's Americanism is needed, one may count as such the inclusion of his *Hiver* and *Printemps*—

written probably long before he dreamed of becoming a citizen of the New World—on one of the programs of the festival of the American Society of Composers, Authors, and Publishers, in the fall of 1939.

The music of *Henry F. Gilbert* is so racy of the soil that it stamps its composer as one of our first nationalists. He was one of the original Wa-Wan group, and his intense nationalism may have been one of the reasons for the tardy recognition he received, particularly in the opening years of the twentieth century. Born in Somerville, Massachusetts, September 26, 1868, he studied first at the New England Conservatory, and then became MacDowell's first American pupil. During his student years, from 1889 to 1892, he earned his living playing the violin for dances and in theatres. This hack work disgusted him, and he determined to keep his music apart from the routine of getting money to feed himself. He became first a real-estate agent, then a foreman in a factory, a raiser of silk-worms, and finally a bread and pie cutter in a restaurant at the Chicago World's Fair. There he met a Russian prince who had been a friend of Rimsky-Korsakoff's, and who, when he recovered from the unconventional advances of the bread and pie cutter, was able to tell the young American much about Rimsky-Korsakoff and other members of the "neo-Russian" school.

Gilbert was always interested in composers who used folksongs and native material in their music, and his journeys after 1895, when he inherited a small sum of money, took him wherever he could find kindred spirits. He was so stirred when he heard of the coming première of Charpentier's *Louise* in Paris, knowing that it made use of popular themes, that he worked his way to Europe on a cattle-boat to hear the first performance.

It was not until 1911, when he was forty-two, that he really came to the attention of the musical public. It was in April of that year that the Boston Symphony played the *Comedy Overture on Negro Themes*, which disturbed the audience considerably but impressed itself on its hearers immediately as something new. As Olin Downes remarked, "There were some who thought that the opening was undignified, and stopped thinking at that place." [4]

The *Overture* had originally been intended as a prelude to an operetta based on the *Uncle Remus* tales of Joel Chandler Harris. Gilbert had actually completed his sketches for the operetta and then found that exclusive stage rights had been granted to another composer. So he could use only the overture, which he rescored for a larger orchestra. The first theme was a Negro melody from the Bahamas; the second a tune sung by the roustabouts of the Mississippi steamboats, *I'se Gwine to Alabamy, Oh!* The middle section was a witty, rollicking fugue on the *Old Ship of Zion*. In spite of the audience's dismay at the first performance, Gilbert had given his material such genuine, spontaneous treatment that he began to be talked about, and two years later he was invited to write an orchestral work for the Litchfield County Festival in Norfolk, Connecticut.

For this occasion he wrote his *Negro Rhapsody*, which pictured first a Negro "shout," alternating a savage dance tune and a spiritual; then a glorification of the spiritual, in which the barbaric elements gradually gave way to the loftier, nobler phase. This final triumph of the spiritual offers a direct contrast to John Powell's *Negro Rhapsody*, in which there is a reversion to paganism.

Gilbert's next work to bring him further recognition was his *Dance in the Place Congo*, based on five songs of the Louisiana Creole Negroes. It was first composed as an orchestral piece, but the composer later wrote a ballet scenario, to which it was finally performed at the Metropolitan in New York, March 23, 1918. This is one of Gilbert's best works. The tropical grace of the Creole tunes is subtly emphasized, while the gloomy, tragic note of the slave dances in the old Place Congo of New Orleans forms a weird and fantastic background. First comes the *Bamboula*, then some light moments which rise to frenzy, interrupted at

[4] *Musical Quarterly*, January, 1918.

last by the booming of the great bell that summons the slaves back to their quarters. Then a pause and a cry of despair.

There were also several works not based on American folk-songs. Long before Gilbert gained the recognition that came with the *Comedy Overture,* David Bispham had sung his setting of Stevenson's *Pirate Song* ("Fifteen Men on a Dead Man's Chest"), and the Russian Symphony Orchestra in New York had given a single performance of his *Salammbô's Invocation to Tanith,* for a soprano and orchestra. There was also a Symphonic Prelude to Synge's drama, *Riders to the Sea,* in which Gilbert made use of an old Irish melody. This was first written for small orchestra, to be played at some performances of the drama at the Twentieth Century Club in Boston, in 1904. Later Gilbert expanded the work, and it was performed at the music festival of the MacDowell Memorial Association at Peterborough, September, 1914. He also composed a one-act opera that has not yet been performed—*Fantasy in Delft,* with the scene laid in seventeenth-century Holland. Gilbert lived to be not quite sixty years old, and died May 19, 1928.

The death of *Charles Tomlinson Griffes,* April 8, 1920, was a cruel loss to American music, for it took away one of our most promising talents when he was only thirty-six years old and had written a mere handful of works. But that handful was enough to give him a permanent place among our composers, and a number of his pieces continue to appear regularly on concert programs.

His product fell into three distinct periods. First came the student period, when he was definitely under the influence of his German teachers, Rüfer and Humperdinck. It was then that he wrote German songs. In his second style Griffes leaned toward the French Impressionists, and also showed his fondness for the Russian Orientalism that was to appear as the mysticism of his later works. *The Lake at Evening,* from the three tone-pictures for piano, and *The White Peacock,* from the *Roman Sketches* for piano, show him in this period and demonstrate his power of impressionistic description. *The White Peacock* was arranged by the composer as an orchestral piece and has achieved something of a vogue.

The third period shows an advanced trend; a grasping for something less rigid than the tempered scale, a medium to sound the overtones he wanted us to hear. It was during this period that Griffes composed his Piano Sonata and his larger orchestral works. The Sonata has the intellectual consistency of a Schoenberg, a pursuit of tonal logic without the sacrifice of poetic conception. The themes are clearly defined, but it is their development that is interesting rather than the themes themselves.

The most important orchestral work is *The Pleasure Dome of Kubla Khan*, a tone-poem. It was first performed, in 1920, under circumstances that were tragic, for the labor of its composition was partly responsible for the illness that caused the composer's death. When he knew the work was to have a performance by the Boston Symphony Orchestra, he set himself to copying out the parts. He was tired and busy with his regular work of teaching music at a boys' school, and when he had finished the parts he fell ill with an attack of pneumonia. Word of his great success was brought to him just before he died.

For *The Pleasure Dome of Kubla Khan*, Griffes took his inspiration from Coleridge's poem; the lines that describe the "stately pleasure dome," the "sunny pleasure dome with caves of ice, the miracle of strange device." In writing his music Griffes gave his own imagination free rein in his description of the palace, and of the revelry that might well have taken place there. The vague, foggy beginning suggests the sacred river, which ran "through caverns measureless to man down to a sunless sea." Then the outlines of the palace gradually rise, "with walls and towers girdled round." Sounds of revelry and dancing rise to a wild climax and then suddenly break off. The original mood returns, and we hear again the sacred river and the "caves of ice."

All this is colorful music, and so is the *Poem* for flute and orchestra, which was first played by Georges Barrère with unforgettable mastery. In the orchestration of the *Poem*, Griffes surpassed even the *Pleasure Dome*. This is the most mature of his works. Starting in a gray mood, it develops into a dance movement of Oriental rhythm and color, strange and fragrant.

Among Griffes' works for piano, the best known are the *Roman Sketches*. First comes *The White Peacock*, who makes his bow in a languorous chromatic passage. *Nightfall* brings the strange sounds of the early evening, an almost oppressive quiet. *The Fountain of the Acqua Paola* shows the rise and fall of the water, the shimmering lights of the foam. Its kinship with the *Jeux d'Eau* of Ravel shows the tremendous influence the French composer had on the work of Griffes' second period. The last piece of the set, *Clouds*, starts with a lofty chordal passage, suggesting the high and massive cloud banks.

The songs are still much used on recital programs, from the early settings of German poems, through those of texts by Fiona MacLeod, to the later songs in which he showed that he was finding a really personal expression—*An Old Song Re-Sung*, the *Sorrow of Mydah*, and others of their kind.

Griffes was born in Elmira, New York, September 17, 1884. He was talented in other fields than music. He could draw well with pen and ink, he made excellent water-color landscapes, and later in life he worked in etchings on copper. When he was in high school he decided to be a musician, and he went to Berlin to study for the career of concert pianist. It was not until he studied theory with Humperdinck that he decided to be a composer. Then he came back to America, in 1908, and took the position of music teacher at the Hackley School in Tarrytown, New York, which he held until his death in 1920.

How much further he might have gone had he lived longer no one can say. Probably his ideals were high enough to have saved him from being spoiled by the recognition and success that were just beginning to come to him. At any rate, it is significant to note that his works have held their place in the repertoire, and that the last decade has witnessed no falling off in their appearance on programs.

John Beach belongs to the older generation of our "modernists." He was born in Gloversville, New York, October 11, 1877, and studied first at the New England Conservatory of Music, under Chadwick. Then for a while he taught piano in the Northwestern Conservatory, in Minneapolis, and theoretical subjects at the University of Minnesota, and later lived for a time in New Orleans. In 1910 he went to Paris, where he spent seven years, studying fugue and composition with Gédalge, and piano with Bauer. He has also studied with Loeffler and with Malipiero. He served in the World War on the Italian front, and then returned to live in New York. His orchestral works include *Asolani* (1920), *Phantom Satyr,* a ballet (1924), and *Orleans Alley* (1925). For chamber orchestra he has written another ballet, *Mardi Gras* (1925); *Angelo's Letter,* with tenor or baritone solo (1926); and *Enter Buffoon* (1929). There is also a dramatic prelude, *Pippa's Holiday* (1926), for soprano and orchestra; and his several works of chamber music include: *Naïve Landscapes* (1917), for piano, flute, oboe, and clarinet; a *Poem* for string quartet (1920); and a *Concert for Six Instruments*—violin, viola, cello, flute, oboe, clarinet.

Among the nationalist pioneers, *Arthur Farwell* must have his place, and not only for his association with such men as Henry F. Gilbert. Even though Farwell may be more important to American music for what he typifies and represents than for the actual music he has produced, he is one of those who first became discontented with the traditional European patterns that American music was following, and as a crusader he deserves an honorable place in our musical annals.

At the very beginning of the century he resented so keenly the fact that commercial publishers turned their backs on American composers who tried to be individual, that he joined with Clarence Birchard in founding the Wa-Wan Press, an organization with the avowed intention of issuing unsalable works by Americans, and with a special welcome to works that developed in interesting fashion any folk-music to be found on American soil. This was in 1901, and for eleven years the Wa-Wan Press helped to launch a number of Farwell's fellow-composers: such men as Henry F. Gilbert, Edgar Stillman Kelley, Harvey Worthington Loomis, and others. At the end of the eleven years the founders felt that the work was done, and handed over the catalog of compositions to the firm of G. Schirmer, Inc., in New York.

Farwell did not decide to become a musician until he had graduated from the Massachusetts Institute of Technology at the age of twenty-one. He was born in St. Paul, Minnesota, April 23, 1872, and although he had violin lessons as a child, there was no opportunity to hear much music in his home city. It was when he went to Boston that he heard a symphony orchestra for the first time, and after this his principal reason for staying at the engineering school was that it kept him in Boston, where he could hear the concerts every week. The day he graduated he had an interview with George W. Chadwick, and he decided to become a composer.

After four years of study in Boston he went abroad to work with Humperdinck and Pfitzner in Germany, and with Guilmant in Paris. When he came back to America, in 1899, he became lecturer on the history of music at Cornell University, and began his first experiments with Indian music. In the following years he made frequent journeys to the Far West, lecturing, and studying the songs of the Indians in the Southwest, and the folk-songs of the Spanish Californians.

When Gaynor was elected mayor of New York, in 1910, Farwell was appointed to the newly created position of Supervisor of Municipal Music. Through this position he was able to carry out some of his ideas for pageants. He wrote incidental music for Louis Parker's *Pageant Play,* and for *Joseph and his Brethren.* He composed and conducted the music for the presentation

UNFAMILIAR IDIOMS

of Percy MacKaye's *Caliban,* which was given in the Lewisohn Stadium in 1916.

In 1915 Farwell succeeded David Mannes as director of the Music School Settlement. Then, in 1918, he went to California, where he spent nine years teaching at the University of California in Los Angeles and in Berkeley, organizing choruses and composing music for pageants. In 1927 he went to East Lansing, Michigan, where he now conducts theoretical courses and gives lectures on music history at the Michigan State College.

Farwell used to say that his interest in folk-music lies in his being a spiritual descendant of the tribe of Tom Sawyer and Huck Finn, and that as such he gets "a great kick out of a rip-snorting development of a good old American tune." The first of his Indian compositions for orchestra was *Dawn,* played for the first time at the St. Louis Exposition, in 1904. His next large Indian score was called *The Domain of Hurakan*—the wind-god of the Central American Indians. For piano, he has written a group of *American Indian Melodies;* a *Navajo War Dance; Impressions of the Wa-Wan Ceremony* (from the Omaha tribe); *Pawnee Horses;* and a *Fugue Fantasia.* He has also made settings of Negro melodies, and cowboy and prairie songs.

These folk-song developments, however, are only a small part of Farwell's creative work. The opus numbers of his works run to one hundred and three. He has in his time tried innovations, one of them with a form that has an analogy to the choral-prelude of the Reformation. This appeared in his *Mountain Song,* which he termed a symphonic song-suite—with movements based on the themes of choral songs, the audience singing the songs whenever the form of the piece demands it. This technique was also used in the *Symphonic Hymn on March! March!* and in the *Symphonic Song on Old Black Joe.*

Among Farwell's recent works, the most important is perhaps the orchestral suite, *Gods of the Mountain,* after the play by Dunsany. This had its première in Minneapolis in 1929, and has had frequent performances elsewhere. He has also been devoting himself to a *Rudolph Gott* symphony, which is based on a fragment of something over a hundred bars by an ill-fated friend who was one of the composer's greatest inspirations.

Although he is close to seventy, Farwell is by no means through with innovations and experiments. They are too much a part of his nature for him ever to abandon them. He may be less aggressively nationalistic than he was thirty years ago, but he still feels that a creative artist is lost if he does not keep close to his own land and people, and in some degree reflect them. But he should not be thought of simply as a "folk" composer, for whatever he has done in that field (and he is happy to have done it) is far outweighed by his freely created work. His whole outlook explains, perhaps, why he has lent so much of sympathy and encouragement to his younger colleague and former pupil, Roy Harris.

ROY HARRIS

It was Farwell who gave *Roy Harris* his first musical training, and it was because the older man recognized a kindred spirit that he sought to interpret his young colleague when he wrote of him several years later in the *Musical Quarterly*, January, 1932. The opening words of that article were: "Gentlemen, a genius—but keep your hats on!"

It would be gratifying to believe that there was a striking significance in the utterance of this exclamation a century after Schumann had hailed Chopin, and it is entirely possible that Harris may prove to be one of the outstanding figures of the twentieth century.

There are several factors in his favor. First of all, the wide recognition he has won was not achieved by any facile bid for popularity. He has not given the public music easy to listen to, or even pleasant according to accepted standards. He has never hesitated to promote his own interests, nor is he by any means one who hides his light under a bushel, but he has never written

Roy Harris

music merely to tickle his listeners' ears. He has set himself ideals and high-minded standards which he has followed sincerely and without compromise, and yet he has become one of the most widely performed of our composers, and certainly the best represented on phonograph records.

If any question of sincerity arises, it concerns not Harris himself but his audience. When a composer becomes the fashion among a cult of the intelligentsia, we may often wonder how genuine its appreciation of his product may be. It is fair to ask how many have jumped aboard the bandwagon merely because Harris has been widely discussed, and how large a proportion of his followers really grasp his intentions and are capable of evaluating the worth of his music. But Harris himself is very much in earnest and believes sincerely in what he is doing.

When he first appeared on the scene, in the late 'twenties, he seemed the answer to all our prayers. Here was a genuine American, born in a log cabin in Oklahoma, like Lincoln, tall, lanky, rawboned, untouched by the artificial refinements of Europe or even the stultifying commercialism of cosmopolitan New York; a prophet from the Southwest who thought in terms of our raciest folk-tunes. Small wonder that we called him the white hope of American music.

Added to his background was a keen intellect and a questioning mind, a temperament incapable of accepting tradition merely because it was tradition; a mind that asked whether there was not a better way, a more flexible medium for the expression of creative thoughts. Impatient of teachers and academic attitudes, he has examined all music with a critical eye and has come to the conclusion that the past masters created masterworks in spite of the restrictions and limitations of tradition rather than because of them. And so through prodigious energy and rigorous intellectual discipline he has created music which is indubitably his own, quite unlike the music of anyone else. What its permanent value may be is another matter.

It may be that Harris's mental powers will prove to be his

downfall; that the racy, native flavor that is his birthright will not stand too much intellectualizing; that he is giving his natural voice too objective a treatment. Certainly he asks a great deal of his contemporary listener, for at present it requires an analytical mind and ear as well as an emotional sensitivity to enjoy his work. When we have absorbed his idiom, then we shall see if he reaches our emotions, and if he does, he is a great composer. But that is something which will be determined in the future, not in the present.

It is no simple matter to describe or explain Harris's idiom in a few words. Arthur Mendel, one of the earliest and warmest of Harris's admirers, treated one phase of it as successfully as anyone, perhaps when he wrote of Harris in *The Nation*.[5] He said, in part:

> The composer ... must devote all his attention to perfecting a clear and powerful medium of expression, which means—in a period like this, when old formulae have lost their power—a new medium.
> This has been one side of the work of leading "modernists" all over the world: Schoenberg changing the interval-formation of chords and melodies and experimenting with atonality; Stravinsky working at new rhythms, orchestral colors, polytonal effects; Hába working with quarter-tones; everyone everywhere reshaping our conceptions of consonance and dissonance, and the relations between them. Roy Harris, instead of basing his work on novelty in the sensuous materials of the art, focusses his attention on the structure of music. ... [He] is trying to work out an idiom in which the structure shall be based on the self-determined growth of the melodic material, not on any superimposed form. In theory, he is attempting to do in music what was done long ago in poetry—to free it from limitations corresponding to rhyme, meter, and conventional forms. ... He feels that the composer of the future must free himself of these shackles. His music must be just as cogent and logical and structurally perfect as he can make it. But its form must be determined by its content. It must grow as a plant or an animal grows, along lines dictated by its own inner necessity, not imposed on it from above.

[5] "A Change in Structure," January 6, 1932.

All of which embodies a worthy aim, one which should enrich the art of music; but it will be several years yet before we may decide whether Harris's natural talents will flower in such surroundings or whether his exceedingly conscious striving for a new vehicle for his thoughts will smother his message and prevent it from finding its most fruitful outlet.

He was born in Oklahoma, February 12, 1898, of pioneer parents who staked a claim and tilled a farm. Malaria drove the family to California where they continued farming in the Gabriel Valley. Here Roy spent his youth and early manhood and had his grammar and high-school education. When he was eighteen he started a farm of his own, and spent his leisure time studying Greek philosophy.

When America entered the World War, Harris served as a private in the army. After a year he returned to Southern California, and gave himself largely to study. He entered the Southern Branch of the University of California, began to study harmony, and delved into Hindu theology. In the daytime he drove a truck, and in the evenings attended classes.

During his boyhood he had played a little on the piano, the clarinet, and the organ, but it was not until after the War that his real interest in music grew. It was while he was studying harmony and theory that he approached Arthur Farwell, still in California, and asked to become his pupil. Farwell taught him for two years, and later remarked,[6] "I was convinced that he would one day challenge the world."

While Harris was working with Farwell he composed a Suite for string quartet, and an *Andante* for orchestra, which was chosen from a mass of submitted manuscripts for performance by the New York Philharmonic-Symphony at the Stadium Concerts in the summer of 1926. Shortly after this he went abroad to study in Paris with Nadia Boulanger. During his first year there (1927) he composed his Concerto for string quartet, piano and clarinet,

[6] *Musical Quarterly*, January, 1932.

and the next year his Piano Sonata. These works represented a tremendous advance over the somewhat groping *Andante* and were instrumental in winning for him a Guggenheim Fellowship.

In 1929 he suffered an accident which fractured his spine. He partially recovered in a Paris hospital, and then returned to New York for an operation. During his six months' convalescence he composed a String Quartet, and he believes that it was the enforced absence from a piano which freed him from the restrictions of the piano keyboard and rendered his technique more fluent.

Harris's vogue dates from these years, and the early American performances of the Concerto and the Piano Sonata. With performances came recognition from other quarters, in addition to commissions for new works. In 1931 the Pasadena Music and Arts Association awarded him a fellowship which would provide him with leisure for creative work. There were no conditions attached to the award except that he produce according to his capacity and ability. Later, in 1933, Harris moved to Princeton to become teacher of theory and composition at the Westminster Choir School, where he remained until 1938. At present he lives in New York, where he devotes the bulk of his time to composition and does some teaching and lecturing.

Harris is interesting and important in two directions: in the nationalism of his speech, and in his attempt to create a new idiom. In 1929 Paul Rosenfeld had several comments to make on the native character of his early works, most specifically of the Concerto for string quartet, piano and clarinet (which he called a Sextet), and the Piano Sonata. In describing the former [7] he wrote of the "irregularity and looseness" of the "melodic conduct," which

> makes it affect one like the sight of a body reeling from side to side, staggering a little and yet never actually losing its balance. Cowboys walk in that fashion, extremely awkwardly and extremely lithely; and so personal a piece as the scherzo of Harris's sextet brings to mind noth-

[7] *An Hour with American Music* (Philadelphia: J. B. Lippincott Company, 1929).

ing so much as the image of a little cowboy running and reeling about on the instruments, toppling but never falling.

Of the Piano Sonata, Rosenfeld said that it

carries the pathos of many lives beside his [Harris's] own. Its gaunt homely forms seem charged with the feeling of many struggling, patient, tragical existences on this continent; on the farms, in the homes, long ago, here now.

It may be that those of us who know Harris, who have fallen under the spell of his personality and have heard his drawling, Southwestern speech, imagine these native elements in his early works. But if they are actually present, it is thoroughly apparent that they came there naturally, without any conscious effort on Harris's part. The subsequent experiments with forms and idioms are more objective and studied, and it remains to be seen whether the native flavor will stand formalizing, or will virtually disappear.

Certainly it is not so apparent in the *Symphony 1933*, in which the composer is preoccupied with an elaborate formal structure. In describing his intentions Harris wrote: "In the first movement I have tried to capture the mood of adventure and physical exuberance; in the second, of the pathos which seems to underlie all human existence; in the third, the mood of a positive will to power and action." Then follows an extended description of the work's construction, and the development of its material.

The principal theme of the first movement offers considerable contrast, between the development of a short rhythmic motive which is constantly reiterated (so insistently that in listening to its recording on the phonograph one may at times wonder whether the record is not marred and the needle traveling repeatedly in the same groove), and the unfolding of a lyric melody that continues in a long unbroken line and gives the feeling of a yearning idealism. The second movement undoubtedly succeeds in its purpose; its dirgelike melody is poignant without becoming tragic, and the listener may grasp its import and its beauty without the need of consulting Harris's extended explanation of its form, which he terms a "free use of the Rondo principle."

The last movement, representing the "positive will to power and action," is a variation development of the theme stated in the opening. It is, explains the composer, "a free use of contrapuntal devices, canon, imitation, etc., in which the characteristics of the theme are extended into autogenetic melodic designs of varying lengths and contours." And while Harris seemed preoccupied with other matters in the first two movements, he has, unconsciously perhaps, embodied more of his native spirit in this last movement.

The Symphony was first performed by the Boston Symphony Orchestra, in Boston, January 26, 1934. A week later, on February 2, Koussevitzky played it in New York, and at that time the Columbia Phonograph Company made a recording of the work. In Boston, H. T. Parker [8] found the Symphony "American, first, in a pervading directness, in a recurring and unaffected roughness of speech—an outspoken symphony. . . . He is also American," Parker wrote, "in broad design, full voice, a certain abruptness in the progress of his symphony."

In New York, Olin Downes disputed this view.[9] He considered "the technical formulae . . . creditable enough" but thought "the music . . . labored and the thematic material very sparse. . . . It sometimes repeats, but seldom progresses."

Closely akin to the *Symphony 1933* is a work introduced the following year, which had been commissioned by the RCA-Victor Company for recording. This is the comparatively brief "American Overture," *When Johnny Comes Marching Home*, which under the title, "From the Gayety and Sadness of the American Scene" had been performed by the Los Angeles Symphony under Nicolas Slonimsky, December 29, 1932. In this work we find Harris still intent on developing an "autogenetic" form, one that grows naturally from its content, but also incorporating considera-

[8] *Boston Evening Transcript*, January 27, 1934.
[9] *New York Times*, February 3, 1934.

ble native flavor which is apparent throughout in spite of the elaborate treatment it receives.

In the leaflet which accompanies the recording of the Overture, Harris sets forth his aims. When he was commissioned to write the work, he explains, he was presented with a very specific set of problems.

First the work should express a gamut of emotions particularly American and in an American manner. Secondly, the form of the work being an Overture should be complete in itself and yet indicate that it was only a concentrated announcement of materials and moods which could unfold in a development of much greater length. Thirdly, the work must give these impressions and yet be eight minutes in length and divided into two well-balanced equal parts.

The moods which seem particularly American to me are a certain noisy ribaldry, a sadness, a groping earnestness which amounts to suppliance towards those deepest spiritual yearnings within ourselves; and finally a fierce struggle of will for power, sheer power in itself. There is little grace and mellowness in our midst. That will probably come after we have passed the high noon of our growth as a people.

With the moods of ribaldry, sadness, suppliance and willful power in mind I chose an American theme which is not only well known and loved but capable of extended development: "When Johnny Comes Marching Home." This was one of my father's favorite tunes. . . . He used to whistle it with jaunty bravado as we went to work on the farm in the morning and with sad pensiveness as we returned at dusk behind the slow weary plodding of the horses.

These impressions have undoubtedly influenced me in determining the use of this theme. . . . The first half of the work expresses openly and directly the ribald quality of the theme itself and its transformation into a slow, sad mood. . . . The last section . . . treats the mood of struggle for power and ends in an unresolved continuance of that struggle.

Thus it will be seen that the underlying program of the Overture is almost identical with the Symphony. And though the material is different the treatment is largely the same, with the same high-pitched ejaculations in the brasses and the same abrupt ending. Both works are unmistakably written by the same hand, using methods which some would call characteristic of the Harris individuality and which the unfriendly would term mannerisms.

Since Harris was so specific in telling what impressions he intended to convey, it is important to learn how faithfully and vividly these ideas may affect the listener. What would one hear in the piece if one were ignorant of the composer's intentions? This question must, of course, be answered by the individual listener, and no doubt the answers will vary considerably; but there is undeniably a jauntiness in the opening measures which does indeed suggest a carefree ribaldry, while the second section has a pensive brooding that is certain to leave its mark. In the final section the effect is less definite; some may, indeed, feel the "struggle for power" while others may be lost in a seemingly futile confusion.

In the later *Symphony for Voices,* Harris appeared to be carrying out his doctrines of form somewhat dogmatically. As a result the native elements are considerably obscured, if not completely hidden. This work, written for the Westminster Choir in 1936, is the second of the major works for chorus, following by two years the *Song for Occupations* which was commissioned by the League of Composers, and performed by the Westminster Choir.

Both works are settings of texts by Walt Whitman, and each is composed for an eight-part a cappella chorus. In the *Symphony for Voices* Harris uses a three-movement pattern to present once more the same basic contrasts he set forth in the Symphony *1933* and in *Johnny*. The first movement is buoyant, taking its text from Walt Whitman's *Sea-drift:*

> Today a rude brief recitative,
> Of ships sailing the seas, . . .
> Of unnamed heroes in the ships . . .
> Of dashing spray, and the winds piping and blowing, . . .

The second movement is subtitled "Tears," and again the lines are from *Sea-drift* and the music brings us an almost hysterical wail of anguish. The finale is once more the dream of power, and the words are drawn from Whitman's *Inscriptions:*

UNFAMILIAR IDIOMS

>Of life immense in passion, pulse, and power,
>Cheerful, for freest action form'd under the laws divine,
>The Modern Man I sing.

Whether a chorus of human voices is the proper medium for the kind of music Harris composed in this work is questionable. Certainly the demands made of the voices are cruel, and sometimes they are as hard on the listener as they must be on the singers. In the opening passages of the first movement the male voices continue an almost annoyingly persistent ostinato on the words "Of ships sailing the seas," while the sopranos intone the words that follow in a high, virtually monotonal line in a piercing tessitura.

The second movement is as dismal as Harris evidently intended it to be, and the triple fugue of the last movement is effective but harshly unvocal. It is true that the work as a whole has its moments of idealism, of aspiration, but they are too often submerged in the complex problems of the structure.

Others of Harris's orchestral works include a *Chorale* for six-part string orchestra (1932), a Second Symphony (1936), a prelude and fugue for string orchestra (1936), *Farewell to Pioneers* (1936), and a *Time Suite*, which was commissioned by the Columbia Broadcasting System and first performed over its network August 8, 1937. Presented with the desirability, if not the necessity, of composing a work within definite time limits, Harris proceeded to make a virtue of his problem by making time units not only the physical dimensions of his work but also its philosophical basis and reason for being. Hence the six movements were designed to occupy, respectively, one minute, two minutes, three minutes, four minutes, five minutes and four minutes. At the initial performance these durations varied considerably; the five minute movement consumed two seconds short of six minutes, and none of them occupied the exact amount of time it was intended to last; but then, the actual length of time was only a part of the scheme, which embodied not only philosophical but social and political ideas as well.

"The minute," said Harris in a preliminary announcement, "becomes a unit of space in music just as the square foot is a unit to the mural artist. We need to fill that minute as an organic thing for which the music seemingly has grown." He then proceeded with a detailed explanation of the work:

The first movement ["Broadway"] marked presto, is a study in asymmetrical rhythm. The second ["Religion"] is a study in two old church modes, the Phrygian and Lydian, and is purely contrapuntal, scored for muted strings and treated in the vocal style.

The three-minute movement ["Youth"] takes the form of a Fantasy. It is very free in form, and pagan or pantheistic in spirit. It reflects spontaneity, the spontaneity of youth, and unregimented natural growth.

By direct contrast the March, or fourth movement, is completely regimented. It seeks to capture the idea of "The March of Time" and symbolizes the growth of transportation and communication. I might call this a "Time Movement" within a "Time Suite," because the fourth movement is in four sections, each one minute long. The stylized sound of a train whistle connects each movement. This, together with an ascending pitch, expresses the idea of humanity longing for progress, the idea of motion.

Further contrast is supplied in movement 5 ["Philosophy"], whose background is built on a descending scale. This is a development of the second movement but broader in scope and orchestration. It is a study of diatonic and chromatic scales, the material and foundation of all music.

The Finale ["Labor"] is a study in rhythms again, as in the opening movement, but it is symmetrical as well as asymmetrical. Power is its mood and its expression is made in a fast, agitated tempo, which grows progressively more deliberate and stronger, culminating in a broad, powerful climax. This tries to show in music the resolution of chaos into order.

This was an ambitious program to embody in nineteen minutes of music, and it is not surprising that, to one listener at least, it did not register all of its polymorphous message. It also leads us back to the question we put a few pages earlier, whether the Harris intellect may not come to destroy the artist. We may well hope that it will not, for in spite of the cerebration that at times seems to smother and submerge it, the native talent is still there.

It is richly in evidence in three of his most mature works: the Quintet for piano and strings; the Quintet for two violins, two violas, and cello; and the Third Symphony.

Of the first-named, Arthur Mendel wrote: [10]

> The Quintet . . . is as concentrated as anything Harris has written and it is consistently polyphonic to an extent that might be expected to rule out easy triumphs. It is full of elaborate canonic device and subtle thematic development, and as one becomes more and more absorbed in these intricacies one forgets more and more the factors that give it direct appeal to the casual listener. What are these factors?
>
> First of all, exceptional melodic beauty. . . . Even among Harris's themes, the melody upon which the first two movements of this work are based is a rarity. . . . This, incidentally, is his first melody that can really be called ternary. The theme is so eminently singable, so strongly diatonic and tonal in feeling, that one is surprised to realize that it contains every note of the twelve-tone scale.
>
> In addition to its beauty of thematic material, the Quintet makes its appeal particularly through great variety of texture and color. A common complaint about Harris's music is that it is all on one plane of intensity, that it never relaxes. There is a certain truth in that observation (whether or not it is ground for complaint), and this uniformity of emotional pitch only makes variety of texture the more welcome.

The work is in three movements: a Passacaglia, consisting of the theme referred to and six variations on it; a Cadenza, in which the various instruments rhapsodize in turn on the material of the same theme; and a triple Fugue, on three subjects. Perhaps it shows, as Mendel claims, that Harris's intellect, vigorous as it is in this work, has not overwhelmed his ear and his heart. Lazare Saminsky [11] calls the Passacaglia "a work of genius and the best piece of American music that has been written during the three hundred years of its history."

The Third Symphony, too, has called forth superlatives. Writing in *Modern Music*,[12] George Henry Lovett Smith said:

---

[10] *Modern Music*, October–November, 1939.
[11] *Music of Our Day* (New York: Thomas Y. Crowell Company, 1932).
[12] October–November, 1939.

So far, it is safe to say, there is no work equal to it in American music-making. For significance of material, breadth of treatment and depth of meaning; for tragic implication, dramatic intensity, concentration; for moving beauty, glowing sound, it can find no peer in the musical art of America.

And Arthur Mendel, in the *Victor Record Review* [13] (both the Quintet and the Third Symphony, as well as many other works by Harris, have been recorded):

There are works of Harris that are simply packed full of so many things, each in itself beautiful, that they get in each other's way. In the Third Symphony, on the other hand, Harris's style has been skilfully pruned. It is as rich as anything he has ever written, only clearer and simpler. It will, I believe, become a part of the orchestral repertory [as a matter of fact, it was chosen by Koussevitzky as the one American work on the programs of the 1940 Berkshire Festival], and it will make both performers and listeners realize that they have put away some of Harris's earlier works too soon. They will then value it not only for its own great qualities, but also as a key to other music of Harris which did not invite them as clearly at first, but in which there are just as great and lasting beauties.

In addition to the works mentioned above, Harris has composed a *Folk-Song Symphony* for chorus and orchestra which received the award of the National Committee for Music Appreciation in May, 1940; a String Sextet (1932); a set of Variations on a Theme, for string quartet, the theme being derived from the initials of Mrs. Elizabeth Sprague Coolidge (1933); a third String Quartet, consisting of four preludes and fugues; a Trio, commissioned by Mrs. Coolidge (1934); a second Piano Sonata; a Fourth Symphony, for Tommy Dorsey's jazz orchestra; *Western Landscape,* for the dancer Doris Humphrey and her group; and numerous other works. In 1940 he wrote a symphonic work on commission from the Chicago Symphony Orchestra: *American Creed,* in two movements, "Free to Dream" and "Free to Build." He has also written music for the film, *One Tenth of a Nation,* a

---

[13] April, 1940. The quotation has been slightly rearranged by the author.

study of Negro rural education made by the Rockefeller Foundation.

He has composed few short pieces, and one of them, a *Poem* for violin and piano (1935) is among the most satisfactory of all his compositions. It shows his ability to continue a long, unbroken melodic line, and represents Harris at his best, as the poet and dreamer, unselfconscious and spontaneous.

If Harris can achieve such detachment in all his works, if he can outgrow the necessity for explaining and being explained, and, having developed his idiom to the point where he can forget it, can devote himself exclusively to the emotional content of his music, then he may truly come to fulfill the prophecies of his admirers.

AARON COPLAND

While racially Harris seems to derive definitely from the Scotch-Irish elements of his ancestry, *Aaron Copland* embodies the Russian-Jewish element transplanted to American soil. Thus we find that while Harris reflects the prairies and vastness of the West, Copland brings us the sophistication of the cosmopolitan cities on the seaboard. Both composers are nationalists, but each tells us of a different phase of American living.

Copland's colleague, Virgil Thomson, is credited [14] with the remark, "Aaron Copland's music is American in rhythm, Jewish in melody, eclectic in all the rest," which seems a fair and just summation. For a number of years he turned to jazz as his rhythmic basis; he often employed Jewish folk-melodies in his scores, particularly in such works as his trio, *Vitebsk*, a study on a Jewish theme; and in his tonal idiom he has adopted polytonalism, dissonant counterpoint, and even quarter-tones—whatever has suited his purpose.

At first his use of jazz was direct and conscious. He seemed to be one of the few who could make of it something flexible, who

[14] David Ewen, *Composers of Today* (New York: The H. W. Wilson Company, 1934).

might come to use it subjectively and become its master rather than its servant. These jazz touches made their appearance subtly, unobtrusively in his early works, until in his piano Concerto they burst forth in full, exciting vigor. Many observers felt that a composer had arrived who had the power to sustain his rhythmic interest in the jazz pattern, and to continue his polyrhythms to the point of actual development. Most of the jazzists had been episodic, content with momentary ejaculations of their odd rhythms and the monotony of their regular pulsations. Copland had built a larger structure; as an architect he brought to mind skyscrapers, steel bridges, the quick-paced life of cities.

But it was not to be; not, at any rate, obviously, on the surface. After the Concerto (1927) Copland himself severed the direct relation of his music to jazz. He has used it since, but only indirectly; he has felt its emotional limitations. He is at present chiefly concerned with writing music for the new American audience, opened to composers through the radio and the phonograph. This audience, he feels, will come to have a profound effect on the general musical language of our composers. In his own case, he sees a simplification of language and idiom which is symptomatic. And, as he remarks: "The writing of important music in a simple style is not easy; it presents a problem which is likely to occupy us for some time."

The most recent products of this attitude are the orchestral *Music for Radio*, which was commissioned by the Columbia Broadcasting System in 1937; and the operetta for children, *The Second Hurricane*, written in collaboration with Edwin Denby and first produced at the Grand Street Playhouse, New York, April 21, 1937.

In contrast to the detailed explanation which Roy Harris felt called upon to offer with his *Time Suite* (which was commissioned in the same series) Copland felt unable even to name his piece, and the broadcasters asked members of the audience to suggest names. From some thousand replies, they selected *Saga of the Prairie*, which, representing a listener's reaction, may indicate that music may be all things to all men, no matter what the composer or his commentators may write about it. As for Copland, his only explanation of the piece was that "it lasts about ten minutes, starting allegro vivace, forte, and ending quietly."

The Second Hurricane was an interesting experiment. Copland was glad to write a work for school performances, for he felt that American composers have, to a degree, come up against a stone wall in addressing their music to the usual run of symphony audiences. Therefore if modern composers can only reach the youth of the country, their future will be more soundly assured.

Denby's libretto dealt with wholly modern matters: airplanes, a radio station, flood relief. In his score, Copland kept in mind the average talents and capabilities of children of high school age. His melodies were broad, strongly rhythmed, and easily sung. The orchestral scoring was colorful, but simple; and discretion took the place of experiment in the contemporary nature of the harmonic texture. The initial performances were notably successful, and the work has been published so that it will be available in schools throughout the country.

Copland's background helps to explain him, and his music. He was born in Brooklyn, November 14, 1900, of Russian-Jewish parents. The family name was originally Kaplan, but his father, on landing in England in 1876, was supplied by immigration officials with an impromptu spelling of his name, as it sounded when he pronounced it. So Copland it has been ever since.

After his graduation from the Boys' High School in Brooklyn, Copland started the study of harmony and composition with Rubin Goldmark in 1917. After four years he went to Paris, to the American school at Fontainebleau, and finally studied with Nadia Boulanger. He came home in 1924, and has since been active in New York as a composer and as a lecturer. He was the first composer to receive a Guggenheim Fellowship (1925–27); he has been a lecturer at the New School for Social Research, New York; and he has been an active worker in helping to advance the interests of his fellow composers. With Roger Sessions he inaugurated and maintained for several years the Copland-Sessions Concerts, which presented programs largely devoted to the works of young and as yet unrecognized American composers. He was also the founder of the American Festivals of Contemporary Music which are held at Yaddo, in Saratoga Springs, New York. He is a member of the faculty of the Tanglewood School, in Lenox, Massachusetts, of the Boston Symphony Orchestra.

His first work of distinction had its initial performance at Fontainebleau—a Scherzo-Humoristique for piano, *The Cat and the Mouse*. While he was abroad he wrote a one-act ballet, named *Grohg*, which was never performed in its original form, but which later formed the basis of another work. Howard Hanson conducted in 1925 an excerpt from *Grohg*, entitled *Cortège Macabre*, but aside from that performance the entire work seemed laid aside and forgotten. When the RCA-Victor Company announced a $25,000 prize for a symphonic work in 1929, Copland immediately set to work on a *Symphonic Ode*, but about a month before the competition was to close he realized that he could not finish the *Ode* in so short a time. As a last resort he took *Grohg* from his shelves, extracted a set of three dances from it, called them a *Dance Symphony* and mailed it to the judges. These gentlemen decided that no single work submitted was worthy of the entire prize, but, dividing the award into five parts of $5,000 each, included the *Dance Symphony* as one of the winners. The other awards went one each to Ernest Bloch and Louis Gruenberg, and two to Robert Russell Bennett.

The *Dance Symphony* was first performed by the Philadelphia Orchestra under Stokowski in April of 1931, and had its first New York hearing April 10, 1937 at a Philharmonic-Symphony concert under Rodzinski. At that time the critics took into consideration the fact that it was actually an early work, but recognized that in spite of its derivations, and the influence of Ravel and Stravinsky, it was characterized by expert craftsmanship.

Another comparatively early work which Copland refurbished and rescored for later performance is his First Symphony, which was originally performed by Walter Damrosch and the New York Symphony in 1925 as a symphony for organ and orchestra. On that occasion the solo part was played by Nadia Boulanger. In its revised form the work has been played in Berlin (1932), by the Chicago Symphony (1934), and by the Boston Symphony in Boston and New York (1935).

Neither of these early works, however, is as important as the two pieces which first brought Copland his recognition, and in which jazz appeared unashamed: the suite, *Music for the Theatre*, and the Piano Concerto. The former, for small orchestra, was composed at the Peterborough Colony in the Summer of 1925 and had its first performance in November of the same year, by Koussevitzky and the Boston Symphony. In December it was performed at one of the League of Composers concerts in New York. It is an extremely effective piece, and is still heard not infrequently.

The Concerto was written in 1926 and the composer played it the following year with the Boston Symphony Orchestra. In this work the piano part is eloquent. Copland has taken jazz formulae and developed them so that they are formulae no longer. Some complained that the work had no spiritual value, only animal excitement; but what else has jazz?

Since the Concerto there have been the *Two Blues* for piano, and a very severe set of Variations; two pieces for string quartet, *Rondino* and *Lento Molto* (later arranged also for string orchestra); the trio *Vitebsk*; the *Symphonic Ode* which was temporarily laid aside during the RCA-Victor competition but which was completed and then performed by the Boston Symphony in 1932; an orchestral work called *Statements*, commissioned by the League of Composers, 1935-36; a ballet entitled *Hear Ye! Hear Ye!* performed by the Chicago Civic Opera Company in 1934; *El Salón México*, first heard over the NBC chain under Sir Adrian Boult; and an *Outdoor Overture* (1939).

The problem of judging Copland's recent works is difficult; he is still developing his medium. It is possible that his abandonment of jazz as a direct influence, and his seeking for simplification is causing him to grope. At any rate, he does not seem to have as firm a hand on his materials as he did when he produced his *Music for the Theatre* and the Piano Concerto. As W. J. Henderson wrote in his review of the New York performance by the Boston Symphony of Copland's *Symphonic Ode:* [15]

> Strength and even imagination are found in this composition. But there is the unfailing subterfuge of the modernist when old-fashioned music seems imminent. Something is done to thrust it mercilessly aside, a screech, a crash, or a smash and the mold is broken.

Where, however, a specific problem is posed, Copland can be counted on for a thoroughly satisfactory solution, as is illustrated by his film music for *The City, Of Mice and Men,* and *Our Town.*

LOUIS GRUENBERG

Louis Gruenberg is another composer who tried to conquer jazz, to develop its pattern so that its rigidity would be overcome and it might rise above mere entertainment. So we have his *Jazettes* for violin and piano; the *Four Indiscretions* for string quartet; *The Daniel Jazz,* for high voice and eight solo instruments; *The Creation,* a Negro sermon for a similar combination; and the *Jazz Suite* for orchestra, which was introduced by the Boston Symphony in 1930. But all of these works, as well as the earlier *Hill of Dreams; The Enchanted Isle;* the Symphony No. 1, which won its share of the RCA-Victor prize in 1930; and even the opera he wrote to John Erskine's libretto, *Jack and the Beanstalk,* were eclipsed by the stir his *Emperor Jones* caused when it was produced at the Metropolitan Opera House, January 7, 1933.

For here was undoubtedly the most expertly wrought American opera that had yet been produced, which Olin Downes quite truthfully characterized [16] as "the first American opera by a com-

---

[15] *New York Sun,* March 4, 1932.
[16] *New York Times,* January 8, 1933.

poser whose dramatic instinct and intuition for the theatre seem unfailing, and whose musical technique is characterized by a very complete modern knowledge and a reckless mastery of his means."

Yet in seeking to make an opera of Eugene O'Neill's play about the Pullman porter who made himself "Emperor" of an island in the West Indies, Gruenberg set himself a tremendously difficult, perhaps an impossible, task. Not that his music for the play is ever inappropriate. The interludial outcries of the chorus, the orchestral comments on the drama, with rhythms not unlike the *Sacre du Printemps* of Stravinsky, and the dramatic fervor of the spiritual, *Standin' in the Need of Prayer*, were all in keeping with the intensity of the drama, but it is doubtful whether they added a new dimension to it. As Paul Rosenfeld has remarked: [17]

What the music actually does is externally to accentuate what was already given by O'Neill, to work theatrically on the spectator while leaving the playwright to perform the veritable labor and touch the emotions.

It may be that O'Neill himself had originally provided all the music that was necessary for the effectiveness of his play. In his original version, the beat of a drum started off-stage toward the end of the first scene, accelerating slowly and terrifyingly throughout the action, gradually pounding its way into the listener's consciousness. Gruenberg incorporated this drum beat into his score, but its elaborations were superfluous. It was far more effective in its naked simplicity.

Nevertheless, in spite of the fact that music may be uncalled for in a drama that can stand so eloquently on its own feet, Gruenberg's savage music, with its explosive detonations, its howls and outcries, and what Olin Downes termed its "evil orchestral chuckles," did provide the most finished and theatrically effective American opera that the Metropolitan has yet produced.

Gruenberg was born in Russia, August 3, 1884. He was brought

[17] *Discoveries of a Music Critic* (New York: Harcourt, Brace & Company, 1936).

to America when he was two years old, and received most of his education in this country. At one time he was a pupil of Busoni. He has lived in Brooklyn, and at present makes his home in Los Angeles.

His style has undergone a number of changes, and he has gradually worked out for himself definite convictions which, he says, have taken the place of former vague conjectures. In reply to questioning on the subject, he has very kindly supplied a statement of his artistic creed, which deals with the emphasis and value he feels he must put on each of the several component parts of music. I quote his own words:

Melody is the actual blood of a composition. Without a definite line, easily recognizable, no matter where placed on a score, a composition may sparkle in the orchestra like a veritable jewelry shop in Bagdad, without achieving any other effect than a sauce alone does without meat. Therefore, even a trivial melody is better than none at all.

Emotion, being alone of all ingredients in art or life, the very essence of actual, not imaginary, experience, is the most important of all. With it, generations are bridged over, humanity welded together (regardless of laws, races, religions, and all other paraphernalia invented by human beings). Sorrow and joy, the foundation of emotion, are universally understood and reach us all without being subjected to the criticism of our brains. Therefore, music that does not spring from *Emotional* experience, goes the way of all manufactured matter.

Harmony, formerly consonant in character, is in danger of being as boresome now that it is founded on dissonance. Since it is inconceivable that new combinations can be invented with the physical restraints of the half-note system, neither the third-note nor the fourth-note being practical as long as instruments have not been newly revised—it would seem that a mixture of consonance and dissonance is preferable to either alone. At least this method has the advantage of contrast.

Beauty, only distinguishable in its primitive state, is a matter of development, as much as any other sense. It can only occur when the critical faculty has been eliminated. Beauty is invisible to the brain.

Counterpoint is important only as an enrichment of the melody. If too much of it is used, either it obscures the most important element in music, the melody, or the ear is confused and incapable of accepting the combined effect. So-called horizontal music is purely academic in value.

Therefore, a strong melodic line with an occasional counterpoint is enough, judging from the masterpieces of the past.

Technique, that is, the knowledge adequately to express one's emotions on paper, so that they may be capable of being reproduced (regardless of whether set for orchestra, piano or voice) is absolutely essential in the formative phase of a writer. It is a positive danger after a certain maturity has been reached, for with an adequate technic, one is more than apt to create without waiting for the vitally essential emotional experience. Therefore, technical proficiency is as dangerous as technical awkwardness is powerless.

Rhythm, in our generation placed upon a pedestal of greatest power, is but a minor element. It is empty of value, and of all elements in music, the quickest to bore the listener.

In conclusion [writes Gruenberg] I reject, as emphatically as I am able, ALL systems that tend to cramp the emotional sweep of one's impression. This includes fugues, third-tone, fourth-tone or twelve-tone systems, trick orchestrations, and other easily acquired technical matter.

Another opera had been produced before *The Emperor Jones,* the setting of John Erskine's *Jack and the Beanstalk,* which was presented by the Juilliard School of Music, November 19, 1931. This was a work which its authors sub-titled, "a fairy opera for the childlike." Erskine's libretto put its own interpretation on the age-old fairy story, and made of the cow a philosopher who comments on the situations, and on human nature in general.

For all this satiric fun-making, Gruenberg supplied a score that was singularly appropriate. Even though it was composed several years before the composer had supplied the artistic creed we have just quoted, he released in *Jack and the Beanstalk* a flow of melody which had been carefully concealed in earlier works. Olin Downes wrote of the score: [18]

It is couched in wholly fanciful, impersonal and melodic terms. The composer of *The Enchanted Isle* . . . ; of the *Jazz Suite;* the *Daniel Jazz;* and the *Creation,* which the League of Composers has presented us, has been willing to become, as Mr. Erskine's libretto puts it, hap-

[18] *New York Times,* October 4, 1931.

pily childlike in his score. It is as if Mr. Gruenberg sat himself down in a mood of relaxation and careless pleasure in his task, and, reinforced by the technic that he has won so hardly and so well, tossed off a series of scenes with the informality of a set of sketches for a children's play. But this is done with complete authority and sureness.

It may be that Gruenberg has learned from his own experience that a consummate technique can at times prove a composer's undoing. Certainly some of the criticisms leveled at his First Symphony read almost like his own remarks on the subject. This work was first introduced in Boston by the Boston Symphony, February 10, 1933, and when it was played by the same orchestra in New York March 4, the reviewer of *Musical America* remarked: [19]

Mr. Gruenberg's lengthy symphony is another example of mastery of a medium, with ideas not sufficiently cogent to make the work arresting. The four movements contain all manner of idioms, from the Strauss of the Salomé period to the Stravinsky of Petrouchka time, orchestral effects galore, considerable rhythmic interest, and varied orchestral timbres. But thematically the symphony speaks to us with no conviction.

When the League of Composers commissioned Gruenberg to write an orchestral work, in 1934, he responded with a *Serenade to a Beauteous Lady*, which was first performed by the Chicago Symphony April 4, 1935. It consisted of five movements in dance rhythms, which proved to be concise, expertly orchestrated and full of genuine musical fancy.

The latest opera Gruenberg has written was composed especially for radio performance, on commission from the Columbia Broadcasting System, and first produced over its network September 17, 1937. In this work the composer attempted to fit his subject to his medium, and to make tone take the place of color and action. Thus, trees, clouds, a waterfall, birds, snakes, monkeys, must be heard as they cannot be seen. The libretto was drawn from a novel, *Green Mansions*, by W. H. Hudson, and although the subject offered ample opportunities for the treatment Gruen-

[19] March 10, 1933.

berg proposed to give it, the opera did not altogether accomplish its purpose. Perhaps the performance was inadequate; at any rate it was by no means as effective as radio adaptations of works originally created for the stage have been.

Added to the many prizes Gruenberg has won is the thousand dollars awarded his Quintet for piano and strings in the chamber music contest of the Lake Placid Club. Two movements of this work were heard over the radio (NBC) August 26, 1937, and it was played for the first time in its entirety at the Lake Placid Club the following September 5. Besides these works, which have had major performances, there are two String Quartets, two Piano Concerti, a Second Symphony, and a large number of smaller instrumental pieces. Another opera is in preparation, to a libretto by Philip Moeller.

EMERSON WHITHORNE

When *Emerson Whithorne's* symphonic poem, *The Dream Pedlar*, was played in New York by the Philadelphia Orchestra, February 18, 1936, Lawrence Gilman remarked: [20]

> The music which Mr. Whithorne has woven about his dream of the little pedlar and the mysterious article of merchandise is luminous . . . full of pleasant sounds and fairy evocations; and if it sometimes suggests that what the Little Pedlar was really selling was a second-hand score of "Pelléas et Mélisande," why, there is no harm in that. Mr. Whithorne is a man of taste.

All of which is a fair characterization; not particularly in its reference to Debussy, but in the suggestion that Whithorne is really a combination of romanticist and impressionist. He is rarely the realist, and while he uses polytonality on occasion, and never hesitates at invoking acrid dissonance to gain the effects he wants, he always seems more interested in an impressionism designed to produce atmosphere, rather than in any devices advanced for their own sake alone.

[20] *New York Herald Tribune*, February 19, 1936.

The Americanism of his music is a matter that is open to debate. Certainly he has not gone about the production of a nationalistic speech in any self-conscious fashion, even though he has turned to the native scene for a number of his works: cosmopolitan New York in the suite for piano, *New York Days and Nights*, and a series of transcontinental impressions in *The Moon Trail*. Also, he particularly states that he uses syncopation, not jazz. Apparently he is mainly interested in making his music a personal, individual expression, and is content to let the nationalistic phases of his product take care of themselves.

He was born in Cleveland, Ohio, September 6, 1884, and studied there with James H. Rogers. Later he went to Europe, where he worked with Leschetizky and with Robert Fuchs in Vienna. From 1907 to 1915 he was in London, where he composed, taught piano and theory, and wrote musical criticisms for the *Pall Mall Gazette*. From London he returned to America, became music editor for publishing firms, and then, in 1922, retired so that he might devote all of his time to composition.

It was in London that he composed his first serious music: pieces for piano, songs and song cycles, and a string quartet, *Greek Impressions*. *New York Days and Nights* was composed after he returned to America, and it was this work which first brought him to the public attention. Originally written for piano, the suite was later scored for orchestra and performed by symphony societies, in motion picture theatres, and in special arrangements for jazz bands. In 1923 it was chosen to represent America at the Salzburg Chamber Music Festival.

The work consists of four pieces. First comes "On the Ferry," with moaning horns, shrieking whistles, rhythmic chugging of paddle-wheels, and mendicant musicians. This is followed by "Pell Street," depicting Chinatown. Next, "A Greenwich Village Tragedy" tells of the section where an episode becomes an epic, where trysting turns to tragedy. The finale, "Times Square," paints flashing colors, swirling crowds, ribaldry and mirth, with snatches of popular tunes flashing through the nightly revels.

UNFAMILIAR IDIOMS

In his *Poem* for piano and orchestra, which Walter Gieseking introduced with the Chicago Symphony in 1927, Whithorne shows his preoccupation with persistently syncopated rhythms, which, the composer insists, are not jazz. Again, in *Fata Morgana*, for orchestra, he presents a constant recurrence of patterns interrupted by restless rhythmic changes. This work was first played by the New York Philharmonic-Symphony in 1928.

Impulsive rhythms again play an important part in *Moon Trail*, presented by the Boston Symphony Orchestra, December 15, 1933. Here the expertly scored music, vivid and aptly descriptive, paints four scenes: "Death Valley," "The Devil's Kitchen," "Palos Verdes," and "Surf at Malibu." In addition to the rhythms, the arresting thematic material, tumultuous and impetuous, is often strikingly original.

The Dream Pedlar is of course the work which shows Whithorne as a romanticist. The score shimmers with the delicate tones of the harp and of strings *divisi*, and the pleasant sounds of the celesta. Whithorne himself told of the incident which inspired his work:

> A number of years ago I was strolling . . . along the left bank of the Seine in Paris. . . . I came upon a small crowd gathered about a little pedlar, who, for a few sous, was apparently selling some article of merchandise. . . . Suddenly there was an altercation in the centre of the crowd . . . all were voicing their anger at the little pedlar. Then in tones of strident self-defense he cried: "I am only selling you blind ones a glorious sunset; look at it and be grateful that you have bought beauty at so small a price."

When the piece had its première performance by the Los Angeles Symphony, January 13, 1931, the critic of the Los Angeles *Examiner* called it a work that was "descended from the past and nurtured on the present."

Whithorne's orchestral works include also three symphonies, two of them given their first performances by the Cincinnati Symphony under Eugene Goossens—the first, January 12, 1934, and the second, March 19, 1937. Neither of them is based on any program. Of the first Whithorne remarked that he intended it to "mirror certain human experiences which are expressed in a forthright manner." The second is reflective, and somewhat somber in mood. It was the 1939 choice for the Juilliard publication award. A *Fandango* was played by Sir Thomas Beecham in 1932, and *Sierra Morena* was performed in May, 1939, by the NBC Symphony Orchestra under Monteux.

In the field of chamber music Whithorne has followed his early *Greek Impressions* with a Piano Quintet, which was performed first at a League of Composers concert in New York, and in the following year (1929) at the Coolidge Festival in Washington; and with a String Quartet, composed in 1930. The latter is a vigorous work, with definitely outlined themes and restrainedly modern treatment. There are also a Violin Sonata and numerous works for piano.

For voice, Whithorne has used the poems of Countee Cullen for two notable works. One of them, *Saturday's Child*, is scored for tenor and soprano with chamber orchestra. It deals with Negro racial traditions, the love for the dance, the intense rhythmic instinct. The other Cullen setting, *The Grim Troubadour*, for medium voice and string quartet, has a warmth and richness of melody that is not always found in Whithorne's music to an equal degree.

There are also a ballet and some incidental music for the theatre. The ballet is *Sooner and Later*, originally written for performance at the Neighborhood Playhouse on Grand Street, New York. The scenario for this work, by Irene Lewisohn, deals fantastically with three states of existence: a primitive tribal life, a mechanized city routine, and a resultant crystallized era where there are no more primal passions, where feeding is accomplished by scientific apparatus, and relaxation is provided by a synthetic mood induced by an instrumental, vocal, and color prelude. The incidental music was written for the New York Theatre Guild production of *Marco's Millions*. Here Whithorne used authentic Chinese themes, and attempted to imitate native instruments with wood-winds, a

UNFAMILIAR IDIOMS

violin with wire strings, cello, guitar, mandolin, celesta, muted trumpet, gongs, tam-tams, and drums.

WALTER PISTON

Walter Piston has been associated with the Harvard Division of Music, first as a student, later as assistant professor, and more recently as chairman, succeeding Edward Burlingame Hill. Piston is something of a neo-classicist. Nicolas Slonimsky [21] once described him as "a builder of a future academic style."

There are composers [Slonimsky wrote] who seek new colors, new rhythms, new harmonies. Walter Piston codifies rather than invents. His imagination supplies him with excellent ideas, and out of the material he builds his music without words, descriptive titles and literature. He is an American composer speaking the international idiom of absolute music.

All, however, are not agreed as to Piston's importance. On the occasion of a performance of his Concerto for orchestra the reviewer of *Musical America* wrote: [22]

. . . Of beauty, it has none, only a brittle, etched something, conceived in a purposeful manner, instead of with inspiration. To praise it would be to have praised some of our composers twenty years ago who wrote tone poems *à la* Richard Strauss; we knew better than that. Mr. Piston twenty years later writes a concerto for orchestra *à la* Paul Hindemith. The imitator of today lacks authenticity quite as did his predecessors two decades ago.

In addition to being a neo-classicist, Piston approaches the atonalists at times, even though he does not join them unreservedly. In the Suite for orchestra, to quote Slonimsky again: [23]

the old system of tonality all but breaks down; Piston fights desperately the tonic-dominant complex; and to avoid fifths and octaves suggestive

---

[21] *American Composers on American Music*, edited by Henry Cowell (Stanford University Press, 1933).
[22] February 25, 1936.
[23] *Op. cit.*

of tonality, he builds his themes on the augmented fourth and major seventh, these two banners of the dodecuple system.

Yet, in spite of these formulae of the European modernists, Slonimsky insists that

the Suite is an American work, and Piston is nothing loath to incorporate a "blues" interlude in the score. "Snare-drum with wire brush" marks the four-four time, and the crooning melody is woven against it in the best manner of symphonic Broadway.

Piston was born in Rockland, Maine, January 20, 1894. In his youth his interest in music was only incidental, for he intended to become an artist, and graduated from the Massachusetts School of Art in 1914. When he entered Harvard, from which he graduated in 1924, he became more interested in music, but principally from an intellectual point of view. He tried independently to establish fundamental musical laws. From Harvard he went abroad, to study with Nadia Boulanger. After his return to America, he joined the music faculty at Harvard.

He first came to the attention of the American public when Koussevitzky conducted his *Symphonic Piece* with the Boston Symphony, March 23, 1928. The Suite for orchestra was composed in 1929, and had its first performance several years later, April 1, 1932, by the Philadelphia Orchestra under Stokowski. These orchestral works were followed by the Concerto for orchestra, introduced by the Boston Symphony, March 29, 1934; a Prelude and Fugue for orchestra (1934); and a Concertino for piano and chamber orchestra, commissioned by the Columbia Broadcasting System and first performed June 20, 1937. In addition, there is a First Symphony commissioned by the League of Composers in 1936 and completed the following year; a ballet, *The Incredible Flutist;* and a Concerto for violin and orchestra, first performed by Ruth Posselt and the Boston Symphony Orchestra in March, 1940.

In the field of chamber music Piston has written two String Quartets (1933 and 1935); Three Pieces for flute, clarinet and bassoon (1926); a Sonata for flute and piano (1930); a Suite for oboe and piano (1931); a Trio for violin, cello, and piano (1935); and a Sonata for violin and piano (1939). He has also published a book on musical theory, *Principles of Harmonic Analysis*,[24] and a second book on harmony is in preparation.

QUINCY PORTER

Quincy Porter is a composer who has devoted himself largely to chamber music, and to making the string quartet a form responsive to his idiom. Through his pioneer New England ancestry he derives by heritage from early American sources, but whatever native elements are inherent in his music have come there naturally, and not through any conscious effort of his own.

Hence we find that certain rhythmic patterns subtly reflect American ways of doing things, and occasionally we feel that some of these rhythms derive from the same spirit that gives rise to jazz. But even though these devices are subtle, never obvious, Porter's music is rarely obscure; it establishes a contact with the average listener as well as with the sophisticated musician. It shows, too, that its composer's chief interests are color, rhythm, and melody.

Altogether, Porter has composed six string quartets, the first in 1923 and the sixth in 1936. Several of them have been widely performed, particularly the third, which was published in 1936 by the Society for the Publication of American Music, and has been recorded on phonograph records by the Gordon String Quartet. There are also two Sonatas for violin and piano; a Quartet for clarinet and strings; a Sonata for piano; and a Suite for viola alone.

For orchestra, there are four major works. The earliest, for strings, was the *Ukrainian Suite*, composed in 1925. Next comes a Suite in C minor, 1926; then a *Poem and Dance*, 1932; a First Symphony, composed in 1934 and awarded honorable mention in

[24] Boston: E. C. Schirmer and Company, 1933.

the New York Philharmonic-Symphony Society's prize competition in 1937, which had its first performance by the Society, with the composer conducting, April 2, 1938; a *Dance in Three-Time*, commissioned by the St. Louis Chamber Orchestra, 1937; and an orchestral work commissioned by the Columbia Broadcasting System, *Two Dances for Radio*, 1938.

Of the Symphony, Lawrence Gilman wrote: [25]

> The symphony is in three movements—an Allegro moderato, an Andante, and an Allegro finale. The texture of the music is firmly woven, the idiom mildly contemporary, the flavor quite dry—about four-fifths French vermouth with a dash of Parisianized vodka. Igor, the fallen Czar, lurks in the background.

Porter was born in New Haven, Connecticut, February 7, 1897, the son of a professor at the Yale Divinity School. He graduated from Yale in 1919, and two years later from the Yale School of Music, where he was a pupil of Horatio Parker and David Stanley Smith. Later he went to Paris to study with d'Indy, and then returned to America for further work with Ernest Bloch.

For six years he taught at the Cleveland Institute of Music, and then, in 1928, went to Paris on a Guggenheim Fellowship. He came back to Cleveland three lears later, and after another year at the Institute accepted an invitation to Vassar College, where he was for several years professor of music. In 1938 he was appointed dean of the faculty at the New England Conservatory of Music in Boston—the post formerly held by the late Frederick S. Converse.

RICHARD DONOVAN

Richard F. Donovan is also a former student of the Yale School of Music, and in 1940, when David Stanley Smith retired as dean of that institution, Donovan was appointed acting dean. His studies were also carried on at the Institute of Musical Art in New York, and for a short time in Paris with the great organist,

[25] *New York Herald Tribune*, April 3, 1938.

Widor. He was born in New Haven, Connecticut, on November 29, 1891, and is now conductor of the Bach Cantata Club there, as well as organist and choirmaster of Christ Church. Before joining the Yale faculty he taught at the Institute of Musical Art, at the Taft School, and at Smith College.

Donovan has been one of the group most interested in the development of music at Yaddo since the first Festival of American Music, held there in 1932; in 1940 he was conductor of the chamber orchestra that played there, and his *Serenade* for flute, violin, and cello, figured on the programs. He has written a symphonic poem, *Smoke and Steel* (1932), for orchestra; *Wood-Notes* (1926) and a Symphony (1937), for chamber orchestra; many choral works, both sacred and secular; a Sextet for wind instruments and piano (1932); Four Songs for soprano and string quartet (1933); a Trio for violin, cello, and piano (1937); and a Suite for piano (1933), published by *New Music*.

He tries to avoid the inhibitions which he feels are apt to result from the exclusive use of either the old "tried and true" or the "up-to-date" idioms of musical speech. He believes that a fresh and individual tonal texture can be obtained by drawing whatever is needed from the general body of music, and then adding whatever the composer's personal preferences and tastes may dictate.

RICHARD HAMMOND

Richard Hammond, musical son of John Hays Hammond, and brother of the inventor, John Hays Hammond, Jr., is another Yale man. He was born August 26, 1896, in Kent, England, where his parents were living at the time. After graduating from Yale, he served in the Navy during the World War, and then had further musical training from Emerson Whithorne, Mortimer Wilson, and Nadia Boulanger. With Whithorne he founded the Composers' Music Corporation, a publishing house devoted to the furtherance of contemporary music. He has been a member of the executive board of the League of Composers, and has written on contemporary musical matters for *Modern Music* and other journals. His works have been played chiefly under the auspices of various societies dedicated to the cause of new music. They include: for orchestra, *Five Chinese Fairy Tales* (1921); *The Sea of Heaven* (1929); *West Indian Dances* (1930); *Suite after reading "The Woman of Andros"* (1930); Sinfonietta (1931); two suites of *Dance Music* (1933 and 1937); and a suite, *Excursion* (1937); *Voyage to the East* (1926), for medium voice and orchestra; several works for chamber orchestra and for chorus; a Sonata for oboe and piano (1924); and three ballets.

LAZARE SAMINSKY

Lazare Saminsky has been characterized [26] as representing the lyric spirit of the Hebrew in modern music, just as Ernest Bloch represents the epic spirit. Saminsky occupies a unique position in our musical life: as director of music at the Temple Emanu-El in New York (since 1924) he has been one of the prominent leaders in Jewish musical circles; as a composer he has shown considerable independence, combined with an artistic tolerance that recognizes sincerity wherever it exists; and as a writer and critic he has proved penetrating and forceful.

Although he has lived in America only since 1920, his thirty-ninth year, he feels very definitely, and justly, that America has had a greater influence on his creative work than anything he had known before he came here; that it has eaten so deeply into his creative being that American influences and images have crystallized within him almost without his being aware of the process. Thus, he feels, America has contributed to his musical emotion and thought the directness, the rhythm, the western clarity which every artist of Oriental extraction needs.

He is intensely the modernist; to quote Domenico de Paoli,[27]

[26] By Leigh Henry, in *Lazare Saminsky, Composer and Civic Worker* (New York: Bloch Publishing Company, 1930).
[27] *Ibid.*

he "employs without hesitation any means which seem to him adapted to his expressive goal, and of which he has need *at the given moment.* He is quick to free himself from one medium when his emotion changes and to reach out for another more apt to express his idea." Yet he believes that it is the communion with the spirit and rhythm of our time that makes a modern composer; not the liberal use of any method, or harmonies called modernisms. He admires Schoenberg, for example, but he revolts against modernistic artifice.

Saminsky believes in the eternal youth of the racial element in art; he thinks that when it is allied with a sensitiveness to modern life and thought it provides the highest type of creative stimulus. So he has turned to Hebrew melodies and Russian song, and has tempered their influence by his contact with fellow composers and musicians, and, since 1920, his life in American surroundings.

He was born near Odessa, Russia, October 27, 1882. Though he was musical from childhood, he was first trained in languages, higher mathematics and political economy. He did not start to study music seriously until he was fifteen. When he was twenty, his family met financial ruin, and he became a private tutor in mathematics and Latin. Then he received a scholarship in the Moscow Conservatory, but was expelled in 1906 for joining a revolutionary group and taking part in political demonstrations. He moved to the Conservatory at Petrograd, and continued his studies. He began to compose, and gradually acquired a reputation as his pieces were performed. After the Armistice, he left Russia, went to Paris and then to London, and finally came to America in 1920.

Before he came to this country he had composed two symphonies, a number of separate orchestral works, some chamber music, a four-act opera, and some ballet music. Since he has been in America he has added three symphonies to his list, an opera-ballet based on Poe's *Mask of the Red Death* and entitled *Gagliarda of the Merry Plague* (first produced in New York, February 22, 1925); several large choral works; and for orchestra, a suite, *Ausonia;* a group of "poems," *Stilled Pageant; Three Shadows; Pueblo—A Moon Rhapsody;* and *To a Young World.*

De Paoli has written a vivid description of the *Merry Plague:* [28]

He [Saminsky] has kept the macabre atmosphere undiluted and contrived to create musically an hallucination, precisely like that vision in Poe's tales. The music ushered in by the muffled voices of two muted trumpets reveals in well crystallized, well ordered and variegated forms, in clear architectural equilibrium, a tumultuous frenzied life, of ever restless rhythm and changing color, a life propelled by an impetus which seems impossible of restraint but which, nevertheless, allows for ample lyric pauses. A music, briefly said, well related to the story, lucid and neat in spite of that impetus which drives irresistibly to one end.

When *Three Shadows* was given its première by the New York Philharmonic-Symphony, February 6, 1936, the critics were divided on its merits. Designed as a tonal tribute to Edwin Arlington Robinson, the work was divided into three sections: "Omen," "A Poet and Grass," and "A Dirge." The *Musical Courier* [29] reported that

Mr. Saminsky has created these thoughts in adept musical expression. An eerie quality of mysticism permeates the music, giving at all times a sense of uncertainty and indecision. Curious orchestral effects, novel and completely original, sound throughout the three short pieces. . . . The thirty-two-foot organ pedals are used with a rolling pattern on the piano, and in other places, to enhance the mystic aroma of the composition, strings and wood-winds in the higher registers sound with no supporting bass.

Musical America,[30] on the other hand, found Saminsky's means of expression "arbitrary rather than inevitable, cerebrated rather than poetically inspired," and said that while the second piece established the most tangible mood, it was "difficult on one hearing to sense the inherent relationship between the spirit of any of the poetic excerpts involved and the tonal garment provided."

[28] *Ibid.*
[29] February 15, 1936.
[30] February 25, 1936.

In addition to his composing, Saminsky has contributed dozens of articles on music to current magazines, and is the author of two published books: *Music of Our Day*,[31] and *Music of the Ghetto and the Bible*.[32]

FREDERICK JACOBI

In one of his articles Saminsky has helped to characterize the next composer on our list, *Frederick Jacobi*, by remarking [33] that through its Hebraic strain and pitch, some of Jacobi's music has proved "that an ardent allegiance to American ways in art and thought may very well blend with an exotic peculiarity of utterance." This sentence explains and characterizes Jacobi clearly and tersely; the man blends in his style several elements that are indubitably American—at first consciously, perhaps, but later spontaneously.

His background helps to account for his typically American cosmopolitanism. Born in California, May 4, 1891, he was educated largely in New York, at the Ethical Culture School, and in music, with Paolo Gallico and Rubin Goldmark. Then he studied in Berlin, with Paul Juon at the Hochschule für Musik. When he returned to America, he became assistant conductor at the Metropolitan Opera House, from 1914 to 1917, and then went West to study the life and music of the Pueblo Indians in New Mexico and Arizona.

After the World War—in which he served as a saxophone player in the Army bands—he made his home in New England, at Northampton, Massachusetts; and since 1936 has been a teacher of composition at the Juilliard School in New York.

The study of Indian music had a definite and immediate effect on his own writings; it resulted in his *String Quartet on Indian Themes* (1924), and in the *Indian Dances* for orchestra (1927–

---

[31] New York: Thomas Y. Crowell Company, 1932.
[32] New York: Bloch Publishing Company, 1934.
[33] *Musical Courier*, May 21, 1932.

28). But although he used folk-melodies consciously in these scores, and believes that there is far greater beauty and importance in Indian music than is generally admitted, he sees no necessity for basing an American music on the songs of either the Indians or the Negroes.

Jacobi does not believe strongly in nationalism in music, particularly a nationalism which is consciously sought. The composer, he feels, is too busy trying to create an expressive line, a satisfactory whole, to occupy himself, while composing, with matters other than those which are purely musical. If he does his job carefully and well, and if he has talent, the question of expressing his race, his nationality, his time, and even his emotions, will take care of itself. For, Jacobi remarks, these elements tap the subconscious and operate best when left to themselves.

While he is thoroughly modern, and contemporary, Jacobi believes primarily in "line"—melody, which is at once an idea and its development. He is no atonalist, for he feels that tonality offers a pivot, a focal point, a base on which an architecture may be constructed; and architectural planning is the essence of music.

The Indian pieces were the first to bring Jacobi to the attention of a wide public, even though he had composed a number of earlier works. And while these Indian pieces attached the folk-music label to him for a number of years, his later works have shown that this was but a passing phase of his career. The second String Quartet (published, like the first, by the Society for the Publication of American Music), is a far more mature work than its predecessor, and shows a more flexible technique and a more personal idiom. The opening movement may be a bit enigmatic in its introduction, but it soon comes to melodic patterns which are clear, and which appeal in spite of biting dissonances. The slow movement has warmth and genuine beauty, while the finale is humorous and brilliant. The work was first played by the Pro Arte Quartet at a concert of the League of Composers in New York, February 18, 1935.

Aside from smaller pieces, Jacobi's other important works are the Concerto for cello and orchestra; a Piano Concerto; and the *Sabbath Evening Service* which was commissioned by the Temple Emanu-El in New York.

The Jewish *Service* (1930–31) established Jacobi as one of the important Hebrew composers of the country. With melodies patterned after ancient Hebrew hymns, it offers moments of irresistible poignancy, of a passion that never sacrificed dignity. As David Ewen remarked,[34] Jacobi "recaptured the spirit of Hebrew music and yet created something intrinsically his own."

The Cello Concerto was given its première performance in Paris, at the École Normale, May 30, 1933, and was subsequently published abroad. The first movement provides suspense and animation through a syncopated rhythmic pattern, and the entire work shows originality and an authentic racial quality. The Piano Concerto was composed in 1934–35, and in 1936 was given several performances in New York and Brooklyn, and at the American Composers' Concerts in Rochester, with the composer's wife, Irene Jacobi, playing the solo part. This work shows its American character in "Charleston" jazz effects, and in an Indian flavor which harks back to Jacobi's earlier period. A Violin Concerto was first performed by Albert Spalding with the Chicago Symphony Orchestra in March, 1939, and again with the New York Philharmonic in October of the same year, in the festival of the American Society of Composers, Authors, and Publishers. In April, 1940 Jacobi's *Ave Rota* (Three Pieces in Multiple Style for small orchestra) figured on the programs of the tenth annual Festival of American Music in Rochester.

ROGER SESSIONS

Perhaps *Roger Sessions* might be grouped with the experimentalists; yet, while his music is often stark and austere, he never appears to indulge in cacophony for the sake of aggressiveness. His dissonances seem the inevitable result of what Nicolas Slo-

[34] *Musical Courier*, October 22, 1932.

nimsky has well termed [35] the "icy flame" of a New Englander.

Sessions was born in Brooklyn, New York, December 28, 1896, of a long line of New England ancestors. In 1911 he graduated from the Kent School in Connecticut, and in 1915 from Harvard. For the following two years he studied at the Yale School of Music under Horatio Parker, and then, from 1917 to 1921, taught musical theory at Smith College. Meanwhile he had met Ernest Bloch, who encouraged his early efforts at composition, and took him, as assistant, to the Cleveland Institute of Music. When Bloch resigned in 1925, Sessions left too, and spent eight years abroad: two of them on a Guggenheim Fellowship, three as a Fellow at the American Academy in Rome, and two on a Carnegie Fellowship.

Since his return to America in 1933, he has been active as a teacher of composition: first at the Dalcroze Institute in New York, later at the University of California Summer School, and at Princeton University, where he is now assistant professor of music. He is also president of the International Society for Contemporary Music.

Among his early efforts, the most important is the orchestral suite from his incidental music to Leonid Andreieff's play, *The Black Maskers*. Originally written in 1928, this is still the most widely performed of his works. It shows the influence of Bloch, emotional, expansive, with considerable orchestral imagery. Equally important are the three Choral Preludes for organ, written in Florence in 1926. These are in effect studies in counterpoint, with a slight touch of melancholy which evokes a nostalgic mood.

These works were followed by three more written abroad— the First Symphony (1927), a Piano Sonata (1930), and a Concerto for violin and orchestra (1932). Slonimsky has analyzed Sessions' idiom briefly and clearly: [36]

---

[35] *American Composers on American Music* (Stanford University Press, 1933).
[36] *Op. cit.*

Melody with Sessions is paramount. . . . Sessions derives his art of melody from the idea of a human voice. This may be the reason why he is so eminently successful in writing slow movements—by far the most difficult art in composition. To give the melody a living shape, he resorts to fractional repetitions of the melodic line, incorporated in the greater melodic design. . . . In order to secure a perfect form, the composer employs brief identical figures usually at the end of a period, as a sort of reminiscent quotation, long enough to be recognizable, but sufficiently short not to suggest a recapitulation. It is a device similar to that of a terza rima in poetry, as in Dante's *Inferno*.

Since his return from Europe, Sessions has composed his Second and Third Symphonies, three Dirges for orchestra, and a String Quartet. The last-named was played during the annual Coolidge Festival at the Library of Congress, Washington, April 11, 1937, by the Coolidge Quartet. It proved to be a work in orthodox form, but with considerable modern feeling. It did not, to quote Francis Perkins,[37] turn back toward romanticism, nor "stray in the direction of the diatonic." In his review, Perkins supplied a somewhat detailed description of the Quartet:

The work merits much praise for the composer's mastery of form, the clear and definite quality of his ideas and the skill and resource shown in his treatment of them in a homogeneous, well-integrated style. The slow movement, an adagio with a short allegretto interlude, gives an occasional impression of taking its time during its closing section, but here the composer indulges in his broadest expressions of lyricism. A muted passage and the closing chords, where the harmonic coloring is most warm and pronounced, are among the most imaginative measures of the work. The progress of the first movement has a pleasing directness. The lively finale, almost a "perpetuum mobile," is of a character more general to the period than its two predecessors.

The Quartet has been recorded by the Galimir String Quartet.

PHILIP JAMES

Among the winners of prize competitions, *Philip James* is out-

[37] *New York Herald Tribune*, April 12, 1937.

standing. In 1932 his *Station WGZBX*, for orchestra, won the first prize ($5,000) in a contest sponsored by the National Broadcasting Company; in 1936 his overture, *Bret Harte,* was awarded honorable mention in a contest, conducted by the Philharmonic-Symphony Society of New York, for which no one was given the cash prize; in 1937 his Suite for string orchestra was chosen for publication by the Juilliard School in New York; and in 1938 his orchestral *Song of the Night* won the $500 prize in a contest fostered by the New York Women's Symphony.

James was born in Jersey City, May 17, 1890. During the World War he served for two years in the infantry, and after the armistice he became commanding officer of the A.E.F. General Headquarters Band, commonly known as General Pershing's Band. At various times he has been an organist in churches in and around New York, conductor for the theatrical productions of Winthrop Ames and for Victor Herbert operettas, conductor of the New Jersey Orchestra, which he helped to found, and of the Brooklyn Symphony Orchestra. From 1929 to 1936 he conducted the Bamberger Little Symphony on radio station WOR, Newark, and he has appeared as guest conductor with several of the country's major orchestras, among them the Philadelphia and the National Symphony of Washington. Since 1927 he has been associated with the music department at New York University, as chairman since 1933.

Station WGZBX is altogether characteristic of James's best work. It shows him to be something of a modernist in spirit and idiom, in this instance using his method and materials satirically and with humor, as he depicts the mad hurly-burly of the radio offices and studios, static and interference on the air, with the honey-sweet voice of a crooner entering the chaos at odd moments. His *Kammersymphonie,* too, is modern in feeling, its Scherzo providing a tricky combination of multiple rhythms which would try the patience of any but a skilled conductor.

The overture, *Bret Harte,* was actually the composer's third attempt to catch what he termed "the romance, the boisterousness,

UNFAMILIAR IDIOMS 173

the animation, and the many other abstract qualities of the people of Bret Harte and the West," a people and a section of our country, James adds, "whose glamour has been bedimmed through the eyes of Hollywood as well as by the mawkishness of the radio 'hill-billy' singer." The work was performed by the New York Philharmonic-Symphony Orchestra December 20, 1936. In general, the professional critics seemed to like it, even though some of them felt that it was a bit overscored and somewhat loosely constructed.

One of James's important essays in choral music is his setting of Vachel Lindsay's *General William Booth Enters Heaven,* first performed by the Downtown Glee Club of New York, under Channing Lefebvre, May 3, 1933. When this piece was published the reviewer of *Musical America* [38] found that it possessed "a rhythmic variety and freedom that are arresting, all finely integrated in setting forth the poet's words. The climax on the words, 'Oh shout salvation,' " this critic wrote, "is stupendous." On the occasion of the New York performance, however, the critics were not unanimous in praising the work. Henry Beckett [39] felt that the composer "missed the poet's robust vigor and his passion for the dim beauty at the heart of things." In Beckett's opinion, "the occasional vulgarity of Salvation Army methods is overemphasized and the genuine religious frenzy and desperate hope of forgotten men are insufficiently presented."

Yet despite such reservations, James is one of the more important of our contemporary composers, and the recognition he has gained seems entirely deserved. He has composed in various forms, including chamber music with a String Quartet and a Piano Quintet. His earlier works include the frequently performed *Overture on French Noëls;* a *Sea-Symphony;* and an orchestral tone-poem, *Judith;* a Suite for chamber orchestra; numerous choral pieces; several works for organ; and many secular and sacred songs. He is a member of the American Society of Com-

---

[38] April 25, 1933.
[39] *New York Evening Post,* May 4, 1933.

posers, Authors, and Publishers, and in 1933 he was elected to membership in the National Institute of Arts and Letters.

BERNARD WAGENAAR

Although *Bernard Wagenaar* is not a native American, having been born in Arnhem, Holland, July 18, 1894, he has now been with us for almost twenty years, and since 1923 has been a faculty member of leading educational institutions—from 1923 to 1927 at New York's Institute of Musical Art, and since 1927 at the Juilliard Graduate School. His most recent orchestral work to enjoy a major performance is his Triple Concerto for flute, harp, and cello, with orchestra, written for his friends, Georges Barrère, flutist, Carlos Salzedo, harpist, and Horace Britt, cellist, and performed by them with the Philadelphia Orchestra, March 18 and 19, 1938, in Philadelphia, and March 22 in New York.

Following the New York performance, a conflict of opinion arose between the two leading critics. Lawrence Gilman was not particularly impressed. He wrote, in part: [40]

> Concerning the values of Mr. Wagenaar's composition, certain doubts arose. Sometimes it appeared as though Mr. Wagenaar were amusing himself with experiments, or even spoofing Euterpe—though one should probably reject that notion, for Mr. Wagenaar has long been known as a composer of unassailable artistic sobriety, and it is hard to imagine him teasing Euterpe or scattering orange peels in her path or otherwise assailing her immortal dignity. One is inclined to feel that . . . his taste [is] a bit—well, exuberant. Undoubtedly he is an excellent musician, an able craftsman . . . but the work as a whole is too long, and it lacks aesthetic tact.

Olin Downes, however, was altogether delighted with the very elements which annoyed Mr. Gilman. In his weekly article for the following Sunday's music section,[41] Mr. Downes took occasion for what seemed a direct reply to his older colleague. Pay-

---

[40] *New York Herald Tribune*, March 23, 1938.
[41] *New York Times*, March 27, 1938.

ing no compliment to Wagenaar's earlier, more serious works, he wrote:

> The musical success of the week . . . was that of Bernard Wagenaar's triple concerto. . . . This writer is constrained to add that the success was as pleasant as it was astonishing to him. Whether Mr. Wagenaar, had he followed previously chosen paths of extreme atonality, would have caused this commentator to commend music of a kind that he had been condemning is not now the point. For Mr. Wagenaar, where the concerto was concerned, was no longer an ego in a tower of ivory. He was writing for the public!
> He appeared to be writing a concerto that aimed, in a modern and artistic way, to please. . . . [He] may or may not continue to consider the public pulse, or appear to do so, in further compositions. . . . We may encounter a symphony number three [42] from his pen, more portentously dissonant than anything he has thus far produced. But take notice: on one occasion he wrote to entertain, and he produced an art-work of value. He did not sacrifice his standards in so doing. He composed with skill and enthusiasm, with a concrete purpose that reached his audience.
> Some of Mr. Wagenaar's contemporaries could afford to take a leaf from this book. If they will look upon composition as a direct means of communication with their fellow-man they will find themselves in good company. Among their companions will be Monteverdi, Palestrina, Gluck, Haydn, Mozart, Beethoven, Wagner, and others too numerous to mention.

Wagenaar first came to this country in 1921, when his fellow-Hollander, Willem Mengelberg, was conducting the New York Philharmonic. He joined the orchestra as violinist and also as harpsichordist, pianist, organist, and, on occasion, as player of the celesta. Two years later he started his teaching career in New York.

Aside from the Triple Concerto, he has not written much light-hearted music. His three symphonies are altogether serious in intent, and marked by various experiments in atonality and other latter-day devices. He will not, however, discuss his own idiom

---

[42] Mr. Downes apparently overlooked the fact that a third symphony had already been performed at the Juilliard School in January, 1937.

or his purposes. "Being a composer," he protests, "I feel entirely incompetent to answer any such questions regarding my own music."

Two of his symphonies were introduced by the Philharmonic Society. The first was played by Mengelberg in 1928, while the second enjoyed the exceedingly rare distinction of being one of the few American works performed by the orchestra while Toscanini was its conductor. The work, given three performances in November, 1932, was notable for its economic and skillful construction, showing its composer to be an excellent craftsman. The Third Symphony was introduced by the orchestra of the Juilliard School, with the composer conducting, January 23, 1937. In the following summer it was played at Chautauqua, under Albert Stoessel.

For small orchestra Wagenaar has composed a *Sinfonietta*, introduced by the Philharmonic under Mengelberg in 1930. This was the only American work chosen in that year by the International Society for Contemporary Music for performance at the Liège Festival. A *Divertimento* for orchestra, which received an Eastman School Publications Award, was first performed in 1929, by the Detroit Symphony under Gabrilowitsch, and has subsequently received a number of performances by major orchestras.

In the field of chamber music, Wagenaar has written three String Quartets, a Sonata for violin and piano, and a Sonatina for cello and piano. The Sonata and the Third String Quartet are published by the Society for the Publication of American Music. The Sonatina is music of intellectual rather than emotional appeal, but healthy and vital withal, and marked by an individuality that does not depend too much on the stark harshness of its angular dissonance.

WERNER JOSTEN

The year 1921 saw another talented foreigner emigrate to our shores—*Werner Josten*, a German born at Elberfeld, June 12,

1888. He had been a pupil of Rudolf Siegel in Munich and had studied further in Paris. Returning to Germany when the War broke out, he had eventually become assistant conductor at the Munich Opera House. Since coming to America he has become a naturalized citizen, and from 1923 has been a professor of music at Smith College. Here his revivals of old operas have attracted particular attention. Aided by the college music department he has given the first stage performances in America of several works by Monteverdi and Handel, and in the Spring of 1938 he presented the first performance since 1723 of Johann Joseph Fux's opera, *Costanza e Fortezza*.

Josten's own music, however, does not derive from the eighteenth century. He is distinctly of the present day in his viewpoint and his expression. Yet, though he seems at times affected subconsciously by the style of the later Stravinsky, with what Olin Downes terms "harmonic astringencies and tonal combinations of the dry, stark Stravinskian manner," he achieves a subtle blending of the old and the new by tempering his acerbities with exquisite lyricism, with long-breathed, sustained melodic lines, and striking and imaginative harmonic and contrapuntal structure.

Among his most important works for orchestra is the *Concerto Sacro*, completed in 1927, which, like his more recent music for the ballet, *Joseph and His Brethren* (produced by the Juilliard School of Music in March, 1936), unquestionably shows the influence of the severe religious atmosphere of his childhood home. The two parts of the *Concerto Sacro* were introduced separately by major orchestras (No. 2 by Koussevitzky and the Boston Symphony in 1929, and No. 1 by Stokowski and the Philadelphians in 1933), but they form a single work, inspired by a triptych painted for the Isenheim altar at Colmar in Alsace, by the sixteenth-century Rhenish master, Mathias Grünewald.

The first Concerto depicts "The Annunciation" and "The Miracle," while the second comprises a "Lament" (that of Mary after the Crucifixion), and a final division called "Sepulchre and Resurrection," which the composer describes as an "instrumental motet." Behind his music Josten has placed a background of plainsong, with suggestions of the spirit and methods of the pre-Bach German composers. The result is highly successful in providing music of lofty and noble purpose. One may readily agree with Lawrence Gilman's observation [43] that "the religious sentiment expressed throughout, with its blend of mysticism and naïveté, is conveyed with rare subtlety and tact. The flame of devotional tenderness and exaltation burns with singular purity."

Josten has also written two Symphonies (one for strings alone); two ballets in addition to that named above—*Batouala* and *Endymion*; a *Serenade* for orchestra; *Jungle*, a symphonic movement; Sonatas for violin, for piano, and for cello; a String Quartet; and several large-scale choral works.

JOHN DUKE

A colleague of Josten's at Smith College is *John Woods Duke*. Duke was born in Cumberland, Maryland, July 30, 1899, and graduated from the Peabody Conservatory, in Baltimore. Then he studied in New York, with Brockway, and in 1923 was appointed to the Smith faculty. In 1929 and 1930 he was in Europe, studying piano with Artur Schnabel and composition with Nadia Boulanger. He was chairman of the music committee at Yaddo for the summer of 1936, and has been editor for the Ampico Recording Laboratories.

Most modernists, he feels, would call his works rather conservative in idiom, for he does not think it necessary to evolve a new tonal language, or even to depart very radically from the harmonic system employed in the works of Bach, in order to be truly contemporary in spirit and message.

He has written an Overture in D Minor, for string orchestra (1928); a Suite for unaccompanied cello (1934); a Fantasie in A Minor for violin and piano (1937); a Trio for violin, viola, and cello (1937); and numerous songs.

[43] *New York Herald Tribune,* October 22, 1933.

HARL McDONALD

Harl McDonald is a product of the Far West. Born July 27, 1899, on his father's cattle ranch in the high Rockies above Boulder, Colorado, he grew up in Southern California, where irregular schooling allowed ample time for musical training in an unusually musical household. He started to compose at the age of seven, and some of his earliest pieces were published. As a young man he toured as accompanist with several well-known concert artists, and in 1921 played his first Piano Concerto with the San Francisco Symphony. Then followed a period of study in Germany, and the performance of his symphonic fantasy, *Mojave*, by the Berlin Philharmonic, in 1922, and by Coates in London during the same season. In 1922 he taught at the Académie Tournefort in Paris, and then returned to the United States, at first teaching privately and appearing in recital. During the 1925–26 season he taught at the Philadelphia Academy of Music, and in 1927 was appointed to the faculty of the University of Pennsylvania. This connection he maintained until the spring of 1939, when he became manager of the Philadelphia Orchestra.

As a composer McDonald defies classification, for his vocabulary ranges from the strident, and to some hearers painful, yelling used in the neo-primitive *Songs of Conquest*, to the restrained, highly conventional language of his Second String Quartet, or the calm, serene beauty of the *Hebraic Poems* for orchestra. He believes that if composers find it necessary to speak in a musical language which employs tom-toms, shrieks, and ear-shattering combinations of tone, and if they speak with conviction, they are able to contribute wonderful things to our art. If, however, the twentieth-century composer is merely contributing to the everchanging fashion in tonal tricks when he makes his excursions into new fields, McDonald holds that he has descended to the level of the designers of women's clothes. He wonders if, after all, the purist is not today's radical, persisting in his ideal of ascetic purity in an age of experiments.

McDonald's orchestral works include four symphonies. The first, *Santa Fe Trail*, was introduced by the Philadelphia Orchestra in November of 1934, first in Philadelphia and a few days later in New York. This is frankly program music, seeking to recreate something of the spirit and experience of the pioneers, yet it succeeds in setting forth moods and atmospheres rather than falling into the trap of too literal descriptiveness. The first movement deals with the explorers; the second reflects the spirit of the life in the Spanish settlements; while the third and last represents the many influences—Hispanic, Nordic, and American-Indian—which combined to form the spirit and substance of the Southwest.

The Second Symphony, a *Rhumba Symphony*, was introduced by the Philadelphia Orchestra in October of the following year. Here the composer adopts advanced idioms to depict the idea he suggests in the sub-title, *Reflections on an Era of Turmoil*. He succeeds admirably in presenting graphically the modern restlessness, the hectic, brooding emotionalism, and the avid lust for wild and fiery pleasure that outwardly characterize much in the present era. The scherzo of the symphony, *Rhumba*, has had numerous separate performances, and has had wide circulation on phonograph records.

The Philadelphia Orchestra, assisted by the University of Pennsylvania Chorus and a soprano soloist, Vera Resnikoff, presented McDonald's Third Symphony in January of 1936. The sub-title of this work is *Lamentations of Fu Hsuan*, and the music is in effect a setting of a group of Chinese poems. The Fourth Symphony, introduced by the Philadelphians in April, 1938, is given no sub-title, nor is it based on any avowed program. At the time of its first performance the composer remarked that while this work was no exception to the rule that all music is in a sense autobiographical, he would refrain from boring his listeners with details of experiences that were important to him as a composer but would be most improper as part of the program notes. A novel feature of the work was the introduction of a cake-walk as the scherzo. The composer explained that the patterns of this dance came to his mind as a part of many scenes associated in his memory with different sections of the country, many of them varying greatly in atmosphere, but all intensely American.

In addition to these four symphonies, McDonald has a long list of major works to his credit: an orchestral suite, *Festival of the Workers;* a *Concerto* for two pianos and orchestra; a *Tragic Cycle,* for orchestra; the choral *Songs of Conquest,* first performed by the Mendelssohn Club in Philadelphia, 1937, and later at the Worcester (Massachusetts) Festival in the fall of 1939; two String Quartets; two Trios; and other works, which include two evening pictures, *San Juan Capistrano,* and a rather curious *Lament for the Stolen,* a tonal elegy on the Lindbergh kidnapping, presented by the Philadelphia Orchestra and a chorus in December, 1938.

As a composer, McDonald lacks neither skill nor humor, and as a teacher he is not without resource. On one occasion he teamed the two functions in a practical joke which was thoroughly effective. In December, 1939, the Philadelphia Orchestra under Ormandy played a *Miniature Suite,* by one John C. Smith, who, it appeared, was the Johann Christoph Schmidt who had served Handel as amanuensis. After the critics and the public had unsuspectingly accepted and enjoyed the work, it was revealed as the concoction of Harl McDonald, devised to convince his aggressively twentieth-century students that it was possible for a contemporary composer to write eighteenth-century music.

ARTHUR SHEPHERD

Arthur Shepherd has been busy in recent years adding new works to his already imposing list. Among them are two Piano Sonatas; two String Quartets, the first published by the Society for the Publication of American Music and the second commissioned by the League of Composers (1936); a *Triptych* for voice and string quartet; two Cantatas—*City in the Sea* and *The Song of the Pilgrims;* and, for orchestra, a series of *Dance Episodes on an Exotic Theme.*

The *Dance Episodes* had their première in Cleveland, by the Cleveland Symphony, in October, 1931. They proved distinctly original in thematic material and in development, and were clothed in truly brilliant orchestral dress. *The Song of the Pilgrims* takes for its text a poem by Rupert Brooke, and its musical content and the great craftsmanship with which it was handled moved the reviewer of *Musical America* [44] to characterize it with enthusiasm as "one of the noblest works of its kind yet brought forth in this country."

While Shepherd himself is concerned only with the communicative power of his music and avoids self-conscious attempts at modernism, there are those who detect racial traits in his music, chiefly Anglo-Celtic, resulting perhaps from his English parentage. He was born in Idaho, February 19, 1880, was educated musically at the New England Conservatory, and then went to Salt Lake City, where he conducted a theatre orchestra as well as a symphonic group. In 1908 he was appointed to the faculty of the New England Conservatory, but a few years later settled in Cleveland, where he has lived ever since and has held several positions: assistant conductor of the Cleveland Symphony Orchestra, music critic for the *Cleveland Press,* and since 1927 professor of music and chairman of the music division of Western Reserve University.

When he was twenty-two his *Ouverture Joyeuse* was awarded the Paderewski prize, and several years later, in 1909, he won two prizes from the National Federation of Music Clubs. The work for which he is still best known, however, is the orchestral suite *Horizons,* frequently performed, and published by the Juilliard Foundation. This work is based partly on original material and partly on frontier ballads: *The Dying Cowboy, The Old Chisholm Trail,* and the *Dogie* song. It is full of the raciness, the adventure, the spacious life of the plains, and one of its movements,

---

[44] February 10, 1938.

"The Lone Prairie," has been widely performed as a separate piece.

On March 7, 1940, the first performance of Shepherd's Symphony No. 2, in D minor, was given by the Cleveland Orchestra under the composer's own direction.

SOME OTHER MIDDLE-WESTERNERS

John J. Becker, in St. Paul, Minnesota, has been a solitary and vigorous crusader for musical modernism in the Middle West. Many of the best talents of this section, as Henry Cowell points out,[45] have moved East. But not Becker, who has aggressively championed the cause of musical radicalism in Minnesota, Wisconsin, and Indiana. Becker was born in Henderson, Kentucky, January 22, 1886, and studied with Middelschulte in Chicago and von Fielitz in Berlin, among others. He has conducted numerous choruses and orchestras in St. Paul, St. Cloud, and South Bend, and has taught at Notre Dame University and at the College of St. Scholastica. In recent years he has been director of the Federal Music Project for Minnesota.

He has composed three Symphonies; several Concertos for solo instruments with orchestra; several large choral works; several *Soundpieces* for various string combinations; and numerous stage works, including *Dance Figure; Obongo, Dance Primitive; A Marriage with Space,* for solo and mass recitation with solo and group dancers and large orchestra; and the *Life of Man* (Andreieff), described as a "new musico-dramatic form." Of the "Credo" from a mass of Becker's, Charles Ives is on record as saying that "it is one of the finest, high-moving, stirring pieces of music of its kind I have ever heard. It is the expression of a big man with something great to say and not afraid to say it."

Max Wald is a Chicagoan, born in Litchfield, Illinois, July 14, 1889. He began his studies of music without a teacher, and later

[45] *Op. cit.*

studied theory with Walter Keller and Arthur Olaf Andersen in Chicago. For a time he did theatrical conducting. During the '20's and early '30's, he spent much time abroad, and it was there that his *The Dancer Dead*, for orchestra, was written. This work won the second prize in the NBC 1932 prize contest. He has taught theory at the American Conservatory in Chicago, and is chairman of the theory department at the Chicago Musical College. He has written a *Comedy Overture; Sentimental Promenades;* and *Retrospectives,* for orchestra; some chamber music; and an opera *Mirandolina,* based on Goldoni's play, *La Locandiera.*

Another Middle-Westerner is *Wesley La Violette,* born in St. James, Minnesota, January 4, 1894, who heads the theory department of the De Paul University School of Music, in Chicago, and is director of the De Paul University Press, established for the publication of American music, as well as president of the Chicago section of the International Society for Contemporary Music. He was active in the organization of the first Yaddo Festival.

He has written numerous orchestral works, including a *Requiem* (1925); *Penetrella,* for eighteen-part string orchestra (1928); *Osiris* (1929); *Dedications,* a violin concerto (1929); Nocturne (1932); *Collegiana* (1936); a Symphony (1936); a Chorale (1936); a Piano Concerto, and a Concerto for string quartet and orchestra (both 1937). There is also an opera, *Shylock,* which won the Bispham medal in 1930. His chamber music includes several String Quartets; a Piano Quintet; an Octet; two Violin Sonatas; and other works.

NICOLAI BEREZOWSKY

Nicolai T. Berezowsky was one of the winners of the memorable NBC Competition of 1932, when his *Sinfonietta* was awarded fifth prize. To some critics, Berezowsky's dissonance is self-conscious and mannered, particularly when it is punctuated by moments which are almost naïve in their sentimentality. Nevertheless, his works have been frequently performed and he has been the recipient of several honors, among them a League of Composers commission for a string quartet.

Berezowsky was born in St. Petersburg, Russia, May 17, 1900. He was educated at the Imperial Capella, and before coming to America in 1922 he was first violinist at the Moscow Bolshoi Theatre and music director of the School of Modern Art. For five years after 1922 he was a first violinist of the New York Philharmonic. He appears frequently as a guest conductor of orchestras, and has been a member of the Coolidge String Quartet.

His works include three Symphonies, composed respectively in 1925, 1929 and 1936; two String Quartets; *Toccata, Variations and Finale* for a string quartet with orchestra; a Violin Concerto; a *Concerto Lirico* for cello; two Wood-wind Quintets; a String Sextet; a Piano Sonata; a Fantasia for two pianos; the *Sinfonietta*; and a *Hebrew Suite* for orchestra. The *Concerto Lirico* was dedicated to Gregor Piatigorsky, the cellist, who played it with the Boston Symphony in February, 1935. Although one reviewer found the work "dry, derivative, and consciously contemporary in conception," [46] others were interested in the novel experiment of omitting the cello section of the orchestra from the score, and assigning parts which would normally be taken by the cello to various wind instruments and to the violas. Thus, the solo instrument had no competition in tone quality.

Of the String Sextet, as performed at the Coolidge Festival in the Library of Congress, in April, 1940, Francis D. Perkins [47] wrote:

> ... after a short and early threat of experiment with dissonant harmonies [it] ... exhibited an auspicious degree of lyric sensitiveness, especially in the adagio, where an occasional slight sense of length was offset by a poetically meditative quality which characterized the movement as a whole. The swift movements were high-spirited, and the use of rhythmic variety and contrast was an effective feature. These could be hailed, for the most part, as deftly wrought music, marking an advance in the composer's creative career.

[46] *Musical America*, March 10, 1935.
[47] *New York Herald Tribune*, April 15, 1940.

OTTO LUENING

Otto Luening holds extremely practical ideas about the problems of the American composer. He has been (and says he still is) called in turn "conservative, ultra-modern, a stylist, vulgar, imposing, a melodist, folksy, insane," mostly by critics or audiences familiar with one or two of his works. He believes that a composer should write for all types of mediums, should do some experimenting, compose for any occasion he is called upon to supply music for, expand all forms after having mastered them, create new forms, and generally interest himself and make himself useful wherever he can. Then, Luening points out, his immortality will be decided by audiences, critics, colleagues, and time—which may mean the next two hundred years, so he need not worry about it.

The rest of his credo concerns itself with the present:

In America the composer needs to worry *a great deal* about having his works published, performed (not once but repeatedly), recorded, broadcast and paid for via publishers' fees and performing fees. These matters are the direct concern of every composer in America, every performer, all sponsors, music lovers, audiences and musicologists.

Luening was born in Milwaukee, June 15, 1900. From 1914 to 1917 he studied in Munich, and from 1917 to 1920 in Zürich, with Jarnach and Busoni, among others. During these years he was active as a flutist and as a conductor of opera and light opera. From 1925 to 1928 he was coach and executive director of the opera department at the Eastman School in Rochester, also assistant conductor, and later conductor, of the Rochester American Opera Company. From 1930 to 1932 he worked on a Guggenheim Fellowship, and for the following two years was associate professor at the University of Arizona. Since 1934 he has been associated with Bennington College, Vermont, where he heads the music department.

He has a long list of works. For orchestra there are two Symphonic Poems; a Divertimento; two Symphonic Interludes; a Serenade; a Dirge; a Symphony; a Suite for strings; and a work entitled *Americana*. For chamber orchestra the list includes a Symphonietta; a *Prelude to a Hymn-tune;* and a Concertino; while the chamber music works add up to more than twenty—among them three Quartets; two Sonatas for violin and piano; a Sextet; a Piano Sonata; and many others. Luening has also written an opera, *Evangeline,* in four acts.

ERNST BACON

A close friend of Luening's, and even a collaborator with him in one short piece, is *Ernst Bacon,* who heads the music school of Converse College, in Spartanburg, South Carolina. Born in Chicago, May 26, 1898, Bacon studied at Northwestern University and the University of Chicago, as well as with Raab and Gunn, before going abroad, where, particularly in Germany and Austria, he continued his studies, in piano with Bree and in composition with Karl Weigl, and concertized as a pianist. He has also been a pupil in composition of Ernest Bloch and in conducting of Eugene Goossens. Bacon has been very active as teacher, conductor and musical administrator in addition to his creative work. Before assuming his post at Converse, he was the founder and first conductor of the Carmel (California) Bach Festival, Supervisor of the Federal Music Project and conductor of the Federal Symphony Orchestra in San Francisco, and acting professor of music at Hamilton College.

Bacon has a long list of works to his credit, ranging from symphonies to a musical comedy. His First Symphony and one movement of his Second have been played by the San Francisco Symphony Orchestra; his *Country Roads,* a folk suite, by numerous orchestras; his Prelude and Fugue by the Rochester Philharmonic. *Take Your Choice* was a musical comedy produced by the Federal Theater and Federal Music Project in San Francisco, but Bacon is also the composer of music for the theatre in more serious vein: incidental music for *The Tempest* (Shakespeare) and for Paul Horgan's *Death, Mr. President,* scheduled for Broadway production. Several of his works are for soloists with orchestra: *The Postponeless Creature,* for baritone or contralto, on poems by Whitman and Emily Dickinson; *Whispers of Heavenly Death* (Whitman), for baritone or contralto; *Midnight Special,* for mezzo-soprano; *Black and White Songs,* for baritone; *My River,* for mezzo-soprano, again on poems by Emily Dickinson. He has also written numerous songs; a *Suite to the Children,* for two pianos; and several pieces for the latter medium in lighter vein: *Wastin' Time, Kankakee River,* and, with Luening, *Coal Scuttle Blues.* It will be seen that Bacon is no one-idea or one-style man; his music combines sensitivity, warmth of feeling, and humor, in an idiom which is the spontaneous and sincere expression of his ideas rather than a style consciously developed for its own sake. His work has been recognized by the awards of a Pulitzer Scholarship and a Guggenheim Fellowship.

EXOTICS BY BIRTH OR CHOICE

Even though *Arcady Dubensky* is in step with contemporary musical speech, he has little use for any mathematical approach to music. He abhors music which is full of noisy and shrieky effects, written, as he puts it, in the belief that in the future all people will become deaf. He believes that if percussion instruments were taken away from the composers of such works, they would become utterly helpless in the expression of their confused ideas.

For Dubensky, Bach still remains the greatest of modernists, in his daring modulations, in his harmonies, and in the complexity of his ideas. It is, perhaps, this worship of Bach that lies behind the very effective *Fugue for Eighteen Violins,* first performed by the Philadelphia Orchestra under Stokowski in April, 1932, and since that time frequently played by other orchestras. The superb craftsmanship of this Fugue lies in the expert use of extremely limited resources. The eighteen violins are divided into nine groups of two, and the composer has used striking inventiveness in obtaining variety without being able to contrast the tonal coloring of different instruments.

Dubensky was born in Viatka, Russia, October 3, 1890. At the age of eight he started singing in the cathedral choir there, and at thirteen he played the violin in a theatre orchestra. In 1904 he went to Moscow where he graduated from the Conservatory in 1909, after studying violin with Hřimaly and counterpoint with Ilyinsky. In 1911 he became a member of the Moscow Imperial Opera Orchestra, where he remained until 1919. Since 1921 he has lived in New York, where, in 1922, he became a member of the New York Symphony and later of the Philharmonic-Symphony Orchestra, upon the merger of the two organizations.

His works include an opera-miniature, *Romance with Double Bass*, produced in 1916 at the Imperial Opera in Moscow; a symphonic poem, *Russian Bells*; Two Suites for orchestra; the *Fugue for Eighteen Violins*; a "melodeclamation," *The Raven*, based on Poe's poem, and performed by Benjamin de Loache and the Philadelphia Orchestra in 1932; a *Tom Sawyer Overture*, composed for the Mark Twain anniversary in 1935, and first performed by Stokowski and the Philadelphia Orchestra; and a *Suite Anno 1600*, first played by the Philadelphia String Sinfonietta in 1937, and later by the New York Philharmonic-Symphony in April, 1939. This latest work is an attempt to capture the atmosphere and mood of the beginning of the seventeenth century. The general lines of the old forms are followed, but the impression is by no means archaic. A light, melodic touch renders the music agreeable, and in several passages, charming.

Colin McPhee was one of our prominent young modernists in the late 1920's and early '30's, and then more or less disappeared from view. He went to Bali in 1931 for a six months' trip and stayed there for six years, and this trip seems to have been a very fruitful one for him, musically. McPhee was born in Montreal, Canada, March 15, 1901. He was a pupil in composition of Strube,

Le Flem, and Varèse, and in piano of Friedheim and Philipp. His earlier works were often heard on the programs of the International Composers' Guild, the Copland-Sessions Concerts, the Pan American Association of Composers, and the League of Composers. Wallingford Riegger, in a critical article on McPhee,[48] quoted the composer as saying that he had been trying to convey through music "an emotion resulting from contact with daily life —its noise, rhythm, energy, and mechanical daring." He was not writing program music, he explained, but striving for a tonal structure which, while "orderly and complete," should be "as complex as the structure of a large bridge." McPhee had a natural facility which (true son of the twentieth century!) he distrusted. But during the years before his sojourn in Bali he produced a Concerto for piano and orchestra; a *Sarabande* for orchestra; a one-movement Symphony; a Concerto for piano and eight wind instruments, published by *New Music;* a Sonatina for two flutes, clarinet, trumpet and piano; and scores for two very interesting "modernistic" films: *Mechanical Principles* and H_2O.

In Bali, McPhee apparently found what many a modern composer needs: a highly developed tradition and style, disciplined and conventional, yet with conventions which are fresh to the Western ear. This experience seems to have given him a new lease on creative life. In 1936 he produced a symphonic work, *Bali.* He has transcribed a set of three pieces of *Balinese Ceremonial Music* for two pianos. But his more recent music is not confined to an Oriental or pseudo-Oriental style. In response to a League of Composers commission he wrote a choral work, *From the Revelation of St. John the Divine,* for men's chorus, two pianos, three trumpets, and timpani, first sung by the Princeton Glee Club; and in the summer of 1940 he furnished incidental music for Paul Robeson's performance of Eugene O'Neill's *The Emperor Jones.*

Anis Fuleihan is another composer who dislikes attempts at classification, particularly so far as his own music is concerned. He

---

[48] *American Composers on American Music,* edited by Henry Cowell (Stanford University Press, 1923).

disclaims belonging to either the left, the right, or the middle wing. He has little use for ugliness, and he feels that obviously clever or smart music is naïve. Actually, his own product is far removed from Germanic backgrounds, for he avoids long melodic lines, and anything resembling heroics.

In some respects his work shows his Near-East heritage; he is of Arabian descent, born, April 2, 1900, on the Island of Cyprus. Educated principally in British schools in the Near East, he came to New York in 1915, where he studied piano with Alberto Jonàs. For a number of years he was active as a concert pianist, and composer of ballet music—for the Neighborhood Playhouse, Adolf Bolm, and the Denishawn Dancers. In 1925 he went to Egypt, and for three years toured the Near East as a pianist. Returning to America in 1928, he again appeared here as a concert pianist, and as a radio conductor. In 1932 he joined the staff of G. Schirmer, Inc., music publishers, and in the spring of 1939 he was awarded a Guggenheim Fellowship in composition.

The major performances of Fuleihan's works date from 1935, when the Cincinnati Symphony introduced his *Mediterranean Suite*. A year later New York had an opportunity of hearing the *Preface to a Child's Storybook*, when it was played by the National Orchestral Association. On New Year's Eve, 1936, the Philharmonic-Symphony Society, under Barbirolli, gave the première performance of Fuleihan's First Symphony, and Olin Downes found it to be "music of a subjective hue, often exciting and often gorgeous." [49] "He dares," the critic continued, "to put down much that is untraditional and that seems natural to him." The Symphony had an unusually cordial reception from both audience and critics.

It is no doubt Fuleihan's experience and gifts as a pianist that have rendered most effective his two Piano Concerti—the first for piano with strings, and the second with full orchestra. The earlier work was first played by the composer at the Saratoga Festival in September, 1937, and in the following January with the Na-

[49] *New York Times*, January 1, 1937.

tional Orchestral Association in New York. It showed craftsmanship and imagination, as well as resourcefulness in obtaining variety of color from the strings.

The Concerto for piano and full orchestra was played by Eugene List with the New York Philharmonic-Symphony in December, 1938. It too showed a command of the medium, for it was ably written, rhythmically interesting, and executed in vivid, bold, orchestral colors. Fuleihan's further works include a *Symphonic Episode;* a Suite for chamber orchestra; a symphonic poem, *Calypso; Fiesta,* for orchestra; a *Symphony Concertante* for string quartet and orchestra, performed by the New York Philharmonic-Symphony in April, 1940; a Concerto for two pianos and orchestra; a Sonata for piano; a set of Preludes for string quartet; and a number of shorter pieces, including songs and choruses.

MARION BAUER

Some twenty years ago, *Marion Bauer* was considered by many to be a radical member of the musical left wing, but today, in comparison with contemporary experimentalists, she is decidedly "middle-of-the-road." Her style has not changed materially, she is still an impressionist at heart; it is merely that the conservatives have come to use a vocabulary that was held radical a couple of decades ago.

Whatever changes Miss Bauer's style has undergone have been adopted chiefly to fit the demands of the larger forms in which she has been composing, as in the Viola Sonata, the *Dance Sonata* for piano, and the orchestral *Sun Splendor*. There are also incidental music to *Prometheus Bound;* a String Quartet; *Pan,* described as a choreographic sketch for a film; the earlier *Fantasia quasi una Sonata* for violin and piano; and numerous shorter pieces in various forms.

Miss Bauer was born in Walla Walla, Washington, August 15, 1887. She studied music with her sister, Emilie Frances Bauer, and in New York with Henry Holden Huss, Eugene Heffley, and Walter Henry Rothwell. In Paris she worked with Raoul Pugno, Nadia Boulanger, Campbell-Tipton and André Gédalge. In addition to composing she is active as a teacher and journalist: she holds the positions of associate professor of music at New York University and New York editor and critic of the *Musical Leader*. As an author she has continued the series she started in *How Music Grew* [50] (written in collaboration with Ethel R. Peyser) by writing another book with Miss Peyser, *Music Through the Ages*,[51] and with a clear treatise on present-day composers and their idioms, *Twentieth Century Music*.[52]

Mary Howe merits the attention she has received for a number of orchestral works which avoid traditional patterns. One of the earliest of them, and perhaps the most widely played, is the brief *Sand*, which is aptly descriptive, and which Leopold Stokowski told the composer had "given him a new conception of staccato." Even earlier than *Sand*, however, are the *Poema*, which dates from 1926, and the majestic *Dirge*, composed in 1931, and first played by the National Symphony in Washington in 1932.

Mrs. Howe is a native of Richmond, Virginia, born there April 4, 1882. She studied in America with Ernest Hutcheson, Harold Randolph, and Gustav Strube, and in Germany with Richard Burmeister. Practically all of her life has been lived in Washington, where she is vice-president of the Friends of Music in the Library of Congress, and has directed two choral societies.

Others of her orchestral works include a *Spring Pastoral; Stars; Whimsy; Coulennes; American Piece;* and *Castellana,* for two pianos and orchestra. Her list of chamber music numbers a Sonata for violin and piano; a String Quartet performed at Yaddo, September, 1940; a Suite for string quartet and piano;

---

[50] New York: G. P. Putnam's Sons, 1925.
[51] New York: G. P. Putnam's Sons, 1932.
[52] New York: G. P. Putnam's Sons, 1935.

and a Fugue for string quartet. For mixed chorus and orchestra she has composed a *Chain Gang Song* which was performed at the Worcester (Massachusetts) Festival in 1925.

Although *Carl Eppert* gives to his music such specific titles as *Traffic, Speed,* or *Vitamins,* he does not consider himself a realist. He uses such titles, he confesses, chiefly to whet the imagination of the average listener, while as a composer he confines himself to impressionism. He does not go in for such realistic devices as riveting machines, auto horns and whistles.

Traffic, which was awarded third prize in the NBC contest of 1932, is actually the opening movement of *A Symphony of the City,* the other movements being: "City Shadows," "Speed," and "City Nights." This Symphony, as a whole and in its separate movements, has enjoyed numerous performances by major orchestras. For orchestra there are also a fantasy, *The Argonauts;* a tone-poem, *The Pioneer; A Little Symphony;* a Symphony in C minor; a satirical portrait, *Escapade;* a suite, *Vitamins;* and a Concert Waltz Suite. Eppert has also composed music for symphonic band, a number of choral works, and considerable chamber music.

He was born in Carbon, Clay County, Indiana, November 5, 1882, and studied in Chicago, and in Germany. At present resident in Milwaukee, where he organized and for four seasons conducted the Civic and Symphony Orchestras, and has been associated with several conservatories, he has also been active as a conductor and teacher in Terre Haute, Indiana, in Seattle, and in Berlin. Although his name has a German sound and his musical training is German, he is descended on both sides from men who fought in the American Revolution.

Paul White is a musician who came to the Eastman School faculty with considerable experience. Born in Bangor, Maine, August 22, 1895, he was a graduate of the New England Conservatory in Boston and studied violin with Ysaÿe and composition and conducting with Eugene Goossens. For a number of years he played first violin in the Cincinnati Symphony Orchestra, and he has been guest conductor of the Boston, Cincinnati, Rochester, and the New York Philharmonic-Symphony Stadium Orchestras. In addition to his duties at the Eastman School, he is associate conductor of the Rochester Civic Orchestra.

White considers himself a liberal in his own compositions, for while he speaks the language of the present day, he feels that a composer should have at his disposal the technics of all ages. Although he is a strong supporter of his fellow American composers, he is no blind chauvinist, and the only work in which he can be said to be a nationalist is *The Voyage of the Mayflower*, for orchestra and chorus, which was performed first at the Eastman Festival in 1935, and later by the Philadelphia Orchestra under Stokowski.

The most widely played of his works is the less important suite of *Five Miniatures*, performed by nearly every major orchestra in the country, including the Philadelphia Orchestra in its coast-to-coast tour. These pieces are trifles written with the utmost ingenuity, and raising to concert-hall level the pest of radio orchestras, the vibraphone. Both the *Miniatures* and *The Voyage of the Mayflower* have been published, as have a Sonata for violin and piano and a Sinfonietta for string orchestra or string quartet. In manuscript White has a Symphony in E minor; a *Pagan Festival* overture; another overture, *To Youth*; *Feuilles Symphoniques*; and shorter pieces for orchestra.

Mark Wessel is one of the most talented of the former pupils of Arnold Schoenberg. Twice awarded a Guggenheim Fellowship and also the recipient of a Pulitzer Scholarship, he has to his credit a Symphony; a *Symphony Concertante* for piano and horn with orchestra; *Holiday* and *Song and Dance* for orchestra; a Concertino for flute and chamber orchestra; a Sextet for woodwind and piano; a String Quartet; a Quintet; *The King of Babylon*, a Symphonic Poem for orchestra, chorus and mimers, which won honorable mention in the 1938 contest of the New York Philharmonic-Symphony Orchestra; and other works.

He was born in Coldwater, Michigan, March 26, 1894, and was graduated from Northwestern School of Music. He has taught piano and theory at Northwestern, and more recently has been professor of piano and composition at the University of Colorado.

Ulric Cole has composed a number of major works, and her *Divertimento* for string orchestra and piano has received a number of performances recently, bringing her to the attention of the public. Herself a pianist, she has appeared as soloist in several of the performances, notably with the Cincinnati Symphony under Goossens in the Spring of 1939. The *Divertimento* is in three movements: "Toccata," "Intermezzo," and "Fantasia."

Miss Cole was born in New York in 1905, and studied in Los Angeles, in New York with Goetschius, Lhévinne, and Goldmark, and in Paris with Nadia Boulanger. Her works include two Sonatas for violin and piano, one of them published by the Society for the Publication of American Music; a Concerto for piano and orchestra; a Suite for orchestra; a String Quartet; a Piano Quintet; a Suite for Trio; and a Fantasy Sonata for piano.

OTHER COMPOSERS IN UNFAMILIAR IDIOMS

Continuing alphabetically the list of composers who logically belong in this chapter, we come first to the two Achrons, both foreign-born (one in Poland and the other in Russia), and both resident in America for a number of years. *Isidor Achron* (Warsaw, 1892) is a pianist, and in 1937 played his Piano Concerto with the New York Philharmonic-Symphony. *Joseph Achron* (Losdeye, 1886) is a violinist who has lived in America since 1925. He has composed three Violin Concerti; two Sonatas for violin and piano; a Children's Suite for piano, clarinet and string quartet; and numerous orchestral and chamber music works. He has devoted much attention to Hebrew subjects. His *Golem Suite* was chosen for the Venice Festival of the International Society for Contemporary Music.

Paul Hastings Allen lived in Italy for many years, and much of his music was written there. He was born in Hyde Park, Massachusetts, in 1883, and studied at Harvard. As early as 1910 his Symphony in D major won a Paderewski prize. His first opera, *Il Filtro*, was sung in Genoa in 1912, and another, *Milda*, in Venice in 1913. His largest work in this form is *The Last of the Mohicans* (based on Cooper), produced in Florence in 1916. *Cleopatra* was written on commission for the Italian publisher, Sonzogno. In 1928 he returned to this country, and since that time has been active in publishing in Boston. His orchestral works include two Symphonies (1912 and 1937), a Serenade (1928), *Ex Hocte* (1930), and *O Munasterio* (1912). He has also written chamber music and choral works.

At times *David Barnett* (New York, 1907) leans toward the conservative, as, for example, in the orchestral *Divertimento* which was played at the Lewisohn Stadium in New York in 1933; but his idiom nevertheless tends toward the present day. Active principally as a pianist and teacher, he has composed a number of works in the larger forms, several of them published in Paris.

Evelyn Berckman (Philadelphia, 1900) has been represented frequently at the League of Composers concerts, and at the Yaddo Festivals. Largely self-taught, she was prevented from achieving a career as pianist by a paralysis which she blames on highly incompetent instruction. She had composed before this happened, and afterwards concentrated on composition. She has written numerous orchestral and chamber-music works, as well as music for two ballets, *From the Odyssey* and *County Fair*.

Eugene MacDonald Bonner (Washington, North Carolina, 1889) studied at the Peabody Conservatory in Baltimore. He also worked with Boise and Brockway, and from 1911 to 1917 he lived and studied in England. After the World War, in which he served in the United States Artillery, he remained in Paris, studying with the conductor and composer, Albert Wolff. He returned to America in 1927 to take up critical work with *The Outlook* and later the *Brooklyn Daily Eagle*. He is the composer of *White Nights* (1925), performed in April, 1939, by the New York Philharmonic under John Barbirolli; *Whispers of Heavenly Death* (three Whitman poems for soprano and orchestra, 1922); four operas: *Barbara Frietchie, Celui qui épousa une femme muette, The Venetian Glass Nephew,* and *The Gods of the Mountain;* incidental music for *The Young Alexander;* and some chamber music.

Theodore Ward Chanler (Newport, Rhode Island, 1902), a pupil of Ernest Bloch and Nadia Boulanger, was first heard from when his Sonata for violin and piano was performed at the Copland-Sessions concerts in New York. He has also composed a Mass for two women's voices; a Suite for piano, entitled *Five Short Colloquies;* and two series of *Epitaphs,* for voice and piano. In April, 1940, Chanler was commissioned under the terms of the Award in Composition offered jointly by Town Hall (New York) and the League of Composers to write a work for Dorothy Maynor, Negro soprano, to sing in the next season's Town Hall Endowment Series.

Louis Cheslock (London, 1899) was brought to America at the age of two, and studied at the Peabody Conservatory in Baltimore, where he is now an instructor. He is also assistant concertmaster of the Baltimore Symphony Orchestra. His compositions include a Symphony; several Tone-Poems for orchestra; a Violin Concerto; a French Horn Concerto; a String Quartet, a Violin Sonata; and several choral works.

Avery Claflin (Keene, New Hampshire, 1898) is known chiefly for his opera, *Hester Prynne,* which was performed by the Friends and Enemies of Modern Music in Hartford, Connecticut, in 1935. Although actively engaged in business, he has also composed a Symphony; a *Moby Dick Suite* for orchestra; some chamber music; a one-act opera, *The Fall of the House of Usher;* and a ballet.

Among the composers who lead a double life musically, *Vladimir Dukelsky* (Pskoff, Russia, 1903) is a highly interesting figure. As *Vernon Duke* he has contributed dashing tunes to the *Ziegfeld Follies* (1936); *The Show Is On;* the *Garrick Gaieties;*

Three's a Crowd; and the recent *Cabin in the Sky*. A pupil of Glière in Russia, he left his native country following the Revolution, and after living in Paris and London, settled in America in 1929, eventually becoming a citizen. He uses his own name for his serious compositions, which include two Symphonies; two Piano Concerti; a piece for piano and orchestra, *Dédicaces;* an oratorio, *The End of St. Petersburg*, performed in 1938 by the New York Schola Cantorum; some chamber music; three ballets; and a two-act opera, *Demoiselle Paysanne*.

Henry Eichheim (Chicago, 1870) continues to clothe the ritual and mystery of the Orient in a music understandable in Western concert-halls. Following his orchestral suite, *Burma* (1927), and his *Java* (1929), he has more recently composed *Bali* (1933), a series of Variations based on Balinese music which he heard in a temple court at Denpassar. When the composition was first performed by the Philadelphia Orchestra, Lawrence Gilman [53] pronounced it "a fascinating web of tone, cunningly wrought, perturbing, not easily to be forgotten." In addition to his earlier works, the *Oriental Impressions* (1922), the *Chinese Legend* (1924), and others, Eichheim's recent compositions include a *Japanese Nocturne*, commissioned by Mrs. Elizabeth Sprague Coolidge in 1930; a *Korean Sketch* for orchestra; and a Sonata for violin and piano, performed at the Pittsfield (Massachusetts) Festival in 1934. The composer was educated at the Chicago Musical College, and for a year was a member of the Theodore Thomas Orchestra. From 1890 to 1912 he was one of the first violins of the Boston Symphony, and then retired to devote himself to composing and occasional recitals. He has made many journeys to the Far East in search of material and native instruments for his Orientally inspired music.

Albert I. Elkus (Sacramento, California, 1884) was the 1935 winner of the Juilliard Publication Award, with his *Impressions from a Greek Tragedy*, for orchestra. He is a graduate of the Uni-

[53] *New York Herald Tribune*, December 6, 1933.

versity of California, and a pupil of Bauer, Lhévinne, and Schalk. In 1935 he was appointed professor of music at the University of California.

Herbert Elwell (Minneapolis, 1898), in 1926 a Fellow at the American Academy in Rome, and a pupil of Ernest Bloch and Nadia Boulanger, is still best known for *The Happy Hypocrite,* originally music for a ballet and subsequently arranged as a Suite for orchestra. In the latter form it won the Eastman Publication Award. For a number of years Elwell has been music critic for the *Cleveland Plain Dealer* and program-annotator for the Cleveland Symphony. In 1935 he was appointed assistant director of the Cleveland Institute of Music, where he heads the theory and composition departments. His works include a String Quartet; a Quintet; a Piano Sonata; and a Sonata for violin and piano.

Amedeo de Filippi (Ariano, Italy, 1900) was brought to the United States as a child of five years. He was awarded a four-year scholarship at the Juilliard School, where he studied with Rubin Goldmark, and has since been active as a conductor and violinist in the theatrical field. For the theatre he has composed incidental music for plays and motion pictures; for orchestra, a Suite (1920), a Concerto (1928), and a Symphony (1930); and for chamber music combinations, a String Quartet (1926); a Piano Quintet (1928); a Sonata for viola and piano (1929) which was performed at the Westminster Festival at Princeton, New Jersey, in 1936; and numerous other works.

Rudolf Forst (New York, 1900) was winner of the third prize in the NBC chamber music contest in 1937. The String Quartet which won the award was the first of two works in this form. Largely self-educated, he undertook post-graduate work with Daniel Gregory Mason at Columbia University, and then became instructor of violin at the New York College of Music. His works include a Symphonic Rhapsody (based on two Ozark folktunes) (1937); a Symphony (1937); a *Symphonietta* for strings (1936); a *Sonata da Camera* (1937); and a Sonata for cello and piano (1932).

As a composer, *Isadore Freed* (Russia, 1900) considers his mission to be that of an organizer in the new language of music, aiming to relate our music with the great heritage of music from 1400 to 1900. He was brought to this country at the age of three, studied at the Philadelphia Conservatory of Music and the University of Pennsylvania, and later with Ernest Bloch and Vincent d'Indy. His orchestral works number two suites published in Paris, *Jeux de Timbres* (1931) and *Triptyque* (1932); an earlier suite, *Vibrations* (1928); a symphonic rhapsody, *Pygmalion* (1926); a Ballad for piano and small orchestra (1925); a suite, *Pastorales* (1936); and a Symphony (1937). He has also written two String Quartets and other chamber music works.

The tragic death of *Aurelio Giorni* (Perugia, Italy, 1895–Pittsfield, Massachusetts, 1938) removed a talented and welcome figure from our musical life. He had been widely known as the pianist of the Elshuco Trio. His Sonata for cello and piano was one of the early works chosen for publication by the Society for the Publication of American Music (1924). He had also composed a symphonic poem, *Orlando Furioso* (1926); a Symphony in D (1936); a *Sinfonia Concertante* for piano with orchestra; a String Quartet (1936); a Piano Quintet (1926); a Piano Quartet (1927); a Piano Trio (1934); Sonatas for flute and piano (1932), violin and piano (1924), clarinet and piano (1933); and numerous other works. At the time of his death he was teaching composition at Smith College.

Carl Hugo Grimm (Zanesville, Ohio, 1890) has been a teacher of composition and organ at the Cincinnati Conservatory of Music since 1931. A pupil of his father (author of several treatises on harmony) and Frank Van der Stucken, he has himself composed a long list of works: four Symphonic Poems; a Suite for orchestra; a Suite for chamber orchestra; a String Quartet; a Fantasia for two clarinets, cello and piano; a Serenade for wind instruments; many works for chorus; and numerous songs. His *Erotic Poem* was awarded a thousand-dollar prize by the National Federation of Music Clubs in 1927, and his *Song of Songs*, a choral work, won a similar prize awarded by the MacDowell Club. His *Abraham Lincoln* was first performed at the American Composers' Concerts in Rochester in 1931. Idiomatically, Grimm uses the harmonic combinations which grow out of exotic scale forms, many of them Oriental. He works on a system of unusual cadence forms which tend to grow more involved and colorful. He seems to have a predilection for dark tinges.

During the last decade *William Franke Harling* (London, 1887) has been in Hollywood as composer and arranger for the Paramount studios, and in recent years has not frequently been heard from in the concert halls. His chief claim to fame still lies in his opera, *The Light from St. Agnes,* which the Chicago Civic Opera Company produced in 1925. He also composed the music for *Deep River,* a lyric drama produced in New York in 1926; as well as a *Jazz Concerto,* a *Venetian Fantasy, Chansons Populaires* (on themes by Berlin, Kern and Gershwin) and numerous songs and choral works.

Ethel Glenn Hier (Cincinnati, 1889) was one of the two women awarded Guggenheim Fellowships in music for the season of 1930–31. The other was Ruth Crawford. A pupil of Stillman Kelley, Percy Goetschius, and Ernest Bloch, Miss Hier has also been profoundly influenced by association with such modernists as Alban Berg, Egon Wellesz, Schoenberg, and Malipiero. In addition to numerous shorter works for voice and for piano (including her suite, *A Day in the Peterborough Woods*), she has written several Quartets for voice, violin, cello and piano; a Suite for string quartet; a Sextet for flute, oboe, violin, viola, cello, and piano; a setting of *America the Beautiful* for chorus and orchestra; and a ballet for orchestra—*Chorégraphe.*

Herbert Inch (Missoula, Montana, 1904) is a Fellow of the American Academy in Rome (1931), and a graduate of the Eastman School of Music. He teaches at Hunter College, New York. His works show some reflection of modern European trends, and are marked by vigor and energy. For orchestra he has composed a Symphony (1932); a Piano Concerto (1937); *To Silvanus*

(1933); an earlier *Variations on a Modal Theme* (1927), as well as a Suite for small orchestra (1929); and a Serenade for woodwinds and strings (1936). His chamber-music list includes a Quintet (1930); *Mediterranean Sketches* for string quartet (1933); a Sonata for piano and cello (1934); a Divertimento for brass instruments (1934); a Piano Sonata (1935); and a String Quartet (1936).

Although *Boris Koutzen* (Uman, Russia, 1901) might be labeled a modernist, he claims a romantic rather than an intellectual approach to creative work. He feels that however revolutionary his peculiarities of idiom may seem to the layman, they are the result of a slow evolution which has produced in the composer a product that is actually natural and orthodox. A pupil of Glière, he played in orchestras in Russia and in Berlin until he came to the United States in 1924 and became a violinist with the Philadelphia Orchestra. In 1930 he became head of the violin department at the Philadelphia Conservatory, and he is a member of the NBC Symphony Orchestra, organized for Toscanini's leadership. His orchestral works include a poem-nocturne, *Solitude* (1927); a Symphonic Movement for violin and orchestra (1929); a symphonic poem, *Valley Forge* (1931), presented by the National Orchestral Association, and by the NBC Symphony Orchestra, in 1940; a Symphony (1937); and a Concerto for five solo instruments (1934), which has been played by the National Orchestral Association and, in February 1940, by the Boston Symphony Orchestra. He has also two String Quartets (1922 and 1936); a Sonata for violin and piano (1928); a Trio for flute, cello, and harp (1936); and numerous smaller works.

George McKay (Harrington, Washington, 1899) is distinctly a product of the Northwest. Except for study with Sinding and Palmgren at the Eastman School, of which he was the first graduate in composition, and some teaching in other sections of the country, he has spent all his life in his native territory, where he is now Associate Professor at the University of Washington. His works show his environment, particularly his *Fantasy on a*

Western Folksong; his *Harbor Narrative;* his American dance symphony, *Epoch;* and his *Symphonic Prelude in American Idiom.* He has also composed three Sinfoniettas (1925, 1929 and 1933); a *Machine Age Blues* (1935); works for symphonic band; and a considerable number of works for chamber music combinations.

It is a good many years since *Leo Ornstein* (Russia, 1895) ceased to shock concert-goers as the impish youngster who dealt in note-clusters. Today Ornstein has achieved a highly respected niche as a piano teacher in Philadelphia, and he seems content to leave experiments to others. *The Wild Men's Dance* and *A la Chinoise* were the piano pieces which attracted the most attention on his recital programs, but he also has a lengthy list of orchestral works, including a Piano Concerto (1923); a Quintet (1929); a Quartet (1929); two Sonatas for violin and piano; a Cello Sonata, and a Piano Sonata. In 1935 he was commissioned by the League of Composers to write an orchestral work; this was the *Nocturne and Dance of the Fates,* first performed by Vladimir Golschmann and the St. Louis Orchestra in February, 1937.

Solomon Pimsleur (Paris, 1900) chooses arresting titles for his works, *e.g., Dynamic Overture, Impetuous Toccata and Fugal Fantasia, Fiery Sonato* for trio, and *Impetuous Sonata* for violin and piano. He came to the United States at the age of three, and studied with D. G. Mason and Rubin Goldmark. His *Symphonic Ballade* has been played by the New York Philharmonic-Symphony Orchestra. He has written numerous orchestral, choral, and chamber music works.

Alois Reiser (Prague, 1887) was winner of the second prize in the NBC Music Guild contest of 1936, with his second String Quartet. His earlier Cello Concerto was awarded second prize in the 1931 Hollywood Bowl competition. In his youth a pupil of Dvořák at the Prague Conservatory, he came to New York in 1905, and is at present musical director at the Warner Brothers and Fox Studios in Hollywood. He is the composer of an opera, *Gobi* (1912); several tone-poems: *A Summer Evening* (1907),

From Mt. Rainier (1926), and *Erewhon* (1931); a *Slavic Rhapsody* for orchestra (1927); two String Quartets (1916 and 1930); two Trios (1910 and 1931); and a more recent Sonata for violin and piano.

Le Roy J. Robertson is the composer of a Quintet which was chosen by the Society for the Publication of American Music in 1936. A graduate of the New England Conservatory of Music, he studied also with Ernest Bloch and Hugo Leichtentritt. He is professor of music at Brigham Young University.

Edward Royce (Cambridge, Massachusetts, 1886) has become so distinguished as a teacher of composers that the casual observer is likely to overlook his own compositions. Nevertheless, Royce has to his credit two major orchestral works, *The Fire-Bringers* (1926), and *Far Ocean* (1929), both of them performed at the American Composers' Concerts in Rochester, and the latter published by the Eastman School; a set of Piano Variations in A minor, which has been played repeatedly by Harold Bauer and other pianists; and numerous shorter pieces and songs. He studied at Harvard and in Berlin, then founded the piano department at Middlebury College, Vermont. He spent a number of years at the Ithaca (New York) Conservatory, and since 1923 has taught composition at the Eastman School. Gaining from his father, Josiah Royce, a philosophical insight into music, he has been able to make a rational analysis of the ever-changing patterns that modern music assumes, and to balance the relative values of the old and the new. The radical, he holds, is right in maintaining that the chief unchangeable law is that there must be change; but he is wrong if he holds that the secessionist complex is an unconditional guarantee of perfection. As for dissonances, he feels that although up to and including twelve notes they may occur, they must be clearly audible; their emotional content must be discoverable; and their resolution, by some method, must be sought or implied. In all complexity, he continues, there must be some simplicity; and in all simplicity there must be some complexity.

Although the continued foreign residence of *Timothy Mather*

Spelman (Brooklyn, New York, 1891) prevented his countrymen from hearing more of him, two of his works have had recent performances at the American Composers' Concerts in Rochester: *Pervigilium Veneris* for soli, chorus, and orchestra in 1934, and the Symphony in G minor in 1936. Spelman was educated at Harvard and in Munich, and for many years made his home in Italy. For orchestra he has composed two symphonic poems, *Christ and the Blind Man* (1918), and *Dawn in the Woods* (1937); two suites, *Barbaresques* (1923) and *Saints' Days* (1925); and a Symphony in G minor. He has also written choral works, several pieces of chamber music, two one-act stage works, and a three-act opera, *The Sea Rovers*.

Alexander Lang Steinert (Boston, 1900), a pupil of Loeffler, d'Indy, Gédalge, and Koechlin, enjoyed three years at the American Academy in Rome. His orchestral works number *Nuit Méridionale* (1926); *Leggenda Sinfonica* (1931); *Three Poems by Shelley*, with soprano solo (1932); and a *Concerto Sinfonico* with piano solo. He has also a Sonata for violin and piano (1925); a Trio (1927); and a Sonata for piano solo (1929).

Burnet C. Tuthill (New York, 1888) has labored diligently and effectively in the cause of the American composer, and has for many years been treasurer of the Society for the Publication of American Music, founded by his father and himself. Until 1922 music was an avocation for Tuthill, but in that year he became manager of the Cincinnati Conservatory. Since 1935 he has been associated with the Memphis College of Music, becoming its director in 1937. His orchestral works include a pastorale, *Bethlehem* (1934); a rhapsody, *Come Seven* (1935); and a symphonic poem, *Laurentia* (1936). His long list of chamber music contains mostly works for wood-wind combinations, for he is himself an excellent clarinetist. There are also a Sonata for violin and piano (1937); a Sextet for strings (1937); and, for band, a march, *Dr. Joe* (1933), and a Symphonic Overture (1937).

5

NEWCOMERS

ONE of the most encouraging phases of our musical development is the constant appearance of new faces in the ranks of our composers, most of them belonging to young men and women with fresh and novel ideas and undoubted talent. We have almost an embarrassment of riches, creating such keen competition that no matter how generously our major orchestras, choral societies, and opera houses open their doors and their programs to these new works, it would be impossible to make a place for all that the newcomers have to offer.

Appraisal of their work is a difficult and dangerous task. By the time another decade has passed some of them will have established their reputations firmly, and their works will have become part of the standard repertoire, while others will already have enjoyed their brief moment of fame, and subsided into obscurity. It is apparent, however, that to command attention the young composer of the 1930's and '40's has had to have considerably more to say musically than his predecessor of the 1920's. The time has passed, we hope for all time, when it was necessary only to introduce an automobile siren, a vacuum cleaner, an airplane motor, or a riveting machine into a score to achieve international notoriety. We have become sated with the merely sensational. Nowadays our composers must, and in general do, base their claims to a hearing on more solid foundations.

It is worth noting that the great majority of the new arrivals are largely American trained. Many of them, it is true, have worked abroad, some enjoying the bounty of the Guggenheim or Pulitzer grants, but often this has been largely for the purpose of broadening their experience and adding a finishing touch to what they have learned at home. This situation is partly but not altogether due to the fact that most of Europe's greatest teachers are now resident in America; many of our leading teachers are themselves Americans—Howard Hanson, Edward Royce, Frederick Jacobi, Aaron Copland, Roger Sessions, Roy Harris, the late Rubin Goldmark, and others.

JUILLIARD ALUMNI

The philanthropists who either bequeathed or gave of their bounty to found professional training schools have been richly vindicated in the creative field, for a gratifying number of our newer composers have studied in these institutions. From the Juilliard Graduate School comes *Vittorio Giannini*, a pupil of Rubin Goldmark, and in 1932 a Fellow of the American Academy in Rome. Born October 19, 1903, in Philadelphia, the young Giannini studied first with his mother, then for a short time in Milan, and finally at the Juilliard School.

His list of works includes a Suite for orchestra (1931); a *Symphony in Memoriam Theodore Roosevelt*, commissioned by the New York State Theodore Roosevelt Committee (1935); Concerti for piano and orchestra (1935), and for organ and orchestra, commissioned by the Vienna Gesellschaft der Musikfreunde (1937); four produced operas—*Lucedia* (Munich, 1934), *The Scarlet Letter* (Hamburg, 1938), *Beauty and the Beast* (commissioned by the Columbia Broadcasting System and given a radio performance November, 1938), and *Blennerhasset* (radio performance, Columbia Broadcasting System, November, 1939); a *Requiem* for double chorus, soli, and orchestra produced in Vienna, May, 1937; and for chamber music combinations: Sonatas for violin and piano (1936) and piano solo (1934); a Trio (1934); a String Quartet (1930); a Piano Quintet (published by

Vittorio Giannini

the Society for the Publication of American Music, 1933); a Quintet for wood-winds (1934); a Madrigal for four voices and string quartet (1939); and a *Triptych* for voice and string orchestra (1937). His Concerto for two pianos was performed by Luboschutz and Nemenoff in January of 1940. A new opera, *Casanova*, on a libretto by Robert A. Simon, is in preparation.

When *The Scarlet Letter* was produced at the State Opera in Hamburg, the composer's distinguished sister, Dusolina Giannini, sang the leading soprano role. One of the critics [1] termed Giannini

a conventional architect who employs the well-weathered bricks of the trade for the foundation of his edifice and then decorates its orchestral façade with the familiar Italian ornament that custom never seems to stale. . . . Linear or strident modernisms are as foreign to Giannini's mode of thought as the cold, clear texture of the present Italian school with its brittle witticisms, sharp edges, and glistening surfaces.

Giannini is altogether frank regarding his idiom, and it is somewhat refreshing to find a composer who confesses simply that the goal he seeks is beauty, and that he is willing to accept any method that will help him achieve it. When his Piano Concerto was performed by Rosalyn Tureck with the National Orchestra Association, Francis Perkins [2] found it "unashamedly romantic," but added:

At a time when economy of utterance and keeping emotion rather in the background are still among favored tendencies in contemporary music, the opulence and expansiveness of Mr. Giannini's score proved welcome. He did not hesitate to dwell upon frankly expressed melodies, while his orchestral coloring proved warm and vivid.

Another prominent Juilliard alumnus is *Paul Nordoff*, twice awarded a Guggenheim Fellowship (1933 and 1935) and also winner of the Bearns Prize from Columbia University for his Prelude and Variations for piano (1933). His *Secular Mass* was commissioned by Eugene Ormandy and given its première per-

---

[1] Geraldine de Courcy, *Musical America*, July, 1938.
[2] *New York Herald Tribune*, March 23, 1937.

formance by that conductor with the Minneapolis Orchestra in March, 1935. Three years later, when Ormandy had become conductor of the Philadelphia Orchestra, the work was performed by that organization, in Philadelphia and New York.

Born in Philadelphia, June 4, 1909, Nordoff studied first at the Philadelphia Conservatory, and in 1927 won a Juilliard Fellowship and entered the graduate school as a composition pupil of Rubin Goldmark and a piano pupil of Olga Samaroff. He is now active as teacher and lecturer, and is an instructor in composition at the Philadelphia Conservatory. In 1940 he won the Pulitzer Scholarship.

Among his first important works was a set of modernized settings of Stephen Foster melodies, composed at the suggestion of John Erskine, and published abroad. In 1934 he played his Piano Concerto with the Groningen Orchestra in Holland, and in 1934 he heard his *Triptych*, three songs with Dryden texts, sung at the Juilliard School. His *Prelude and Three Fugues* for orchestra were played in their original version for two pianos at a League of Composers concert in New York, March, 1933, and one of the Fugues was performed in its orchestral form by Stokowski and the Philadelphia Orchestra, in April, 1937. More recent is the Concerto for two pianos and orchestra, which was performed by the composer and Allison Drake with the Federal Symphony Orchestra of New York, May, 1939. Francis Perkins [3] found it "ably written," and remarked that "the second movement, a largo, gave the greatest impression of creative imagination and emotional content."

In addition to these works, Nordoff has composed two String Quartets (1932 and 1935); a Piano Quintet (1936); a Sonata for violin and piano (1932); incidental music to *Romeo and Juliet* and *St. Joan* (for Katharine Cornell); and about seventy songs. He has also written an opera, as yet untitled.

Bernard Herrmann, Juilliard graduate, has concerned himself largely with the development of composition for radio perform-

[3] *New York Herald Tribune,* May 8, 1939.

ance. He has had considerable experience in this field, as musical director of the American School of the Air and the "Columbia Workshop," and since 1938 as a staff conductor of the Columbia Broadcasting System. As a creative musician he feels that any serious-minded composer naturally uses whatever tonal devices suit his needs, but personally Herrmann feels he must have modern devices to express what he wants to say. Much of his music has been inspired by an American background, and he has derived much pleasure from his attempt to transmute the feelings his surroundings evoke, rather than to follow the latest neo-classic vogues from abroad.

Accordingly, the titles of his major works reflect native surroundings: a *Currier and Ives Suite, The Skating Pond* for orchestra (1935); a tone-poem, *The City of Brass* (1934); Orchestral Variations on *Deep River* and *Water Boy* (1933); and, most ambitious of all, a dramatic cantata, for male chorus, soloists and orchestra, *Moby Dick*, composed in 1937 and given its première performance by the New York Philharmonic-Symphony in April, 1940.

Herrmann was born in New York City, June 29, 1911. He founded and conducted the New Chamber Music Orchestra which gave concerts in New York and at the Library of Congress, and he has been active in various movements to promote the cause of new music. In addition to the works with descriptive titles, he has composed a Sinfonietta for string orchestra (1935); a Nocturne and Scherzo for orchestra (1936), performed at the American Composers' Concerts in Rochester in January, 1938; a Violin Concerto (1937); a String Quartet (1932); and numerous shorter works.

The performance of *Moby Dick* on April 11, 1940, in Carnegie Hall, was the occasion for a good deal of press comment, both before and after the event. Francis D. Perkins [4] found that Herrmann's treatment of the large orchestra he employed was masterly. "It reveals," Perkins wrote,

[4] *New York Herald Tribune,* April 12, 1940.

a remarkable command of the resources of instrumental color and timbre, an exceptional ability to depict with convincing vividness a wide variety of emotional hues and atmospheres. . . . Mr. Herrmann's power for dramatic suggestion is best revealed in his instruments, although both the singers and the orchestra contributed to the sense of impending tragedy which marked the work as a whole . . . much of the time Mr. Herrmann's orchestration proved much more memorable than his musical ideas themselves. . . . But yet, *Moby Dick* gave reason to look forward with interest to his next work of this type, *Johnny Appleseed*.

In addition to the last-named piece, Herrmann has a new Symphony and a "fiddle (not violin)" Concerto, based on three old breakdown tunes, in preparation.

A. Lehman Engel, educated first in Cincinnati, and later at the Juilliard School under Goldmark, is perhaps better known as a choral conductor than as a composer. As organizer and director of the Madrigal Singers, a unit of the WPA Music Project, he has introduced many contemporary works by Americans, and has brought to light many pieces by forgotten composers of the past. His own works include four orchestral pieces—*Jungle Dance* (1930), *Introduction and Allegretto* (1932), *Scientific Creation* (1935), and *Traditions* (1935); a number of choral pieces; a String Quartet (1934); and a Piano Sonata (1936). He has also composed much for the stage—incidental music to Eliot's *Murder in the Cathedral* (1936), O'Casey's *Within the Gates* (1934), Aristophanes' *Birds* (1935), and other plays. He has written two operas, *Medea* (1935), and *Pierrot of the Minute* (1927); and a ballet, *Phobias* (1933).

Engel was born in Jackson, Mississippi, September 14, 1910. In addition to his studies at the Cincinnati College, the Cincinnati Conservatory, and the Juilliard School, he has worked with Lora and Trucco in New York, and with Roger Sessions.

There are other newcomers on the Juilliard list who have achieved varying degrees of prominence, among them *Norman Cazden* (New York City, 1914); *Arthur Cohn* (Philadelphia,

1910); *David Holden* (1912); *Elie Siegmeister* (New York City, 1909); and *Julia Smith* (Texas, 1911). Cazden's String Quartet was performed at the Westminster Festival (Princeton, N.J.) in 1936; Cohn has a long list of chamber music and orchestral works; Holden's *Chamber Music for Piano and Strings* was selected by the Society for the Publication of American Music in 1939; Siegmeister has lent his talents to political causes with his *May Day*, and *Hip-Hip Hooray for the NRA*; and Miss Smith saw the production of her opera, *Cynthia Parker*, with Leonora Corona in the title role, at Denton, Texas, February, 1939.

Jerome Moross (Brooklyn, New York, 1913) studied for a year at Juilliard, and in the early 1930's was one of the young composers' group in New York to which Herrmann and Siegmeister also belonged. Moross has written a symphony; *Paeans* and *Biguine*, both orchestral works published by New Music; and, in response to a commission from the Columbia Broadcasting System in 1938, *Tall Story*, for orchestra. His manuscript works also include two ballets and a full-length opera. He is on the musical staff of Paramount Pictures, in Hollywood.

Tragedy overtook one of the Juilliard group at a cruelly early point in his career when, on August 4, 1940, *Charles Naginski* was drowned in a lake at Lenox, Massachusetts, where he was attending the Berkshire Festival of the Boston Symphony Orchestra. Naginsky was born in Cairo, Egypt, in 1909, and came to this country in 1927, later adopting American citizenship. He studied with Rubin Goldmark at the Juilliard School for five years, and also with Roger Sessions. He had composed a Sinfonietta, a *Children's Suite*, a ballet entitled *The Minotaur*, and several other works. He had won the Walter Damrosch Fellowship for study at the American Academy in Rome, in 1938, and much had been expected of him.

As a tribute to his memory, the musicians who were gathered at Yaddo in September, 1940, played his Sinfonietta at the conclusion of the programs of both days of the music-making, under the baton of Richard Donovan, of Yale. Of the first performance, Howard Taubman wrote: [5]

> The work is filled with decisive energy. No matter that the ideas are not all personal or memorable; Mr. Naginski manipulated them with the air of a man who was at home with an orchestra, and who reveled in its opportunities for color, rhythm, and contrast.

THE EASTMAN GROUP

The Eastman School of Music in Rochester, New York, has produced its share of our recent composers, a number of them already discussed in preceding chapters. Among the younger of them, *Gardner Read* came to wide public attention by winning the New York Philharmonic-Symphony prize of one thousand dollars, with his first Symphony, in 1937. When the work was performed, in November of that year, it impressed at least one of the critics [6] as possessing well defined musical ideas, and "passages of appealing lyric eloquence," even though it could stand "more conciseness and simplicity."

Read was born in Evanston, Illinois, January 2, 1913, and while still a high-school student attended music courses at Northwestern University. In the summer of 1932 he was awarded a scholarship to the National Music Camp at Interlochen, Michigan. While there he met Howard Hanson, who urged him to apply for a scholarship at the Eastman School. Having won this, he studied in Rochester for four years, with Royce, White, Rogers, and Hanson. In 1938 and 1939 he traveled in Europe on a Cromwell Fellowship.

In his own music, Read has been deeply influenced by impressionism, and he remarks that if he must be pigeon-holed, he might venture to call himself a "modern romanticist." Like Giannini, he confesses to being one of those "die-hards" who still believe

[5] *New York Times*, September 8, 1940.
[6] Francis Perkins, *New York Herald Tribune*, November 5, 1937.

that music is an art which should express beauty, and, to use his own words, "that a good melody is worth a carload of exotic chords and perverse rhythms."

In addition to the Symphony, his orchestral works include a symphonic poem, *The Lotos Eaters* (1932); a symphonic suite, *The Painted Desert* (1933); another symphonic suite, *Sketches of the City* (1933), performed by the Rochester, Chicago, and Cincinnati Orchestras, and published by the Juilliard Foundation; a Fantasy for viola and orchestra (1935); and a Prelude and Toccata (1937). His works also include a Piano Sonata (1935); a Passacaglia and Fugue for organ (1936); and a set of songs for mezzo soprano and thirty-eight instruments, *From a Lute of Jade* (1935).

David Diamond studied at the Eastman School from 1932 to 1934. Before that he had worked at the Cleveland Institute, and afterwards he continued with Sessions and Boepple at the New Music School, and with Nadia Boulanger at Fontainebleau. Born in Rochester, New York, July 9, 1915, he has already enjoyed several distinctions: the Elfrida Whiteman Scholarship in 1935, the Juilliard Publication Award for his *Psalm for Orchestra*, a commission from the League of Composers, in 1937, and a Guggenheim award in 1938.

Diamond has a long list of works. In addition to the *Psalm*, his orchestral works include a Sinfonietta (1934), a Symphony (1935), a Violin Concerto (1936), a Serenade for strings (1937); an *Elegy in Memory of Ravel* (1938); a *Heroic Piece* (1939); a Concert Piece written for the New York High School of Music and Art, and a Concerto for chamber orchestra, which figured in the September, 1940, programs at Yaddo. His Sonata for cello and piano, composed in 1936, was published three years later in an issue of *New Music*. Somewhat angular, melodically and harmonically, this work is compact structurally, and reveals a predilection for a long-breathed thematic line. Other chamber music works are a Piano Sonata (1936), a Violin Sonatina (1937), a Trio (1937), a Quintet for flute, three strings, and piano (1937), a Divertimento for piano and small orchestra (1936), a Chamber Symphony (1936), and a highly sophisticated Sonatina for two pianos, published in 1937 by the Proem Press. In April, 1940, the Eastman Festival programs included his *Variations on an Original Theme*, for orchestra.

Frederick Woltmann received his Bachelor of Music degree from the Eastman School in 1937, and in the same year was awarded a Juilliard Fellowship at the American Academy in Rome. Born in Flushing, New York, in 1908, he studied music as a child, and for a season sang in the boys' chorus of the Metropolitan Opera Company. He studied other arts at Columbia University—architecture, drawing, painting, and stage design, but a scholarship at the Eastman School led him to the study of composition under Bernard Rogers and Howard Hanson.

A number of his orchestral works have been performed at the American Composers' Concerts in Rochester—a Rhapsody for horn and orchestra (1935); a Symphony, *Songs for Autumn* (1937); *Variations on an Old English Folk-tune* (1939). He has also composed a Piano Concerto (1937); a tone-poem, *The Pool of Pegasus* (1937); a *Scherzo* (1937) and a *Poem* (1933), each for eight instruments; as well as numerous shorter works. His "The Coliseum at Night" from *Two Impressions of Rome* was performed by the New York Philharmonic Symphony under Mitropoulos during December of 1940.

Burrill Phillips, born in Omaha, Nebraska, November 9, 1907, was graduated from the Eastman School in 1932, and after receiving his Master's degree in the following year, was appointed a faculty member, teaching theory and composition. His *Selections from McGuffey's Reader*, given the Eastman Publication Award, had its first performance at the American Composers' Concerts in 1934, and was later played by the Minneapolis and the Hollywood Bowl orchestras. In this orchestral work, the composer uses three well known American poems, presenting them musically in the simple manner of the McGuffey Readers: *The One-Hoss*

Shay, The Courtship of Miles Standish, and *The Midnight Ride of Paul Revere.*

Another orchestral work, *Courthouse Square,* was introduced at the American Composers' Concerts in 1935, and later performed as a ballet at the Eastman Festival in 1937, while Stokowski and the Philadelphians played it in April of the same year. It depicts in colorful fashion various phases of small town life. Also on Phillips's list are a *Grotesque Dance from a Projected Ballet* (1932); two other ballets, *Princess and Puppet* (1935) and *Play Ball* (1938); a *Symphony Concertante* (1933); a Piano Concerto (1937); and several shorter works. His *Concert Piece* for bassoon and strings and his *Dance* for orchestra were played at the tenth Eastman Festival, and his String Quartet figured on a League of Composers program of the works of young composers in April, 1940.

Wayne Barlow, born in Elyria, Ohio, September 6, 1912, is another of the composers educated at the Eastman School who are now teaching there. He also studied for a season with Arnold Schoenberg. Barlow feels that the music of our time is more closely akin in spirit to the music of the centuries preceding the seventeenth than to the music of the immediate past. He believes in the importance of a good melody and in linear treatment of voices, and maintains that recently-developed devices should be available to the composer when he wants to use them, which, he points out, is far different from the composer's being a slave to the devices.

His works include a Poem for orchestra, *De Profundis;* a choral ballet, *False Faces;* a cantata, *Zion in Exile;* a String Quartet; a Sonata for violin and piano; and several songs. The Eastman Festival programs in April, 1940, included two new orchestral works by Barlow, *The Winter's Past* and *Three Moods for Dancing.*

The Eastman roster further includes *Hunter Johnson* (Benson, North Carolina, 1906); *Kent Kennan* (Milwaukee, Wisc., 1913);

Gail Kubik (Coffeyville, Oklahoma, 1914); and *Irvine McHose*. Johnson had his training in Rochester, where he graduated in 1929. He then taught in the music school of the University of Michigan until 1933, when he received the Rome prize. He has written a Symphony and a Prelude for orchestra; an Andante for flute and string orchestra; a Concerto for piano and small orchestra; *Letter to the World*, for Martha Graham and her dance group; and several pieces of chamber music, including a Piano Sonata. Kennan's *Night Soliloquy* has been recorded by the Eastman School Orchestra for Victor; Kubik's most extended work is a setting of Vachel Lindsay's *In Praise of Johnny Appleseed*, for orchestra, chorus, and baritone solo; and McHose, at present an Eastman faculty member, has composed, among other works, a Concerto for oboe and orchestra which treats old tunes in modern fashion.

There are also a number of composers, not mentioned elsewhere in this volume, whose works have been performed at the American Composers' Concerts at the Eastman School, the annual Eastman Festival of American Music, or the more recently founded Symposium. The list includes:

Martha Alter (Orchestral Introduction and Song from *Bill George*, March, 1932; Suite for violin, piano, and percussion, May, 1932; *Anthony Comstock*, a ballet, May, 1934); *Victor Alessandro* (*Serenade* for strings, November, 1936, January, 1937; Sinfonietta for Wind Instruments, April, 1937); *Russell Baum* (*Variations on a Theme of Paganini*, for orchestra and piano, October, 1935; *Passacaglia and Fugue*, January, 1938); *William Bergsma* (*Pioneer Saga*, April, 1939); *Abraham W. Binder* (*Valley of Dry Bones*, October, 1936); *Anthony Donato* (*Three Imitations* for string quartet, May, 1937); *Alvin Etler* (*Music for Chamber Orchestra*, April, 1939; Etler received a Guggenheim Fellowship in 1940); *George Foote* (*Variations on a Pious Theme*, April 2, 1931—also performed by the Boston Symphony, February, 1935); *Harold Gleason* (*Prelude on a Gregorian Theme*, October 29, 1931); *Henrietta*

NEWCOMERS

Glick (*Paris, 1927*, symphonic suite, April, 1931); *William P. Grant* (Symphony in D minor, Adagio and Scherzo, October, 1936); *Edmund Haines* (*Symphony in Miniature*, April, 1940); *Arthur Henderson* (Sonata for violin and piano, April, 1937); *Frank Hruby* (*Satirical Suite*, April, 1939); *Dorothy James* (Excerpts from *Paolo and Francesca*, opera, April, 1931; *Three Orchestral Fragments*, March, 1932); *Gerald Keenan* (*Andante, Interlude,* and *Finale,* for horn and strings, April, 1935); *Homer Keller* (*Serenade* for clarinet and strings, January, 1938; in December, 1939, Keller's first Symphony was awarded the $500 prize of the Henry Hadley Foundation); *Gordon Kinney* (*Concert Piece* for piano and orchestra, November, 1936); *A. C. Kroeger* (Symphony in E Flat, February, 1931); *Edward Kurtz* (Scherzo, March, 1932); *Irving Landau* (*Free Variations* for orchestra, May, 1933; Sinfonietta, November, 1934); *Erik Leidzen* (*Fugue with Chorale*, October, 1936); *Marjorie T. MacKown* (Theme and Variations, for cello and orchestra, December, 1934; Piano Quartet, April, 1936); *Hugh McColl* (*Romantic Suite in Form of Variations*, October, 1936); *Joseph La Monaca* (Three Dances from *The Festival of Gauri*, May, 1934); *Walter Mourant* (*Five Inhibitions*, January, 1937; *Three Dances*, October, 1939); *Robert Nelson* (*Ballet Suite* for orchestra, February, 1931); *Robert Palmer* (*Poem* for violin and orchestra, January, 1939, April, 1939); *Owen Reed* (Symphony, April, 1939); *Herman Rudin* (Prelude and Dance from *Impressionistic Suite*, October, 1932; Suite for strings, May, 1934; *Symphonic Fragments*, November, 1934; Quartet, April, 1937); *Gustave Soderlund* (*Symphonic Interlude*, April, 1935); *Charles Vardell* (*Joe Clark Steps Out*, January, 1934, April, 1939; *Folk Symphony from the Carolina Hills*, April, 1938); *Lazar Weiner* (*Prelude, Dance, Little Story*, May, 1934); *York Wynn* (*Night Clouds*, April, 1939).

FROM THE CURTIS INSTITUTE

While our records show only two composers from the Curtis Institute to be presented in this chapter, *Samuel Barber* and *Gian-Carlo Menotti*, these men have achieved such wide recognition that they have assumed prime importance among the newcomers.

Barber, a nephew of Louise Homer, was born in West Chester, Pennsylvania, March 9, 1910, and by the time he was twenty-five years old had won several of the prizes most coveted by young composers: in 1928 and in 1933 the Bearns Prize from Columbia University, and in 1935 both the Pulitzer Scholarship and the American Prix de Rome. He won the Pulitzer award again the next year, thereby becoming the first composer to achieve this honor twice. At the Curtis Institute he studied conducting with Fritz Reiner, singing with Emilio de Gogorza, and composition with Rosario Scalero.

The work that won the 1933 Bearns Prize was the Overture to *The School for Scandal*, composed in 1932. The next major orchestral work, written in the following year, was entitled *Music for a Scene from Shelley*, taking for its inspiration certain lines from *Prometheus Unbound*. It was given its first performance in March, 1935, by the New York Philharmonic-Symphony, under Werner Janssen, and on this occasion the reviewer for *Musical America*[7] wrote: "The young man has written an appealing work . . . investing a broad melody with shimmering color and tender mood. Great originality is not apparent, but great promise is."

Barber's *Symphony in One Movement* was composed while he was a Fellow at the American Academy in Rome, and had its first performance in Rome by the orchestra of the Augusteo, under Molinari, late in 1936. Artur Rodzinski introduced it to the United States with the Cleveland Orchestra, in Cleveland in

---

[7] April 10, 1935.

Samuel Barber

January, 1937, and in New York during the following month. In the summer of the same year, Rodzinski conducted the Symphony at Salzburg and in London, announcing that he considered Barber one of the greatest of American composers. The work had a performance also by the New York Philharmonic-Symphony Orchestra in March of the same year, when Francis Perkins commented:[8]

> The symphony reinforced the impression of marked ability and promise made by the composer's earlier orchestral work. It presents clearly defined musical ideas of considerable cogency in an instrumental garb wrought with unusual mastery; the orchestral medium combines clarity with an exceptionally well developed knowledge of the resources of the orchestral palette; the colors are selected and blended by one who has a definite idea in this regard and knows how to attain it.

In November of 1938 a signal honor came to Barber: Arturo Toscanini chose his *Adagio for Strings*, and his *Essay for Orchestra*, as the first American works to be presented under his direction of the NBC Symphony Orchestra. This choice caused considerable resentment among left-wing musicians, for they felt that Barber was too conservative for such a distinction, but on the general public the works made a favorable and musicianly impression. The *Adagio* was performed by the New York Philharmonic-Symphony in January, 1940.

Barber's chamber-music works include a Serenade for string quartet; a String Quartet in B minor; a Sonata for cello and piano; and *Dover Beach*, for medium voice and string quartet. A choral work, *God's Grandeur*, written in free polyphonic style with plentiful dissonance, was performed at the Westminster Festival in Princeton, New Jersey, in May, 1938.

Menotti represents something of a phenomenon in American music; before he was twenty-six he had completed, and seen produced, an opera of such sparkling gayety and charm that it disarmed all criticism. He is also unique in being a foreigner who

---

[8] *New York Herald Tribune*, March 26, 1937.

came to America to study music. Born in Milan, July 7, 1911, he was from childhood steeped in the traditions of the theatre. From his family's box at La Scala, he heard the works of Mozart, Rossini, Wagner, Puccini, Verdi, Bellini, and Donizetti. With other members of his family (he was the sixth of ten children) he played chamber music. In 1928 he came to America with his mother, to study with Rosario Scalero at the Curtis Institute, and he has lived in this country ever since.

Although he had already composed numerous shorter works, his opera, *Amelia al Ballo* (*Amelia Goes to the Ball*), was his first large work of any kind. Begun when he was twenty-two, its composition took two and a half years, the composer writing his own libretto. The work was first produced by the opera department of the Curtis Institute under Fritz Reiner, in Philadelphia and New York. After the New York performance, Francis Perkins wrote in the *Herald Tribune:* [9]

> The music and the book, both in a vein of amusing satire, are a remarkably deft and mature work for a young man of twenty-five. . . . In reproducing the general style of this genre of opera [opera bouffe] and doing so with notable lightness and sureness of touch the composer has not provided an imitation of Rossini or some earlier specialist in this form but has written a score distinctly his own. It would be possible to name a few influences, but these have been merged in an individual and exceptionally effective style, suggesting the development of a technique and craftsmanship in writing for the lyric stage which should carry the composer far.

The following season, in March of 1938, the work was produced at the Metropolitan Opera House, New York, and with notable success, even though the larger auditorium was not as well suited to the intimate nature of *Amelia* as was the smaller New Amsterdam Theatre, where the Curtis Institute had presented it. After the first performance at the Metropolitan Lawrence Gilman wrote, in part: [10]

[9] April 12, 1937.
[10] *New York Herald Tribune,* March 4, 1938.

It is essentially Latin in its plot, its characters, its psychology, its motivation . . . and its score is written with a sense of the stage, an innate awareness of what will be effective in the theatre, a wit and gusto and deftness that are the product of two centuries or so of operatic tradition and inheritance. . . .

Occasionally the hand is a bit heavy, and the orchestra would seem better suited to the comedy if it were more transparent and lighter in texture. . . . But this is an astonishing piece of work, and arouses the liveliest curiosity regarding Mr. Menotti's future output.

It was not long before Menotti was able to satisfy, partially at least, the critics' and public's curiosity as to what he would do next, for the National Broadcasting Company commissioned him to write an opera for radio, which was produced by that organization in April, 1939. Its title was *The Old Maid and the Thief*, and once more the composer supplied his own libretto for a satirical farce. After the performance, Francis Perkins, who had predicted after hearing *Amelia* that the young composer's craftsmanship would carry him far, had this to say: [11]

Mr. Menotti's score resembles that of "Amelia" in its skill and craftsmanship, its ability to reproduce and emphasize the atmosphere of scenes and situations, and while its style continues to be primarily that of Latin opera buffa, there are fewer moments when it recalls any particular master in that field. . . . In general, it emphasizes the impression of waxing individuality and understanding the particular demands of music of this genre made by its predecessor. It is distinguished more by craftsmanship and effectiveness than by unusually salient ideas, but the craftsmanship is remarkable.

Aside from his operas, Menotti has composed only a few works that have been performed in this country. In 1931 a piano composition, *Variations on a Theme of Robert Schumann*, won the Carl F. Lauber Music Award; and his *Pastorale* for string orchestra and piano was performed by the Philadelphia Chamber String Sinfonietta in 1935, and at the Saratoga (New York) Spa Music Festival in 1937.

[11] *New York Herald Tribune*, April 23, 1939.

FROM OTHER SCHOOLS AND TEACHERS

Other institutions, too, have contributed their share of newcomers among the composers. One of the most individual talents of them all, *Robert Guyn McBride,* received virtually all of his training in the Far West, at the University of Arizona. Born at Tucson, February 20, 1911, the young McBride made his first approach to music in thoroughly up-to-date fashion. At ten he started playing the clarinet, then the oboe, the saxophone, and the piano. He was constantly busy in school bands, local theatre orchestras, and jazz bands. At the University he specialized in public school music, and received his Bachelor's degree in 1933. Two years later he took his Master's degree in composition, and then joined the faculty of Bennington College in Vermont. In 1937 he was awarded a Guggenheim Fellowship.

His works point to his youthful occupations, not only in their idiom but also in the subjects which they portray: the *Go Choruses* (commissioned in 1936 by the League of Composers), based on the adventures of a jazz band where each player in turn takes a chorus of the tune and "goes" with it; the jazzy *Fugato on a Well-known Theme,* and *Jingle Jangle* and *Swing Stuff* (all three recorded by RCA-Victor); and finally, *Workout* for chamber orchestra.

Not all of McBride's works are of as light a texture, however; if he chooses, he can be grim and unrelenting. When his *Prelude to a Tragedy* was introduced to New York by the Philharmonic-Symphony in November, 1935, Lawrence Gilman wrote in the *Herald Tribune:* [12]

> This Prelude ... is spare, compact, austere, disdaining rhetoric and the lush lamentings of romantic grief. It is hard-visaged music, stern, implacable, full of the hammer strokes of Destiny—not the C-minorish Destiny of the early gods, not borrowed properties out of Beethoven's sublime storehouse, but a private Destiny of Mr. Mc-

[12] November 21, 1935.

Bride's; something that he has known and experienced in his own imagination.

In similar vein is *Depression* (1934), a sonata for violin and piano; but brighter moments, and the composer's breeziness of spirit, are manifest in his *Mexican Rhapsody* for orchestra (1934), in the ballet, *Show Piece* (1937), and in the Prelude and Fugue for string quartet (1936). In July, 1940, McBride and the Gordon String Quartet gave the first performance of a new Quintet entitled, characteristically, *Wise-Apple Five*.

While McBride, with Otto Luening, is teaching music to the young ladies of Bennington, another comparative newcomer, *William Schuman*, is performing a similar service at that other shrine of progressive education, Sarah Lawrence College, in Bronxville, New York. Like Luening and McBride, Schuman has been a Guggenheim Fellow (1939 and 1940). Born in New York City in 1910, he is a graduate of Columbia University, and a composition pupil of Persin, Haubiel, and Harris, and has studied at the Mozarteum Academy in Salzburg, Austria.

Two of his works have been performed by the Boston Symphony Orchestra: the second Symphony, in February, 1939, and an *American Festival Overture* the following October and November. The Symphony proved to be an unconventional work, with abundant dissonance and a construction which indicated that the composer has an independent, inquiring mind. The Overture opens with three notes which Schuman describes as the call for getting groups of New York boys together for "an auspicious occasion." The development of subsequent material is lively and spirited, even though the work suffers slightly from looseness of construction in the fugal section.

Schuman's first Symphony was composed in 1935, scored for a chamber orchestra of eighteen instruments. He has also a Prelude and Fugue for orchestra (1937), a number of choral works, and three String Quartets (1936, 1937 and 1940). His cantata, *This Is Our Time*, on a text by Genevieve Taggard, was performed on July 4, 1940, by the New York Philharmonic-Symphony Stadium Orchestra and the People's Philharmonic Choral Society, under the baton of Alexander Smallens.

Frederic Hart, Schuman's colleague on the music faculty of Sarah Lawrence College, was born in Aberdeen, Washington, on September 5, 1898, and received his musical education in Chicago, New York and Paris. He studied piano with Glenn Dillard Gunn, Ernest Hutcheson, and Elizabeth Quaile, and composition with Arthur Olav Andersen, Mortimer Wilson, Rubin Goldmark, and Nadia Boulanger. Although he has published a considerable number of songs and piano pieces, he first came to public attention through his *Romance of Robot*, a one-act satirical opera produced by the Federal Music Theatre, which achieved no less than twenty performances in 1937. He also has in manuscript a three-act romantic light opera, *The Wheel of Fortune;* a String Quartet; a Suite for string trio; and a Concert Overture for orchestra.

Aaron Copland may claim several of his younger colleagues as pupils, among them *Paul Frederic Bowles* and *Israel Citkowitz*. Bowles was born in New York City, in 1911, and studied with Virgil Thomson as well as with Copland. His interest in folk-music has taken him to Spain, Northern Africa, the Sahara, the Antilles, and South and Central America. No doubt his residence in these lands lent verity to his most widely known work, the ballet, *Yankee Clipper*, for this imaginative piece describes the adventures of a young farmer who goes to sea and voyages around the world. At every port music appropriate to the locale helps to establish the color and atmosphere. The score depicts many and varied moods, and shows its composer to be an excellent craftsman, possessed of a vivid imagination. The work was first performed by the Philadelphia Orchestra in April, 1937, and, in February, 1938, by the Ballet Caravan in New York.

Bowles has written other music for the stage, particularly the incidental music for WPA productions of *Horse Eats Hat* and Marlowe's *Doctor Faustus,* and for the Helen Hayes-Maurice Evans *Twelfth Night*. He has also composed a Suite for small orchestra; a piece for nine instruments entitled *Melodia*; a Trio; a three-act opera, *Denmark Vesey*; a Cantata; and several shorter pieces.

Citkowitz, born in Russia in 1909, was brought to America as an infant. His study with Copland was supplemented by work with Roger Sessions and with Nadia Boulanger, and he has taught composition at the Dalcroze School of Music in New York. Specializing in chamber music, sometimes with voices, he has heard his works performed mostly by those groups that foster and promote contemporary music. His first String Quartet was performed at the first Yaddo Festival, at Saratoga, New York, in 1932; his *Sonatine* for piano at the Vienna section of the International Society for Contemporary Music (1933); and his *Song Cycle to Words of Joyce* at the London section of the same organization. The Dessoff Choirs gave a New York performance of his sensitive setting of William Blake's poem, *The Lamb*, composed in 1936, while the New Singers presented his *Songs of Protest* (1936).

It is in his songs that Citkowitz shows his lightest touch, for as David Ewen once wrote: [13]

> Citkowitz spins a gossamer web of the most delicate material. In his tonal palette there are only pale colors—grays, lavenders and mauves. But with these colors, Citkowitz etches moods with most subtle artistry. . . . His piano sonatina and his first string quartet may have a greater pretentiousness and a wider scope, but they can never match the artistic perfection of his songs.

Sessions, who had a hand in Citkowitz's training, was also one of the teachers of *Ross Lee Finney*, a composer who may boast an imposing list of teachers: Donald Ferguson at Northwestern University, Edward Burlingame Hill at Harvard, Sessions, and in Europe, Malipiero, Alban Berg, and Nadia Boulanger. Finney was born in Wells, Minnesota, December 23, 1906, and is at present associate professor of music at Smith College. During the

[13] *Musical Courier*, September 16, 1933.

season of 1937–38 he was awarded a Guggenheim Fellowship and also a Pulitzer award, the latter for a String Quartet.

Finney is not particularly interested in nationalism, at least a self-conscious nationalism, for he feels that his own Americanism will render it impossible for his music to be anything but American. Being known as a conservative holds no horrors for him; conscious modernism, he feels, would be far worse. He is concerned chiefly with composing music that will express his own individuality with as fine a technical command as he can achieve.

His orchestral works include a Piano Concerto (1934); a Violin Concerto (1936); and a *Prelude for a Drama* (1937). A choral work, *John Brown,* was composed in 1939, and the dance drama, *Masse Mensch* (1936) was given nine performances at Smith College. His chamber-music list numbers a Trio (1931); two Piano Sonatas (1932 and 1933); a Sonata for violin and piano (1934); and two String Quartets (1935 and 1937). In September, 1940, at Yaddo, he sang his own *Bletheris, a Monody, from the Hamlet of Archibald MacLeish,* with chamber orchestra accompaniment.

DANTE FIORILLO

Dante Fiorillo, one of the most talented of the newcomers, has shown a singular ability to escape attention. Although he has several times been awarded a Guggenheim Fellowship, and in 1939 was granted a Pulitzer award, his name appears in none of the important reference books and encyclopedias. Born in New York City, July 4, 1905, he was a cello student at Greenwich House Music School, but is altogether self-taught in composition. For a time he taught music at Harlem House, New York City, but at present devotes all of his time to composition.

His output has been enormous; at the time of his winning the Pulitzer prize, it was announced that the award had been made on the basis of eight of the twelve symphonies he had written. In addition to these works there are several Partitas for orchestra;

several Concerti for various instruments with orchestra; a number of String Quartets; several Piano Quintets and Trios; numerous Sonatas for piano and for other instruments; a Horn Quintet; and other pieces for orchestra and for organ, as well as songs and choruses. "In fact," Fiorillo remarks, "I've tried everything."

Although his work is known and highly respected by a few musicians, he has been accorded few conspicuous performances. The New York Civic Orchestra, the Chamber Orchestra of Philadelphia, the New York Philharmonic-Symphony Chamber Orchestra, have given an occasional playing to his works, and he has had hearings at the Yaddo Festivals and at the New School for Social Research, but as far as major organizations are concerned, his music has been sadly neglected. That this neglect is undeserved seems altogether probable. When Ralph Kirkpatrick played Fiorillo's Concerto for harpsichord and strings with the Durieux Ensemble, it was clear that this composer has no lack of interesting things to say, or means to say them with.

The Bush Conservatory, in Chicago, was responsible for the early training of *Robert L. Sanders*, and in 1925 awarded him a Master's degree. At the same time he won the American Prix de Rome and lived at the American Academy from 1925 to June, 1929. He has come into prominence largely through being a co-winner, with Charles Haubiel, of the New York Philharmonic-Symphony contest for a short symphonic work, in 1938. Sanders' piece was entitled *Little Symphony in G,* and it was first performed, under the composer's baton, by the Philharmonic-Symphony in February, 1939. It proved to be a pleasant piece, described by the reviewer of the *New York Times* [14] as "an attractive sheaf of music which will probably be welcomed by the nation's orchestras."

For this, the reasons are simple: a few folksy tunes, fitting harmonic raiment and unpretentious musical forms. . . . Indeed, the most ad-

[14] February 27, 1939.

mirable thing about this music may well be the fitness of manner to matter.

In January, 1940, the *Little Symphony* was played by the Indianapolis Symphony, and later in the same month repeated by the New York Philharmonic-Symphony. Sanders was born in Chicago in 1906, and in addition to his studies at the Bush Conservatory he worked abroad with Respighi, Bustini, and Dobici. At present he is a faculty member of two institutions: the University of Chicago and the Chicago Conservatory of Music, and is also assistant conductor of the Chicago Civic Orchestra.

Several years before winning the Philharmonic-Symphony prize, Sanders had heard another of his works performed by the same organization, when *Saturday Night,* a "barn dance" was played in February, 1934. This piece, subsequently published, is built on four original melodies, and adheres closely to traditional form. Other works include a Violin Concerto (1935); a Suite for Large Orchestra (1928); the symphonic *Scenes of Poverty and Toil* (1935); a Trio (1926); a Violin and Piano Sonata (1929); a Cello and Piano Sonata (1932); a String Quartet (1929); and several choral works.

A *Symphonic Intermezzo* by *Florence Grandland Galajikian* (Maywood, Illinois, 1900) was awarded the fourth prize in the NBC orchestral contest of 1932. She is a graduate of the Northwestern School of Music and Chicago Musical College, and a pupil of Rubin Goldmark and Albert Noelte. She was awarded a scholarship to study with Respighi in 1935, but the Italian composer's illness and death prevented its being used. She is at present active as a teacher of piano and composition in Chicago. She has also composed a *Tragic Overture* for orchestra (1934); a Fantasie for violin and piano (1930); an *Andante and Scherzo* for string quartet (1935); several choral works; and a ballet, *Transitions* (1937).

Because of his research in the fields of acoustics, aesthetics, musicotherapy, and kindred subjects, *Paul Creston* might conceivably be placed among the experimenters, but his music does not altogether justify such a classification. Leonard Liebling made this distinction clear when he reviewed Creston's Suite for saxophone (or clarinet) and piano. He wrote: [15]

> Here is something in contemporary style which will please the advance guard and not offend the reactionaries and standpatters. Creston's form and construction move along conservative lines, but his harmonies and rhythms speak the tonal language of the moment. If there is concordance in dissonance, you can find it here, much to the satisfaction of any sort of taste. Freshness in ideas, clever colors, and a certain healthy brightness seem to prove that Creston does not write merely because he has technic, but chiefly because he feels creative urge. His new suite has atonal freedom, with the result that the integrated passage writing is especially alive and flexible.

Creston was born in New York, October 10, 1906, and is self-taught in harmony, theory and composition. He did, however, study other branches of music with Randegger and Déthier, and organ with Pietro Yon. At present he is organist and choirmaster at St. Malachy's Church in New York. He was awarded a Guggenheim Fellowship in 1938, and again in 1939. Among his works are a Prelude and Dance, and a Symphony, for orchestra; a Partita for flute, violin, and strings; and a long list of chamber-music works, several of which have been performed at the Yaddo and the Westminster Festivals, and elsewhere. His *Two Choric Dances* were performed by the National Symphony Orchestra in Washington under Hans Kindler, on March 3, 1940. His Concertino for marimba and orchestra was played at Yaddo in September, 1940. Perkins [16] found it "graceful and melodic and advantageous for the soloist, while not of unusual consequence in regard to its musical ideas." But then, as someone has remarked, it would be hard to be very significant on the marimba.

David Van Vactor is another winner of a prize from the New York Philharmonic-Symphony Society, for his Symphony in D

---
[15] *Musical Courier*, July 1, 1938.
[16] *New York Herald Tribune*, September 9, 1940.

was awarded first prize in the contest of 1938, and received its première performance in January, 1939. The following April it was played by the Chicago Symphony and in November by the Cleveland Orchestra.

Van Vactor was born in Plymouth, Indiana, in 1906, and received most of his education at Northwestern University, where he is at present an instructor. When he graduated from the University he went to Vienna to study the flute with Niedermayr, and during the summer of 1932 he lived in Paris, studying the flute with Moyse and composition with Paul Dukas. Meanwhile he had become a member of the Chicago Symphony Orchestra.

His orchestral works include a symphonic prelude, *Masque of the Red Death* (1932), which won honorable mention in the Swift Competition; a Chaconne for strings (1928); an overture, *Cristobal Colon* (1930); a Passacaglia and Fugue in D minor (1933); an *Overture to a Comedy* (1935); a Concerto Grosso (1935); the prize-winning Symphony (1937); and a Concerto for flute and twenty-one instruments (1931). In addition there are a number of chamber-music works, and a ballet, *The Play of Words* (1934).

There are many others of our younger composers who have received the major part of their training at home. *Radie Britain* (Amarillo, Texas, 1903) studied at the American Conservatory in Chicago before she went to Paris for work with Dupré, and to Germany to study with Noelte. Many of her works have won prizes; the amusing *Theme and Variations on the Old Gray Mare* winning one in her home state of Texas (1934). Her more serious works include a *Heroic Poem* for orchestra (1929), a *Southern Symphony* (1937), choral and chamber-music works, and a ballet.

Mark Brunswick (New York City, 1902) studied with Goldmark, Bloch, Boulanger, and Sessions. He is known best for his Ballet-Suite from *Lysistrata,* and his Symphony for chorus and orchestra. *William D. Denny* (Seattle, Washington, 1910), awarded the Prix de Rome in 1939, is a graduate of the University of California (Bachelor's and Master's Degrees) who supplemented his work at home by studying under Dukas in Paris.

Oscar Levant (Pittsburgh, 1906) is perhaps entitled to a volume of his own, and he has, in fact, provided us with a merry one,[17] but unfortunately our book must confine itself to his compositions, rather than to the startling fund of information and ready wit displayed in his own remarkable work, or on the *Information Please* radio program. Suffice it to note, therefore, that he studied piano with Stojowski and composition with Schoenberg, and that in addition to popular songs his works include a Piano Concerto (1936); a String Quartet (1937); an orchestral Nocturne (1936); and music for sound films.

Two American institutions have been responsible for training *Allan A. Wilman* (Hinckley, Illinois, 1909)—the Knox College Conservatory at Galesburg, Illinois, and the Chicago Musical College. He has also studied privately in Chicago, and with Boulanger in Paris. In 1935 he was awarded the Paderewski Prize, and his works include a *Ballade of the Night* for voice and string quartet, performed at the 1937 Eastman Festival; a symphonic poem, *Solitude*, performed in 1936 by the Boston Symphony; a Symphonic Overture (1935); a Piano Sonata (1930); and a Suite for violin and piano (1937).

Robert Mills Delaney (Baltimore, Maryland, 1903), a Guggenheim Fellow in 1929–30, and in 1933 winner of a Pulitzer prize for his setting of Benét's *John Brown's Body*, studied both at home and abroad. In the United States he worked at the University of Southern California and in Paris he was a student of Nadia Boulanger at the École Normale de Musique and a private violin pupil of Capet. On completion of his training he became a theory instructor at the School of Music in Concord, Massachusetts, and later was music director at the Santa Barbara School in California. His long list of works includes a *Don Quixote Symphony* (1930); a Symphonic Piece No. 1 (1935) and a

[17] *A Smattering of Ignorance* (New York: Doubleday, Doran and Company, 1940).

Symphonic Piece No. 2 (1937); many choral works in addition to *John Brown's Song* (1931); several String Quartets; and an early Violin Sonata (1927). His *Work 22* was performed by the New York City Symphony Orchestra, a unit of the WPA Federal Music Project, in March, 1940.

Normand Lockwood (New York City, 1906) supplemented his studies at the University of Michigan School of Music with work abroad under Boulanger and Respighi. He has been the winner of several prizes: the Prix de Rome (1929-32); the Swift Award (1935); and in 1938 the $500 prize offered by G. Schirmer, Inc., for a choral work, *Out of the Cradle Endlessly Rocking*, dedicated to the World's Fair in New York. Since 1933 he has been associate professor of theory and composition at Oberlin College in Ohio. Aside from a Symphony, which was performed in April, 1935, by the Chicago Symphony Orchestra, and some chamber music, almost all of Lockwood's major works are for chorus: *Drum Taps* (1930); a *Requiem* (1931); *The Hound of Heaven* (1937); and many shorter pieces.

When Lockwood's Quintet for piano and strings was played at Yaddo, in September, 1940, Francis D. Perkins wrote: [18]

> Much of this was impressive and revealed salient individuality of style. The opening adagio in particular gave a sense of unusual expressive intensity, of an instrumental medium skilfully brought to the service of the desired emotional atmosphere. Imaginative appeal was also in evidence elsewhere, including the well contrasted third section, an allegro in rondo form. But the marked effectiveness of the work as a whole was somewhat weakened by its length; the finale was rather discursive and episodic and had its repetitious moments. The vigor and percussiveness which marked the piano part had their value in the expressive significance of the music, but the frequent appearance of such characteristics detracted from their ultimate effect.

Even though he is older than most of the men and women in this chapter, *Tibor Serly* (Hungary, 1900), has come to the pub-

[18] *New York Herald Tribune*, September 9, 1940.

lic's attention as a composer so recently that he seems to belong with the newcomers. Although a number of his works had enjoyed earlier American performances (among them a Sonata for violin and piano, in New York, 1923), it was not until the Philadelphia Orchestra played his first Symphony, in January, 1937, that he became known to the general public. He was brought to this country as a small child, and after private study at home, with A. W. Lilienthal, he went to Europe in 1931. Three years later he graduated from the Budapest Royal Academy with honors in composition, which he studied under Kodály. He has been a viola player in the Cincinnati Symphony Orchestra (1927–28), in the Philadelphia Orchestra (1928–36), and in the NBC Symphony Orchestra. In addition to the Violin Sonata and the Symphony, his works include a String Quartet (1924); a Viola Concerto (1929); two Symphonic Movements for winds and percussion (1932); and other pieces.

Anton Bilotti (New York City, 1904) seems to be unique in this group as an American composer who received all of his musical training abroad. At the age of nine he was taken to Naples to study at the Royal Conservatory. He was awarded a scholarship at the Naples Conservatory, and then studied with Busoni. Later he was one of the few pupils of Vladimir De Pachmann. After a debut in New York in 1921, he made his headquarters in Paris for twelve years, and then returned to America. His works include a number of published piano pieces, and a Concerto for piano and orchestra which he performed with the National Orchestral Association in New York (March, 1938).

Ray Green occupies the post once held by Ernest Bloch—that of head of the composition department at the San Francisco Conservatory of Music. Green is a pupil of Bloch, too, as well as of Elkus and Milhaud, and has studied conducting with Pierre Monteux and Gregorian chant with Silva. He is a native of Cavendish, Missouri, where he was born in 1908. He has won scholarships and prizes of the San Francisco Conservatory, the

University of California, and the Carnegie Foundation, and is a member of the advisory board of *New Music*. His compositions include a Concertino for piano and orchestra; a Prelude and Fugue for orchestra; music for *The Birds* of Aristophanes; and several pieces of choral and chamber music.

6

EXPERIMENTERS

THIS is an age of change and revolution in many fields, as the hectic fourth decade, just closed, bore ample witness. In music, the fires of revolt were kindled almost as soon as the century was born, and there has been a merry blaze ever since.

But while this has been true all over the world, we must not forget that the spirit of experiment, freedom from convention, a certain "cussedness" are in the American blood. And where should we have been without it? From Roger Williams, Patrick Henry, and John Adams to Thomas Edison, Henry Ford, and "Wrong-Way" Corrigan, impatience with convention has been one of our salient characteristics.

It has not been lacking among our composers. The most daring heresies of Europe were not unprecedented here, even though our own rebels were not known at the time to either their foreign or their American contemporaries. Experimenters, pioneers, forgers of new paths, composers of the future, crackpots, musical anarchists, downright fakers—we have had our share of them all.

The difficulty is that to their contemporaries they all sound very much alike, especially at first hearing. The notoriety-seeker who tries as hard as he can to shock the public and the critics, and the true pioneer, boldly hewing out a new language—both are apt to sound simply unintelligible to the untutored, and often even to the tutored. This results in great injustices. The builder of the music of the future may be dismissed as a fraud or a lunatic, while the real fraud is listened to respectfully by an audience that has been taught that it must be tolerant. It is not fair, but there doesn't seem to be much we can do about it. On the whole, it would be better to let a few frauds escape detection than to suppress, out of narrow-mindedness, a really original and creative voice. There was once a time when our critics and our audiences were reluctant to listen to music that did not speak to them in familiar accents, when young composers had to struggle for a hearing, when ticket-holders canceled their subscriptions because "modern" music was inflicted on them. Perhaps we are going too far in the other direction now, and listening to music good and bad with a tolerance that borders on indifference.

Two things are sure, at any rate. The first is that only posterity will be able to pass definite judgments on our contemporaries. The other is that our rebels cannot all be right, for they disagree among themselves.

Probably they are not all wrong, either. History is full, as we have often been told, of bold and original spirits who have been misjudged and wrongly condemned by their contemporaries. So it behooves us to think twice before dismissing unfamiliar sounds as mere noise. Few of us can find the staff of life among the extremists. But they add spice to our diet, and so we welcome them collectively, even though at times we forget to welcome them quite so cordially as individuals.

Among those whose point of view it is easiest to understand is the group of composers who have felt that the musical language needed enrichment in the form of new scales, new instrumental colors, and the like. They differ from our composers in "Unfamiliar Idioms" only in the degree of unfamiliarity, and of course the line between the two groups cannot be drawn with complete accuracy.

SCIENTIFIC INNOVATORS

Hans Barth is an American apostle of quarter-tone music. He has built a piano with two keyboards, and two sets of strings, tuned a quarter-tone apart, upon which he has given many recitals of his own and other composers' music. He has also appeared with several major symphony orchestras playing his own Concertos, both "half-tone" and quarter-tone. Barth was born in 1897, in Leipzig, Germany, and came to this country as a young child. He is a well-known teacher and writer on piano technique, as well as composer. His works include a Suite for strings, brass, and kettledrums, and a Concerto for piano and strings, both quarter-tone; two other Piano Concertos; two Piano Sonatas; an opera, *Miragia*; and a *Pantomime Symphony*.

Many musicians who agree with Barth that the half-tone is too large to serve as the smallest unit of our tonal system disagree with him in their feeling that the mere simple division of our "artificially" tempered semitones for two is too arbitrary and systematic a procedure. *Joseph Yasser*, a theorist rather than a composer, who was born in Lodz, Poland, April 16, 1893, believes that tonality is an evolving thing, and that its history justifies the assumption that just as our tonal system (the diatonic) contains seven primary and five auxiliary tones, so the tonal system of the next evolutionary stage will consist of twelve primary and seven auxiliary tones. The tempering of this system would result in a division of the octave into nineteen equal parts. Yasser has worked out his viewpoint in minute detail and created an impressive theoretical structure.[1] His interest is in explaining tendencies, both past and future, rather than in the practical application, in composition or performance, of the principles he has enunciated.

Arthur Fickenscher, who heads the music department of the University of Virginia, in Charlottesville, carries the subdivision of the semitone as far as sixty tones to the octave, and has invented an instrument, the "Polytone," designed to further research in pure intonation. He was born in Aurora, Illinois, in 1871 (many of our experimenters are no youngsters!), and is

[1] *A Theory of Evolving Tonality* (New York: American Library of Musicology, 1932).

a graduate of the Royal Conservatory in Munich, Germany. He has composed several orchestral works: *Willowwave and Wellaway, Day of Judgment, Out of the Gay Nineties,* and *Variations on a Theme in Medieval Style,* all since 1925; and several pieces of chamber and choral music.

The music of *Ruth Crawford,* which is constructed in elaborate and intricate patterns, both formal and rhythmic, is not intended for a mass audience. Miss Crawford was born in East Liverpool, Ohio, in 1901, the daughter of a Methodist preacher. She studied with Weidig, and in 1930 received a Guggenheim Fellowship for study in Berlin and Paris. During the late '30's she lived in Washington, where the work of her husband, Charles Seeger, in the Resettlement Administration and in the Federal Music Project of the WPA, brought her into contact with American folk-music. In this connection she collaborated with John and Alan Lomax in the editing of the second volume of *American Folk-songs and Ballads.* But in her own music she is as far as possible from folk-song. Seeger, in Henry Cowell's *American Composers on American Music,*[2] wrote that Miss Crawford's music could "very well find a permanent place in a small repertoire of an intellectual sort for a particular group of people who were interested in that sort of thing." In 1933 Miss Crawford's *Three Songs* for contralto, oboe, piano, and percussion, with orchestral ostinato, were chosen as one of two American works on the programs of the Festival of the International Society for Contemporary Music in Amsterdam. Her works include also a Violin Sonata; a String Quartet; *Three Movements* for wind instruments and piano; *Two Movements* for chamber orchestra; four *Diaphonic Suites* for flute, oboe, clarinets, and celli; and numerous other pieces.

The Mathematical Basis of the Arts is the title of a book by *Joseph Schillinger;* it reveals his attitude towards composition in a nutshell. Schillinger was born in Kharkov, Russia, in 1895, graduated from the St. Petersburg Conservatory in 1918, and held various posts as conductor and composer under the Soviet

[2] Stanford University Press, 1933.

government. In New York he has taught at Teachers College of Columbia University and at the New School for Social Research. His work as a teacher has not been confined to music but has included mathematics and the fine arts. Many Broadway composers have studied with him. He is the author of several orchestral works, including a *Symphonic Rhapsody* commissioned by the Soviet government to celebrate the tenth anniversary of the October Revolution, and of considerable music for chamber combinations and for the stage.

Two of our experimenters—Ruggles and Ives—have called forth ecstatic superlatives from their admirers, and are undoubtedly men of great originality.

UNICORN AND LION

The Americanism of *Carl Ruggles* goes deeper than the mere facts of his American birth, ancestry, and residence, so his admirers say. In a most readable article on Ruggles in Cowell's *American Composers on American Music*,[3] Charles Seeger writes:

Of course no orchestra is big enough: parts just naturally clamor unceasingly for extra horns and clarinets. Then again, there are only twelve semitones per octave, and everyone knows that is a pitiful number, especially when you have only eight octaves and, at least theoretically, no melody may repeat a given tone until at least nine or ten others have intervened. Furthermore, a melody starts way down in the bass and ascends: first thing you know it has reached a height where the characteristic tone-quality desired cannot be maintained— the first string of the cello can only go so far. Substitute after substitute, the limits of the gamut are there, and the melody is still full of energy to soar. Or perhaps a fine resounding chord, *fortississimo*, with about ten different constituents, simply must follow while all eight horns are ripping out a line in unison—there are not enough instruments in any orchestra in the country. And so on. Is it the composer's fault?

In Europe the same wants are felt. But there, if a man does not quickly learn to forget them and to confine himself to the use of the

[3] *Op. cit.*

means available he is not "routine," not *gründlich*, and the reproach is usually sufficient to put him in his place.

Or listen to Cowell, writing in the *New Freeman* back in May, 1930:

> Ives has built up a style on a direct basis of the idiosyncrasies of early American folk-music. Ruggles has taken the European standard of perfection, and gone it a step better than anyone in Europe.

These are strong words, but they sum up much of the character of Carl Ruggles. He is a perfectionist, forever polishing and refining and whittling away at his work. His object is the sublime grandeur that one finds in Bach and Handel. He composes partly by his own principles of melodic and harmonic structure, which have been called "formulae" by those who do not like them, and which inevitably call to mind the "tone-rows" of Schoenberg. But he is a healthy, rebellious, Rabelaisian, outdoor Yankee. As he himself says:

> All real composers create their own formulas—I know I have created formulas of my own and some moderns have said 'Ah, too bad, he goes by formula, if he wouldn't do that he would be a good composer,' but I make the point that a real composer should be able to break the formula, to bust it all to hell when he felt it necessary to bust it; otherwise you are the victim of your own formula, you have created only a Frankenstein monster.[4]

Ruggles was born on March 11, 1876, in Marion, Massachusetts. His ancestors were New Bedford whaling masters. From his mother he inherited his musical inclinations and received his earliest musical impressions. At an early age he learned to play the violin, and at nine appeared in a Lord Fauntleroy costume, as an infant prodigy, before President Cleveland, who was summering in Massachusetts. He went to Harvard, and later migrated to Winona, Minnesota, where he organized and conducted a symphony orchestra. He lives in Arlington, Vermont, in

[4] Interview, *New York Herald Tribune*, February 10, 1935.

a made-over schoolhouse that contains a music room forty feet square, and he likes to compose on "select pieces of wrapping-paper of varying colors and sizes, ruling his own staff-lines about one inch apart so that the notes are grand and fat, made often as not with colored crayon." [5] Clearly, Carl Ruggles is a real American in one sense at least: he loves bigness!

One is largely dependent on what his friends have had to say about him, because his music has not often been heard. His *Men and Mountains* and *Portals* have, however, been played by symphony orchestras in this country and abroad. *Sun Treader* was on the programs of the Barcelona Festival of the International Society for Contemporary Music. His music was first introduced on the programs of the International Composers' Guild, in which Varèse was the moving spirit, and such hearings as it has had have been owing largely to the efforts of Varèse and Henry Cowell.

A hint has been given of Ruggles's principle of non-repetition of notes in a melody. Reiteration (repetition without intervening notes) he finds occasionally useful, but other kinds of repetition at short intervals weaken the melody, he feels. His early works were frankly homophonic, and he finds melody the *sine qua non* of music. But his style has become increasingly polyphonic, and abounds in imitative complexity.

Of course one could not do justice to such phenomena as Ruggles in a few paragraphs, even if one had had greater opportunities for listening to his music. Either he is a great genius or he is crazy. Perhaps he is both; he would not be the first. At any rate he is a colorful figure, no doubt worth hearing, and very well worth reading about. Lawrence Gilman called him "the first unicorn to enter American music . . . the master of a strange, torrential, and disturbing discourse."

It was Gilman, too, who called *Charles E. Ives* "an unexampled creative artist of our day, probably the most original and extraordinary of American composers." The adjectives are richly

[5] Seeger, *loc. cit.*

deserved. Ives, in the first place, is almost unique in the way he went on for many years composing the most amazing works, and in an amazing quantity, without attracting, or apparently desiring, the least public notice. When Schoenberg, Stravinsky, Strauss, and a host of others were youngsters with all their startling innovations still ahead of them, Ives, completely out of sight, was writing pieces embodying many of their most startling "discoveries." Of course there is no implication that European composers knew Ives's work or were influenced by it; until very recently he was practically unknown, even in America.

He was born October 20, 1874, in Danbury, Connecticut. His father, George E. Ives, was a bandmaster, at the age of sixteen, in Grant's army. The story is told that Lincoln, referring to the band of Ives Senior (The First Connecticut Heavy Artillery Band) remarked to Grant, "That's a good band." "It's the best band in the Army, they tell me," Grant replied, "but you couldn't prove it by me. I know only two tunes: one of them is Yankee Doodle, and the other isn't."

It was not only a generally musical bent and the sound of band music in his ears that Ives got from his father; it was a genuine boldness and adventurousness in musical matters, which characterized the father no less than the son. For George E. Ives worked with a quarter-tone instrument many years ago, and was a ceaseless experimenter in acoustics. It is said that he placed several bands on different levels to try the effect of music coming to the listener in different planes. And along with the conventional harmony and counterpoint which he taught his son, we may be sure there was also many a hint about the unexplored possibilities of music, about chords constructed in fourths, and the like.

Ives spent four years at Yale, under Horatio Parker—who must have been astonished at the unheard-of musical notions of his pupil—and studied the organ with Dudley Buck. He was a church organist for some years: "Master Ives [who on the occasion referred to, had played Rossini's overture to *William Tell*, arranged by Dudley Buck, a Bach Toccata, *Home, Sweet Home*, the organ Sonata in F Minor of Mendelssohn, and other pieces] deserves and receives great praise for his patient perseverance in his study of the organ, and is to be congratulated on his marked ability as a master of the keys for one so young. We predict for him a brilliant future as an organist," wrote James Montgomery Bailey in the *Danbury News* for June 12, 1890.

In 1898, after graduating from Yale, Ives became a clerk with the Mutual Life Insurance Company, and later formed his own firm, Ives & Myrick, in which he was active until 1930, when ill health caused him to retire. Thus he was never a professional musician—at least not since those early days of church organ playing—and has composed entirely for his own pleasure in the leisure afforded him by his business activities. Moreover, he has never sought public attention, and his music has become known almost in spite of him. It was in the period from 1906 to 1916 that most of his major works were written. Since that time he has written mostly songs, hundreds of them, ranging from the simplest *Lieder* to those containing the most biting and aggressive dissonance and the most freakish rhythms.

The accidents of inexpert music-making in the country town, the "heterophonies" caused by the sounds of two bands playing at once as they marched along the streets, the efforts of a musician who had lost his place to get back into step with the rest, the wheezing of a reed-organ badly in need of a tuning, the authentic and by no means inexpert playing of the country fiddlers—all these and many more memories of American small-town life are dear to the heart of Charles Ives, and are reflected in his music. Thus, according to Henry Cowell [6]:

A good example of the Ivesian individual-part writing is in the latter part of *Washington's Birthday*, in which the orchestra changes from an Allegro to a slow movement. The viola, however, is still full of the feeling of the Allegro, so continues to play an altered version of it against the rest of the orchestra's Adagio! In the same work, in the Allegro, the flute-player feels that the tempo should be faster; so he

[6] *Op. cit.*

plays it faster than the rest of the men, and his measures come out a sixteenth-note shorter than those of the rest of the orchestra on this account.

"Washington's Birthday" is the first movement of a symphony, *Holidays,* of which the other movements are "Decoration Day," "Fourth of July," and "Thanksgiving."

The Second Piano Sonata is, the composer says, "an attempt to present (one person's) impression of the spirit of the literature, the philosophy, and the men of Concord, Mass., of over half a century ago." This *Concord Sonata* was written between 1911 and 1915, and was published in 1919; it is in four movements: 1. "Emerson;" 2. "Hawthorne;" 3. "The Alcotts;" 4. "Thoreau." The first movement is based on themes representing musical evaluations of Emerson's prose and of his poetry. The Hawthorne movement is a fantastic scherzo. The third movement, devoted to the Alcotts, is quiet and meditative, calling up visions of the village of Concord, of the old Alcott house beneath the elms, and of the spinet-piano on which Beth used to strum old Scotch airs, and play at Beethoven's Fifth Symphony. And this is Ives's cue to construct a rhapsody on the opening motive of the Fifth—the "Fate" theme—which he views as "the soul of humanity knocking at the door of the Mysteries, radiant in the hope that it will be opened." For the Thoreau movement, "if there shall be a program," writes the composer, "let it follow his thought on an autumn day of Indian summer at Walden—a shadow of a thought at first, colored by the mist and haze over the pond:

> Low anchored cloud,
> Fountain head and
> Source of rivers. . . .
> Dew cloth, dream drapery—
> Drifting meadow of the air. . . ."

The mood of stillness passes, and Thoreau is off for a walk through the woods, down to the lake, along the railroad, seeking to become one with Nature and suit his mood and tempo to hers.

The Sonata was first heard in its entirety in a recital by John Kirkpatrick in New York's Town Hall, on the evening of January 20, 1939. The next day, Lawrence Gilman wrote in the *New York Herald Tribune:*

This sonata is exceptionally great music—it is, indeed, the greatest music composed by an American, and the most deeply and essentially American in impulse and implication. It is wide-ranging and capacious. It has passion, tenderness, humor, simplicity, homeliness. It has imaginative and spiritual vastness. It has wisdom and beauty, and profundity, and a sense of the encompassing terror and splendor of human life and human destiny—a sense of those mysteries that are both human and divine.

Others felt that while the work had many of the qualities Gilman credited it with, it lacked, on the whole, organization, differentiation, cogency. But there were few who came away untouched.

In addition to the works already mentioned, Ives has written some four Violin Sonatas; another Piano Sonata; two Cantatas; two Overtures; a String Quartet; three Symphonies (*i.e.*, four in all), of which the first two are in strict conventional form; three orchestral Suites, the first consisting of a group of three *New England Scenes:* "Boston Common," "Putnam's Camp (Redding, Connecticut)," and "The Housatonic at Stockbridge;" some quarter-tone music for two pianos; and many pieces for small chamber groups. This is by no means a complete list; his works employ almost every device known to modern music, including polyharmony and polytonality, atonality, infinite rhythmic variety and complexity, melodic idioms compounded of wide and difficult leaps, *sprechsingen*. The amazing audacity of his music combines with his great personal reserve and reticence to make a musical personality quite unique. He scorns popularity won by easy methods, and for the composer who chooses the primrose path to success he has expressed his opinion: "his business is good—for it is easy to sell the future in terms of the past—and there are always some who will buy anything."

ATONALISTS

Two of our experimenters are definitely atonalists, and it happens that they have each written about the other in that *vademecum* of the student of modern American music, *American Composers on American Music*.[7]

Adolph Weiss was born September 12, 1891, in Baltimore, Maryland. His father had been a piano pupil of Busoni, and the son learned to play the bassoon, which he has done professionally in the New York Philharmonic-Symphony Orchestra, in Hollywood, and elsewhere. Weiss studied composition with Weidig in Chicago, Lilienthal and Rybner in New York, and Schoenberg in Vienna. In 1932 he won a Guggenheim Fellowship. He works along lines similar to those laid down by the Viennese atonalists, although Schoenberg is said to consider Weiss too independent a personality to be called his pupil. But like Schoenberg, Weiss works with twelve-tone "rows;" or he builds up an entire work on the basis of one or two intervals. Of his *American Life* Riegger writes, "I feel that it reflects our sentimentality, our nervous energy, and something of our morbid love of the sensational, just as I sense something of the ironical to be present in the *Kammersymphonie*." Both these works are orchestral, and for orchestra Weiss has also written a *Ballade;* a Theme and Variations, played by Monteux and the San Francisco Orchestra in 1935; and *Five Pieces*. His other works include four String Quartets; a cantata, *Libation Bearers;* some chamber music for wood-wind instruments; some songs and piano pieces; and the first act of an opera, *David*.

"Complex, indefinite, facetious" is how Weiss describes the personality of *Wallingford Riegger*. Riegger was born in Albany, Georgia, on April 29, 1885. His early musical education he obtained in Indianapolis, and he later studied with Goetschius in New York and with Stillman Kelley and Hekking in Berlin.

[7] *Op. cit.*

EXPERIMENTERS

He has held various teaching posts, has served in an administrative or advisory capacity such organizations as the Yaddo Festivals, the Pan American Association of Composers, New Music Publications and Quarterly Recordings, and the Dance Division of the Federal Theatre Project of the WPA, and has done editorial work for music publishers.

His early works were romantic in style: the Trio in B Minor won the Paderewski Prize in 1921, and *La Belle Dame sans Merci*, for eight instruments and four singers, the Elizabeth Sprague Coolidge prize in 1924. But he later became an aggressive champion of modern tendencies, and an avowed atonalist. The *Study in Sonority*, for ten violins, was his first work in the new idiom to win public attention. It was first played by Howard Hanson and the Rochester Orchestra, and later by Stokowski and the Philadelphia Orchestra. Then came Three Canons, for woodwinds; a Fantasy and Fugue, for organ (two players) and orchestra; a Prelude and Fugue for orchestra; *Dichotomy* and *Scherzo*, for chamber orchestra; a String Quartet, played at Yaddo in September, 1940; and much music for the modern dance.

Dancers, not having studied harmony, are not prejudiced against the "modern" idiom [Riegger writes in a letter to the author], so from that standpoint I have enjoyed working with them, and have developed a great versatility of style. . . . The recent change of outlook on the part of the American dancers (originating with Martha Graham—about 1930) is extremely important for the composer. The dancer, instead of interpreting a *morceau* of Ravel, Villa-Lobos, or Hindemith, creates first the choreography and then calls upon the composer to write music for it. Inasmuch as the Modern Dance is not stylized but much more organic than the ballet, no set piece of music will do. The composer watches the dance, endeavors to catch the mood, and notes down the rhythmic design—(such as 10 bars of $\frac{4}{4}$ time; 6 bars of $\frac{5}{8}$; 12 bars of $\frac{3}{4}$, with the accent on the second beat; then four sevens; etc., etc.!!). To create within such a straitjacket taxes one's ingenuity; fortunately, the dancer is willing to make a concession now and then.

Riegger has furnished music for such leaders of the Modern Dance as Doris Humphrey, Charles Weidman, Martha Graham, Hanya Holm, Tamiris, and others.

"NEW MUSIC"

Henry Cowell is the friend of all modern tendencies and the tireless proponent of all modern works. In his books, *American Composers on American Music,* and *New Musical Resources;* in the concerts which he has organized at the New School for Social Research in New York, and for the Pan American Association of Composers, in Europe and America; in his lectures in many parts of the world; in his quarterly publications and recordings of New Music, issued under that title; and in countless other activities, he has been one of the most ardent and effective champions of modern American music of the nonconformist variety.

Cowell was born in California on March 11, 1897. He studied the violin as a child, but when he was eight he gave his instrument away. He decided that composing was his destiny, and he proceeded to follow it, not deliberately breaking the rules of harmony, but simply not learning them and paying no attention to them. Charles Seeger was one of his teachers, but Cowell is largely self-taught. He is in the truest sense of the word an experimenter, for it is the materials of music and their expansion that chiefly interest him. His early fame came from his use of the term "tone-clusters" and from his employment of them in his music. He was not the first or the only composer to use clumps of tones as sonorous material. Ives had written "chords" that must be played with a board or a ruler. But Cowell specialized in the production of new tone-colors from the piano. He pays no attention to prejudices and habits of thought, such as the notion that the keyboard is the part of the piano that should be used for tone production. No—Cowell rubs, pats, plucks, punches the strings, the sounding-board, the case. And in so doing he has produced some new and wondrous sounds, which have nothing but the un-

EXPERIMENTERS

conventionality of their origin against them. Probably he has produced more raw material for composition than actual music; but that is often true of pioneers.

In 1931, he received a Guggenheim Fellowship for the study of comparative musicology—specifically, the music of exotic and primitive peoples—in Berlin. It was in that same year, too, that Cowell induced Professor Leon Theremin, inventor of the ether-wave instrument that bears his name, to construct an instrument for the execution of all sorts of complicated rhythms, which they dubbed the Rhythmicon. From one to sixteen sounds in a given time-interval are made by this instrument, at the pitches which correspond to their metric frequency in the overtone series. Cowell has written a four-movement orchestral suite, *Rhythmicana*, in which this instrument is employed.

Cowell's tendencies as a composer are dual. On the one hand, he has a certain Celtic fondness for the weird, the colorful, the whimsical—even, at times, the sentimental. On the other, he is full of the scientific spirit. *Synchrony*, for orchestra and dancers; *Polyphonica*, for twelve instruments; a Piano Concerto; these and many other compositions represent the modern scientific experimenter in Cowell. The Suite for "string and percussion piano" and chamber orchestra, (in three movements, "The Banshee," "The Leprechaun," and "The Fairy Bells") represents the application of his technique acquired by experiment to the ends of expressiveness and color effect.

The list of Cowell's works is far too long for inclusion here. And besides, it is what he stands for, what he has made possible, and what he has done to help his fellow composers that make him most important. Whatever one thinks of the value of his music, or of this innovation or that, or even of much of the music he has helped to make known, he has been a unique and incomparable factor in seasoning our musical fare, and in adding color and life to the American musical scene.

Associated with Cowell in the New Music Society has been *Gerald Strang*, who started the New Music Workshops in 1933, and succeeded Cowell in 1936 as director of the Society and editor of the New Music Edition. Strang was born a Canadian (Claresholm, Alberta, February 13, 1908), and graduated from Leland Stanford University in 1928. He later studied at the University of California and the University of Southern California. Like Cowell, he is particularly interested in comparative musicology. He also resembles Schoenberg, whose assistant he has been since 1935 in the Music Department of the University of California in Los Angeles, in his fondness for elaborate canonic device. Thus his *Mirrorrorrim*, for piano, he has explained as follows:

> Dual tonal centers (not tonalities) are used; for the first subject c-b; for the second subject f-f sharp. They lie between the notes of upper and lower staves, forming a focus for inversion. In the development various temporary centers are introduced. Wherever more than one voice appears, the lower staff is a precise inversion of the upper staff, based on the appropriate tonal center. The last half of the composition is a note for note reversal of the first half with certain time changes and bar changes introduced for rhythmic reasons.

He has composed chiefly chamber music: a Quintet for clarinet and strings; two String Quartets; Percussion Music for three players; a Passacaglia for string quartet; and various pieces for small combinations. He has also written a Suite for chamber orchestra; a choral work, *Vanzetti in the Death House*; and *Incidental Music for a Satirical Play*.

FROM FRANCE

Californian also, although by adoption, is *Dane Rudhyar*, who came to America from France as Chennevière-Rudyard. His *Poèmes Ironiques* and *Vision Végétale* figured on a dance recital program in the Metropolitan Opera House as early as 1917. These reflected the influence of the Stravinsky of *Le Sacre du Printemps*. He was also represented on the first program of modern music given by the International Composers' Guild, in New York, on December 17, 1922. He was born in France in 1895, and received his education there. He is very much interested in mysticism and the philosophies of the Orient, and his works are a part of his philosophical structure. He rejects our subservience to European tone systems, and believes that what he calls "cut-and-dried keyboard scales" should give way to melodic continuity between successive notes. His works are atonal, but he believes that they appear chaotic only to those who have not understood the principles of unity other than tonality upon which they are based. Rudhyar's works for orchestra and chamber orchestra include *The Surge of Fire* (1921), *To the Real* (1923), *Ouranos* (1924), a Symphony (1928), *Hero Chants* (1930), and a *Sinfonietta* (1931). In 1934 he completed the piano score of a symphonic poem with recitation, *Paean to the Great Thunder*, the first member of a trilogy called *Cosmophony* which is intended to express stages of development of mystic consciousness. In recent years, Rudhyar has devoted himself increasingly to writing and painting, on the basis of "a new cosmological outlook," and little has been heard from him, musically.

Two others among our prominent experimenters have been immigrants from France. *Carlos Salzedo*, the Henry Cowell of the harp, was born in Arcachon, France, on April 6, 1885. He graduated from the Paris Conservatoire with honors in both piano and harp, and has a world-wide reputation as a virtuoso of the harp, and also as inventor of a modern harp—said to compare to the old "as an aeroplane to an ox"—and of many new and strange effects to be obtained from the instrument. He has been active in organizations of modern composers and of harpists. All his music features the harp, either singly or in groups of as many as seven. *The Enchanted Isle*, for harp and orchestra, has been performed by Salzedo with all the leading symphony orchestras of the country, as has his Concerto for harp and seven wind instruments. *Pentacle*, five pieces for two harps, and *Préambule et Jeux*, for harp, four wind instruments and string quintet, were commissioned by Mrs. Elizabeth Sprague Coolidge in 1928 and 1929.

In 1920, Salzedo joined the pianist E. Robert Schmitz in organizing the Franco-American Musical Society, later Pro Musica, and in 1921 he assisted Edgar Varèse in the formation of the International Composers' Guild. He was active in the direction of both societies, which for several years presented modern music of the radical stripe to American audiences. He was also one of the organizers of the Pan American Society of Composers, in 1928. In 1932 he formed a flute-harp-cello trio, with Georges Barrère and Horace Britt, for which several composers, including Wagenaar, Riegger, and Boris Koutzen, have written special pieces. He initiated the harp department at the Curtis Institute of Music, and teaches at the Juilliard School as well. Many of his works are published, and the Sonata for harp and piano was chosen by the Society for the Publication of American Music in 1925.

The music of *Edgar Varèse* [wrote Lawrence Gilman in 1924],[8] is the pure milk of Modernism. Mr. Varèse makes no such disgraceful compromise with euphony as do his more conventional brethren. Hearing Schoenberg's *Five Pieces* for orchestra, you will remember that Wagner once lived; hearing Casella's *Alta Notte*, you will remember that Schoenberg still lives. Hearing Varèse's *Hyperprism* you remember only Varèse.

Of *Offrandes*, on another occasion,[9] Richard Stokes had this to say:

The alteration is one in the music's very tissue—a sudden break with traditions which run back to the harmonic ratios discovered by Pythagoras. The change of element, like that of some marine creature cast up from water into air, is inevitably disconcerting to all save those whose ears, so to speak, have evolved lungs. At the best, Mr. Varèse's score resembles elocution in a foreign speech. The words are mostly unintelligible, but from the gestures of the music, its facial expression, and the timbre of its voice, one does gain a sense of feeling, of sincerity, and of a remote and alien beauty.

[8] *New York Herald Tribune*, December 17.
[9] *New York Evening World*, April 19, 1928.

From all of which the reader will gather that Varèse is an original. He insists, however, that style must be the result of the exigencies of the musical concept—the one an integral part of the other. He claims that he is not interested in novelty or in orchestral virtuosity, but only in expressiveness. He has long been waiting for the electric instruments which would give form to certain musical concepts beyond the range of existing media and systems. "I refuse to submit myself only to sounds that have already been heard," he said in an interview published in the *New York Telegraph* shortly after his arrival here in 1916.

Born in Paris, December 22, 1885, Varèse was at first interested chiefly in science and mathematics, and planned to attend the École Polytechnique in Paris. At seventeen he decided, against the wishes of his family, to devote himself to music, and specifically to composition. He became a pupil of Roussel and d'Indy at the Schola Cantorum and of Widor at the Paris Conservatoire. In 1906 he organized the Choeur de l'Université Populaire in Paris, which he conducted, and a year or two later the Symphonischer Chor in Berlin. In Germany he was befriended by Richard Strauss and Karl Muck, and studied with Busoni and with Mahler.

After his discharge from the French Army, in the second year of the World War, he came to America, and three years later he founded the New Symphony Orchestra in New York, for the performance of music by modern composers. Rather than modify his policy in this respect, as the directors wanted him to do, he resigned from the conductorship of the organization, and two years later founded the International Composers' Guild, a pioneer group in the presentation of contemporary music. In 1927, Varèse wrote an open letter to the *New York Times* in which he announced the disbanding of the Guild, on the ground that it had fulfilled its function of stirring up interest in modern music. The next year he founded the Pan American Association of Composers, for the presentation of modern music by composers of the two American continents.

Varèse's own music is revolutionary in harmony, melody,

rhythm, and orchestration. This leaves very little ground untouched. His *Hyperprism*, which dates from the early 1920's, employed a small orchestra which included many kinds of percussion instruments (among them sleighbells) and a siren. Then came *Intégrales*, also for chamber orchestra; *Amériques*, for full orchestra ("Amériques-Americas: new worlds on earth, in the stars and in the minds of men"); *Arcana* (described by Stokes as "strong, arrogant, infinitely repellent"); *Offrandes*, for soprano and chamber orchestra; *Octandre*, for chamber orchestra. *Ionisation* (1931) is for two groups of percussion instruments, in the hands of sixteen players. Or rather, it is for instruments of "percussion, friction, and sibilation," excluding all instruments of definite pitch. Slonimsky says it is "in sonata form." *Ionisation* has been recorded by Columbia.

In recent years, Varèse has produced *Density 21.5*, for flute solo and chamber orchestra (1936); *Equatorial*, for organ, percussion, trumpets, trombones, theremin, and bass-baritone voice (1937); and *Espace*, a symphony with soli and chorus. "The world of sound is infinite and only a small and arbitrary portion has been used by composers," he says; and of attempts to classify him: "Right-wing, liberal, left-wing, applied to any Art, what nonsense! I try to fly on my own wings." Opinions may vary on how high Varèse has flown; but nobody will accuse him of not having used his own wings—especially his left! Like Harris, Ruggles, Ives, and not a few others, he has been called the greatest of modern American composers. He feels now that as a composer he has almost finished with hand-played instruments; electric instruments and work with the sound-track on film offer unlimited possibilities which he is actively exploring.

THE CLEVER ONES

Nicolas Slonimsky is hardly known as a composer, though he has written a *Suite in Black and White*, said to be based on counterpoint in consonant intervals, using atonal and polytonal effects, and a *Fragment from Orestes*, built on the enharmonic quarter-tone "mode" of the Ancient Greeks, which was played under the composer's direction in Hollywood in 1933. His reputation is based rather on his work as the friend and interpreter of other composers, both as conductor and as critic. He was born in St. Petersburg in 1895, studied the piano with his aunt, Isabella Vengerova, and composition in the St. Petersburg Conservatory, and migrated to America in 1923. He has been active as critic and teacher in Boston, and has received considerable notice as conductor of concerts of the Pan American Association in New York, Havana, Paris, and elsewhere. His encyclopedic survey *Music Since 1900*, published in 1937,[10] is characteristic of his mind: brilliant, brittle, fascinated by the extraordinary—pedantically interested in detail, important and unimportant. He is a colorful and unique figure.

The once famous *George Antheil* is less famous nowadays. His *Ballet Mécanique*, scored for orchestra with several player pianos and airplane motors, and produced in New York in 1927, represented about the last word in unconventionality, and was hard for even him to outdo. So he had to settle down, and in his soberer mood he has attracted less attention. At one time he said that he had reformed, and that he considered all the music he had written before 1926 too radical and immature. (This of course included the *Ballet Mécanique*, which was written in 1924.) In 1932, however, he wrote a letter to the *Musical Courier* to deny that he had repudiated the *Ballet Mécanique*. He did not repudiate anything he had ever written, he said; he simply did not wish to be known exclusively by that early work all his life. Henry Cowell, who cannot be accused of unfriendliness toward experimenters and musical radicals in general, wrote in 1932 that Antheil's real talent was in discovering very quickly what the latest trend or fad was, and in following it at once. "The idea was," Cowell wrote, "to amuse Paris for a day."

It is difficult to take Antheil seriously, even in his allegedly

[10] W. W. Norton and Company.

soberer and more mature mood. Hollywood has taken him seriously enough to pay him to write music for the films (*Once in a Blue Moon, The Plainsman, The Buccaneer*). And John Erskine collaborated with him in an opera produced by the Juilliard School in February, 1934—*Helen Retires*.

The musical setting provided by Mr. Antheil [wrote the critic of the *Musical Courier*],[11] blending modernistic and jazz idioms, is of the requisite pungency. That it is effective and often tuneful cannot be denied, although the angularity of the vocal lines somewhat obscures the clarity of the words at times. There are frequent passages of lyricism, sometimes flavored with acrid harmonies. The instrumentation is treated with ingenuity, the unexpected being intriguingly prevalent . . .

Lawrence Gilman [12] was less charitable:

Of Mr. Antheil's music, with its blend of Puccini and Strauss, musical comedy and sophisticated jazz, its plebeian humors and its almost unrelieved banality, it is disheartening to speak.

Antheil is a native of Trenton, New Jersey, where he was born on July 8, 1900. He studied with Constantin von Sternberg, in Philadelphia, and had some lessons from Ernest Bloch. At the age of twelve he began to compose, and played modern music in public. For many years he lived abroad, and his works were first played there. His *Zingareska*, a symphony in which jazz was used, was played in Berlin in 1922, and a String Quartet was heard in Paris in 1926. His Symphony in F was played in 1926 in Paris, under Golschmann, and his Piano Concerto under the same auspices the next year. For the Berlin State Theatre he wrote incidental music to Sophocles' *Oedipus*, and in 1929 he became assistant musical director there. His ballet, *Fighting the Waves*, to a text by W. B. Yeats, was produced in the same year at the Abbey Theater, in Dublin, Ireland.

In 1930 Antheil's opera, *Transatlantic*, was performed at the

[11] March 10, 1934.
[12] *New York Herald Tribune*, March 1, 1934.

EXPERIMENTERS

State Theater in Frankfort. Among other ingredients, it employed jazz of an old-fashioned type, in the service of a libretto that presented a caricature of American life. The plot had to do with a beautiful woman of doubtful origin named Helen, who tried to decoy Hector, the hero, candidate for the presidency. There was a feverish struggle for power and for love; scenes at dances, booze parties, political meetings, attempts at murder, until finally Hector rescued Helen from suicide on Brooklyn Bridge and was elected president.

Antheil received Guggenheim Fellowships in 1932 and 1933. In addition to the works already named, he has written a *Capriccio*, for orchestra, performed by Howard Hanson in Rochester in 1934; *Archipelago*, for orchestra, played on a General Electric broadcast in 1935; a ballet, *Dreams*, on a scenario by André Derain, for the American Ballet company; and an *American Symphony* (1937).

In addition to his musical pursuits, Antheil is said to study astronomy and various other subjects. To complete the picture, it should be stated that he also signs a syndicated newspaper column of advice to the lovelorn.

It would be interesting to know what goes on in a lesson in composition given by Antheil, but at least one composer acknowledges him to have been "my principal teacher." The young man in question is *Henry Dreyfuss Brant*, who confesses that at the age of twelve he wrote a string quartet which "attempted to combine the styles of Schoenberg, Stravinsky, Bartók, and Hindemith." Brant was born September 15, 1913, in Montreal, Canada, and studied at McGill University's school of music, where his father taught the violin, and at the Juilliard School. He has won several prizes, has acted as secretary of the Pan American Association of Composers, done some orchestrating for the films, and received commissions from the Yaddo festival and from the American Ballet company. Brant feels that music should express some feeling essential to its period, no matter from what viewpoint or whether directly or indirectly. In order to express intelligibly some phase of the tangled emotional web of the present time, he feels that experimentation in all styles of the present and past, both art-music and folk-music, is probably necessary. He considers that the possibilities of satire, burlesque, etc., in music ("but directed to some *very serious* purpose") are largely unexplored, and very useful as expressive agents for a sound portrayal of the contemporary temper.

Brant is thus an avowed experimenter. "No two of my works," he writes, "have any surface resemblance in technique and style." One of Brant's early interests was in "oblique harmony"—the relations between one voice at one point and another at another, rather than mere horizontal or vertical relations. In principle, there seems nothing very new about that. His *Variations in Oblique Harmony,* to be played by "any four instruments," are published in the New Music edition. He has also written *Miss O'Grady,* an opera; *Entente cordiale,* a satire with music; a *Lyric Cycle,* for soprano, three violas and piano; *Crying Jag,* for military band; a Symphony in B flat minor; a Quintet for oboe and strings; a Concerto for eleven flutes; a Concerto for double bass and orchestra; and a *Sonata Sacra* for hardware and piano. (There is no misprint in the foregoing sentence.)

Nothing, of course, was surer to set the town talking than to spoof the sacred in the days when composers had nothing better to do. But the idea was not new with young Brant. Half a dozen years earlier, in Paris, *Virgil Thomson* had presented the world with his *Sonata da Chiesa* (church sonata), consisting of a chorale, tango, and fugue, scored for trombone, horn, viola, trumpet, and clarinet. This piece made, as the composer himself expressed it, a "funny noise."

But Thomson, unlike many of his fellow-shockers of the middle classes, is, even in conventional terms, a thoroughly trained and accomplished musician. Born in Kansas City, on November 25, 1896, Thomson attended Harvard University, and while in Cambridge studied with Gebhard, Davison, and Goodrich. He later worked with Scalero and with Boulanger. From 1925 to

1932 he lived in Paris and his point of view has been characteristic of the *avant-garde* of that time and place. Among his elders, Satie, Cocteau, and Stravinsky exercised the greatest influence on him, but of course he was no mere follower of any of them. In order to be accepted in the ranks of the smartest set in the Paris of those inter-war days, one had to be one of a kind. Originality was orthodox, unpredictability a convention. In this respect Thomson was no heretic. He could be as unexpected as anyone else. Indeed, it has been suggested that much of Antheil's remarkable success in attracting public attention was due to Thomson's sage counsel. However, Thomson himself was not much in the public eye until he burst upon the American scene in 1934 with *Four Saints in Three Acts,* an "opera" on words by Gertrude Stein. That occasion, however, proved to have been worth waiting for. After initial performances in Hartford, by the Friends and Enemies of Modern Music, this curio was presented in a two weeks' Broadway run, and in Chicago, and even attained inclusion in the *March of Time* broadcast.

Measured in columns of newspaper comment, *Four Saints* was a huge success. And since it seems unlikely that the world will again have leisure for such fooling for some time, perhaps it is worth while to recall for a moment what it was that caused such a stir. First of all there was a "libretto" prepared by Maurice Grosser from words by Gertrude Stein, whose *Capitals, Capitals* Thomson had previously set. This was undoubtedly like no other libretto that has ever been, in that it purposely made no sense whatever, although it had something to do with the Spanish Saints, Ignatius and Teresa. The most quoted passage was:

Pigeons on the grass alas. Pigeons on the grass alas. Short longer grass short longer shorter yellow grass. Pigeons large pigeons on the shorter longer yellow grass alas pigeons on the grass. If they were not pigeons what were they?

When one realizes that the text went on like this indefinitely, with occasionally more variety but rarely more meaning, it is hard to believe that people actually sat still in the theater, having paid for their tickets, and listened to it for two hours and a quarter. Of course, there was more than the text. There was the Negro cast, chosen, according to the composer, because the Negro sings with greater ease than his white colleague, puts himself more readily into the various moods demanded by the opera, fanciful and devotional, sings with a clarity of English diction never equaled by white singers, has no intellectual barriers to break down, no *arrières pensées* about the "apparent nonsense" he is singing, is satisfied with the pure beauty of the sound of the words and the music and hence could not possibly give a tongue-in-cheek performance. There is no denying that much of this is true, and the singers for the most part gave such a simple, serious, unsuspecting performance as almost to embarrass the listener who did not find the joke funny enough to warrant the playing of such a trick on them.

And there was the music. One would not have expected it to please the critics, but praise came for it from high places. Gilman [13] called it "deceptively simple, a little self-consciously candid and naïve, actually very wily and deft and slick, often subtly and wittily allusive, distinguished in its artful banality." The critic of *Musical America* [14] wrote that Thomson had handled meaningless recitative so that it carried more conviction than the song-speech of almost any American opera that could be called to mind, and found that the lesson of this was that one must perhaps do away with word-meanings if one wanted one's music to mirror the text. "Handel keeps company with Arthur Sullivan, Rossini with Victor Herbert." Carl Van Vechten thought that only in *Pelléas et Mélisande* could a parallel be found to the originality of conception of the work. Olin Downes,[15] who was careful to state that "the trail of foppishness and pose and pseudo-intellectuality is over it all," put his finger on a central point when he wrote:

[13] *New York Herald Tribune*, February 21, 1934.
[14] February 25, 1934.
[15] *New York Times*, February 25, 1934.

... Mr. Thomson ... wore lightly what is obviously a real knowledge of prosody and a great skill in combining music and text. He showed that he knew very well the half, if not the whole, of opera technique. ... The combination was funny where the text by itself would have been obvious and labored—would in fact have missed fire. Then when he wanted to make a phrase tell he found for it a rhythm, accent, and shape of the melodic line that fitted the words like a glove. Once in a while the Stein text relapses into something like a meaning, or a feeble joke. Quick as a flash, the composer pounces upon it, throws it, with a singular adroitness, straight at the audience's head, and this with such reckless ease and certainty of aim that one is hardly aware until it is over of the cunning of it.

In short, *Four Saints* made an impression. The composer had skill, wit, intelligence, and a knowledge of how to avoid the expected. These abilities he has put to work in a long series of works, including a *Symphony on a Hymn Tune*, a second Symphony, several choral works, a large number of pieces for small combinations, and considerable incidental music for films and plays. The latter include the WPA Negro version of *Macbeth*, Leslie Howard's production of *Hamlet* and Tallulah Bankhead's of *Antony and Cleopatra*, and *Injunction Granted*, for the WPA's Living Newspaper. Perhaps the most productive use of his talents has been in the scores he wrote for the government documentary films, *The Plough That Broke the Plains*, and *The River*. Unfortunately, however, these quite serious and propagandistic films offered no opportunity for Thomson to make use of his greatest gift, which is his accurate ear for prosody. But the music he wrote for them is effective and appropriate, without being startling in any way.

All of Thomson's gifts, which perhaps do not quite add up to those of a composer, make him an admirable critic, with a keen insight and a sharp and witty tongue. He has written often for *Vanity Fair, Modern Music*, and other journals. His book, *The State of Music*,[16] published in 1939, is a witty, fearless, and on the whole very sensible discussion of the position of music and

---

[16] New York: William Morrow and Company, 1939.

the musician in contemporary society, full of things which only Thomson has the keenness and audacity to say, presented, of course, in the most provocative manner possible. In the autumn of 1940 he succeeded to the post of the late Lawrence Gilman as critic of the *New York Herald Tribune*.

What happens when exceptional talents of a not really creative order are applied first to things for which they are not suited and then to purposes that bring out the best in them, is illustrated in the case of *Marc Blitzstein*. Blitzstein was born in Philadelphia, March 2, 1905. He studied at the University of Pennsylvania, at the Curtis Institute (piano with Siloti, composition with Scalero) and abroad with Boulanger and Schoenberg. He is an accomplished pianist, lecturer, and writer on music, and until the last few years he seemed to indulge an unrequited love for composition, producing the regulation originalities and new departures expected of any bright young man looking for recognition in advanced circles. His sketch *Triple-Sec* was included in the *Garrick Gaieties*, and his pieces were played at the Copland-Sessions Concerts, the League of Composers concerts, and the first Yaddo Festival.

He has made an allegory of his development as a composer in *I've Got the Tune*, a radio song play which he wrote on commission from the Columbia Broadcasting System. This tells the story of Mr. Musiker, the composer, who has a tune, and no words to fit it. From Mrs. Arbutus, the Park Avenue patroness of the arts, comes the suggestion: "The moon is a happy cheese tonight, I swoon," etc. At an initiation ritual of the Purple Shirts, Musiker hears the tune sung to the words "How peaceful is our captain!" against a background of whistles, bombs, machine guns, and sirens. The tune reappears in many forms. But Mr. Musiker is about to abandon the quest and return to his Ivory Tower when he comes upon a group of students singing radical songs of revolt to threadbare Salvation Army tunes. They are looking for a new tune, and he is looking for the words. "This is like a breath of fresh air," he shouts. "Here's where my tune belongs."

The intended moral, obviously, is that the mission of the composer today is to write music for the masses, music of hope and music of revolt. Blitzstein thinks this is a turning point in the history of music and all art, in its way comparable to the rise of instrumental music which followed the domination of the church in the middle ages, or to the Industrial Revolution which brought the middle class into the concert hall. His music is by turns dissonant, consonant, conservative, or radical, according to the purpose or the occasion. He believes that composers today have obligations which surround the obligation of writing good music—namely, social obligations, and he attempts in his music to fulfill some of those obligations.

In all countries in these years of turmoil, artists have turned their talents to what they considered social ends. The political left wing in particular has enlisted many outstanding talents. Blitzstein's first work of this tendency to attract attention was *The Cradle Will Rock*, a remarkably strong play with music, originally scheduled for production by the Federal Theater Project of the WPA, and later presented by Orson Welles's Mercury Theater, in December, 1937. This was another allegory, the import of which was the stupidity, greed, and cruelty of the rich. Presented on a stage without scenery, and with music of a sparse and simple texture, *The Cradle Will Rock* was an effective and biting play which attracted audiences steadily during a run of some months. In it, Blitzstein was perhaps at once more and less than a composer: he was a playwright who wrote his own music. The play was the thing, and the music contributed greatly to its power, though it was hardly of sufficient interest to be enjoyed purely as music. Blitzstein also supplied incidental music for the Orson Welles production of *Julius Caesar*, and, with Virgil Thomson, for the film, *Spanish Earth*. In January, 1940, he produced *No for an Answer*, a successor to *The Cradle Will Rock*.

This is not the place to debate questions of social and economic policy, or the role composers should have in political action. Perhaps there are no rules, and each composer must decide for himself. The contribution that music can make to politics has been much discussed; it seems clear that it must be a minor one. But no matter what one may think of Blitzstein's political views, it is only fair to say that whatever the effect of his music on politics, the effect of political beliefs on his music has been to give it a conviction and a direction which it had hitherto seemed to lack.

Well, there they are—the brave, the foolhardy, and the reckless, a salty and peppery stew. Pick out the pieces that tempt your palate. Or leave the whole pot-full alone, if you'd rather. It's a free country, and nobody has to listen to anything he doesn't want to. But remember that everyone has a right to listen to the things you think are crazy or worse. Some of the best people were wrong about Berlioz, Wagner, and Debussy. And, on the other hand, many composers were greeted as heroes in their own time who are forgotten today. Posterity is supposed to do the deciding, and of course the weight of numbers is on posterity's side. But meanwhile we might as well make up our own minds, since we won't be here to know the ultimate verdict anyway!

7

FOLK-SONG AND RACIAL EXPRESSIONS

IF FOLK-MUSIC itself were the concern of this book, the present chapter would be an extended one indeed. Research in this field has made great progress in the last few years, and there is now a considerable body of what is referred to as American folk-music.

The question: What is American folk-music? should logically be preceded by the more general: What is folk-music? The narrower the definition, the less accurate. Most students seem to agree that folk-music is that which expresses in simple, unsophisticated accents the feelings of a people. If we accept this principle, such academic questions as: Must it be anonymous? Must it be old? How old? Is Jazz folk-music? and a hundred others need not be answered here. We incline to the broadest definition, and are not too shocked to hear either *Old Black Joe* or the *St. Louis Blues* called a folk-song.

So then, what is *American* folk-music? We may claim that any folk-music which belongs either to the whole American people, or to any racial, sectional, or occupational group of Americans, is itself American. This eliminates the question of origin, which must be got out of the way if we are to include the vast body of Anglo-Saxon melodies, or any other tunes which have come from abroad; for obviously, the only really indigenous folk-music of any considerable age belongs to the only really indigenous people —the Indians.

There was a time when our nationalist composers felt that to be American composers they must use this Indian material. But they overlooked the common-sense consideration that any truly nationalistic use of folk material must be based on the complete assimilation of that material as a part of one's musical background: it must be "one's own" material that one uses, and not merely the melodies of primitive peoples who happen to inhabit the same continent. This fact is now generally recognized, and Indian material is ordinarily confined to such uses as might be made of any other primitive or exotic melodies.

FROM INDIAN SOURCES

There have been, however, several composers who have occupied themselves particularly, though not exclusively, with the music of the American Indian. Some of these composers have been discussed elsewhere, but two of them in particular should be presented here: *Charles Sanford Skilton* and *Frederick Ayres (Johnson)*.

Skilton is one of our older contemporaries, having been born August 16, 1868, in Northampton, Massachusetts. After his graduation from Yale he studied music in Berlin, and later with Dudley Buck and Harry Rowe Shelley in New York. He has always maintained an interest in church music, is the composer of a Communion Service in G, commissioned by Grace Cathedral in Topeka, Kansas, and is a member of the examining committee and national convention board of the American Guild of Organists. Skilton held several teaching positions before he became, in 1903, professor of organ, theory, and music history at the University of Kansas. It was in 1915 that he first became interested in Indian music, when an Indian pupil offered to teach him tribal songs in exchange for harmony lessons. He later taught at Haskell Institute, a government school for the Indians, where he was able to pursue further his interest in the subject. His first works on Indian themes were the *Deer Dance* and the *War Dance*, originally for string quartet and later rewritten for orchestra. They constituted the first part of the *Suite Primeval*, of which the second part followed four years later, its four movements all based on primitive songs: "Sunrise Song" (Winnebago); "Gambling Song" (Rogue River); "Flute Serenade" (Sioux); and "Moccasin Game" (Winnebago).

Skilton has written several dramatic works. His music to Sophocles' *Electra* was commissioned by Smith College for a performance by the Class of 1889. *Kalopin* is an Indian opera in three acts, based on the earthquake in New Madrid in 1811 and the legendary causes attributed to it by the Chickasaw and Choctaw Indians. *The Sun Bride*, another Indian opera, in one act, was given its first performance over an NBC network in the spring of 1930. Skilton has also composed music to Barrie's *Mary Rose*; a two-scene opera with prologue, *The Day of Gayomair*; and numerous orchestral works, pieces for chamber music combinations, and choruses.

Frederick Ayres Johnson (usually known as *Frederick Ayres*) did not use actual Indian material, but he caught the spirit of the West—its great mountains and broad plains—in his music. His early years were all spent in the East. He was born March 17, 1876, in Binghamton, New York, went to Cornell University, and studied music with Edgar Stillman Kelley and Arthur Foote. In his later life he became a spokesman for the Rocky Mountain section, making his home in Colorado Springs, where he died, November 23, 1926. His best known work is an overture, *From the Plains*, and he composed also a String Quartet; a Sonata for violin and piano, and one for cello and piano; two Piano Trios; and various piano pieces and songs, including the vivid cycle, *The Seeonee Wolves*.

Harvey Worthington Loomis (1865–1930) was one of the composers whose music was published by the Wa-Wan Press. A pupil of Dvořák, he made settings of Indian melodies which gained him a considerable reputation, notably *Lyrics of the Red Man*, for piano. *Thurlow Lieurance*, born in Iowa in 1878, is known principally for his immensely popular song, *By the Waters of Minnetonka*. He has written numerous other songs, and an opera, *Drama of the Yellowstone*.

THE ANGLO-SAXON HERITAGE

All folk-music in this country other than that of the Red Men has roots in some foreign land, and there are undoubtedly as many strains of it as there are nationalities and races in our great cosmopolitan population. Those strains which belong to nations having a strong musical culture of their own—Germany, France, Italy, Spain, Hungary, Bohemia, etc.—or which represent comparatively small numbers in this country, are usually not thought of as American folk-music, no matter how long the songs may have been here or what modifications they may have undergone on American soil. Those strains, on the other hand, which belong to peoples who in the last century or two, at least, have had no strong musical culture—the peoples of the British Isles and of Africa—tend to be adopted as our own.

John Powell has become the undisputed leader of the group which believes in the fundamental importance to the cultural life of the nation of American folk-music derived from Anglo-Saxon sources. Creator of the Virginia State Choral Festival, he has been a moving spirit in the annual White Top Mountain Folk Music Festival, and a friend to all who are interested in our Appalachian tunes and ballads. Although in late years he has produced relatively few new works of his own, those that he has composed have been based on traditional material.

Most recent is *A Set of Three*, an orchestral suite using Virginia tunes. The first of its three parts is entitled "Snowbird on the Ashbank," the name of one of the tunes on which the movement is based. The second part, "Green Willow," derives from a song the composer heard in Giles County, while the finale, "Haste to the Wedding," utilizes several traditional folk-dance tunes. In his settings, Powell has adhered closely to the modes

ASCAP

John Powell

of the original melodies: the Mixolydian, Dorian, and Ionian.

Although separate movements of the work had been given previous performances, the Suite as a whole had its initial presentation by the New York Philharmonic-Symphony Orchestra in February of 1940. Those who heard it on that occasion were impressed by the composer's skillful and effective instrumentation, and by the manner in which the essential flavor of the songs was preserved.

Several years earlier than a *Set of Three* is the orchestral *Natchez on the Hill,* performed for the first time at the Worcester (Massachusetts) Festival in 1931. Since that time it has received many hearings by major orchestras and on the radio. The tune from which the piece takes its name is a close relative of *Turkey in the Straw,* and the two other country dances which appear in the score are typical country-fiddler tunes. The three folk-tunes are attached to each other in a novel pattern, somewhat akin to rondo form, but with a third theme taking the place of a recurrence of the first theme. It is a form that the composer has used also in "Snowbird on the Ashbank," in which the succession of themes may be represented by the letter-symbols A-B-C-B-A.

Powell's Virginian antecedents and environment have given him a sense of profound nearness to the forerunners and founders of the nation. He believes intensely in the value of those ethnic and cultural forces which actuated the molders of our past, and he would preserve them in their integrity for the benefit of contemporary and future times and to ensure the persistence of those impulses and ideals which the world has come to regard as typically American. This conviction is reflected in the way he preserves the modal nature of his folk-material and strives to induce his style from the innate character of the material itself, avoiding incongruous progressions and cadences or extraneous chromaticisms.

He was born in Richmond, Virginia, September 6, 1882. His father, John Henry Powell, was headmaster of a girls' school, and his mother was a descendant of Nicholas Lanier, court musician to Charles the First of England. As a child he had music lessons at home, and then went to Vienna to study with Leschetizky and Navrátil. He became an excellent pianist, and as such was able to introduce his own works to a large public. The piece which first established his reputation in America was based, not on Anglo-Saxon material, but on Negro airs. This was the *Rhapsodie Nègre* for piano and orchestra, first produced in 1919, and since that time repeatedly performed by the composer with major orchestras throughout the country.

When he used Negro material, in the *Rhapsodie* as well as in several earlier works, Powell was careful to point out that he was seeking to interpret the Negro as a race; he was not voicing America. The *Rhapsodie* begins and ends on a primal note, pagan, orgiastic; the idealization that creeps in during the middle section cannot maintain itself against the primitive instinct. The work is intense in a fervor that rises to fury, and was composed with the consummate craftsmanship that marks all of Powell's works.

The sociological aspects of the *Rhapsodie* were discussed by the late Donald Francis Tovey, who once wrote:

Mr. Powell has the profoundest respect for the Negro as artist and human being. But profound sympathy is very different from the facile sentimentality that refuses to recognize the dangers that threaten two races of widely different stages of evolution that try to live together. The "Rhapsodie Nègre" is music, not political propaganda; but it will be soonest understood by those who, whether from personal knowledge of the composer or from the capacity to recognize emotional values in music, manage to understand from the outset that this is not only an eminently romantic, but also a thoroughly tragic piece.

Others of Powell's works include a *Sonate Virginianesque*, for violin and piano (1919), which seeks to present certain of the more amiable aspects of Virginia plantation life before the Civil War; an overture, *In Old Virginia* (1921); a *Sonata Noble*, for piano; a suite for piano (also arranged for small orchestra) entitled *At the Fair;* a *Symphony in A* (1937); and a Piano Concerto which is still in manuscript.

FOLK-SONG AND RACIAL EXPRESSIONS 273

Basically the same Anglo-Saxon tradition is represented by *Percy Aldridge Grainger,* who symbolizes in his person as well as in his music the essential unity of the English-speaking races. Grainger was born in Melbourne, Australia, July 8, 1882, and did not come to this country until he was thirty-three years old. Although his early studies were in Germany, with Kwast and Busoni, his fundamental musical kinships were with his fellow students—the Dane, Sandby, and the Englishman, Cyril Scott. He was a friend and disciple of Edvard Grieg and has been active in propagating his music.

At the age of eighteen he went to London, where he became immensely popular as a pianist, and he has actively carried on a concert career ever since. In 1917 he interrupted it to enlist in the American Army, where he became a bandsman, playing the oboe and the saxophone, and taught in the Army music school. Soon afterwards he took out American citizenship papers, and has made his home in this country ever since, with frequent journeys to other parts of the globe—to Scandinavia, where he has done a good deal of folk-song collecting; to the Orient; and to Australia and New Zealand, where he is a prophet far from being without honor in his own country. For several years he was head of the music department in New York University.

He is best known for his brief settings of folk-tunes of the British Isles: *Country Gardens, Irish Tune from County Derry, Mock Morris, Molly on the Shore, Shepherd's Hey,* and many others. In recent years he has specialized in making his music accessible to all sorts of vocal and instrumental combinations by clothing it in the most flexible scoring.

Grainger's services to American folk-music do not consist only in his *Tribute to Foster,* for five solo voices, solo piano, mixed chorus, orchestra, and musical glasses (a characteristically unorthodox scoring, by the way). Much of the credit for the increased interest in folk-music in this country is his, both through the popularity of his transcriptions of similar English material and because of his yeoman service on the concert platform to transcriptions of such American folk-classics as Guion's *Turkey in the Straw* and *Arkansas Traveler.*

Grainger's personal sincerity and generosity are as remarkable as his talents. Paradoxically, his very sincerity has at times brought on him the completely undeserved charge of charlatanism. Thus, when he decided to marry, and wanted the whole world to know of the beauty of his bride and of his love for her (as lovers proverbially do) he wrote the piece *To a Nordic Princess,* dedicated to Ella Viola Strom Grainger, which was played at the wedding ceremonies, held in the Hollywood Bowl before an audience of some twenty thousand people. It is the old story, tersely summarized by Jean Cocteau when he said, "It is impossible both to be sincere and to seem sincere." Grainger has chosen to be sincere, to the amusement of the cynical, the abbarrassment of the conservative, and the delight of those who really know him. His thoughts on questions of musical style, jotted down for the benefit of the present writer, are characteristic:

I find no "modern" or "futuristic" music modern enough [he writes]. All the new music I hear (in which I am vitally interested) sounds to me amazingly old-fashioned. Ever since I was about ten or eleven years old (in Australia) I have heard in my imagination what I call "free music"—music that is not tied down to the slavery of scales, intervals, rhythm, harmony, but in which the tones dart, glide, curve like a bird in the air, a fish in the sea, and in which changes of pitch and changes of tone-strength can occur with the smooth gradualness we see in nature. . . . At present [1937] I am writing such "free music" for six Theremins—the Theremin being perfectly able to carry out my intentions. In the last few years I have become keenly interested in the older music of Europe . . . and in Asiatic music. . . . I feel that all music (primitive music, folk-music, art-music in Asia and Europe) probably had a common origin, certainly should have a common appeal. I feel at home in music of all races, all periods, all styles. And I feel that every serious musician should know as wide a range of musics as we all know in the other arts (literature, sculpture, painting, architecture, etc.)

But in spite of this universalist feeling for music, outlook upon music, I also feel that music should have local roots—should express the feelings of its country, race, nationality just as it also expresses the individual, personal feelings of its composer. . . . I think I can express my view on universality and nationalism in music as follows: "local sowing, universal harvest."

I do not think my music, or my musical outlook has changed (essentially) since I was 10, in Australia. My life (as a composer and musician) has been an attempt to carry out the ideals and intentions I had formed at that age—ideals formed mainly upon Bach in music, the Icelandic Sagas, and Anglo-Saxon poetry in literature.

Lamar Stringfield won a Pulitzer award in 1928 for his orchestral suite *From the Southern Mountains,* in which, as in all his music, he aimed to voice a distinctively American message. For he feels that the only way a composer can appeal to men of all nations is to speak of the things he knows best in the ways he knows best, and for Stringfield the natural idiom is in the tradition of Anglo-Saxon folk-music. He was born in Raleigh, North Carolina, in 1897, and lived in the mountains of the western part of that state during most of his youth. At first he planned to study medicine, and pursued music only as an avocation, studying with his older sisters and brothers. He served in the Army from 1916 to 1919, and then turned to the study of music as a profession. At the Institute of Musical Art, in New York, he graduated with the artist's diploma in flute-playing, and for the next few years he played and conducted in New York with various orchestras and chamber-music ensembles. In 1930 he promoted the organization of the Institute of Folk Music at the University of North Carolina, and shortly afterwards he became the musical director of the North Carolina Symphony Orchestra. He was later appointed regional director of the Federal Music Project of the WPA, and in 1938 joined the staff of the Radio City Music Hall as associate conductor.

He has written a symphonic poem, *Indian Legend;* a suite, *Moods of a Moonshiner;* a symphonic ballad, *The Legend of*

John Henry, and numerous shorter works, including the colorful *Negro Parade.* He has also published a collection of *Thirty and One Folk-Songs from the Southern Mountains.*

It is worthy of note that almost all of those who have been most interested in collecting and using the materials of our Anglo-Saxon heritage come from the South, where for many reasons a sense of racial and national and even regional homogeneity is both felt and fostered. The present volume cannot in most cases treat of composers or transcribers who have worked mainly in the smaller forms of the song, the piano piece, and the short chorus. But it may reasonably be argued that these are the most appropriate of all forms in which to treat folk-song, and there are some who have contributed notably to the understanding and popularity of the Anglo-Saxon folk heritage who are not chiefly composers of large works.

Associated with John Powell in collecting, preserving, and making known the Anglo-Saxon folk music of the Southeastern states has been *Annabel Morris Buchanan.* As lecturer, recitalist, writer on folk-music, collector of some two thousand tunes, Advisory Chairman of Folk Research for the American Federation of Music Clubs, Director of the Virginia State Choral and White Top Festivals and mother of four children, Mrs. Buchanan has not had much leisure for composition. Her published works include mainly transcriptions of folk-songs for chorus and a few original compositions based on folk-tunes. Best known are the two collections *Folk Hymns of America* and *White Top Folk Trails.* She has become recognized as an authority on this material, has written on it for many publications and reference works, and lectured on the modality of American folk-music to the International Music Congress in New York, in September, 1939. She was born at Grossbeck, Texas, October 22, 1889, was educated at Landon Conservatory in Dallas, and studied privately with Emil Liebling and Cornelius Rybner.

An attractive and picturesque worker in the same field has

been John Jacob Niles, who has published numerous collections of the songs of the Southern mountaineers and has brought them to life in vivid recitals in which he has sung these ballads and carols to delighted audiences. There are many others who have contributed importantly to our knowledge of the folk-songs of the Southern hill-folk, the cowboys, etc., whom it would be pleasant to discuss here if space allowed. But their names must not go unmentioned: Cecil Sharp, the pioneer, from England; Howard Brockway, and Loraine Wyman, John A. and Alan Lomax, George Pullen Jackson, Franz Rickaby—these are only a few.

Representing the Southwest is *David Wendell Fentress Guion*, born in Ballinger, Texas, December 15, 1895. Guion has written a few works in the larger forms: *Shingandi*, a Primitive African Ballet, for large symphony orchestra; a Suite for orchestra; and others. But he is best known for his very popular transcriptions for piano of *Turkey in the Straw, Sheep and Goat Walkin' to Pasture*, and the *Arkansas Traveler*, and for his arrangements of Cowboy songs and Negro songs and spirituals. Guion studied at the Royal Conservatory in Vienna, and has taught composition at the Chicago Musical College and elsewhere. He is an accomplished pianist, and has often played his own compositions in public. One of his boasts is that his kinship with the Cowboy is more than figurative: he is as much at home in the saddle as on the piano stool.

NEGRO COMPOSERS

There are many reasons why folk-music should be particularly cultivated among the Negroes. Cut off from many of the comforts, pleasures and social interchanges of their white fellow-citizens as they have often been, and naturally musical and gifted with singing voices as so many of them are, they inevitably have turned to music as a recreation and solace. Something in them responded to the white man's music almost as soon as they heard it, and it was not long before they had molded out of it an idiom characteristically their own. Where the ingredients come from and in what proportions they have been blended—these are not questions that concern us here. The fact is that, whatever their origin, they have been combined in a characteristic folk-idiom of the Negro—an idiom in many ways as distinctive as that of any of the much-touted folk-musics of distant lands. This is genuinely American folk-music, too, for whether the components come from Ireland, Scotland, or the Congo (and no doubt some of them come from each of these, and from many more places as well) they have been put together here to make up a folk-music that exists nowhere else.

Furthermore, while the white composer may or may not be conscious of his membership in a racial or national group, the Negro could not forget his if he would. His position in society forces on him an awareness of his fellowship in a community of color. His achievements may be so remarkable as to transcend the color line, and win from critics and public superlatives that any musician, white or black, might envy—as in the cases of Marian Anderson, Dorothy Maynor, Roland Hayes or Paul Robeson. Yet off the platform he is not often accepted as an equal member of society. But the human tragedy is the artist's opportunity; circumstances, which deny him so much, offer him in richer measure than any of his white colleagues the chance to speak for a race. He wishes, of course, to be judged by standards that have nothing to do with color, and so he must be, whether or not he makes use of the rich store of material that chance has left upon his doorstep.

Among the pioneers in bridging the gap between raw folk-material and art-music is *Henry Thacker Burleigh,* who is in his fifth decade of service as soloist in the exclusive St. George's Church in New York. He was born December 2, 1866, in Erie, Pennsylvania, was active as a church singer in his youth, and in 1892 won a scholarship for study with Dvořák at the National Conservatory in New York. It need hardly be stated that the play of influence between Burleigh and the composer of the *New*

World Symphony was mutual: Dvořák listened with enthusiasm to the Negro songs Burleigh sang for him.

Burleigh's arrangements of Negro spirituals were among the first to achieve wide popularity, and his *Deep River* is known throughout the land. His harmonizations are far from naïve or primitive; if anything they are cast a bit too much in the vein of European and American art-music, and tend to clothe these simple melodies in somewhat too familiar dress. But Burleigh's service to the popularization of the spiritual cannot be overemphasized.

William Levi Dawson, who since 1931 has been Director of the School of Music and of the Choir at Tuskegee, was born in Anniston, Alabama, in 1899. He studied composition and orchestration at Washburn College, Topeka, Kansas, and at the Horner Institute in Kansas City. He took a Master of Arts Degree at the American Conservatory in Chicago, and shortly afterwards became the first trombonist in the Chicago Civic Orchestra, the first Negro to occupy such a position, it is said. One of his qualifications for the job was the fact that none of the other applicants could read the alto clef. "I couldn't read it either," he later explained, "but Mr. Stock liked my attempt."

In 1930 and 1931, Dawson won the Rodman Wanamaker contest for composition. His *Negro Folk Symphony No. 1* was played several times by Leopold Stokowski and the Philadelphia Orchestra, and broadcast over the Columbia network. He is also the composer of a Scherzo for orchestra; several choral works; a Trio; and a Sonata for violin and piano.

R. Nathaniel Dett is one of the composers who owe a debt of gratitude to Percy Grainger for helping to make their works known; his lively *Juba Dance* is a very popular item in the pianist's repertoire. Dett has made many successful settings of spirituals, and is the author of several larger works, including the *Ordering of Moses,* for soloists, chorus and orchestra, performed at the Cincinnati and Worcester Festivals of 1937 and 1938, respectively, and by the Oratorio Society of New York in March, 1939.

Dett was born on the Canadian side of Niagara Falls, October 11, 1882, and studied at Oberlin. He has for many years been in charge of the music at Hampton Institute, and conducts the famous Hampton Choral Union. He was one of the composers commissioned by the Columbia Broadcasting System to write a work for radio in 1938.

Clarence Cameron White won the Bispham medal in 1933 for his opera *Ouanga*. His musical education was at Oberlin Conservatory and in Europe under Zacharewitsch and Coleridge-Taylor. He was born in Clarksville, Tennessee, August 10, 1880. He is a violinist, and his pieces for violin, among them the *Bandanna Sketches* and the transcription of *Nobody Knows the Trouble I've Seen*, have figured on the programs of Kreisler, Spalding, and other famous violinists. He has also written a *Negro Rhapsody* for orchestra, and a String Quartet on Negro themes, and has edited a collection of Negro spirituals.

By far the most widely recognized Negro composer today, however, is *William Grant Still*, who has been the recipient of the Harmon Award, the Rosenwald Fellowship, a Guggenheim Fellowship (several times), and commissions from the Columbia Broadcasting System, from Paul Whiteman, and from the New York World's Fair of 1939. Still was born in Woodville, Mississippi, May 11, 1895, and studied at Oberlin and later with Chadwick and Varèse. He learned the trade of arranging and orchestrating and practised it for W. C. Handy, Paul Whiteman, Don Voorhees and such musical shows as *Earl Carroll's Vanities*, *Rain or Shine*, and the unforgettable *Shuffle Along*. But his aims are serious, and he even figured at one time on the programs of so "advanced" an organization as the International Composers' Guild.

His *From the Land of Dreams*, which was performed at a concert of that organization in New York in February, 1925, caused a storm of protest. "Is Mr. Still unaware," wrote Olin Downes, "that the cheapest melody in the revues he has orchestrated has more reality and inspiration in it than the curious noises he has manufactured? Mr. Varèse has driven his original and entertaining music out of him."

But this was a mere excursion on Still's part, and it is characteristic of him that when he has outgrown a piece or a style he turns his back on it, or preserves what there may be in it that he can use and discards the rest. Thus he now considers his *From the Journal of a Wanderer*, first performed in 1926 at the North Shore Festival in Evanston, Illinois, with Frederick Stock conducting, a "lesson in what not to do!" And his *Darker America* (1924), published by the Eastman School of Music, he criticizes as fragmentary, containing too much material not sufficiently well organized.

About 1925, Still decided definitely to devote himself to the development of the Negro idiom and the treatment of Negro subjects in his programmatic works. Three of his larger works form a trilogy: *Africa*, the *Afro-American* Symphony, and the Symphony in G Minor. *Africa* has been revised no less than five times. The first version appeared in 1930; the sixth in 1935. It is in three movements: "Land of Peace," "Land of Romance," "Land of Superstition." The *Afro-American* Symphony also dates from 1930. Both works have been played widely, here and abroad. The Symphony in G Minor was introduced by Stokowski and the Philadelphia Orchestra in December, 1937. *Kaintuck*, for piano and orchestra, commissioned by the League of Composers, had its first performance in 1935, in Los Angeles, and *Lenox Avenue*, commissioned by the Columbia Broadcasting System, was first heard over the air in May, 1937.

Still has also written several stage works: *La Guiablesse* and *Sahdji*, ballets; *Blue Steel*, an opera; *Troubled Island*, another opera to a libretto by Langston Hughes; and considerable film music. His Cantata, *And They Lynched Him on a Tree*, with text by Katherine Garrison Chapin, wife of Solicitor-General Francis Biddle, was first performed under the baton of Artur Rodzinski at the Stadium concerts of the New York Philharmonic-Symphony Orchestra, in June, 1940. It is scored for two choruses, contralto solo, and orchestra. Howard Taubman, in the *New York Times*, wrote: [1]

Mr. Still has written with utter simplicity and with deep feeling.... A few harsh, cruel chords evoke the brutal crowd. The music achieves its greatest eloquence in the pages devoted to the Negro men and women and especially to the solo sung by the boy's mother. Using themes that are akin to spirituals, he gives her poignant, searching music.

Mr. Still and Miss Chapin throw light on the tragedy of a lynching as poets should. And they end with the plea:

"O trust your brother and reach out your hand!
And clear the shadow, the long dark shadow,
And clear the shadow that falls across the land."

The constant progress which Still has made promises well for his future. Already in the fifteen years since he first came to public attention he has gained such recognition as comes to few composers, white or black.

In contrast to the number of American composers in general, which has increased enormously in the last twenty years, the roster of those enlisted under the banner of folk-song has not grown perceptibly longer. In part this is due, no doubt, to the realization, mentioned above, that the development of a national folk-song idiom is neither so simple nor so imperative a matter as it was once thought to be. On the other hand, it is partly because many composers who do not belong to any "folk-song school" have nevertheless become increasingly conscious of their national heritage, and have employed themes and subjects of a folk or nationalistic nature in some of their works. We cannot recapitulate all the instances here, but before leaving the subject entirely it would be well, perhaps, to cast a glance back at a few of the many men who have occupied themselves with American materials of one sort or another. Cadman, Farwell, and Gilbert were

[1] June 26, 1940.

among the early enthusiasts. Damrosch (*The Scarlet Letter*, *The Man Without a Country*), Goldmark (*The Gettysburg Address*), Mason (*Lincoln Symphony*), and Converse (*Flivver Ten Million*) are among those of the older generation who have interested themselves in American subjects, while making more or less use of nationalistic melodic materials. And among the younger men, the names of Harris (*Johnny Comes Marching Home*, *Folk-Song Symphony*, and a generally American melodic tinge), Copland (*The Second Hurricane*, film music), Moore (*The Pageant of P. T. Barnum*), Herrmann (*Moby Dick*), Gruenberg (*Emperor Jones*)—these are only some that spring to mind.

Finally, to return to one of the points from which this discussion started, there is jazz, which is certainly very close to being the folk-music of our city dwellers, at least. But let us ring down the curtain quickly before the brickbats begin to fly; let the obstreperous sounds of Broadway and their echoes be confined within a separate chapter.

8

BROADWAY AND ITS ECHOES

It is not by accident that the word "jazz" does not appear in the title of this chapter. For the word has almost as many definitions as definers; jazz is all things to all men. And even the broadest definitions would not embrace all our popular music, which, with its echoes in "art music," forms the subject of this chapter.

Despite all the changes that have taken place in our musical life, it remains true that we who concern ourselves mainly with "serious music" are apt to take a somewhat snobbish attitude toward popular music, and there is a tendency to feel that in the musical history of America it doesn't really count. Now *count* is just what it does do, not only four beats in a measure, but avid listeners by the ten-millions. We should not think of suggesting that the value of music is to be determined strictly according to its popularity as measured in numbers of people—much less by that popularity at any one given time. Still, it is essential that we get a little perspective on ourselves and our tastes. Much of the music we value from the past is important to us, we say, because it is so characteristic of its period, or because it expresses the spirit of its time so well. But if that is really what makes music important, how can we deny that the music which is listened to, sung, and whistled daily by the vast majority of our fellow citizens has an importance which we must recognize? "God must love the common people," and if the common people love a style of music which at first does not appeal to us, maybe we had better look into it a bit more closely and see what it is that they do love.

American popular music is mostly jazz, in the widest sense of that mysterious word. But not altogether; some of our most successful musical-comedy and operetta composers stem rather from the traditions of Franz Lehar, Oskar Straus, Reginald De Koven, and Victor Herbert than from those of the hot spots of New Orleans and Chicago. It will be well to discuss two of these men first, before we plunge into the murky waters of jazz discussion, where many strong swimmers have been known to falter.

Rudolf Friml, who was born in Prague (then the capital of Bohemia and later of Czecho-Slovakia), December 7, 1881, studied in his native land with Jiranek and Dvořák, and first came to America as accompanist to the great violin virtuoso, Jan Kubelik, in 1901. Shortly afterwards he appeared here as a concert pianist, and played his Piano Concerto with the New York Symphony Orchestra. It was not long before he forsook the concert platform for the musical-comedy and operetta stage—not as performer, but as composer of what has become some of the best known and most widely sung light music of the century. *The Vagabond King*, *The Firefly*, *Katinka*, *High Jinks*, and *Rose Marie* are but a few of the best known stage works to come from his pen; while all America has hummed and whistled such tunes as *Sympathy*, *Allah's Holiday*, *Chansonette*, the *Indian Love-Call*, and the *Donkey Serenade*.

Sigmund Romberg also comes from Central Europe: he was born in Hungary in 1887, and studied to be a civil engineer at the University of Bucharest. In America he first played the piano in Hungarian orchestras, but soon began an extraordinarily successful career as composer of light music for the stage. Some of the productions for which he has written the music are *Maytime*, *Rosalie*, *The Student Prince*, numerous *Passing Shows*, *Blossom Time*, and *New Moon*; and among his most popular songs are *Auf Wiedersehn*, *Will You Remember?*, and *Lover Come Back to Me*.

JAZZ

It is significant, perhaps, that Friml and Romberg—our most successful composers of popular music who are not writers of jazz—were born in Europe. Today almost all of the American-born popular composers have had more or less to do with jazz. For jazz, as may be seen, is a distinctly American phenomenon—perhaps the most distinctly American one that has yet appeared in the field of music, though there are those who would not feel that this was a matter for congratulation.

What is jazz? It may be defined, says an expert,[1] as "an American musical dialect strongly influenced by the Negro." "An American musical dialect"—there is understatement for you! Say rather *the* idiom in which American dance music has been cast since about 1915. And the term "American dance music" must be taken in the widest sense, the same sense in which a gigue of Bach or a minuet of Mozart is German dance music. The origin of the word jazz is obscure. Perhaps it was derived from proper names: Razz's Band in New Orleans, Chas. ("Chaz") Washington in Vicksburg; or from an old minstrel term *jasbo,* meaning a sure-fire turn or trick; or from the French word *jaser*. Perhaps it originated in New Orleans, where Lafcadio Hearn reported finding it in the Creole dialect spoken there; or in Chicago, where it is said to have had originally a less than respectable meaning.

Wherever the term originated, its use spread, and so did the thing itself, from Chicago, during the year or so before America entered the war. Apparently it had existed among Negro instrumentalists for years before that, but it was not nationally known, among both white and black races, until one or two New Orleans bands had moved north to Chicago, about 1914.

But before we trace its history further, we must venture a statement about what jazz consists of. For a while, everything noisy, and coarse, and slapstick in popular music was called jazz; but

---

[1] Winthrop Sargeant, "Jazz," *International Cyclopedia of Music and Musicians,* edited by Oscar Thompson. Dodd, Mead & Company, 1939.

nowadays we realize that the jazz idiom, like many another style, has certain characteristics which can be described in the ordinary, polite terms of musical analysis.

Its chief, but not its only, distinguishing characteristic is in its rhythm. Jazz depends on syncopation. Now syncopation is an effect well known to the religious composers of the Middle Ages, so it must be stated at once that the use of syncopation in jazz is something not in principle new, but new in scale and effectiveness. Jazz is a music originally intended to stimulate dancing, or bodily movement in some form—tapping, clapping, stamping, jumping up and down, etc. For this purpose it sets a regular $\frac{4}{4}$ beat going. But instead of simply grinding out four beats and two accents, a primary and a secondary, in each measure, it *implies* as many of these accents as possible, and leaves them for the moving body of the listener to fill in. A Sousa march is calculated to set your feet in motion by sounding accents at a tempo that fits the swing of your legs; by sympathetic vibration, as one might say. Jazz accomplishes the same thing in a subtler and more compelling way by dodging the accents you expect, so that you feel an almost irresistible urge to fill them in yourself.

In dodging these obvious accents, it employs various devices. One is to delay or anticipate the accents, a device which was a favorite of Schumann's, but which he never used, needless to say, in the systematic way, or the regular, even-walking tempo of jazz. Another is to set up conflicting accents—groupings which temporarily obscure the underlying $\frac{4}{4}$ without ever really swamping it. This, too, is not a new device in itself: cross-rhythms have been known from the Elizabethans (and earlier) to Brahms. A third device is the almost complete suppression of all accents, simultaneous with the use of both the other devices to disguise the basic rhythm. Rhythmic music without accents is not new either; listen to a Bach organ fugue. But the particular way in which all these devices have been combined in jazz is new. Its consistent, continual use of them all, in tempi chosen to produce the maximum physical reaction—that is what is new about jazz rhythm. Ragtime was a crude, elementary step in the direction of jazz rhythm; but where one leaves off and the other begins no one can state exactly.

Jazz has its distinguishing characteristics in harmony and melody, as well. They are less original than its rhythmic character, but no less essential. The harmony tends, like the rhythm, to have a very simple basis, disguised by a good deal of elaboration. Rudimentary root-progressions are dressed up with many seventh-chords and non-harmonic tones. "Barber-shop" chords are not neglected. Added-sixth chords and dominant-seventh chords tend to take the place of simple triads. Partly harmonic and partly melodic is the use of "blue" notes—mostly the lowered third and seventh degrees of the scale, to produce a mode which is neither major nor minor, but characteristically jazz. The melodies themselves are mostly very simple, basically, and are often pentatonic in flavor, as are the Negro spirituals to which jazz is closely related. They are almost always in four-bar phrases, grouped in threes and fours to make twelve, sixteen, twenty-four, and thirty-two bar units.

So far as its rhythmic characteristics are concerned, all jazz shares them, though of course they are sometimes used with great originality and sometimes with none. But the melodic and harmonic characteristics vary according to the type of jazz. And here we enter a field of discussion as full of hair-line distinctions as a seminar in musicology, and as bristling with class-discrimination as the society pages. All jazz musicians, probably, and certainly all jazz critics (there are many of them nowadays) resent the snobbish attitude of academically-trained musicians toward what they insist is a folk-art. But among themselves they have their own snobberies, and the neatness of their categories is a source of unending bewilderment to the outsider.

This much seems true: there are two main streams of jazz. The one has its source truly in folk-art, the exuberant strumming and tootling of the unlettered Negro musician, and the crooning and shouting of the untrained colored singer. The other flows off from this into the channels of commerce. That is, it makes use of much of the folk-idiom in furnishing music on a large scale for the music counters, the record booths, the big night clubs and dancing places, the broadcasting stations, and the slot-machine phonographs.

The scorn of the jazz enthusiasts for this "commercial" music is unlimited, even though Tin Pan Alley (as the popular music business is familiarly known) has numbered among its cohorts such famous names as Kern, Berlin, and Gershwin. These men, and many others to be mentioned, have written the tunes that all America has sung. Yet listen to one of the best informed critics of jazz, Winthrop Sargeant, writing in his book, *Jazz Hot and Hybrid:* [2]

> Its melodies [those of jazz] are not handed down comparatively intact from generation to generation, as are most folk melodies. Nor do the people who create it, or who participate in its creation (which, with much of it, amounts to the same thing), fall neatly into the categories—composer, performer, and audience—that are associated with the production of concert music. . . . A tune may be "composed," as we understand the term, by a Tin Pan Alley song-writer. In itself it will, ninety-nine cases out of a hundred, be a wholly uninteresting bit of melodic claptrap, almost indistinguishable from thousands of others of its type, written according to an invariable and childishly unimaginative formula, and destined to be forgotten within a few weeks of its appearance. This feeble specimen of the tunesmith's art may then reach the hands of a clever arranger with a fund of practical musicianship and a good ear for instrumental effect. This gentleman will dress it up with adroit devices of modulation and instrumentation, giving it a semblance of extended form and forestalling its inherent monotony with various recipes for contrast. Next, the composition, if so it may now be termed, passes into the hands of one of the more ambitious sorts of dance orchestra, and is carefully rehearsed. The players, however, do not stick to the letter of the arranger's score, as symphonic musicians do to the notes of a symphony or an overture. They worry and cajole the rhythms and phrases of their solos, extemporizing here and there, introducing "breaks" (or short improvised

[2] New York: Arrow Editions, 1938.

cadenzas) of their own devising, and otherwise ornamenting the printed skeleton that has been provided for their collective guidance.

... The composer, that towering artistic figure of concert music, occupies here a very lowly if not entirely unnecessary role. In the end, his "composition" is almost completely lost sight of, or at best serves as a mere framework on which more interesting things are hung.

Now, while Sargeant's description of the processes by which a tune becomes a "special arrangement" is accurate enough, he has certainly underestimated the role of the composer, even in this "commercial" sort of music, to which another jazz critic, Wilder Hobson, author of *American Jazz Music*,[3] would hardly apply the term jazz at all. A theme by Haydn and another by Handel served Brahms for two grandiose sets of Variations, in which our interest is certainly centered in the elaborations rather than the theme itself; but what would these Variations have been without Haydn and Handel?

"SWING" AND ITS PERFORMERS

Hobson is interested in the truly folk side of the jazz development, that side which has come to be known in the last few years as "swing." In this art, the printed notes ("I can read 'em, but I can't separate 'em," one jazz artist is said to have explained!) are completely out of sight, if not always out of mind, and the players give free rein to their fancy, improvising freely on the mere harmonic basis of an agreed tune, or sometimes even without that common ground. This art abounds, therefore, in polyrhythms, in highly dissonant "counterpoint," and in melodic invention of an extremely free and soaring nature. It is often noisy, but not necessarily so. And its very existence proves that jazz is a definite style, whose conventions are so well understood by those who practise it that they can improvise simultaneously something which often makes a piece of music.

It is this art that has had in recent years the most fervent

[3] New York: W. W. Norton and Company, 1939.

devotees—the word is used with design, for if ever there was a cult, "swing" is it. It has a whole vocabulary that is Greek to the uninitiated. Some of it is funny, and characteristic of the American slang passion for calling nothing by its right name. Some of it is most expressive; and some reflects the disarming naïveté of the untutored Negro musician. Thus, for example, an early "spasm" band of New Orleans numbered among its members two individuals who rejoiced in the names of Stale Bread and Family Haircut. "Corn" to the swing fan is the old-fashioned, sticky quality that keeps a band or a musician from being "hot." A "sweet" band is one that plays primarily from written notes (and consequently preserves a fairly smooth harmonic and instrumental texture). "Dirty" tone is the rough, breathy quality which some jazz singers and players cultivate. (Hobson, incidentally, well points out the "vocalization" of instrumental tone and style, with glissandi, portamenti, vibrati, flutter-tongue effects, and so on, that characterizes jazz playing.)

Like every cult, swing has its devils—the "corny" ones. And it has its idols, some of whose names, at least, should be recorded here. Ordinarily, performers as such are outside the province of this book. But in swing, or hot jazz, as has been pointed out, the player is often composing as he goes along, and never simply playing what someone else has written. So each of the following names belongs to someone who, in addition to his function as a mere performer, has made creative contributions to the art of jazz as well. They include:

Louis Armstrong,[4] one of the very top names in jazz, famous Negro trumpet player; born in New Orleans in 1900, played first there, later in Chicago, and in recent years in New York, various capitals of Europe, and anywhere else he has wanted to. Of him Virgil Thomson has written that he is "a master of musical art comparable only . . . to the great *castrati* of the eighteenth century. His style of improvisation would seem to have

---

[4] See *Swing That Music* (an autobiography). Longmans, Green & Company, 1936.

combined the highest reaches of instrumental virtuosity with the most tensely disciplined melodic structure and the most spontaneous emotional expression, all of which in one man you must admit to be pretty rare." [5]

William ("Count") Basie, Negro pianist and leader of one of the leading big bands—big, that is, for a "swing" band, consisting of more than a dozen men.

Leon Bismarck ("Bix") Beiderbecke, Chicago cornetist, who, because his untimely death in 1931 ended playing which is described as unique in tone, rhythm, and melodic line, endlessly inventive, yet restrained, is reverenced to an extraordinary degree among swing musicians and enthusiasts.

Jimmy and *Tommy Dorsey,* brothers, each of whom leads a famous band. Jimmy plays the clarinet and alto saxophone; Tommy is a virtuoso on the trombone. For Tommy Dorsey's band, Roy Harris wrote his Fourth Symphony.

Edward K. ("Duke") Ellington, who perhaps vies with Louis Armstrong for the title of best known Negro jazz musician. Ellington, born in Washington, D.C., in 1899, is a brilliant jazz pianist, leader, and composer—not only a collaborator in composition, like all these men, but a composer in his own right. It should be said that the members of his band "compose along with him," but the basic ideas, melodic, orchestral, and formal, are his. His band is one of the larger groups. Through his records and his radio broadcasts, Ellington enjoys one of the biggest reputations in the field. He played for several years in Paris, and is well known throughout Europe as well as at home. *Mood Indigo* and *Solitude* are among his best known pieces.

Benny Goodman,[6] clarinetist extraordinary, whose talents and whose very well managed publicity together have crowned him "King of Swing." (It is not so many years since Whiteman was

---

[5] "Swing Music," Virgil Thomson, *Modern Music,* May–June, 1936.
[6] New York: *The Kingdom of Swing* (an autobiography): Stackpole Sons, 1939.

the "King of Jazz"; that King is not dead, so long live the Kings!) Nothing is too good for Goodman, neither the Waldorf-Astoria, where he played regularly for a time, nor the Mozart Clarinet Quintet, which he has played and recorded with the Budapest Quartet, nor Béla Bartók, who wrote a work for him and the violinist Szigeti. Conservative critics have found his playing of the classic repertoire perhaps a little academic, but in no way objectionable; commerce has smiled on him, for he has had perhaps the most sensational success of recent years in the field of jazz; and yet the jazz authorities include him in their Pantheon. The gods are not so good to many.

William Christopher Handy, sometimes called the Father of the Blues, composer of the most famous blues tune, the *St. Louis Blues*, born November 16, 1873 in Florence, Alabama, son of a Negro preacher. The *Memphis Blues* is Handy's, too; likewise the *Beale Street* and *Yellow Dog*. The *Memphis Blues* was published in 1912, and the *St. Louis* shortly afterwards; both are still favorite tunes among all types of jazz musicians.

Coleman Hawkins, who, according to Hobson, "has been to the tenor saxophone what Armstrong has to the trumpet." He has been a member of bands led by Joe Oliver, Fletcher Henderson, and "Count" Basie, among others.

The brothers *Fletcher* and *Horace Henderson*, the former a noted Negro band leader, and the latter a pianist, arranger, and composer (of the "hot jazz" rather than the "commercial" type). Fletcher Henderson is also a pianist. The Henderson brothers have specialized in scores designed to support and furnish a background for brilliant solo improvising by members of the band.

Gene Krupa, an outstanding jazz drummer. The term "drummer" really means percussionist, of course, for drums are only a part of the equipment of the "rhythm section," which, in addition to piano and plucked string instruments (banjo, string-bass, guitar), includes a battery of what used to be known as "traps."

The era of using tin pans, cowbells, and anything else both unconventional and noisy to give the effect of great vitality is largely past. The jazz drummer of today relies on subtler and more genuine means of stimulating his comrades and infusing them with the tempo. It is for them at least as much as for any listeners that he plays.

Meade ("Lux") Lewis, famous "boogie-woogie" pianist, who, at the time (1936) when he made some recordings which have been very popular, was washing automobiles in a Chicago garage. An element of his style is the use of an ostinato figure in the left hand, in some characteristic, rolling rhythm, with free improvisation in the right.

"Wingy" Mannone, one-armed trumpeter, who is the reported source of the remark that he "couldn't separate 'em."

Milfred Mole, trombonist, whose attractive name is immortalized on records made by "Miff Mole and his little Molers."

Loring ("Red") Nichols, who often played with "Miff" and was well known some years ago to record buyers and radio listeners as the leader of "Red Nichols and his Five Pennies."

Joe ("King") Oliver, trumpeter, originally from New Orleans, where he taught and inspired Louis Armstrong to play the trumpet; later of Chicago, where his band at the Lincoln Gardens attracted great attention in the early 1920's.

Bill Robinson, the king of tap-dancers, whose feet are as expressive a pair of musical instruments as any percussion instrument very well could be. Robinson is not as young as he used to be, but as late as the New York World's Fair of 1939 his dancing in *The Hot Mikado*—a partially jazzed version of the Gilbert and Sullivan classic—was telling more than volumes of analysis and criticism ever could about the nature and the origins of jazz.

"Pee Wee" Russell, clarinetist and saxophonist, specialist in improvisation of the "hotter" and "dirtier" variety. (For "dirty," an older generation would have said simply "tough.")

Bessie Smith, "Empress of the Blues," some of whose robust and heartfelt singing was gathered into a special memorial record album shortly after her death in an automobile accident in 1938.

Joe Sullivan, Chicago pianist, whose conservatory training did not spoil him for hot jazz, and who has played with Louis Armstrong, Benny Goodman, and others at the top of the business.

Jack Teagarden, remarkable trombonist, originally from Texas, who has belonged to several leading bands including Louis Armstrong's and Paul Whiteman's. (The latter organization, although it has varied considerably through the years, and has adapted itself to changes in style and taste, has always specialized in the "sweet" or "symphonic" type of jazz, leaving little or no room for improvising. But many of the best improvisers are also first-class technicians on their instruments, and it is as such that such men as Teagarden and Beiderbecke have found places in Whiteman's band.)

Thomas ("Fats") Waller, Harlem-born Negro pianist, who is a brilliant jazz improviser as well as the composer of some published tunes.

Teddy Wilson, young Negro pianist, who has also played the harpsichord both in jazz and in concert performances of eighteenth-century music.

The foregoing is of course by no means a complete list, but it includes many of the most familiar names and admired personalities of "hot jazz," "swing," or whatever else it is now or will shortly be called. The humorous aspects of the subject have not been neglected, not because we take a superior and amused attitude toward the phenomena of jazz, but because humor is an essential element of this folk-art. It is *with,* not *at,* the men with the funny names that one laughs; for their humor is far from unconscious, and it is not only a matter of names. Or even of words. Chuckles as well as raucous laughter are often in this music itself, and the only unconsciously ludicrous element is the attitude which insists on taking it like a sacrament. But then, there are those who can listen to the most rollicking gigue of Bach, or sit through a good performance of *Die Meistersinger,* without cracking a smile.

BROADWAY COMPOSERS

This has been a pleasant excursion. But now we must return to a subject a little nearer home,—to men in the field of popular music who are, despite Mr. Sargeant's disparaging remarks, composers, in the usual sense of the word. Perhaps not all of them in quite the usual sense, for they include men who can't write down the tunes they invent, or, if they can write them, can't harmonize them fully, or orchestrate them. This fact has been cited by those who would deny them the name of composer altogether. But does a man have to know the alphabet to be a poet? Despite the obvious truth that many of the most successful tunes are very much alike, and that it seems as if any clever person could manufacture tunes which would be as good as some of them, the fact remains that in defiance of the most careful calculations of the cleverest people, some tunes "take hold" and some don't, and it is foolish to maintain that even the best luck and the best "plugging" can give a man without native melodic invention a series of song-hits. Granted that melodic invention is only one part of the composer's task; but, in this field at least, it is the absolutely essential part, and for every one with a gift for tunes there are a dozen who can edit and arrange them acceptably for him.

Along with Handy, two of the Negro pioneers of jazz were the brothers *J. Rosamond Johnson,* born in Jacksonville, Florida, August 11, 1873, and *James Weldon Johnson,* who was born in Jacksonville, June 17, 1871, and died June 26, 1939. In their early years, both were interested in music for the comedy and vaudeville stages. Later, however, the elder brother, James, became a poet and public figure of great prominence among his race, and from 1916 to 1930 was Secretary of the National Association for the Advancement of Colored People. The younger brother turned his attention more to the Negro spiritual and to music education among the Negroes, serving as Director of the Music School Settlement for Colored People in New York. Together the brothers wrote a song that has become known as the Negro National Anthem, *Lift Every Voice and Sing*.

Another pair of brothers who were prominent in popular music very early in the Century are the *Von Tilzers, Harry* (born July 8, 1872, in Detroit, Michigan) and *Albert* (born March 29, 1878, in Indianapolis, Indiana). Their names are associated with the popular music of yesterday, not with jazz. Albert wrote such songs as *Forever Is a Long Time*, and *I'll Be with You in Apple-blossom Time;* Harry is the composer of many old-time hits, including *Take Me Down Where the Würzburger Flows; Wait Till the Sun Shines, Nellie;* and *I Want a Girl*. Harry Von Tilzer entered the music publishing business just about at the turn of the century, and has had his own publishing firm since 1902.

George M. Cohan has had a notably successful career in the theatre, as song-and-dance-man, as actor, producer, director, playwright, and composer, without having had much to do with anything that could really be called jazz. Cohan was born July 4 (N.B.), 1878, in Providence, Rhode Island, and had written song successes before he was twenty-one years old. Some of his successful musical productions were *Forty-Five Minutes from Broadway, Little Nellie Kelly, The Rise of Rosie O'Reilly*, etc., while his songs include *Give My Regards to Broadway, I'm a Yankee Doodle Dandy, Mary is a Grand Old Name*, and of course the never-to-be-forgotten *Over There*, the biggest hit of the First World War days. For this song, Congress awarded Cohan a medal, which was presented to him by President Roosevelt.

Popular composers are not in the habit of winning medals or awards, or of looking for them. Their reward, which in some few cases has been very large, comes in the money that a song brings in. But when a song written in 1918 and rejected then by the composer as unsatisfactory, is reclaimed from the scrap-heap some twenty years later to please a radio singer, promptly becomes an outstanding success, and is crowned with an award by a so-called National Committee for Music Appreciation, that should be news.

As *Irving Berlin* himself said, upon receiving the award at a dinner in September, 1940, "I can tell you one thing; this is the closest I've ever been to good music." It all depends on what one means by "good," and no one can deny that Berlin has written better songs than *God Bless America*. But apparently it just fitted in with the popular mood during the days when Europe was destroying itself as fast as it could. Berlin set up a board of trustees to receive the royalties and spend them for the benefit of the Boy Scouts and Girl Scouts of America, and within two years something like $50,000 had accumulated!

It is fitting that this popular substitute for a national anthem should have been written by one who has enacted a typical American success story. Born Izzy Baline, May 11, 1888, in Russia, the son of a Jewish cantor, he was brought to America as an infant, and still carries the scar on his forehead caused by a knife that was dropped by someone from an upper bunk in the steerage section of the boat in which he crossed the Atlantic. He grew up on New York's lower East Side, the same environment that produced Al Smith, George White, and many other New York celebrities. He was not fond either of school or of the more prosaic forms of work, and at an early age he ran away from home to pick up a living as best he could as a busker—that is, a sidewalk and saloon entertainer. Later he was a singing waiter at Nigger Mike's in Chinatown. It was while he was there that he wrote his first song, *Marie from Sunny Italy*. That is, he wrote the words, and one N. Nicholson, the pianist of Nigger Mike's, wrote the music; Berlin did not blossom forth as a composer himself until some time later. He was fired from Nigger Mike's, eventually, for sleeping while he was supposed to be guarding the cash box.

That was when he decided to go uptown to Tin Pan Alley. And it was a great day for Tin Pan Alley when he did, for, beginning in the lowest ranks of that crowded thoroughfare, he made his way steadily upward and has had one of the most spectacular careers in popular music. For many years now, he has had his own publishing house, and his combined income, from song royalties, the publishing business, and production royalties, has been on a par with the salaries paid to captains of industry. It is a number of years now since he married the daughter of one of those very captains—Ellen Mackay, daughter of the leader of the Postal Telegraph-Commercial Cable combine.

Berlin has written many different kinds of tunes: sentimental ballads, dance tunes, tricky jazz-rhythm novelties. But he has always had his ear to the ground, and has frankly composed tunes to sell as many copies as possible, eliminating whatever he found too intricate or too sophisticated for the widest public. That he has known what to eliminate, and that there has been something left that the public cared for, is strikingly attested by a list of a few of his songs: *My Wife's Gone to the Country; Alexander's Ragtime Band; Everybody's Doin' It; When that Midnight Choo-choo Leaves for Alabam; He's a Devil; Oh, How I Hate to Get Up in the Morning; A Pretty Girl is Like a Melody; When My Baby Smiles at Me; Everybody Step; Lady of the Evening; Who; What'll I Do; All Alone; Russian Lullaby; Always; Blue Skies; Remember; Pack Up Your Sins*. In the season of 1940–41 his latest musical comedy, *Louisiana Purchase*, was continuing the Berlin success tradition.

If *Jerome Kern* (January 27, 1885, New York City) had never written a note of music except for his operetta *Showboat*, he would be entitled to a high place in the annals of American popular music (perhaps one might even omit the word "popular"). For *Showboat* is a contemporary classic, there is no doubt about it, and it voiced in pleasant, tuneful, and sincere music, for a large audience, a genuinely native quality that will be sought in vain in our more pretentious efforts for the lyric stage. *Showboat* treated a folk-subject, and, we make bold to say, treated it with folk-music, of Mr. Kern's own composition, but coming from the heart of the American people and speaking to them in a language they recognized and accepted as their own. Musical shows are usually ephemeral things, but *Showboat* is an exception. First produced in 1929, *Showboat* has been successfully revived several times since, both on the stage and on the screen, and as this book goes to press it is promised yet again for the season of 1940–41. *Can't Help Lovin' that Man of Mine, My Bill, Why Do I Love You,* and other *Showboat* tunes were not the "hottest," latest things when they came out, and are not dated now. They are a very mild and polite form of jazz, yet they are not dull or too sweet or tawdry or any of the unpleasant adjectives that could be applied to many tunes of their age. They have no specific originality. They are just tunes one doesn't tire of. And the most popular of them all (though perhaps not the best), *Old Man River,* is not jazz at all, though its mainly pentatonic melody gives it an authentic Negroid flavor. Kern is the composer of numerous other musical productions, including *Sally, Sunny, Oh Boy, Sweet Adeline, The Cat and the Fiddle,* and others.

Since this is not a book devoted primarily to our popular music, every composer in the field cannot be discussed in detail. Some must be omitted entirely; others can hardly be more than listed; while only for a few is there space for any really informative detail. The following composers have written some of the songs that America has sung most, heard most, and bought most during the first forty years of the twentieth century or so. Excluded are Victor Herbert and Reginald De Koven, for two reasons: first, their music belongs as much to the nineteenth century as it does to the twentieth; and second, they died in 1924, and 1920, respectively, and are therefore fully covered by the present author's earlier volume, *Our American Music*. The composers are presented alphabetically; the songs listed are among their best-known tunes.

MILTON AGER

Born October 6, 1893, Chicago, Illinois.
Pianist, arranger, song-writer, and publisher.
Songs: *I Wonder What's Become of Sally; Ain't She Sweet; Happy Days Are Here Again.*

SHELTON BROOKS

Born May 4, 1886, Amesburg, Ontario.

ASCAP

Jerome Kern

Vaudeville pianist and composer.
Songs: *Darktown Strutters' Ball*; *Swing that Thing!*

HOAGY CARMICHAEL

Born November 22, 1903, Bloomington, Indiana.
Gave up law for musical career; pianist and composer.
Songs: *Stardust*; *Georgia on My Mind*; *Lazy Bones*; *Come Easy Go Easy Love*.

FRANK E. CHURCHILL

Born October 20, 1901, Rumford, Maine.
Composer for Walt Disney animated cartoons.
Songs: *Who's Afraid of the Big Bad Wolf?*; *Whistle While You Work*.

EDWARD E. ("ZEZ") CONFREY

Born April 3, 1895, in Illinois.
Pianist and composer, particularly of a sort of trick or novelty ragtime, of the sort that used to be played by movie pianists to accompany a Mack Sennett comedy. Author of a book, *Novelty Piano Playing*, of which one hundred and fifty thousand copies were sold in its first two months off the press. Originally had ambitions as a concert pianist, and attended Chicago Musical College. His song, *Stumbling*, was an early and striking (if obvious) popularization of cross-rhythms. *Kitten on the Keys*, a piano piece, is something of a classic; likewise *Poor Buttermilk*.

WALTER DONALDSON

Born February 15, 1893, Brooklyn, New York.
Songs: *My Blue Heaven*; *My Mammy*; *How Ya Gonna Keep 'em Down on the Farm?*

GUS EDWARDS

Born August 18, 1878, in Germany.
An old-time vaudeville performer and producer.
Songs: *By the Light of the Silvery Moon*; *Tammany*; *School Days*; *Hello Melody, Goodbye Jazz*.

RAY HENDERSON

Born December 1, 1896, Buffalo, New York.
One of the few popular composers who has had thoroughly conventional training, from private teachers and at the Chicago Con-

servatory. Composer member of the team (and publishing firm) of De Sylva, Brown, and Henderson.

Songs: *My Sin; Sonny Boy; Bye Bye Blackbirds; Follow the Swallow.*

WILLIAM J. ("BILLY") HILL

Born July 14, 1899, Boston, Massachusetts; died Boston, December 24, 1940.

Composer of several songs in "cowboy" idiom—a style that was very popular during the 1930's—and many others.

Songs: *Wagon Wheels; The Last Roundup.*

GEORGE W. MEYER

Born January 1, 1884, Boston, Massachusetts.

Secretary of the American Society of Composers, Authors, and Publishers; composer of sentimental songs characteristic of another day.

Songs: *For Me and my Gal; I Believe in Miracles.*

COLE PORTER

Born June 9, 1892, Peru, Indiana.

A sophisticate among the song-writers, in his handling of both music and word-setting. One of the most successful composers for the Broadway stage, after (in spite of?) musical training at Harvard and the Schola Cantorum in Paris. His *Panama Hattie*, a musical show, opened on Broadway in October, 1940.

Songs: *Get Out of Town; In the Still of the Night; Night and Day; Rosalie; What Is this Thing Called Love?; Begin the Beguine.*

RALPH RAINGER

Born October 7, 1901, New York City.

Studied at the New York Institute of Musical Art; graduated with honors from law school; gave up law, as have several others, for success in the song-writing field.

Songs: *Moanin' Low; Thanks for the Memory; June in January.*

RICHARD RODGERS

Born June 28, 1902, New York City.

Composer member of the famous song-writing team of Rodgers and Hart, who have written many of the most successful Broadway musical productions of the 1920's and '30's, including *Higher and Higher; On Your Toes; Heads Up; A Connecticut Yankee; The Girl Friend; Dearest Enemy.*

HAROLD J. ROME

Born May 27, 1908, Hartford, Connecticut.

An architect by profession; achieved fame in the song-writing field with his music for *Pins and Needles,* a witty revue produced by Labor Stage, adapting the technique of earlier intimate reviews (*Garrick Gaieties; The Little Show,* etc.) to a Leftist point of view.

Songs: *Sunday in the Park; One Big Union for Two; Sing Me a Song of Social Significance.*

ARTHUR SCHWARTZ

Born November 25, 1900, Brooklyn, New York.

Another ex-lawyer (there are many of them among the song-writers) who has also been an English teacher, holds four university degrees, and is a member of Phi Beta Kappa. Won his reputation first through his music for intimate revues: *The Grand Street Follies; The Little Show; Three's a Crowd;* but has also had to do with larger-scale successes: *Flying Colors; Revenge with Music; Band Wagon; American Jubilee.*

Songs: *Dancing in the Dark; You and the Night and the Music; Something to Remember You By.*

ALEC TEMPLETON

Born July 4, 1910, in Cardiff, Wales.

One of the very few Englishmen who have wholeheartedly adopted and been adopted by our popular music, Templeton had an orthodox musical education at the Royal Academy of Music in London, and studied with Walford Davies, among others, who is Elgar's successor as Master of the King's Musick. Templeton's greatest talents are in improvisation (of the more conventional musical type, rather than strictly in the field of swing) and in brilliant satire at the piano. He is a witty ironist and mimic and an excellent pianist, whose blindness since birth seems to have handicapped him almost not at all, as a musician. He has also written a good deal of music outside the popular field, but this, while quite respectable and competent, lacks the great originality of his satiric music like *Bach Goes to Town* and *Mendelssohn Mows 'em Down.*

HARRY TIERNEY

Born May 21, 1890, Perth Amboy, New Jersey.

Best known for his greatly successful *Sweet Little Alice Blue Gown,* he has also written music for several hit shows, including the *Ziegfeld Follies; Irene;* and *Rio Rita.*

Harry Warren

Born December 24, 1893, New York City.

Worked his way up through many grades of the show, movie, and dance-hall business. Composer member of the song-writing team in which Al Dubin writes the lyrics.

Songs: *I Found a Million Dollar Baby (in the five-and-ten-cent store)*; *Would you Like to Take a Walk?*; *Cheerful Little Earful*; *Where do you Work-a John?*

Mabel Wayne

Born July 16, 1898, New York City.

Singer, dancer, and vaudeville entertainer, she scored remarkable successes with such songs as *Chiquita*; *In a Little Spanish Town*; and above all *Ramona*.

Vincent Youmans

Born September 27, 1898, New York City.

One of the great names in the musical comedy field of the 1920's, as composer of such outstanding successes as *Great Day*; *Hit the Deck*; and *No, No, Nanette*.

Songs: *Bambolina*; *Tea for Two*; *I Want to Be Happy*; *Hallelujah*; *More than You Know*.

JAZZ IN THE CONCERT HALL

So much for American popular music in its native habitat—an art of the "peepul," full of life, humor, sentiment, sometimes vulgarity, and not to be despised by anyone who cherishes the folk-songs of Andalusia, Hungary, Java, or the Kentucky Mountains.

But how has it happened that this art of the masses has found echoes in the reputedly rarefied domains of Art with a capital A? Well, America is a democracy, for one thing, and has become increasingly aware of the fact during the 1930's. As always happens, of course, deep, underlying tendencies have found instruments to help them along, and the instruments have received credit for what might have happened even without their intervention. But some of the instruments have really deserved a lot of the credit—conspicuous among them such men as Whiteman, Gershwin, and Grofé.

Paul Whiteman has been called the man who took jazz and "made an honest woman of her." Whiteman was born in Denver in 1891, the son of a public school music supervisor who had been a pioneer in the high school orchestra movement. Whiteman began his career as a symphony orchestra musician, playing the viola in the Denver Symphony Orchestra and the San Francisco People's Symphony Orchestra. When jazz struck San Francisco, in the teens of this century, Whiteman determined to learn the new idiom, and formed a small band. Its development was interrupted by the War, when Whiteman enlisted as a band leader.

His real career dates from his engagement at the Hotel Alexandria in Los Angeles. From there he went to the Ambassador, in New York; to the Palais Royal; to Europe; and to the top of the heap, a fact that was acknowledged by his cognomen, "The King of Jazz." In the "popular music racket," as Isaac Goldberg calls it,[7] kings do not rule for life; and Whiteman no longer reigns. But he is still a prominent figure (no pun is intended), and has held his popularity over an exceptionally long time.

Whiteman's big and, as it turns out, historic gesture came in 1924, when, on the afternoon of Lincoln's Birthday, he hired Aeolian Hall, in New York, and gave a concert which he called "An Experiment in Modern Music."[8] The program included old-time jazz like the *Livery Stable Blues*, "semi-symphonic arrangements" of popular tunes (this became Whiteman's specialty), and "adaptation of standard selections to dance rhythm"; and ended, somewhat incongruously, with Elgar's *Pomp and Circumstance*. The affair made history, not because of the great worth of much of the music presented, but because in it Tin Pan Alley came halfway to meet the serious composer; and it was not

---

[7] *Tin Pan Alley, A Chronicle of the American Popular Music Racket*, by Isaac Goldberg. The John Day Co., 1930.
[8] The full program of the affair is reprinted in the author's *Our American Music*, Thomas Y. Crowell Company. Second Edition, Revised and Enlarged, 1939.

too long before the serious composer reciprocated the gesture. (Carpenter had even anticipated it, as long ago as 1921, in his ballet *Krazy Kat*; but the encouragement that Whiteman gave the *entente* was important, nevertheless.) The deepest and by far the most impressive bow made in the direction of the classic muses on this occasion took the shape of a piece of symphonic jazz called the *Rhapsody in Blue*, by George Gershwin. Of course, the rest is history.

Gershwin had one of the most appealing melodic gifts among all the song-writers, and was the composer of a remarkable string of musical comedy and revue successes: *La La Lucille* (1919); *George White's Scandals* (1920–24); *Lady, Be Good* (1924); *Oh, Kay* (1925); *Strike Up the Band* (1927); *Funny Face* (1927); *Girl Crazy* (1930); *Of Thee I Sing* (1931); *Let 'Em Eat Cake* (1933). From them came tunes which have not been surpassed in Tin Pan Alley: *Swanee* (interpolated in Jolson's *Sinbad*); *That Certain Feeling*; *Fascinating Rhythm*; *Do, Do, Do*; *Fidgety Feet*; *Maybe*; *Sweet and Lowdown*; *The Man I Love*; *'s Wonderful*; *My One and Only*; *Enbraceable You*; and many others.

He was born in Brooklyn, New York, September 26, 1898. As a youngster he studied piano with Charles Hambitzer and harmony with Edward Kilenyi, and at the age of sixteen went to work for the firm of J. H. Remick & Company as a "song-plugger." He soon began to write his own songs and was launched on a career of remarkable brilliance. But he had "higher" ambitions, for which the Whiteman concert offered him the first good opportunity. The *Rhapsody in Blue* was an instantaneous success, and was listened to with rapture by the great American public, and with interest by numerous serious composers who felt it pointed in a direction that seemed to offer interesting possibilities. Two of the most exaggerated tributes and one of the most acid comments on the piece have come from England. In 1930, Albert Coates, the noted conductor, ranked the *Rhapsody* among the "fifty best musical compositions of all time." And Stanley R. Nelson, author of a somewhat fatuous book, *All About Jazz*,[9] wrote of the Tschaikowskian *espressivo* theme in the middle section, "To me, this noble tune is one of the most appealing things in all music." On the other hand, the witty young British musician, Constant Lambert,[10] speaks of the *Rhapsody* as "combining the more depressing mannerisms of jazz with all the formlessness of the nineteenth-century fantasia," and one has to admit that the second half of this reproach, at least, is accurate enough.

Gershwin's next venture in the symphonic field was commissioned by Walter Damrosch for the old New York Symphony Orchestra; it was the Concerto in F, written in 1925. For the *Rhapsody in Blue* the orchestration had been prepared by that remarkable Whiteman cohort, Ferde Grofé, but now that Gershwin had graduated into the ranks of symphony orchestra composers he decided that he must do his own scoring. Still belonging, however, to Tin Pan Alley so far as his income was concerned, Gershwin could afford to do what many of his more distinguished colleagues in the symphonic field must have envied him for—that is, hire an orchestra to play the piece over a few times, and then adjust the orchestration accordingly.

Gershwin played the piano part of the Concerto himself. Damrosch, who conducted, introduced the new work with these remarks:

> Various composers have been walking around jazz like a cat around a plate of hot soup, writing for it to cool off, so that they could enjoy it without burning their tongues, hitherto accustomed only to the more tepid liquid distilled by cooks of the classical school. Lady Jazz, adorned with her intriguing rhythms, has danced her way around the world, even as far as the Eskimos of the North and the Polynesians of the South Sea Isles. But for all her travels and her sweeping popularity, she has encountered no knight who could lift her to a level that would enable her to be received as a respectable member in musical circles.
>
> George Gershwin seems to have accomplished this miracle. He has done it boldly by dressing this extremely independent and up-to-date

---

[9] Heath Cranton Limited, 1934.
[10] *Life and Letters*, Vol. I, No. 2, July, 1928.

young lady in the classic garb of a concerto. Yet he has not detracted one whit from her fascinating personality. He is the Prince who has taken Cinderella by the hand and openly proclaimed her a princess to the astonished world, no doubt to the fury of her envious sisters.

Just who the sisters were, Dr. Damrosch didn't specify. But despite his graceful remarks and Gershwin's best playing, the Concerto didn't quite come off as the *Rhapsody* had done, although it enjoyed a considerable popularity for several years.

In *An American in Paris*, also written for Dr. Damrosch, and presented by him on the same program with the first performance of Bloch's *America*, Gershwin found a subject suited to his idiom, and created a very charming and relaxed bit of writing. It had humor, and gaiety, two of the things jazz could handle best. And its program—the adventures of an American (recognizably the composer himself) three thousand miles from home, opened the door to a "blue" mood and a blues theme that is one of Gershwin's happiest inspirations. Listening to it, one knows what was meant by Constant Lambert, and yet how wide of the mark he was, when he wrote: [11] ". . . jazz has long ago lost the simple gaiety of the charming savages to whom it owes its birth, and is now, for the most part, a reflection of the nerves, sex-repressions, inferiority complexes, and general dreariness of the modern world. The nostalgia of the Negro who wants to go home has given place to the infinitely more weary nostalgia of the cosmopolitan Jew who has no home to go to."

Like everything Mr. Lambert writes, his essay on jazz is intelligent and witty; but this is nonsense. Of course he didn't have *The American in Paris* in mind when he wrote it. But George Gershwin's nostalgia in Paris is one of the answers to Lambert. And the "charming savages" didn't confine themselves to "simple gaiety" in their jazz. On the contrary, the blues is one of the original forms of Negro jazz, and it celebrates the nerves, the sex-defeats if not repressions ("I hate to see de evenin' sun go down, Because my baby, he done lef' dis town"), and the general dreari-

[11] *Loc. cit.*

ASCAP

George Gershwin

ness of life for these same "charming savages." Frustration and homesickness are experiences that do not belong exclusively to savages or cosmopolitans, and jazz is one of the folk-arts in which people have always voiced their emotions over experiences like these.

On February 5, 1932, Gershwin played his Second Rhapsody, for piano and orchestra, in Carnegie Hall, New York, with the Boston Orchestra, under Dr. Serge Koussevitzky. On that occasion, Olin Downes wrote: [12]

> The score . . . is the expansion of a five-minute sequence introduced into the picture *Delicious,* a screen comedy drama, based on a story by Guy Bolton, with lyrics by Ira Gershwin and music by George, produced in 1931. The Rhapsody was written in California in the Spring of the same year and later somewhat revised. Some of the comedy scenes showed the streets of New York, and for the five-minute orchestral sequence Gershwin conceived a "rivet theme" to echo the tattoo of the skyscrapers. The Second Rhapsody had originally the title of "Rhapsody in Rivets."
>
> This rhapsody has more orchestration and more development than the *Rhapsody in Blue.* Its main motive is reasonably suggestive of rivets and racket in the streets of the metropolis; also, if you like, of the liveliness and bonhomie of its inhabitants. There is a second theme, built into a contrasting section. Thus jazz dance rhythm and sentimental song are opposed and juxtaposed in this score. The conception is wholly orchestral . . . But with all its immaturities, the *Rhapsody in Blue* is more individual and originative than the piece heard last night . . . we have had better things from Mr. Gershwin, and we expect better in time to come.

One more serious effort on a large scale was to come from George Gershwin, his "folk opera" *Porgy and Bess,* based on the play, *Porgy,* by Du Bose and Dorothy Heyward, produced by the New York Theater Guild at the Alvin Theater in the autumn of 1935. It was characteristic that when he did get around to writing a jazz opera he wrote it for the theater, and not for the opera house, so that it might be a good show, and not just a musical triumph. All are agreed that it was the former; on the latter ques-

[12] *New York Times,* February 6, 1932.

tion there were dissenting opinions. Brooks Atkinson, drama critic of the *New York Times* [13] remarked that "Mr. Gershwin has found a personal voice that was inarticulate in the original play. The fear and the pain go deeper in *Porgy and Bess* than they did in penny plain *Porgy*." But he had some sensible objections to make:

These comments are written by a reviewer so inured to the theater that he regards operatic form as cumbersome. Why commonplace remarks that carry no emotion have to be made in a chanting monotone is a problem in art he cannot fathom. Even the hermit thrush drops into conversational tones when he is not singing from the topmost spray in a tree. Turning *Porgy* into an opera has resulted in a deluge of casual remarks that have to be thoughtfully intoned and that amazingly impede the action. Why do composers vex it so? "Sister, you goin' to the picnic?" "No, I guess not." Now, why in heaven's name must two characters in an opera clear their throats before they can exchange that sort of information? ... To the ears of a theater critic there are intimations in *Porgy and Bess* that Mr. Gershwin is still easiest in mind when he is writing songs with choruses. He, and his present reviewer, are on familiar ground when he is writing a droll tune like *A Woman Is a Sometime Thing*, or a lazy darkie solo like *I Got Plenty o' Nuttin'*, or made-to-order spirituals like *Oh, de Lawd Shake de Heaven*, or Sportin' Life's hot-time number entitled *There's a Boat that's Leavin' Soon for New York*. If Mr. Gershwin does not enjoy his task most in moments like this, his audience does. In sheer quality of character they are worth an hour of formal music transitions.

Lawrence Gilman [14] took exactly the opposite view:

Perhaps it is needlessly Draconian to begrudge Mr. Gershwin the song-hits which he has scattered through his score and which will doubtless enhance his fame and popularity. Yet they mar it. They are its cardinal weakness. They are a blemish upon its musical integrity ... it is not Gershwin, the apt and accommodating lyricist, who is most conspicuously present in *Porgy and Bess*, but Gershwin the musical dramatist, who has, in certain fortunate moments of this score, been moved to compassionate and valid utterance by the wildness and the pathos and the tragic fervor that can so strangely agitate the souls

[13] October 11, 1935.
[14] *New York Herald Tribune*, October 11, 1935.

of men. These pages will abide, and honor the composer, long after the musical-comedy treacle which drips from other pages has ceased to gladden even those whose favor is scarcely worth the price.

In this case, one is tempted to think that it was the drama reviewer who proved the better music critic. Gershwin was so much a natural part of Tin Pan Alley, and jazz was so natural a part of him, that one must doubt whether his effort to make it a mere ingredient of music in the larger forms ever would have succeeded. The larger forms themselves were not anything he came to naturally, and they always fitted him very loosely. Whether he would have grown into them is a question that can never be answered.

For, at a cruelly early age, and with cruel suddenness, death cut him down in the middle of his remarkable career, on July 11, 1937. He was in Hollywood, working on the score of a new picture, *The Goldwyn Follies*. Two weeks before his death he collapsed at the film studios and was taken to a hospital for observation, with his illness tentatively diagnosed as a nervous breakdown. He seemed to recover, but twelve days later again collapsed, and this time X-ray examination showed a fast-growing brain tumor. An emergency operation was performed, but he did not survive it.

No one questions the eminence of George Gershwin in the field of popular song. And if his accomplishments in more pretentious fields are less firmly established, there can be no question that he put ideas into the heads of many composers who, while lacking his free and easy gift of tunefulness, may turn out to be better able than he to embody jazz in a truly symphonic style. Among his engaging small pieces, the delightful *Preludes* for piano, although they have not seemed to fit into any previous part of this discussion, must not be entirely overlooked. Nor must the part that his brother, *Ira Gershwin* (born December 6, 1896, New York City), played in George's success as adroit and tasteful lyric writer for many of the works mentioned, go without acknowledgment.

Closely associated with the early days of Gershwin's rise to concert fame was *Ferde Grofé*. Born March 27, 1892, in New York

City, Grofé comes of musical stock on both sides. His father, Emil von Grofe (Ferde was born Ferdinand Rudolph von Grofe), was a member of The Bostonians, a noted light opera company which first produced *Robin Hood*, *The Fortune Teller*, and other light opera classics of the '90's. His mother, born Elsa Johanna Bierlich, was a graduate of the Leipzig Conservatory and a concert cellist, following in the footsteps of her father, Bernhardt Bierlich, once a member of the Metropolitan Opera Orchestra with Victor Herbert, and later first cellist of the Los Angeles Symphony Orchestra. Ferde's uncle, Julius Bierlich, was concertmaster of the Los Angeles Orchestra, and in his early days Ferde played viola in the same band. But he did not simply move along in the grooves that had been worn smooth for him. At fourteen he ran away from home, and for some years supported himself as book-binder, truck-driver, bank-clerk, and what have you, playing in dance halls, meanwhile, when opportunity offered.

Whiteman came upon him in San Francisco in 1919, and then and there began a fruitful and influential association that lasted more than a dozen years, during which Grofé worked exclusively with Whiteman. Grofé was one of the first to produce carefully planned, written out, "semi-symphonic" arrangements in the jazz idiom. But it was his arrangement of the *Rhapsody in Blue*, made for that first "Experiment" of Whiteman's, that brought him fame. Since then he has made innumerable arrangements of other men's music, and so distinguished a figure as Deems Taylor has not been too proud to let Grofé make the jazz band arrangement of his *Circus Day*.

But it is as a composer in his own right that Grofé would like to be known. He has written a number of popular tunes, none of which has been outstandingly successful, and, in recent years, a number of suites and other pieces of larger dimensions, including: *Mississippi Suite, Knute Rockne, Three Shades of Blue, Ode to the Star-Spangled Banner, Symphony in Steel, Grand Canyon Suite, Wheels* ("a Transportation Suite"), and *Hollywood Suite*. Grofé conducted a concert of his own compositions in Carnegie

Hall, in 1937, and a second such program was announced for the season 1940–41. You can count on the fingers of one hand the composers who have been able to command similar "one-man shows."

Dana Suesse, one of the few members of the fair sex to compete for Broadway composing honors, has been a staff writer for T. B. Harms and Famous Music, prominent Tin Pan Alley publishers. Born December 3, 1911, in Kansas City, Missouri, she is largely self-taught in music; she has improvised almost as long as she can remember and composed since she was eight years old. At nine and ten she won tri-state prizes offered by the National Federation of Music Clubs. In 1932, Paul Whiteman commissioned her to write a *Jazz Concerto* for piano and orchestra, and the next year he again commissioned her, this time for the *Symphonic Waltzes* for piano and orchestra. In the popular field she wrote the entire scores, in 1936 and 1937, for two successive *Casa Mañana Revues,* presented by Billy Rose at the Fort Worth, Texas, Exposition. She has also written *Two Irish Fairy Tales,* for chamber orchestra, and a Concerto in E minor for two pianos and orchestra. She considers jazz a typical American idiom, but a very limited one, so far as serious composition is concerned, and feels she has said almost everything she has to say in that field. For the larger works she plans to write, she has no intention of restricting herself to the jazz idiom.

FURTHER ECHOES OF BROADWAY

Robert Russell Bennett has been conspicuously successful at combining the glamor and more solid rewards of Hollywood and Broadway with the accolade of such eminent institutions as the Juilliard School. Bennett was born June 15, 1894, in Kansas City, Missouri, the son of musical parents. His mother taught him to play the piano; from his father, who led a band and an orchestra, he learned to play many of the orchestral instruments, some through actual instruction, and more through having to "pick them up" when players were missing from the ensemble. He had been a victim of infantile paralysis as a young child, but recovered his health in the country, and at fifteen he was ready to begin formal musical studies in the city—in harmony, with the veteran Carl Busch. During the years just before the World War, Bennett was in New York as copyist and arranger. For a year he served in the Army, and then he was back, this time on Broadway, where he began his very successful career as an orchestrator of musical comedy scores.

A few years of that were enough to finance a sojourn in Paris, studying with Nadia Boulanger; this was the beginning of Bennett's serious work as a composer. While he was there, in 1927, he won a Guggenheim Fellowship, which was renewed in the following year, and during this period he turned out a considerable list of works, including a Symphony which won honorable mention in the *Musical America* contest that produced Bloch's *America; Paysage,* for orchestra; a one-act opera, *An Hour of Delusion; Endymion,* "an operetta-ballet à l'antique"; and numerous songs, choruses, and pieces of chamber music. There were also *Sights and Sounds,* "an orchestral entertainment," and *Abraham Lincoln, A Likeness in Symphonic Form,* composed in Berlin in 1929 —pieces which won two of the five prizes into which the judges of the Victor contest of 1929–30 split the $25,000 award. Since 1930, Bennett has been in Hollywood, composing, arranging, and conducting music for the films. This is his bread and butter (perhaps we should say ice cream and cake); but he is far from despising it, for he feels the importance and the possibilities in making the music that is listened to by millions. At the same time, his serious composition provides an outlet and a recreation for his leisure moments. Some of the best known musical comedies, revues, and musical films, including *Showboat,* have been scored by Bennett.

The art of scoring for theatre orchestra was informingly and entertainingly described by him in an article in *Modern Music:* [15]

[15] May–June, 1932.

Taking anything from a whistled melody to a piano sketch from its author to the lighted orchestra pit of a theatrical production demands a great many things besides theatrical training but if I were asked what the greatest asset one can have in this work is, I should have to answer, "counterpoint." Here is where the admonition of the teacher to his pupil to avoid forced voice-leading comes into its own. The audience, sitting there watching dimpled knees, and listening to tiny voices singing out familiar intervals in praise of familiar emotions, has no idea what counterpoint is; but let it be stiff, forced, or badly distributed and the knees seem less dimpled, the tiny voices grow tinier, and the general atmosphere becomes charged with an unmistakable *So what?* What the public doesn't know, which is plenty, it very nearly always feels, and that applies to the good things as well as the bad.

Bennett had an opportunity to try out his theories and experience of showmanship in an original work when the Juilliard School presented his opera, *Maria Malibran,* with a libretto by Robert A. Simon, music critic of *The New Yorker,* in April, 1935. The story of the opera concerns the famous singer, daughter of Manuel García, during the two-year visit which she paid to American shores. She had come as a member of her father's troupe, to the Park Theatre in New York, where that city had its first taste of Italian opera from them in the years 1825–27. While she was here, her father married her off to the old and irresponsible Malibran, a French merchant living in New York, ostensibly for 100,000 francs. But immediately after the marriage, Malibran went bankrupt; an annulment followed, and Maria returned in 1827 to Europe and one of the greatest careers an opera singer ever had. Eventually she became the wife of the violinist Charles de Bériot. She lived to be only twenty-eight, dying as a result of a riding accident.

However, it is not history that the opera is concerned with, but romance, and for romance's sake a fictitious episode provides the plot of the piece. Philip Cartwright, an aristocratic young New Yorker, appears on Maria's horizon on the eve of her wedding to Malibran. They are strongly drawn to each other, but it is too late, and Maria must go through with the marriage to which her father has pledged her. Later, when Philip becomes engaged to another woman, Maria attends the engagement reception. Persuaded to sing for the company, she obliges, not with a song of Mr. Bennett's devising, but with what the real Malibran might very well have sung on such an occasion, *Una voce poco fà*, Rosina's air from *The Barber of Seville*, by Rossini. As a second selection, she is to sing an aria from Zingarelli's *Giulietta e Romeo*; but when she appears in the tights of Romeo the assembled company is shocked, and she is escorted from the scene by Philip, whose engagement is broken off, and who now pleads with her to marry him as soon as she can have her own marriage annulled. But she knows that she is made for a career, not for the domestic bliss he offers her, so she must reject him. Their parting makes an effective operatic conclusion.

After the first performance, Oscar Thompson wrote: [16]

> To refer to *Maria Malibran* as an "American opera" is to invite dispute as to what constitutes opera. The work might better be styled a "musical romance," or "a comedy with music." So much of the text is spoken rather than sung, and so much of the music assumes an incidental character in accompanying rather than projecting the dialogue, that Mr. Bennett's occasional lyrical expansions have the casualness of some types of operetta or musical comedy.
>
> Unlike operetta or musical comedy, however, *Maria Malibran* places no reliance on song hits, unless two interpolations of music more than a hundred years old are to be so regarded. *Home, Sweet Home*, which originally did operatic duty in the Bishop-Payne *Clari, the Maid of Milan*, is one of the two. *Una voce poco fà* . . . is the other. They do more than contribute atmosphere for an opera about a singer of the days when they were young. They afford that personage her two chief opportunities to sing. . . .
>
> The slender score makes little or no attempt at musical characterization. . . . The music . . . is expert. If it is somewhat less successful than the book, this is not due to a lack of technical resource. The composer, in an avowal of his aims, explained in advance, as his preferences, almost everything that militates against his work. Among other things, he confessed that he is "not fond of mere melodic inspiration." That is precisely what his opera, if it is opera, lacks and

[16] *Musical America*, April 25, 1935.

needs. The protracted applause bestowed upon the *Barber of Seville* air, neatly incorporated as Maria's showpiece in the reception scene . . . was a commentary no amount of theorizing could explain away.

"Instinctively," Mr. Bennett has said, "my ear demands more than 'gifted music': craftsmanship, cerebral individuality, mechanical resource, harmonic experiment." His score has the latter qualities. "Gifted music" it has not.

Lawrence Gilman [17] was more complimentary and less explicit in his comments on the music. But one could not escape the feeling that there might be a trace of "sour grapes" in Mr. Bennett's scorn for melodic invention. His qualities he has, and no one doubts them. But if to them were added "mere melodic inspiration" would his music be any the worse for it?

Among Bennett's other works are a *Charleston Rhapsody* and an *Adagio Eroico* for orchestra; a *Concerto Grosso* using a small dance band as the *concertino*; a *March* for two pianos and orchestra; and several pieces of chamber and choral music. An experiment that promised much was his music for the colored fountains of the New York World's Fair, 1939; but defects in synchronization largely spoiled its chances of success.

The recipe for American music is simple enough, if you believe *Otto Cesana*. "Take material such as is used in current popular songs, refine it, and that is your subject matter. Orchestration should be symphonic type as represented on various outstanding radio hours. The form—Beethoven is O.K. Put it all together, shake well, and you have American music—maybe. Anyway, that's my story!" he writes, frankly and perhaps a shade naïvely. Cesana was born in Brescia, Italy, July 7, 1899, and came to this country as a boy of six. He began to study music at ten, but family pressure made him take up mechanical engineering as his ostensible life's work. In the end, however, he returned to music, both "classical" and popular. One of his teachers was Julius Gold of San Francisco, and perhaps it is something of Gold's influence that is reflected in Cesana's *Course in Modern Harmony*. He is much in

[17] *New York Herald Tribune*, April 9, 1935.

demand as an orchestrator and arranger for the radio orchestras. And he has written numerous pieces of serious music for orchestra, including two *American Symphonies;* an Overture; a symphonic poem, *Negro Heaven;* a Concerto for two pianos and orchestra, and another for three pianos and orchestra; *Three Moods* (played by the New York Philharmonic-Symphony Orchestra under John Barbirolli in April, 1939); and a ballet-opera *Ali Baba and the Forty Thieves.*

Morton Gould is one of those who has approached jazz "from above" (to use an old-fashioned expression); that is, he did not come to serious music as an alumnus of Tin Pan Alley, but rather the other way around. Born December 10, 1913, in Richmond Hill, Long Island, Gould began to compose when he was four years old, and was something of a pianistic prodigy as well. He studied piano with Abby Whiteside and musical theory with Dr. Vincent Jones, and graduated at the age of fifteen from New York University. In his teens still, he played in public a good deal and attracted some attention as an "elbow pianist"—one, that is, who was not afraid to use his elbows or his whole forearm or anything else that would help him achieve the effect he desired. It would have been easy for him to develop as an eccentric, as so many others have done. But fortunately, financial pressure intervened. He had to earn his living, and Broadway was the best place to do it, he thought. For a time he was on the staff of the Radio City Music Hall, and later of the National Broadcasting Company. Of recent years he has conducted his own programs of "special arrangements" on Station WOR.

Gould has not let his work in the popular field swamp his serious activities, and he has tried to maintain a fruitful connection between the two. He has little use for the "art-for-art's-sake boys." His *Chorale and Fugue in Jazz* was played by Stokowski and the Philadelphia Orchestra in January, 1936; he has played his Piano Concerto with various leading orchestras; and Fritz Reiner commissioned his *Foster Gallery*, a work based on melodies by the immortal Stephen. He has also written three Piano Sonatas; a

Americana Suite; a Cantata; a Symphony; and two *Swing Symphonettes.*

Earl Robinson sprang into sudden prominence in the spring of 1939 with his *Ballad for Americans,* a piece for chorus, solo voice, and orchestra. It is a novel concoction of talk and music, singing the praises of democracy, and it is perhaps for its idea, embodied in a libretto by John La Touche, as much as for its music, that it became immensely popular. It was first introduced in the WPA production, *Sing for your Supper,* where it created a considerable stir. Then it was broadcast on the Columbia Broadcasting System program, "The Pursuit of Happiness," with Paul Robeson taking the solo part. From this hearing its fame and popularity spread—to the symphony orchestras, the movies, and even (although it was of Leftist origin and inspiration) to the Republican National Convention of 1940. Largely on the basis of this great popular success, perhaps, Robinson won a Guggenheim Fellowship for 1940 for work on a musical dramatization of Carl Sandburg's *The People, Yes.* There is no reason to doubt that Robinson may have a fine talent. He has written other songs and choruses with a message, and incidental music for several Federal Theatre plays. But there is also no blinking the fact that the *Ballad for Americans* is a bit old-fashioned and theatrical, and that the fact that it came just at a time when people were particularly conscious of the blessings of the American democracy was largely responsible for its success. On the strength of *God Bless America* alone, Irving Berlin would not have been proclaimed a popular hero, either, at any other time. But voicing the sentiments of the people is no doubt a worthy calling, too, even if no particular originality or distinction is involved. Robinson was born July 2, 1910, at Seattle, Washington, and educated at the University of Washington.

And now it is time to leave Broadway and shut our ears to its echoes without any final estimate of its eternal values set down for all to smile at ten years hence. It is a thoroughfare that teems with life, and it is not waiting for anyone's approval or condemnation. Is jazz only "a decadent and derived art—at its best an ironic comment on Romanticism; at its worst a sentimental expression of a negative emotion" as Constant Lambert [18] would have it? Millions of singing voices deny the slur; millions of moving bodies trample it beneath their feet. This chapter could not close more appropriately than with quotations from a leading American composer of the concert halls. John Alden Carpenter was quoted in a symposium in the *Etude* some years ago as saying: [19] "I am strongly inclined to believe that the musical historian of the year 2000 will find the birthday of American music and that of Irving Berlin to have been the same." If he really made this remark, it embodies an exaggeration that does credit to Carpenter's impulsive generosity. But elsewhere [20] he stated the situation as well in 1925 as it can be stated today:

From the standpoint of Art, it will be interesting to find out if the charm and vigor of jazz can be successfully diluted with the sophistication of the trained creative impulse. In any event, I do not see how it can be ignored by any American composer who feels his native soil under his feet.

[18] *Loc. cit.*
[19] Alexander Woolcott, *The Story of Irving Berlin* (New York and London G. P. Putnam's Sons, 1925).
[20] *Ibid.*

9

TODAY AND TOMORROW

THE most cursory glance through the foregoing pages will have reminded the reader that history knows no date divisions, and that what for convenience we call the twentieth century did not really begin in the year 1900, musically speaking.

It may very well be that future historians will find that the history of our country thus far divides naturally into periods of Exploration and Discovery, Settlement, Expansion (roughly 1790 to 1917), and Maturity (beginning in 1917). The experience of the World War had a profound effect on the American nation, and the year 1917 undoubtedly marks the beginning of a new era in our history.

Throughout the nineteenth century, Europe represented the source of a continual stream of additions to our population, as well as the fountain head of our culture. Yet politically and economically it seemed a different, separate world. Raymond Gram Swing tells of how, in 1914, he sent a cable of five hundred words from Europe to his newspaper on the subject of the Austrian ultimatum to Serbia—the act which led directly to the World War —only to receive the curt acknowledgment from his editor: "Overcabling Serbia!" And yet those five hundred words contained a story of events which were to affect the lives of the readers of that newspaper more importantly than anything else the editor could possibly have found to print on that day.

But if the years 1914–19 taught us that the Atlantic was not as wide a political barrier as we had thought it, they gave us a lesson with almost the opposite meaning, so far as our culture is concerned. They gave us a national consciousness, a self-confidence and an independence we had not had before. Thousands of our men went abroad and brought back fresh impressions of another world, a world not as different from ours as we had imagined. It was, particularly, a world where music and the other arts were held in higher regard and had been brought to a higher degree of development than at home, but perhaps not so much higher as we had supposed.

The World War had two immediate results for American composers. It turned their attention, first of all, from German culture, which had been the predominating influence on our nineteenth-century music, to French culture. And it taught our composers, in larger numbers than ever before, that Europe was not too far away for them to go and inspect its music and musicians for themselves. At first they went in great humility, most of them to Paris, but a good many to Rome, Vienna, Berlin, and London as well, trying to acquire the culture they felt could not be had in their own country. It was not long before they found that, while Europe of the past had endless lessons for them, Europeans of the present were not incomparably above themselves in talent or ambition, and that there was nothing indissolubly linked to European soil about the training they had received. This was not a case of familiarity breeding contempt. It was simply a question of getting rid of the mystical aura that had surrounded the concept "Europe," and finding that the average European was not more gifted or more innately musical than the average American. In some ways the raw material we sent to the European refinery was better than that of the Old World itself.

Until 1917, it may be said, the average American looked on his country as the land uniquely favored by geography and history and uniquely neglected by culture. The World War taught him that both the virtues and the defects of "God's Country" were relative; that we were a nation among nations, subject, despite our great advantages, to the risks and strains of the modern world, and by the same token a contributor in our own right to the world's culture.

At the end of the War we were the one great nation whose economy had grown, instead of having been ruined. Art notoriously follows wealth, and a great influx of European musicians of the first rank came to take advantage of the existence of a new, enthusiastic, and prosperous public. Indeed, as one looks back, it is clear that the bitter experience of War had its compensations for us. It brought us infinitely closer to a musical culture which had something of what we lacked and lacked much of what we had. It was the indirect cause of the fact that many American musicians went to Europe and many Europeans came here—an exchange by which both sides, but particularly ours, in the circumstances, greatly profited.

There were many other ways in which the War experience affected our musical development. Composers cannot exist without listeners and performers, and the number of Americans who came into active contact with music was greatly increased through the patriotic and community activity of the War days. Community singing and community playing, which grew like mushrooms in 1917 and 1918, did not disappear or languish when the War was over.

The spread of community music-making had important results. It was taken up on a huge scale in our schools and colleges, where choruses and orchestras devoted largely to serious music came to be the rule rather than the exception. It is estimated that in 1940 there were some 150,000 to 200,000 school bands and orchestras in the United States.

Now, one of the greatest obstacles in the path of modern composers has been their preoccupation with problems of style, and the existence of a great body of performing musicians with limited techniques has helped in many cases to resolve these problems. The stylistic possibilities of works written for such musicians are limited, and the first step towards solving a problem is to limit it. It was partly an embarrassment of riches, in the shape of the almost unlimited technique of the great professional symphony orchestras, that had produced the quandary.

With schools and colleges turning out musical performers wholesale every year, professional orchestras could be and were formed in many of our smaller cities where they would never have been possible before. Amateur music-making—meaning music-making for fun, whether expert or not—received a great impetus. Musicians were trained faster than economic places could be found for them,—but that problem will be discussed further on.

PHILANTHROPIC FOUNDATIONS

The era of prosperity which corresponded roughly to the third decade of the twentieth century saw many important benefactions of significance to the American composer. In 1919 George Eastman, the camera and film manufacturer, gave $3,500,000 to found the Eastman School of Music, in Rochester, New York. In 1920 he gave an additional $1,000,000, and the school opened in 1921. Under the directorship of Howard Hanson it has done yeoman service for the American composer, taught him, employed him, and played and published [1] his works, on a scale perhaps not equalled by any other American institution. The American Composers' Concerts and Festivals, particularly, to which frequent reference has been made in this book, constitute a unique contribution to our musical life.

Frederic A. Juilliard, New York cotton merchant, died in 1919 and bequeathed about $20,000,000 as a fund to foster the development of music in the United States. The Juilliard Musical Foundation was set up in 1920, and it shortly established the Juilliard School of Music in New York, later divided into the Juilliard Graduate School and the undergraduate Institute of Musical Art, absorbed by Juilliard in 1926. For some time John Erskine was president of the School; in 1937 he was succeeded by Ernest

[1] See Appendix, p. 376.

Hutcheson, whose place as dean was taken by Oscar Wagner, while George A. Wedge succeeded to the post of dean of the Institute of Musical Art. The Juilliard School trains singers, players, and composers, and publishes [2] an orchestral work by an American composer annually.

Forming with Eastman and Juilliard a sort of Big Three among the musical institutions of the country, the Curtis Institute in Philadelphia was founded in 1924 with an endowment by Cyrus H. K. Curtis, publisher of the *Saturday Evening Post,* and has continued with the support of Mrs. Mary Louise Curtis Bok. From 1926 until 1938 Josef Hofmann was director of the Institute; he was succeeded by Randall Thompson.

From the fact that Eastman has been headed by a composer, while Juilliard and Curtis (until recently) have been under the direction of performers, it has come about that of the three schools, Eastman has placed the greatest stress upon composition. Yet all three schools have trained some of our best young singers, players, and composers, as the pages of this book bear ample witness.

At the American Academy in Rome, founded in 1905 to promote the study and practice of fine arts, fellowships in musical composition have been granted since 1921, in the name of the Juilliard Foundation and of Horatio Parker and Walter Damrosch.[3]

The MacDowell Colony, at Peterborough, N.H., founded by Mrs. Edward MacDowell in memory of her husband, and supported through her constant efforts as a summer refuge of artists, composers, poets, and writers, goes on despite the grievous blow dealt it by the fates in the autumn of 1938. In September of that year a wildly destructive hurricane swept over the New England States, laying waste enormous acreages of woodland as far north as the upper White Mountains. The Peterborough Colony was a heavy sufferer, and the damage sustained has as yet by no means been fully repaired. But Mrs. MacDowell's efforts in behalf of

---

[2] See Appendix, p. 377.
[3] See Appendix, p. 382.

the colony have only been redoubled, and it is to be hoped that before long they may be fully successful.

COMPOSERS' ORGANIZATIONS

The 1920's were also the heyday of organizations formed to promote the interests of the contemporary composer. In most of these, the native American at first played the part of an "also-ran" but his importance has steadily increased with the years.

The pioneer among such organizations was the International Composers' Guild—pioneer not only in America, but founded before any of the well-known societies existing for similar purposes in Europe. Its charter is dated May 31, 1921. The latter is a challenging document, or at least it was at the time it was written: [4] "Dying is the privilege of the weary. The present day composers refuse to die. They have realized the necessity of banding together and fighting for the right of each individual to secure a fair and free presentation of his work. It is out of such a collective will that the International Composers' Guild was born." The Guild, like Edgar Varèse, its founder,[5] disapproved of all "isms," denied that there was any such thing as "schools" of composition; recognized "only the individual." The Guild did yeoman service for radicalism in music during its six years of existence; it pressed leading artists into service in its cause; it presented American premières of works by such important modern composers as Stravinsky and Ravel, as well as Ruggles, Rudhyar, Saminsky, Varèse, Salzedo, Still, and other Americans.

It was not long before a group of members became restive under the strongly dominating influence of Varèse, and in April, 1923, they seceded to form the League of Composers, which still carries on, and has been one of the most influential agencies for the propagation of modern musical tendencies in America. The first

---
[4] Excerpts are given in Slonimsky, *Music Since 1900* (New York: W. W. Norton and Company, 1937).
[5] See his remarks quoted on pp. 255-6.

executive board of the League consisted of Arthur Bliss, one of the younger English composers, Louis Gruenberg, Leo Ornstein, Lazare Saminsky, Emerson Whithorne, and several non-composer members. The League made the point that no organization then existing was interested in "the entire range of modern tendencies," and that "a more flexible selection" was needed than that offered by the Guild. It also differed from the Guild by refusing to limit itself to works which had never been heard before. Only two or three times in its history had the Guild repeated any work; the League felt that many works were important enough to deserve re-hearings. Nowadays, of course, this seems obvious enough, and no composer is interested in writing a work which will be heard only once. It is the second and third and tenth performances of works which show the composer that he has reached an audience.

The International Composers' Guild was a bold, idealistic venture which after some six years of existence decided that the task it had set for itself had been to a great extent accomplished, and accordingly disbanded. The League of Composers had its feet on the ground more solidly than the Guild, perhaps, but both organizations may be said to have had in a certain degree the defects of their virtues.

The League has not neglected American composers, particularly in the last few years, when commissions have been given to a considerable number of them for new works.[6] American composers, too, form the backbone of the contributing staff of *Modern Music*, the League's official magazine.

In August, 1922, the International Society for Contemporary Music was formed, as an aftermath of the first International Festival of contemporary music, held at Salzburg, Austria. Leo Sowerby and Ernest Bloch were represented on the programs of this first Festival, and it was not long before a United States Section of the Society was formed. Each Section of the I.S.C.M. operates as a national representative of the movement to foster the composition and performance of modern music, and each Section sends

[6] See Appendix, p. 385.

works annually to be considered by an international jury. At the Oxford Festival, in 1931, Gershwin's *An American in Paris* was played, in the face of vigorous opposition by the members of the United States Section, who did not consider the work truly representative of contemporary American musical activity. But they were overruled, and the international jury definitely reserved the right to dispose as it saw fit of the suggestions proposed by the national sections.[7]

The United States Section performed a particularly valuable piece of work when it published, in 1930, a catalogue of *American Composers of Today* and their works, compiled and edited by Claire Reis and published with the assistance of the Juilliard Foundation. A second edition was published in 1932, and a considerably enlarged one, under the title *Composers in America*, in 1938.[8]

In 1928, the indefatigable Varèse founded the Pan American Association of Composers, in association with Colin McPhee, Carlos Salzedo, Carlos Chavez, leading composer of Mexico, and Julius Mattfeld, then librarian of the National Broadcasting Company, and since 1929 holder of a similar post with the Columbia Broadcasting System. The object was to further the cause of modern music written by composers of the two American continents. It was under the auspices of this association that Nicolas Slonimsky conducted programs of music by Weiss, Ives, Ruggles, Cowell, Salzedo, Riegger and Varèse, the Cubans Amadeo Roldan and Alejandro Caturla, the Spaniard Pedro Sanjuan, and the Mexican Chavez, in Paris (June, 1931) and other European cities, as well as in various Latin-American capitals and in New York. It is interesting to note that this activity preceded the national preoccupation with Pan-American relations, and the "Good Neigh-

---

[7] For a list of American works played at the I.S.C.M. Festivals, see Appendix, p. 389.

[8] New York: The Macmillan Company. To *Composers in America*, the present writers are considerably indebted, as all writers on contemporary American music must be.

bor" policy. Here, at least, Varèse proved to be a man ahead of his time.

The manifold activities of Henry Cowell on behalf of modern American music have already been mentioned. One of his greatest and best organized efforts has been the New Music Society, founded in 1927. It has published *New Music,* a quarterly periodical containing orchestral and chamber-music scores by new composers. It has also issued the New Music Quarterly Recordings [9] and has been active in other ways on behalf of the contemporary composer of radical tendencies. Wallingford Riegger, John J. Becker, and Nicolas Slonimsky have served the Society as associate editors.

MUSIC DURING THE DEPRESSION

All the organizations so far discussed were founded in the days of Prosperity, a happy state that Americans had begun to take for granted as something that would go on getting better "every day in every way." But there came a rude awakening.

The fourth decade of this century entered amid a pandemonium of crashing fortunes. A glamorous bubble had burst, and for a time it seemed as if everything we had hoped for might have gone with it. The years 1929-33 saw America considering for the first time the possibility that its growth might not be unlimited in the future, as it had seemed in the past. There had been panics before, and depressions, and vagaries of the business cycle. But none of them had produced such a widespread and general effect on our whole population. Recovery from them had always, under the influence of expanding frontiers, been fairly prompt. This time we wondered.

Music, it seemed, must be among the first things to suffer. From time immemorial, it had depended largely for its existence upon the patronage of the wealthy, and private philanthropy had never

[9] See Appendix, p. 351 ff.

done more in a corresponding length of time than in the decade just past. Was all this to come to an abrupt end? Where was music to turn for support, now that the rich were no longer feeling rich, and saw nothing but uncertainty ahead?

It would be a callous observer who could look back over the '30's and smugly say that things always work out for the best. And yet things have been accomplished during those difficult years which may spell greater things in the future of American music, and certainly the status of the American composer is in general better in 1940 than it was in 1929.

The crisis brought unemployment on an unprecedented scale to workers in every field of American activity. And in music, as will be seen, special causes were at work which made the situation even more acute. Private charity was not equal to the immense task of supporting the millions of Americans who, in most cases through no individual fault of their own, could no longer support themselves. The Federal Government found it necessary to step in and organize relief activities, and it did so in a way which, for music at least, was of untold value. For instead of simply putting unemployed workers on a dole, a procedure which was widely felt to be "un-American," it organized projects of "made work," on which, for relief wages, they could keep up whatever skills they had against the time when an economic change would make them employable again.

THE FEDERAL MUSIC PROJECT

The Federal Music Project of the Works Progress Administration has been only one small part of a national program about which political discussion still rages. Therefore this book will not be charged with political argument, which lies entirely outside its province, when it points out the invaluable services of the Music Project to American music.

The task of the Project was to put to work as many musicians as possible without competing with those already gainfully employed. In this it has, all things considered, succeeded admirably, and to the satisfaction of the great majority of musicians. It has employed copyists and research workers to augment the staffs of our libraries and help them make available to the public treasures of all sorts which otherwise would have remained hidden for years to come. Research projects have been undertaken which without the WPA would have remained nothing but scholars' dreams. Its main activities, however, have been in performance, and in this field its achievements, while representing only a tiny fraction of the total work-relief program, have been on a colossal scale, compared with anything that had been known in the field of music before.

The WPA has organized some thirty new orchestras of symphonic calibre, as well as other orchestras, bands, dance orchestras and bands, chamber-music ensembles, opera units, and choral groups; and it has made use of the services of soloists as well. Taken altogether, these various units gave, between the inception of the PWA and the autumn of 1939, some 225,000 performances before audiences totaling about 150,000,000 people. Of these, symphony orchestras alone accounted for nearly 20,000 performances and 14,000,000 listeners, and there were some 10,000 chamber-music performances before nearly 5,000,000 people. These are astronomic figures for music. No musical public of such dimensions has ever existed before in the history of the world.

How has all this affected American composers? The WPA has not had a place for them on its pay-rolls, as it has had for other creative workers, and this perhaps shows that music has not yet fully come into its own in the American scheme of things. But indirectly the American composer has benefited greatly by WPA activities. The Project has made the encouragement of American composers an integral part of its basic policy. Over 6,000 different compositions by 1600 American composers, or composers residing in the United States, have been performed by musicians of the Federal Music Project. Three-day festivals devoted exclusively to American works have been held under its auspices. On the programs of the small orchestras and bands (exclusive of dance orchestras) seventy per cent of the works heard have been American, with Grofé, Herbert, Sousa, and Skilton leading the list. The bulk of the repertory of the WPA symphonic orchestras is still made up from the works of European composers old and new; but contemporary American music has had a generous place on their programs.

In addition, the WPA has made possible certain forms of activity that could hardly have succeeded, or might never have been tried, under private auspices. Such a venture has been the Composers' Forums, originated in New York in the fall of 1935, under the direction of Ashley Pettis, and since then carried on in several other cities as well. At the Composers' Forum programs, works by contemporary composers are played, mostly in the presence of the composers, and at the end the listeners have an opportunity to question the composer—in short, to "talk back" to him. The individual remarks and queries are often naïve, ill-tempered, over-enthusiastic, or even frivolous. At times, on the other hand, they make trenchant comments, and cause the composer to throw light on an obscure point. Taken as a whole, they cannot fail to give the composer a better idea of how successfully he is transmitting his message than he could have gained without the Forums.

Undoubtedly the greatest service of the WPA, however, has been the development and fostering of a vastly increased audience for music; a service of which the value is already strikingly evident.

OTHER INSTITUTIONS IN THE 1930'S

It is clear that every point at which American composers can gather together is of importance, particularly if they hear their own and each other's works, exchange ideas and impressions with performers, and attract critical attention. During the 1930's the opportunity to do all these things has been provided by the Yaddo

Festivals, and the Yaddo Music Periods. Yaddo is the name of the estate of the late Mr. and Mrs. Spencer Trask in Saratoga Springs, New York. Using funds left by Mrs. Trask, and administered by the Corporation of Yaddo, the director, Mrs. Elizabeth Ames, and her associates, have provided living and working quarters for a certain number of artists each summer season, and at the end of the summer have presented a series of programs of music, both new and (less often) old, to a small and interested audience. The interchanges of composers and performers are undoubtedly of the highest value to all concerned. At the concerts too many works are presented for digestion at once by the outsider. But since the primary purpose is not to exhibit the works but rather to give the composer the experience of hearing his compositions rehearsed and performed, and comparing them in aims and methods with those of his contemporaries, Yaddo fulfills an important function. It is symptomatic of the change in the status of the American composer, that while no New York newspapers were represented at the first Yaddo Festival, held in the autumn of 1932, it is nowadays self-understood that Yaddo events must be commented upon in detail in the columns of these journals.

Before we leave discussion of the depression period, another institution should be mentioned, one which was born during the lean years, and no doubt owes its origin to their leanness. One of the effects of adversity is always to make people weigh their past conduct and try to discover what is responsible for their misfortune. In politics, this results in reform movements. In New York City a particularly energetic and forward-looking administration came into power when Fiorello La Guardia was elected Mayor, in 1934. Mayor La Guardia is well known for his great interest in music, and for his fondness for conducting an orchestra or a band. (No doubt he is conscious of his limitations, for he rarely undertakes anything more pretentious than a Sousa march.) But that this is no mere pastime or whimsy on His Honor's part is indicated by the warm cooperation he has offered to musical movements in general, and above all by the foundation of the High School of Music and Art in New York City. Here children of musical talent may obtain a high school education through a curriculum that takes full account of their specific needs in the way of technical and theoretical instruction, practice time, orchestral and choral training, and the like. This is a new step forward in the very progressive movement to broaden and deepen American musical education, and it is likely to bear fruit of untold value.

RADIO AND SOUND FILMS

It has been mentioned that the Depression years hit musicians even harder than they did workers in many other fields. The United States Census figures on this subject do not tell a complete story, but they show that as early as 1930 some thirteen per cent of the group classified as "Musicians and Music Teachers" were unemployed, as compared with only about three per cent of workers in the general field of "professional service."

The reasons for this sorry situation are not far to seek. They can be summed up under the heading that covers many of our present-day problems: technological unemployment, which in music is another name for the effects of the development of radio broadcasting and the sound film. The perfection of the latter and the substitution of recorded accompaniments for theatre orchestras threw a host of musicians out of work several years before the general economic crisis. Radio broadcasting absorbed a small proportion of these men, but it had disastrous effects on certain other phases of musical activity.

There is no denying the value of what these inventions will do for America in the long run, or of what they have done already. Radio and sound films both bring new audiences and offer new fields for the composer, and the pages of this book reveal many instances in which composers have taken advantage of the new opportunities. Yet the surface has hardly been scratched, because for every film that has a specially composed score by a serious composer there are hundreds whose musical accompaniment is put together with paste-pot and scissors from the musical resources of the past. And while the broadcasting companies have made gestures toward the composer in the way of "commissions" and prizes, the amount of money involved and the number of composers benefiting, is tiny compared to the total income of the broadcasting organizations and the debt they owe to music.

ASCAP AND PAYMENT FOR PERFORMING RIGHTS

This brings us face to face with a struggle of long standing, which is going through one of its most acute phases as this book goes to press. To understand fully the issues involved, we must go back to the days before the First World War.

One evening in 1913 Victor Herbert was sitting in Shanley's Restaurant in New York, when he noticed that the band was playing music from his *Sweethearts*, which was at that time enjoying a run on Broadway. Now the copyright law of 1909 established minimum damages of $250 and costs for the unauthorized performance for profit of copyrighted music. Was this performance for profit? Herbert said it was; Shanley's said it wasn't. It took Herbert four years to get a final, favorable determination of the issues, and when it came it was from the lips of no less an authority than Justice Oliver Wendell Holmes, voicing a unanimous opinion of the United States Supreme Court.

Herbert's claim had been fought bitterly by an association of hotel and restaurant owners, and he had realized early in the proceedings that an individual composer could not possibly afford to collect his due under the copyright law if he were to be opposed by the combined forces of all the interests who wished to withhold it from him. So he banded together with Sousa, the late Nathan Burkan (an attorney) Gene Buck (author of many Ziegfeld Follies books), and a few others to form the American Society of Composers, Authors, and Publishers—that is, a Society of all those interested in maintaining their rights under the provisions of the law covering public performance of copyrighted music for profit.

By so doing, these pioneers founded an organization which does far more than to seek recognition and fame for the composer and song-writers; it has come to provide for their material needs by collecting and turning over to them payment for the use and performance of their music.

Obviously it was not practical to wait until each separate infringement occurred and then bring suit for damages. It would have required a vast informing organization to keep watch over the thousands of theaters, restaurants, hotels, dance halls, night clubs, and other public places where music was performed for profit. For Justice Holmes had said in the Shanley case: "If the music did not pay, it would be given up. . . . Whether it pays or not, the purpose of employing it is profit, and that is enough." This meant that any person or organization which used public performances of music as an attraction, even though only an "incidental" one, in a place where profit was the aim, must secure the permission of the copyright owner of the music in question. And if it was not practical for ASCAP, as it is now known, to find out about each infringement and then collect, it was no more practical for the law-abiding user of music to attempt to secure the necessary permission in each individual case from the composer, whom he might find it difficult to reach.

For the convenience of both sides, a system of "licensing" was devised, by which ASCAP gave a music-user blanket permission to perform for profit any music by any of the composers it represented, in return for a stated annual fee which bore a definite relation to the size and profit-making potentialities of the place where the music was to be used.

It took some years for this system to become firmly established but after fighting a multitude of lawsuits, in which ASCAP' rights were sustained on every important point, the Society began early in the 1920's to collect enough money to distribute sum of importance among its members.

Then came radio. At first no one knew what the profit-making potentialities of a broadcasting station were, if any. ASCAP satisfied itself with collecting minimum license fees, to establish its right to do so, until the development of radio advertising showed that large profits could be made from this new medium. Then, since music represented a large share of the program attraction offered, ASCAP felt justified in demanding a proportion of the revenue which its copyrights had partly earned.

A new period of legal struggle followed. The broadcasters claimed that broadcast performances weren't "public," weren't "for profit," and weren't anything else that would make them subject to performance fees. But gradually all these arguments were overcome in the courts, and all attempts to amend the copyright laws so as to destroy the composers' rights failed.

By 1932 broadcasting had grown to the proportions of a major industry. After protracted negotiations, an agreement was worked out between the radio stations, who had formed the National Association of Broadcasters, and ASCAP. This provided for the payment of a fixed annual fee by each station for the privilege of using ASCAP copyrights on its "sustaining" (or non-advertising) programs, and of three per cent of their receipts from the sale of advertising time during the first year of the agreement, four per cent the second year, and five per cent the third.

The contracts embodying these terms expired in 1935, but they were then renewed for a period of five years—not, however, without difficulty.

It was at this time, too, that the Federal Government brought suit under the anti-trust laws to dissolve ASCAP as a combination in restraint of trade. The threat of such action has been in the background of ASCAP's quarrels with the broadcasters for years, even though the government dropped the suit after it had actually come to trial. In 1940, when the time came to think about renewing the contracts with the broadcasters, the threat of prosecution was heard again, even though it had been quiescent in the meantime.

The new contract which ASCAP offered the broadcasters in 1940 called for a different allocation of the costs. Previously, the individual stations had been charged both for local programs and for the network programs they had carried. No charge had been made to the networks. Under the new contract, individual stations would be charged only for programs originating locally, while the networks themselves would pay a fee, based on their incomes, for blanket licenses granting them the privilege of performing ASCAP music on any or all of their programs.

These proposals did not appeal to the broadcasters, and they proceeded to devise means of avoiding the necessity of accepting them. The broadcasters have always maintained that the playing of copyrighted music over the air helped to sell printed copies and phonograph records of that music, and that therefore radio should not be charged large fees for "helping the publishers and composers to sell their tunes." While superficially there appear to be elements of truth in this contention, the statistics of the past twenty years tell a different story.

Sheet-music sales reached their highest point in 1927, which was in the infancy of radio, and as the broadcasting and radio-manufacturing industry has prospered, sheet-music sales have shrunk to a small fraction of their volume in that banner year. The cost of manufacture of phonograph records, which was some $48,000,000 in 1921, and after a slump had climbed back as far as $34,000,000 in 1929, amounted to only about $6,500,000 in 1937. Probably even today, although records have regained considerable popularity in the past few years, fewer records are sold than in 1914, and not one-quarter as many as in 1921. Sheet-music copies of the hit tunes of Tin Pan Alley used to be sold in the millions; now few reach the two-hundred-thousand mark.

For these things ASCAP has only one answer—radio; and it is difficult to find any other. Radio is undoubtedly, over the years, building a great new audience for music, and in the end all musicians should benefit by this expansion of their market. But in the meantime, radio is making a great deal of money, while musi-

TODAY AND TOMORROW

cians suffer, and ASCAP insists on securing for its members a share in the profits of the industry which, it maintains, could not exist without ASCAP music.

On that claim rests the ultimate decision between these conflicting interests. The broadcasters, in the face of ASCAP's proffered contract for 1941, professed to believe that they could get along without the copyrights controlled by the Society, even though almost every important popular composer and almost every leading publisher were under contract with ASCAP. To back up their contention, the broadcasters organized Broadcast Music, Inc., a sort of combination publisher and performance-rights agency, owned and controlled by the broadcasters themselves. BMI, as it came to be called, proceeded to acquire catalogs of publishers which were not members of ASCAP, although they were not many, and to solicit the direct submission of manuscripts for publication. It began to publish new songs, and its own arrangements of old ones, on a large scale. On October 1, 1940, the broadcasting systems announced that their sustaining programs for the rest of the year must each contain at least three selections not controlled by ASCAP, and that on January 1, 1941, they would discontinue altogether the use of ASCAP material.

It was hard to believe that a settlement would not be reached before the contracts expired on January 1st; yet to the amazement of onlookers, the opening of the year 1941 witnessed a complete dropping of ASCAP music by the major radio networks. Many small, independent stations signed contracts with ASCAP, but from the four major networks the listeners heard nothing but non-copyright music, and songs of the new Broadcast Music, Inc., which had been hurriedly published by the broadcasters' own organization.

Stephen Foster, of course, proved a gold-mine to the program makers. Even the swingsters seized upon the gentle melodies of "America's Troubadour" and made them veritable orgies of dissonance. George M. Cohan remarked that of the 250,000 songs and pieces which BMI claimed to control, "half are called *Turkey in the Straw,* and the other half are about a girl called Jeanie." The flood of Foster songs reminded some observers that if there had been an ASCAP in Foster's day, the famous song-writer would not have died in poverty.

The stand-bys of the radio repertory—Gershwin, Kern, Berlin, Herbert, Friml, and countless others, were not heard, and the music of the leading serious composers, most of them ASCAP members, was likewise banned—Bloch, Cadman, Carpenter, Damrosch, Grainger, Hanson, Harris, Mason, Powell, Sessions, Sowerby, Taylor, to name but a few. This group has a tremendous stake in the ASCAP radio controversy, for it is the blanket-licensing arrangement, as opposed to the per-program basis which the broadcasters advocate, which makes it possible for the serious composers to be given credit in their ASCAP ratings for their prestige and standing, and thus to receive a proportionately larger payment than the "popular" song-writers. This amounts to a subsidy for the serious composers from the popular group.

As these pages went to press, no final settlement had been reached. The broadcasters seemed determined to test their strength without ASCAP music. The Federal Department of Justice renewed its prosecution of ASCAP, including BMI in its indictment. The latter provisionally agreed to a consent decree in the matter, provided ASCAP would also agree to its provisions. ASCAP hesitated to do so, even with modifications, because it anticipated final victory in the Supreme Court in other pending litigation. However, it seemed likely that some agreement between ASCAP and the Department of Justice would be reached which would perhaps form the basis for new arrangements with the broadcasters as well.

GRAND RIGHTS

ASCAP is not alone in the defense of the performance rights of the American composer, for the Society has not as yet undertaken to collect fees for the so-called "grand rights"—that is, the performance rights on compositions in the larger forms, such as symphonic works—although, as has already been shown, it has allowed for such performances by giving a higher proportionate rating to its symphonist members. But the actual collection of performance fees for grand rights has been left to the composer or his publisher.

There has been an obvious reason for this condition. Until recently there was no large public which clamored to hear these works, as it did the songs of Tin Pan Alley. The American composer of serious music was happy enough if he could get a hearing, without asking for a performing fee, which would only have discouraged performers and conductors from playing his works.

In recent years this situation has changed for the better, as the foregoing pages show. There is a growing public for serious music by contemporary American composers, and it is no longer a rarity for the composer and the publisher of an American symphonic work to receive a fee for its performance. But it is by no means the rule, either, and the composers feel that the salaries paid to star performers are out of proportion to the return, or lack of return, reaped by the creative musician.

A representative group of American composers accordingly formed in 1938 the American Composers' Alliance. Performing fees are only one of the most important subjects that occupy the Alliance's attention. It aims in every way to advance the interests of composers: to foster performances and commissions; to work out standard contracts with publishers, theatrical producers, broadcasters, and other potential "clients"; and to carry on propaganda for the American composer. Already there has been established in close cooperation with the ACA, an American Music Center in New York, under the direction of Harrison Kerr, to act as a clearing house for information and promotional efforts concerning American music of the present day. Clearly the composers need some such organization, to correspond to the Authors' League, or the Dramatists' Guild, for example. Some of its functions, such as the collection of performing fees for grand rights, might perhaps best (and probably will eventually) be handled through ASCAP.

But since ASCAP represents composers, authors, and publishers, three groups which have some interests in common and others which conflict, the advisability of the separate as well as joint organization of these groups has long been recognized by ASCAP itself. The publishers have their Music Publishers' Protective Association; the song-writers are organized in the Song Writers' Protective Association; it is a sign that American music is coming of age when the composers too decide that in union there is strength.

Gene Buck, who heads ASCAP, was one of its organizers, and has been President of the organization since 1923—a genial, able, and widely popular figure who has managed to be in the thick of the fight for the copyright-owners most of the time without sacrificing friendships in every branch of music and fields associated with it. Aaron Copland is president of the American Composers' Alliance, and he, too, in a different sphere, is a uniquely popular and respected personality.

THE NAACC

The National Association for American Composers and Conductors was founded by Henry Hadley, always an enthusiastic crusader for American music, and it continues his crusade, giving programs of contemporary music, maintaining the Henry Hadley Memorial Library, and awarding annually the Henry Hadley Medal for distinguished service in various fields of music. For the season 1939–40 the medal of the society was awarded to Gene Buck as the man who had done most for American music for the season; to Serge Koussevitzky as the outstanding symphonic conductor in the presentation of American works; to Howard Barlow as the most successful American-born conductor of the year; to Roy Harris as the American composer of the most notable attainments during the season; to WNYC, New York City's municipal broadcasting station, for the second time, for doing the most for American music on the air; and to Francis D. Perkins, music critic of the *New York Herald Tribune*, as the critic showing the most practical interest in American music.

PERFORMANCES BY MAJOR ORCHESTRAS

In the spring of 1940, Koussevitzky was also honored at a special dinner given by the Beethoven Association, as one of its last official acts, to acknowledge his services to the American composer. This may remind us that not all the work for American music is done by the organizations formed specially for the purpose. Of the great orchestras of the East, the Boston Symphony Orchestra has been by far the most hospitable to American compositions, both under Koussevitzky and under his predecessor, Pierre Monteux, now conductor of the San Francisco Symphony Orchestra. The veteran Frederick Stock, for thirty-five years conductor of the Chicago Symphony Orchestra, has perhaps played more contemporary American works than any other conductor. Stokowski, too, has given hearings to many of our younger men. Even the New York Philharmonic-Symphony Orchestra, which until recently was the least hospitable to native talent of all the great orchestras, has read the signs of the times.

A few figures may be revealing. In the five concert seasons between the fall of 1925 and the summer of 1930, the Chicago Symphony Orchestra, under Stock, played forty-two American works, including a few repetitions from season to season, but none within a single season. In the same period, the Boston orchestra played thirty-three such works; the New York Philharmonic (later Philharmonic-Symphony) ten.[10] In the five-year period immediately preceding, 1919–24, Pierre Monteux, conducting the

[10] The figures are taken from an article "The Case for American Orchestral Music—1925 to 1930," by Daniel Gregory Mason, *Musical America*, June, 1931.

Boston Symphony, had played no less than forty-four! But in the season 1939–40 alone the Philharmonic played twelve American works, or more than it had played in the five seasons from 1925 to 1930.[11]

In the autumn of 1939, ASCAP proposed to hold a Festival of American Music in New York, and was to have engaged the Boston orchestra to give several programs in this Festival, open to the public without admission. Union difficulties intervened (the Boston Symphony Orchestra is the only one of our large bands that is not unionized), and the Philharmonic-Symphony Orchestra was employed in its place. The Boston orchestra, nothing daunted, proceeded to give its own festival, also free to the public. So the American composer got a double boost. And when Koussevitzky brought his orchestra to New York, he opened both his subscription series there with all-American programs, made up of works which had been played at the Boston festival.

American publishers, too, have been encouraged to do their share. Back in the 'teens of this century, Rudolph Schirmer, then head of G. Schirmer, Inc., pursued a course of remarkable generosity and enlightenment by issuing the works of Loeffler, Carpenter, Bloch, and others. If he had lived in the thirties, he would have had good company. C. C. Birchard & Company, J. Fischer and Brother, and a few other firms have joined the still small roster of publishers (which already included G. Schirmer, Inc., and Carl Fischer, Inc.) who see commercial possibilities in the serious music of the American composer and are willing to take risks in the effort to realize them.

An even more encouraging sign of the times is the recent entry in this field of the Tin Pan Alley publishers. They are not in the habit of encouraging Art for Art's sake, and when a firm like Mills Music signs an exclusive five-year contract with a composer like Roy Harris, we may feel sure that the American composer is no longer a voice crying in the wilderness.

[11] These figures are from articles by Francis D. Perkins in the *New York Herald Tribune*, December 3, 1939, and April 21, 1940.

RECENT RECRUITS

One of the first composers discussed in this book was born in Breslau, Germany, and this fact served an early warning on the reader that the definition of the term American Composer must be a flexible one. We are fortunate that our growth in national consciousness and self-confidence has so far not resulted in any artistic chauvinism. It seems likely that we shall avoid it in the future as well, for we are a very mixed group, and many of us retain a certain kinship with the cultures of the native lands of our forefathers. There can happily never be a definite line drawn between "real" Americans and any other kind, so far as inheritance is concerned; for the proudest boast of our "first" families is that they can trace their ancestry back to those who first came from another land.

We have had occasion to discuss the question of the naturalized American, and have claimed Ernest Bloch, Percy Grainger, and others as our own. In the 1930's we have been lucky enough to receive a rich infusion of Europe's best blood, brought to us as the result of persecution and war. It would be foolish, of course, to claim as American composers men who have made international reputations while still resident abroad, and some of whom may be only visitors. But many of them have come with the firm intention of staying among us. They have become citizens, or are in the process of doing so, and have cast their lot with us. Europe's loss is our immense gain, and in 1940 it seems as if there must be few of the great names of European music that do not appear on the immigration record of recent years.

European performing artists have always visited us. The performer has a limited repertory which he must play to constantly changing audiences, and we have always been one of the most lucrative of listening publics. Many noted players and singers had, in fact, made America their headquarters during and after the first World War. The creative artists and the scholars had deeper roots at home, to which most of them naturally clung as long as they could. But when it became clear to them that their day in Europe was over, most of them came here, determined to help preserve, in this still sheltered land, the best in the cultures they represented. Who are the great names of music in the post-War (or inter-War) period? Stravinsky? Schoenberg? Hindemith? Bartók? Sibelius? Four out of the five are here. Alfred Einstein, formerly music critic of the *Berliner Tageblatt* and editor of the *Zeitschrift für Musikwissenschaft* is at Smith College. Curt Sachs, world-famous authority on the history of musical instruments and many another musicological subject, lectures at New York University. Paul Hindemith teaches at Yale. Darius Milhaud, Nadia Boulanger, Ernst Křenek, Kurt Weill, Mario Castelnuovo-Tedesco,—these and hundreds of other leaders of musical culture in the Old World have come to stay in the New.

Twenty years ago, even ten, we should have been overwhelmed by them, and our native talents perhaps swamped. But 1940 is not 1930, and it really looks as if for once in this topsy-turvy modern world, something had happened at just the right time. America is eager to learn what it can from its distinguished newcomers. But both we and they realize that there are important things which they can learn from us. When eminent foreigners Europeanized American musicians, in former days, they pressed them into a mold from which too often there emerged nothing but a poor imitation of the real thing. The danger of that is past, and happily we have no intention of reversing the rôles. For the process of naturalization, through which it is now their turn to go, does not require the dropping off of anything of value that they have brought with them. On the contrary, it demands that they shall contribute everything that is good to the common store, which we, who preceded them by a few years, have built up.

If chauvinism and national servility are both things of the past, so too, in general, are faddism and the desire to be startling. It is not without significance that the longest chapter in this book is neither *Safe and Sound,* nor *Experimenters,* but rather *Unfamiliar Idioms.* The title will date fast enough; indeed it hardly applies even now to some of the composers treated under it. But it is a fact that the largest number of contemporary American composers are today neither content with the methods of their predecessors nor primarily interested in evolving new ones, but bent instead on saying what they have to say in whatever way seems clearest and best to them, conventional or unconventional. The proportion of these men is even larger than it seems, for of many of those who for convenience of classification are grouped in other chapters the same thing must be said. In that fact there is hope.

Our grandfathers were sure that they lived in the best of worlds, which was steadily growing better. To younger generations their pious optimism seemed for a long time to make them fair game for teasing, and the musical teasing that went on for fifteen or twenty years was often a pretty bitter dose. But it is only the complacent who are fun to shock, and there has been little complacency left in most of us as the '30's rumbled on to their terrible climax.

Today American composers, even more than Americans generally, are alive to their heavy responsibilities in a besieged world. They have felt their strength, and have accepted the great challenge of the times. We need not doubt that they will meet it well.

APPENDIX

A SELECTED LIST OF BOOKS RELATING TO CONTEMPORARY AMERICAN MUSIC

Armstrong, Louis. *Swing That Music.* New York, Longmans, Green and Company, 1936.

Cowell, Henry, editor. *American Composers on American Music; A Symposium.* Stanford University, Cal., Stanford University Press, 1933.

Goldberg, Isaac. *Tin Pan Alley; A Chronicle of the American Music Racket.* New York, The John Day Company, 1930.

Goodman, Benny. *The Kingdom of Swing.* New York, Stackpole Sons, 1939.

Hobson, Wilder. *American Jazz Music.* New York, W. W. Norton & Company, 1939.

Howard, John Tasker. *Our American Music.* New York, Thomas Y. Crowell Company, 1931. Rev. ed., 1939.

Kaufmann, Helen. *From Jehovah to Jazz; Music in America from Psalmody to the Present Day.* New York, Dodd, Mead & Company, 1937.

Mason, Daniel Gregory. *The Dilemma of American Music.* New York, The Macmillan Company, 1928.

——— *Tune In, America.* New York, Alfred A. Knopf, 1931.

Miller, Paul Eduard. *Down Beat's Yearbook of Swing.* Chicago, Down Beat Publishing Company, 1939.

Morris, Harold. *Contemporary American Music.* Houston, Tex., The Rice Institute Pamphlets, V. 21, pp. 83–169, 1934.

Osgood, Henry Osborne. *So This Is Jazz.* Boston, Little, Brown and Company, 1926.

Panassié, Hugues. *Hot Jazz; The Guide to Swing Music.* (Translated by Lyle and Eleanor Dowling.) New York, M. Witmark & Sons, 1936.

Ramsey, Frederic, Jr., and Smith, Charles Edward, Editors. *Jazzmen.* New York, Harcourt, Brace & Company, 1939.

Rosenfeld, Paul. *An Hour with American Music.* Philadelphia, J. B. Lippincott Company, 1929.

Sargeant, Winthrop. *Jazz, Hot and Hybrid.* New York, Arrow Editions, 1938.

Reis, Claire. *Composers in America.* New York, The Macmillan Company, 1938.

Slonimsky, Nicolas. *Music Since 1900.* New York, W. W. Norton and Company, 1937.

Thompson, Oscar, editor. *The International Cyclopedia of Music and Musicians.* New York, Dodd, Mead & Company, 1939.

Thomson, Virgil. *The State of Music.* New York, W. Morrow and Company, 1939.

Upton, William Treat. *Art-Song in America.* Boston, Oliver Ditson Company, 1930.

——— *A Supplement to Art-Song in America, 1930–1938.* Philadelphia, Oliver Ditson Company, 1938.

Whiteman, Paul. *Jazz.* New York, J. H. Sears and Company, 1926.

RECORDED WORKS BY AMERICAN COMPOSERS

[*List compiled by Florence Strauss of* THE AMERICAN MUSIC CENTER, *17 East 42nd Street, New York, from whom information about the recordings may be obtained.*]

C	Columbia	*S*	Schirmer
D	Decca	*T*	Technicord
F	Friends of Recorded Music	*V*	Victor
Ga	Gamut	*Y*	Yaddo Recordings: these are made not primarily for public distribution, and the available information on many of them is incomplete.
Gr	Gramophone		
M	Musicraft		
N	New Music Recordings		
P	Parlophone		
Po	Polydor		
R	Roycroft		
Re	Royale	*	rare or acoustical recording

AMERICAN MUSIC FOR ORCHESTRA, ALBUM
George W. Chadwick—*Jubilee*, from "Symphonic Sketches"
Edward MacDowell—*Dirge*, from "Indian Suite"
John Knowles Paine—*Prelude* to "Oedipus Tyrannis"
Kent Kennan—*Night Soliloquy*
Charles T. Griffes—*The White Peacock*
Eastman-Rochester Symphony Orchestra—H. Hanson (*V*)

ANTHEIL, GEORGE
Sonata No. II (Airplane Sonata—piano): Lydia Hoffmann (*N*)

BACON, ERNST
Of a Feather (song): Ethel Luening, sopr. (*Y*)
There Came a Day (Emily Dickinson): Ethel Luening, sopr.; Lionel Nowak, pf. (*Y*)
The Snow and *The Bat* (Songs): Ethel Luening, sopr.; Gunnar Johansen, pf. (*Y*)

BAILEY, WILLIAM H.
Idless for Violin and Piano: Samuel Siegel, vl.; Gregory Tucker, pf. (*N*)

BALLANTINE, EDWARD
Variations on "Mary Had a Little Lamb" (Piano): Edward Ballantine (T)

BARBER, SAMUEL
Beggar's Song: Benjamin de Loache, bar. (Y)
Bessie Bobtail (Song): Benjamin de Loache, bar. (Y)
Dover Beach (Matthew Arnold): Samuel Barber, bar.; Curtis String Quartet (V)

BARLOW, WAYNE
The Winter's Past (Fantasy for Oboe and Strings): Eastman-Rochester Symphony Orchestra—(V). In preparation

BARROWS, JOHN
Trio for Strings: Lois Porter, vl.; Louise Rood, vla.; Douglas Marsh, vlc. (Y)
Wood-Wind Quintet (Y)

BAUMGARTNER, LEROY
Noch sind die Tage der Rosen (Song with orchestra): Richard Tauber, ten.; orchestra—Hauke (C)

BECKER, JOHN J.
Credo for *a cappella* men's chorus: Greek Byzantine Chorus—Cristos Vrionides (N)

BERGEN, EUGENE
Quintet for Piano and Strings: Gunnar Johansen, pf.; Walden String Quartet (Y)

BERCKMANN, EVELYN
Four Songs: Ethel Luening, sopr. (Y)

BEREZOWSKI, NICOLAI
Quartet No. I. Op. 16: Coolidge String Quartet (V)
Suite for Wood-Wind Quintet: II. Adagio V. Allegro—Barrère Ensemble of Wood Winds (N)

BEYER, JOHANNA MAGDALENA
Suite for Clarinet and Bassoon: II. Lentamente; IV. Allegro Ponderoso: Rosario Mazzeo, cl.; Raymond Allard, bsn. (N)

BLITZSTEIN, MARC
The Cradle Will Rock (Operetta): Original cast, Mercury Production; Marc Blitzstein, pf. (M)

APPENDIX

BLOCH, ERNEST
Avodath Hakodesh—Sacred Service (Chorus and Orchestra): (Privately subscribed for but not yet recorded)
Baal Shem—Three Pictures of Chassidic Life (Violin and Piano):
  I. Vidui (Contrition): Francis Koene and Van Ijzer (*C*)
  II. Nigun (Improvisation): Yehudi Menuhin; A. Persinger (*C*)
    Josef Szigeti; K. Ruhrseitz (*C*)
    Leon Zighera; pf. acc. (*D*)
    Nathan Milstein; Leopold Mittman (*C*)
Concerto Grosso for Piano and String Orchestra
  Curtis Chamber Music Ensemble—L. Bailly (*V*)
  Philadelphia Chamber String Sinfonietta—F. Sevitzky (*V*)
Five Sketches in Sepia (Piano): Harrison Potter (*F*)
Prayer (Violoncello): Gregor Piatigorsky; organ acc. (*P*)
Quintet for Piano and Strings: Alfredo Casella and Pro Arte Quartet (*V*)
Schelomo (Solomon)—Hebrew Rhapsody for Violoncello and Orchestra: Emanuel Feuermann, vlc.; Philadelphia Orchestra—L. Stokowski (*V*)
Sonate for Violin and Piano: Josef Gingold; Beryl Rubinstein (*V*)
  Harold and Marion Kahn Berkley (*Ga*)
String Quartet in B Minor: Stuyvesant String Quartet (*C*)
Suite for Viola and Piano: William Primrose; A. Kitzinger (*V*)
Violin Concerto: Joseph Szigeti and the Paris Conservatory Orchestra—C. Munch (*C*)

BODENHORN, AARON
Stay, oh Sweet (John Donne): Ethel Luening, sopr.; string quartet acc. (*Y*)

BOWLES, PAUL
Letter to Freddy (Gertrude Stein): Ethel Luening, sopr.; Lionel Nowak, pf. (*Y*)
Three Pieces for Piano:
  I. Huapango: Jesus Duron
  II. Cafe sin Nombre
  III. Huapango No. 2—El Sol: Paul Bowles (*N*)

BRAINE, ROBERT
Choreographic Impressions: II. Pavane—"El Greco"; IV. Habanera

—"Lazy Cigarette": Eastman-Rochester Symphony Orchestra—H. Hanson (*V*)

BRANT, HENRY
Lyric Cycle (Eight Songs—text by Cecil Hemley): Helen van Loon, sopr.; Sol Montlack, Clifford Richter, Bertram Brant, violas; Richard Baldwin, pf.—H. Brant (*N*)

BROWN, HAROLD
Prelude for Strings: String Section, Yaddo Ensemble (*Y*)

BUCK, DUDLEY
Festival Te Deum, No. 7, in E♭ Major, Op. 63, No. 1: Trinity Chorus and organ (*V*)

BUSCH, CARL
An Arbor Day Song: Evra Giles, sopr.; pf. acc. (*V*)
Ozarka—Suite (Orchestra):
    I. At Sunset
    II. Hill-Billies' Dance: National High School Orchestra—Maddy (*V*)
Valentine (Song): Helen Jepson, sopr.; pf. acc. (*V*)

BUUCK, PAUL
String Quartet (*Y*)
Suite for Violin and Piano: Bernard Goodman, vl.; Gunnar Johansen, pf. (*Y*)

CADMAN, CHARLES WAKEFIELD
At Dawning (Song): Joseph Hislop, ten. (*Gr*)
From the Land of the Sky-Blue Water (Song): Mary Lewis, sopr.; pf. acc. (*V*)
  Louis Graveure, ten.; pf. acc. (*C*)
Her Shadow (Ojibway Canoe Song): Elsie Baker, sopr. (*V**)
I Hear a Thrush at Eve (Song): Charles Hackett, ten. (*V*)
Shanewis (Opera): Spring Song of the Robin Woman; Elsie Baker sopr. (*V**)

CARPENTER, JOHN ALDEN
Adventures in a Perambulator—Suite (Orchestra): Minneapolis Symphony Orchestra—E. Ormandy (*V*)
Berceuse de la Guerre (Song): Mina Hager, mezzo-sopr.; Celiu Dougherty, pf. (*M*)

APPENDIX

Gitanjali (Song Cycle—Tagore)
   1. When I Bring to You Colour'd Toys: Glenn Darwin, bar.; pf. acc. (*V*)
   6. Light MY Light: Rose Bampton, contr.; pf. acc. (*V*)
The Home Road (Song): Ralph Crane, bar.; pf. acc. (*V*)
The Little Turtle
   In "Songs for Children": Ann Howard, sopr.; pf. acc. (*V*)
Serenade: Gladys Swarthout, sopr. (*V*)
A Song of Faith: Chicago A Cappella Chorus, Orchestra and Organ; Carpenter, narrator—N. Cain, cond. (*V*)
Skyscrapers—Ballet (Orchestra): Victor Symphony Orchestra—N. Shilkret (*V*)
String Quartet in A Minor: Gordon String Quartet (*S*)
Water Colors: On a Screen; The Odalisque: Mina Hager, mezzo-sopr.; Celius Dougherty, pf. (*M*)

CHADWICK, GEORGE W.
Quartet in E Minor
   Second Movement (Andante Semplice): Coolidge String Quartet (*V*)
Jubilee, from "Symphonic Sketches": (See *American Music for Orchestra*—alb.) (*V*)

CHANLER, THEODORE
These, My Ophelia (Archibald MacLeish): Ethel Luening, sopr.; Lionel Nowak, pf. (*Y*)

CHASINS, ABRAM
Three Chinese Pieces (Piano):
   I. Flirtation in a Chinese Garden
   II. Rush Hour in Hong Kong
   III. A Chinese Tragedy: Abram Chasins (*V*)
   Nos. I and II: Benno Moiseivitch (*Gr*)
Fairy Tale (Piano)
Three Preludes (Piano):
   I. No. VI, in D Major, Op. 10, No. 5
   II. No. XIV, in E♭ Minor, Op. 12, No. 2
   III. No. XIII, in G♭ Minor, Op. 12, No. 1: Abram Chasins (*V*)

CLARKE, H. L.
Piece for Oboe and Piano (*Y*)

COHN, ARTHUR
String Quartet No. IV, Op. 24 ("Histrionics"): Galimir String Quartet (*Y*)

COPLAND, AARON
El Salón México: Boston Symphony Orchestra—S. Koussevitzky (*V*)
Music for the Theatre: Eastman-Rochester Symphony Orchestra—H. Hanson (*V*)
Nocturne: Jacques Gordon, vl.; Aaron Copland, pf. (*C*)
Piano Variations: Aaron Copland (*C*)
Scherzo Humoristique—"The Cat and the Mouse" (Piano): (See *Piano Music of the Twentieth Century*—alb.) (*V*)
Two Pieces for String Quartet:
 I. Lento Molto
 II. Rondino: Dorian String Quartet (*C*)
Ukelele Serenade: Jacques Gordon, vl.; Aaron Copland, pf. (*C*)
Vitebsk—Trio for Piano, Violin and Violoncello: Aaron Copland Trio (*C*)
Vocalise: Ethel Luening, sopr.; Aaron Copland, pf. (*N*)

COWELL, HENRY
Movement for String Quartet: Dorian String Quartet (*C*)
Suite for Wood-Winds:
 I. Andante
 II. Jig
 III. Chorale
 IV. Allegro: Barrère Ensemble of Wood-Winds (*N*)
Two Chorales and Ostinato: Josef Marx, ob.; Vivian Fine, pf. (*N*)
Vocalise: Ethel Luening, sopr.; Otto Luening, fl.; Gunnar Johansen, pf. (*Y*)

CRAWFORD, RUTH
Andante for String Quartet: New World Quartet (*N*)

CRESTON, PAUL
Bird of the Wilderness (Song): (*Y*)
Concertino for Marimba and Orchestra, Op. 21: Ruth Stuber, mar. Yaddo Chamber Orchestra (*Y*)
Partita (Orchestra): First Four Movements; Yaddo Chamber Orchestra (*Y*)

Suite for Alto Saxophone and Piano:
  I. Scherzoso
  II. Pastorale
  III. Toccata: Cecil Leeson, sax.; Paul Creston, pf. (*N*)
Two Choric Dances: Yaddo Chamber Orchestra—A. Shepherd (*Y*)

CRIST, BAINBRIDGE
C'est mon ami: Muzio, sopr.; orchestra (*C*)
Seven Chinese Mother Goose Rhymes: Bullock, bar. (*C*)

DAMROSCH, WALTER
Danny Deever (Kipling): Reinald Werrenrath, bar. (*V*)
  Alexander Kisselburgh, bar. (*V*)

DIAMOND, DAVID
Concerto for Chamber Orchestra: Yaddo Chamber Orchestra (*Y*)
Mad Maid's Song: Ethel Luening, sopr.; Otto Luening, fl. (*Y*)
Prelude and Fugue for piano: Leonard Bernstein (*N*)
Sonatina for Violin and Piano: Hildegarde Donaldson, vl.; Gunnar Johansen, pf. (*Y*)

DONOVAN, RICHARD
Adagio (Orchestra): Yaddo Ensemble (*Y*)
Serenade for Oboe, Violin, Viola and Violoncello: Lois Wann, ob.; Bernard Tinterow, vl.; Quincy Porter, vla.; Aaron Bodenhorn, vlc. (*N*)
Suite for Piano:
  I. Prelude
  II. Air
  III. Jig: Edwin Gerschefski (*N*)
Two Songs with String Quartet:
  I. On Her Dancing
  II. Farra Diddle Dino: Grace Donovan, sopr.; Romeo Tata, Hugo Kortschak, Emmeran Stoeber, Harry Berman (*N*)

DUBENSKY, ARCADY
Fugue for Eighteen Violins: Philadelphia Orchestra Strings—L. Stokowski (*V*)
Gossips: Philadelphia String Ensemble—F. Sevitzky (*V*)
The Raven (Melodrama for Speaker and Orchestra): Benjamin de Loache; Philadelphia Orchestra—L. Stokowski (*V*)

DUKE, JOHN
Aria (Violoncello) (*Y*)
Loveliest of Trees (Song) (*Y*)
String Trio (*Y*)
Suite for Viola Alone:
    I. Aria
   II. Scherzo
  III. Cadenza
  IV. Alla Marcia: Louise Rood (*Y*)

EASTHAM, CLARK
Andante for Strings—Elegy: Strings Section, Yaddo Ensemble—M. Holmes (*Y*)

EICHHEIM, HENRY
Bali—Symphonic Variations
Eten Raku—8th Century Ceremonial Prelude: Philadelphia Orchestra—L. Stokowski (*V*)
Japanese Nocturne: Philadelphia Orchestra—L. Stokowski (*V*)

ELLINGTON, DUKE
In my Solitude (Popular Dance Orchestra): Ellington Orchestra—D. Ellington (*V*)
Mood Indigo (Popular Dance Orchestra): Ellington Orchestra—D. Ellington (*V*)
Sophisticated Lady (Popular Dance Orchestra): Ellington Orchestra—D. Ellington (*C*)

ELWELL, HERBERT
The Ousel-Cock (Shakespeare): Ethel Luening, sopr.; Lionel Nowak, pf. (*Y*)

ENGEL, CARL
Triptych: William Kroll, vl.; Frank Sheridan, pf. (*S*)

ETLER, ALVIN
Five Speeds Forward for Flute, Oboe, Viola and Bassoon: David Van Vactor, Alvin Etler, Louise Rood, Joseph Reines (*Y*)
Music for Chamber Orchestra: Yaddo Chamber Orchestra—A. Shepherd (*Y*)
Oboe Quartet (*Y*)

FAIRCHILD, BLAIR
Moustiques (arr. violin and piano—Dushkin): Miquel Candela, vl.; J. Benvenuti, pf. (*C*)

FARWELL, ARTHUR
Alabaster Chambers (Emily Dickinson): Ethel Luening, sopr.; Lionel Nowak, pf. (*Y*)
Cradle Song (William Blake): Ethel Luening, sopr.; Lionel Nowak, pf. (*Y*)

FINE, VIVIAN
Spring's Welcome (Song): Ethel Luening, sopr.; Gunnar Johansen, pf. (*Y*)

FINNEY, ROSS LEE
Bleheris—A Monody from the Hamlet of Archibald MacLeish: Ross Lee Finney and the Yaddo Chamber Orchestra (*Y*)
Sonata: Louise Rood, vla.; Gunnar Johansen, pf. (*Y*)
String Quartet No. II (*Y*)

FOOTE, ARTHUR
A Night Piece: John Wummer, fl.; Dorian String Quartet (*C*)

FORST, RUDOLPH
Divertimento: String Section, Yaddo Ensemble (*Y*)

FREED, ISADORE
The Rebel (Song): Ethel Luening, sopr. (*Y*)

GERSCHEFSKI, EDWIN
Classic Overture: Yaddo Ensemble (*Y*)
Lai (Song): Benjamin de Loache, bar. (*Y*)
New Music for Piano: Edwin Gerschefski (*N*)
Three Piano Pieces (*Y*)
Piece for Saxophone and Piano (*Y*)
Wanting is What (*Y*)

GERSHWIN, GEORGE
An American in Paris: Victor Symphony Orchestra—N. Shilkret (*V*)
Concerto in F Major (Piano): Jesus Maria Sanroma; Boston "Pops" Orchestra—A. Fiedler (*V*)
    Roy Bargy; Whiteman Orchestra—P. Whiteman (*C*)
Porgy and Bess (Opera) . . . Vocal and orchestral excerpts: Law-

rence Tibbett, bar.; Helen Jepson, sopr.; Chorus and Orchestra—A. Smallens (*V*)

Rhapsody in Blue (Piano and Orchestra): Jesus Maria Sanroma; Boston "Pops" Orchestra—A. Fiedler (*V*)
George Gershwin; Whiteman Orchestra—P. Whiteman (*V*)
M. Spoliansky; J. Fuhs Orchestra (*P*)
Transcribed for two pianos by José Iturbi: José Iturbi; Amparo Iturbi (*V*)
. . . Andante—only (arr. for piano solo): George Gershwin (*C*)

Short Story for Violin and Piano: Samuel Dushkin (*Gr*—withdrawn*)

GIORNI, AURELIO

Minuet in G Major—(Violoncello and Piano): Sterling Hunkins, vc.; Arthur Leaf, pf. (*M*)
Trio in C Major—(Violin, Violoncello and Piano): Max Hollaender; Sterling Hunkins; Eugene Kusmiak (*M*)

GOSLEE, GEORGE

Three Sketches for Wood-Winds: Otto Luening, fl.; Alvin Etler, ob.; Richard Korn, cl.; George Goslee, bsn. (*Y*)

GOULD, MORTON

Foster Gallery: Boston "Pops" Orchestra—A. Fiedler (*V*)
Pavane: Boston "Pops" Orchestra—A. Fiedler (*V*)
Satirical Dance: Morton Gould, pf. (*V*)

GRAINGER, PERCY

Brigg Fair (Ten. Solo and Unacc. Chorus): English Singers (*R*)
Norman Stone, ten.; Oriana Madrigal Society—C. K. Scott (*Gr*)
Country Gardens ("Handkerchief Dance"): Minneapolis Symphony Orchestra—E. Ormandy (*V*)
Piano arr. Percy Grainger (*C*)
Handel in the Strand (Clog Dance): New Queen's Hall Orchestra—Sir Henry Wood (*D*)
New Light Symphony Orchestra—Sargent (*Gr*)
In a Nutshell—Suite:
  IV. Gumsuckers' March; Percy Grainger pf. (*C*)

One More Day, My John (Sea Chanty Setting): Percy Grainger, pf. (*C*)

APPENDIX

GREEN, RAY
Sea Calm for *A Cappella* Men's Chorus: Greek Byzantine Chorus—
C. Vrionides (*N*)

GRIFFES, CHARLES T.
By a Lonely Forest Pathway (Song): Glenn Darwin, bar. (*V*)
Alexander Kisselburgh, bar. (*C*)
The Fountain of the Acqua Paola, Op. 7, No. 3—From "Roman Sketches" (Piano): Rudolph Gruen (*R*)
Indian Sketch No. I (String Quartet): Kreiner Quartet (*F*)
Lament of Ian the Proud: William Hain, ten. (*F*)
Piano Sonata: Harrison Potter (*F*)
The Pleasure Dome of Kubla Khan—Symphonic Poem after Coleridge: Minneapolis Symphony Orchestra—E. Ormandy (*V*)
The Sketches Based on Indian Themes: Coolidge String Quartet (*V*)
The White Peacock, Op. 7, No. 1—From "Roman Sketches": Myra Hess (*C*)
Olga Samaroff (*V*)
Columbia Broadcasting Symphony Orchestra—H. Barlow (*C*)
Also in *American Music for Orchestra*—alb. (*V*)

GRISELLE, THOMAS
Two American Sketches:
   I. Nocturne
   II. March: Victor Symphony Orchestra (*V*)

GROFÉ, FERDE
Grand Canyon Suite: Sunrise, The Painted Desert, On the Trail, Sunset, Cloudburst: Paul Whiteman's Concert Orchestra (*V*)
Metropolis: Paul Whiteman's Concert Orchestra (*V*)
Mississippi Suite—A Tone Journey: Huckleberry Finn, Old Creole Days, Mardi Gras: Paul Whiteman's Concert Orchestra (*V*)
Three Shades of Blue—Suite:
   1. Indigo
   2. Alice Blue
   3. Heliotrope: Paul Whiteman's Concert Orchestra (*V*)

GRUENBERG, LOUIS
Emperor Jones (Opera): Standin' in the Need of Prayer: Lawrence Tibbett, bar. (*V*)

GUION, DAVID
Arkansas Traveler (Arr. of Native Folk Tune): Boston "Pops" Orchestra—A. Fiedler (*V*)
Home on the Range (Cowboy Song Setting): John Charles Thomas, bar. (*V*)
Sheep and Goat Walkin' to Pasture (Cowboy Breakdown Setting—Piano): Myrtle Eaver (*V*)
  Percy Grainger (*C*)
Turkey in the Straw (Fiddle Tune Setting): Victor Concert Orchestra—R. Bourdon (*V*)
  Boston "Pops" Orchestra—A. Fiedler (*V*)

HADLEY, HENRY
Concertino for Piano and Orchestra, Op. 131: Eunice Howard; Victor Symphony Orchestra—P. James (*V*)
October Twilight, Op. 95, No. 2: Victor Symphony Orchestra—P. James (*V*)

HAGEMAN, RICHARD
Caponsacchi (Opera): This Very Vivid Morn; Lullaby: Helen Jepson, sopr. (*V*)
Do Not Go, My Love: Nancy Evans (*D*)

HANSON, HOWARD
Merry Mount (Opera): 'Tis an Earth Defiled: Lawrence Tibbett, bar. (*V*)
Symphony No. II ("Romantic"): Eastman-Rochester Symphony Orchestra—H. Hanson (*V*)

HARRIS, ROY
Children's Suite (Piano): Johana Harris (*V*)
Chorale for Strings: Kreiner Sextette (*V*)
Concerto, Op. 2 (Sextet): Harry Cumpson, pf.; Aaron Gorodner, cl.; Aeolian Quartet (*C*)
Four Minutes and Twenty Seconds (Flute and String Quartet): Georges Laurent; Burgin Quartet (*C*)
Piano Quintet: Johana Harris; Coolidge String Quartet (*V*)
Poem: Albert Spalding, vl.; pf. acc. (*V*)
Quartet—See *Three Variations*, etc.
Sonata for Piano: Johana Harris (*V*)

A Song for Occupations (Walt Whitman): Westminster Choir—Williamson (*C*)

Symphony for Voices on Poems of Walt Whitman: Westminster Choir—Williamson (*V*)

Symphony 1933: Boston Symphony Orchestra—S. Koussevitzky (*C*)

Symphony No. III: Boston Symphony Orchestra—S. Koussevitzky (*V*)

Third String Quartet ("Four Preludes and Fugues"): Galimir String Quartet (*V*—in preparation)

Three Variations on a Theme, for String Quartet: Roth Quartet (*V*)

Trio (Violin, Violoncello and Piano): Poltronieri, Bonucci, Casella (*C*)

When Johnny Comes Marching Home—Overture: Minneapolis Symphony Orchestra—E. Ormandy (*V*)

HAUBIEL, CHARLES

Karma (Symphonic Variations): Symphony Orchestra—C. Haubiel (*C*)

HELM, EVERETT

Trio for Flute, Violin and Violoncello: Otto Luening, Morris Levine, Ross Lee Finney (*Y*)

HOVANESS, ALAN

Prelude and Fugue for Oboe and Bassoon: Alvin Etler, Ob.; Joseph Reines, bsn. (*Y*)

HOWE, MARY

Movement from *String Quartet:* Galimir String Quartet (*Y*)

Stars: Maganini Chamber Symphony—Q. Maganini (*N*)

IVES, CHARLES E.

Barn Dance ("Washington's Birthday" Movement from the symphony *Holidays*)

In the Night (Movement from *A Set of Pieces for Theatre Orchestra*): Pan American Orchestra—N. Slonimsky (*N*)

General Booth Enters Heaven (Vachel Lindsay): Radiana Pazmor, sopr.; Genevieve Pitot, pf. (*N*)

Hymn: Ethel Luening, sopr.; Lionel Nowak, pf. (*Y*)

The Last Reader (Oliver Wendell Holmes): Ethel Luening, sopr.; Lionel Nowak, pf. (*Y*)

Six Songs:
  1. Charlie Rutlage
  2. Evening
  3. Resolution
  4. Ann Street
  5. Two Little Flowers
  6. The Greatest Man: Mordecai Bauman, bar.; Albert Hirsh, pf. (*N*)

The Sixty-Seventh Psalm: Madrigal Singers—Lehman Engel (*C*)

JACOBI, FREDERICK

Scherzo for Wood-Winds: Ensemble from the Juilliard School (*N*)

Wood-Wind Quintet: Yaddo Ensemble (*Y*)

JANSSEN, WERNER

New Year's Eve in New York: Victor Symphony Orchestra—N. Shilkret (*V*)

KEENEY, WENDELL

Sonatina for Piano: Johana Harris (*Y*)

KENNAN, KENT

Night Soliloquy: (See *American Music for Orchestra*—alb.) (*V*)

KERR, HARRISON

Study for Violoncello, Unaccompanied: Margaret Aue (*N*)

Trio: Richard Korn, cl.; Aaron Bodenhorn, vla.; Gunnar Johansen, pf. (*Y*)

KROLL, WILLIAM

Little March: Gordon String Quartet (*S*)

KUBIK, GAIL

Four Trivialities for Flute, Horn and String Quartet: David Van Vactor, fl.; Ralph Dunlap, hn.; Malcolm Holmes, Urico Rossi, Louise Rood, Aaron Bodenhorn (*Y*)

LAIDLAW, ROBERT

String Trio: Felix Galimir, Lotte Hammerschlag, Ernst Silverstein (*Y*)

LEICH, ROLAND

Elusive Sleep (Olive Whitney): Ethel Luening, sopr.; Lionel Nowak, pf. (*Y*)

APPENDIX

LOCKWOOD, NORMAND
Quintet for Piano and Strings (Fourth Movement omitted): Johana Harris; Galimir String Quartet (*Y*)
String Quartet: Walden String Quartet (*Y*)

LOEFFLER, CHARLES MARTIN
Adieu pour jamais, Op. 10, No. 2 (arr. for violin and piano by Jacques Gordon): Jacques Gordon, vl.; Carl Deis, pf. (*S*)
Music for Stringed Instruments: Coolidge Quartet (*V*)
Partita (Violin and Piano)
Peacocks ("Les Paons"): Jacques Gordon, vl.; Lee Pattison, pf. (*C*)
String Quintet in One Movement: Gordon String Quartet; Kay Rickert, third vl. (*S*)
Two Rhapsodies, Op. 5:
  I. The Pool ("L'étang")
  II. The Bagpipe ("La Cornemuse"): Bruno Labate, ob.; Jacques Gordon, vla.; Emma Boynet, pf. (*S*)

LUENING, OTTO
Four Songs (Walt Whitman—"Leaves of Grass"): Ethel Luening, sopr.; Otto Luening, fl. (*N*)
Preludes No. II and V (Piano): Edwin Gerschefski (*Y*)
Preludes No. VI and VIII (Piano): Edwin Gerschefski (*Y*)
Prelude to Hymn (Piano): Edwin Gerschefski (*Y*)
Short Sonata for Flute and Harpsichord: Otto Luening, fl.; Ralph Kirkpatrick, harps. (*Y*)
Suite for Soprano and Flute:
  1. Dawnpiece
  2. Nightpiece
  3. Morning Song
  4. Evening Song: Ethel Luening, sopr.; Otto Luening, fl. (*N*)
Three Inventions for Piano: Lionel Nowak (*Y*)

MACDOWELL, EDWARD
Concerto No. II, in D Minor, Op. 23 (Piano): Jesus Maria Sanroma; Boston "Pops" Orchestra—A. Fiedler (*V*)
Dirge, from "Indian Suite": (See *American Music for Orchestra*—alb.) (*V*)

MASON, DANIEL GREGORY
Three Pieces for Flute, Harp and String Quartet:

I. Sarabande
   II. Elegy
   III. Caprice: John Wummer, fl.; Edward Vito, hp.; Eddy Brown Ensemble (*Re*)

McBride, Robert
Fugato on a Well-Known Theme: Boston "Pops" Orchestra—A. Fiedler (*V*)
Let-Down for English Horn with Piano
Warm-Up for English Horn Alone: Robert McBride, E.hn.; Paul Creston, pf. (*N*)
Swing Stuff
Jingle Jangle: Boston "Pops" Orchestra—A. Fiedler (*V*)
Wise-Apple Five (Clarinet and Strings): Robert McBride, cl.; Lois Porter, Claire Harper, Quincy Porter, Aaron Bodenhorn (*Y*)

McDonald, Harl
Concerto for Two Pianos and Orchestra: Jeanne Behrend, Alexander Kelberine, pfs.; Philadelphia Orchestra—L. Stokowski (*V*)
Festival of the Workers (Orchestra): Dance of the Workers
Rhumba Symphony: Rhumba (Third Movement) Phialdelphia Orchestra—L. Stokowski (*V*)
Miniature Suite ("J. C. Smith"): Boston "Pops" Orchestra—A. Fiedler (*V*)
San Juan Capistrano ("Two Evening Pictures"):
   I. The Mission
   II. Fiesta: Boston Symphony Orchestra—S. Koussevitzky (*V*)
Two Hebraic Poems: Philadelphia Orchestra—E. Ormandy (*V*)

Moore, Douglas
String Quartet: Four Movements (*Y*)

Morris, Harold
Second String Quartet: Walden String Quartet (*Y*)

Naginski, Charles
Nonsense Alphabet Suite: Betty Martin, sopr.; Sergius Kagen, pf (*C*)
Sinfonietta: Yaddo Chamber Orchestra (*Y*)

Nowak, Lionel
Suite for Flute and Pianoforte: Otto Luening, fl.; Lionel Nowak, pf (*Y*)

APPENDIX

PAINE, JOHN KNOWLES
Prelude to Oedipus Tyrannis (Orchestra): Eastman-Rochester Symphony Orchestra—H. Hanson (See *American Music for Orchestra*—alb.) (*V*)

PALMER, ROBERT
Sonata for Pianoforte: John Kirkpatrick (*Y*)

PHILLIPS, BURRILL
American Dance (Bassoon and Orchestra): Eastman-Rochester Symphony Orchestra—H. Hanson (*V—in preparation*)

PIANO MUSIC OF THE TWENTIETH CENTURY, ALBUM:
Aaron Copland—*Cat and the Mouse,* Jesus Maria Sanroma (*V*)

PISTON, WALTER
String Quartet No. I: Dorian String Quartet (*C*)
Suite for Oboe and Piano: Louis Speyer; Walter Piston (*T*)
Suite from the Ballet, *The Incredible Flutist:* Boston "Pops" Orchestra—A. Fiedler (*V*)
Three Pieces for Flute, Clarinet and Bassoon:
  I. Allegro Scherzando
  II. Lento
  III. Allegro: Georges Barrère, Fred van Amburgh, Angel del Busto (*N*)

PITTAWAY, R.
Sonata for Piano and Clarinet (*Y*)

PORTER, QUINCY
Dance in Three-Time (*Y*)
Incidental Music to Shakespeare's "Antony and Cleopatra": Yaddo Chamber Orchestra—Q. Porter (*Y*)
Quintet for Flute and Strings on a Childhood Tune: David Van Vactor, fl.; Malcolm Holmes, Urico Rossi, Louise Rood, Aaron Bodenhorn (*Y*)
Sixth String Quartet (*Y*)
String Quartet No. III: Gordon String Quartet (*C*)
Suite for Viola Alone:
  I. Lento—Allegro Furioso
  II. Larghetto Espressivo—Allegro Spiritoso: Quincy Porter (*N*)

POWELL, JOHN
Sonata Virginianesque (Violin and Piano): Eddy Brown, vl.; John Powell, pf. (*Re*)

RIEGGER, WALLINGFORD
Evocation (Piano, four hands): Edwin Gerschefski, Paul Creston (*N*)
Finale from *Trio for Flute, Harp and Violoncello:* Georges Barrère, fl.; Carlos Salzedo, hp.; Horace Britt, vlc. (*N*)
String Quartet: Galimir String Quartet (*Y*)

ROBINSON, EARL
Ballad for Americans: Paul Robeson, bass; American People's Chorus; Victor Symphony Orchestra—N. Shilkret (*V*)

RUBINSTEIN, BERYL
Passepied: Kreiner String Quartet (*V*)

ROGERS, BERNARD
Soliloquy for Flute and String Orchestra: Eastman-Rochester Symphony Orchestra—H. Hanson (*V—in preparation*)

RUGGLES, CARL
Lilacs and Toys from "Men and Mountains": Pan American Orchestra—N. Slonimsky (*N*)

RUSSELL, WILLIAM
Three Dance Movements for Percussion Group: Jessie Baetz, Miles Dresskell, William Russell, Henry Cowell (*N*)

RYAN, THOMAS
Epitaph (Edgar Lee Masters): Ethel Luening, sopr.; Lionel Nowak, pf. (*Y*)

SALZEDO, CARLOS
Chanson dans la Nuit (Harp): Carlos Salzedo (*C*)
Short Stories in Music for Young Harpists: Carlos Salzedo (*V*)
Whirlwind Harp: Sidonie Goossens (*C*)
Concerto for Harp and Seven Wind Instruments: Lucile Lawrence; Barrère Wood-Wind Ensemble—C. Salzedo (*C—withdrawn*)

SCHELLING, ERNEST
Nocturne à Raguze (Piano): Ignace Jan Paderewski (*Gr*)
A Victory Ball: New York Philharmonic Orchestra—W. Mengelberg (*V*)

SCHUMAN, WILLIAM
Choral Etude: Madrigal Singers—L. Engel (*C*)
American Festival Overture: National Symphony Orchestra—H. Kindler (*V*)

Quartettino for Bassoons:
  I. Ostinato
  II. Nocturne
  III. Waltz
  IV. Fughetta: Sam Cohen, Jack Knitzer, Erika Kutzing, Leonard Sharrow (*N*)

SESSIONS, ROGER
Quartet in E Minor: Galimir String Quartet, Guild Recordings

SHEPHERD, ARTHUR
Second String Quartet (*Y*)

SOWERBY, LEO
Comes Autumn Time—Program Overture: Eastman-Rochester Symphony Orchestra—H. Hanson (*V*)
The Irish Washerwoman: Victor Symphony Orchestra—R. Bourdon (*V*)

SPALDING, ALBERT
Etchings, Op. 5: Albert Spalding, vl.; André Benoist, pf. (*V*)
Alabama (Violin): Efrem Zimbalist (*V—withdrawn*)

STILL, WILLIAM GRANT
Afro-American Symphony: Scherzo: Eastman-Rochester Symphony Orchestra—H. Hanson (*V*)

STOCK, FREDERICK
Symphonic Waltz, Op. 8: Chicago Symphony—Frederick Stock (*V*)

STOESSEL, ALBERT
Suite Antique for Two Violins and Chamber Orchestra: Eddy Brown, Albert Stoessel, vls.;—E. Schenkman (*Re*)
Crinoline—Suite in Olden Style (*Re*)

STRANG, GERALD
Sonatina for Clarinet: Robert McBride, cl. (*N*)

STRINGFIELD, LAMAR
Cripple Creek, Op. 41, No. 4—from "From the Southern Mountains" —Suite: National High School Orchestra—J. Maddy (*V*)
Moods of a Moonshiner: Lamar Stringfield, fl.; String Quartet (*Re*)

SUESSE, DANA
Young Man with a Harp—Suite: Caspar Reardon, hp.; pf., perc. (*S*)

TAYLOR, DEEMS
The King's Henchman (Opera):
  Oh! Caesar, Great Wert Thou!—Act I.
  Nay, Maccus, Lay Him Down—Act III: Lawrence Tibbett, bar.; Metropolitan Opera Chorus and Orchestra—Setti (*V*)
A Song for Lovers, Op. 13, No. 2: Rose Bampton, contr.; pf. acc. (*V*)
Through the Looking Glass—Suite: Columbia Symphony Orchestra —H. Barlow (*C*)
Captain Stratton's Fancy (John Masefield): Reinald Werrenrath, bar. (*V—withdrawn*)

THOMPSON, RANDALL
Symphony No. II: Philadelphia Orchestra—E. Ormandy (*V—in preparation*)
Velvet Shoes (Song): Benjamin de Loache, bar. (*Y*)

TRIESTE, ROBERT
Two Pieces for Clarinet and Piano (*Y*)

TUCKER, GREGORY
Three Pieces for Clarinet and Piano (*Y*)
Two Pieces for Clarinet and Piano:
  I. Prelude
  II. In the Clearing: Robert McBride, cl.; Gregory Tucker, pf. (*N*)

VAN VACTOR, DAVID
Divertimento (Chamber Orchestra): Yaddo Chamber Orchestra— D. Van Vactor (*Y*)

VARDELL, CHARLES G., JR.
Joe Clark Steps Out (Mountain Folk Tune—Orchestra): Eastman-Rochester Symphony Orchestra—H. Hanson (*V*)

VARÈSE, EDGAR
Ionization: Thirteen percussion instruments—N. Slonimsky (*C*)
Octandre, for Flute, Oboe, Clarinet, Bassoon, Horn, Trumpet, Trombone and String Bass:
  I. Assez Lent
  II. Très Vite et Nerveux
  III. Grave, à la Mode de Passecaille: Chamber Orchestra—N Slonimsky (*N*)

APPENDIX

WAGENAAR, BERNARD
Sonatina for Violoncello and Piano: Naoum Benditzsky, vlc.; Bernard Wagenaar, pf. (*C*)
A Tale (Piano): Bernard Wagenaar (*C*)

WAGNER, JOSEPH
Pastorale and Burlesque from Serenade for Oboe, Violin and Violoncello: Alvin Etler, ob.; Malcolm Holmes, vl.; Aaron Bodenhorn, vlc. (*Y*)

WEISS, ADOLPH
Songs with Quartet: Ethel Luening, sopr.; string acc. (*Y*)
Three Songs for Soprano and String Quartet (Emily Dickinson): Mary Bell, sopr.; New World String Quartet (*N*)

WHITE, PAUL
Five Miniatures: Boston "Pops" Orchestra—A. Fiedler (*V*)

WHITHORNE, EMERSON
New York Days and Nights:
 Pell Street: Decca Little Symphony Orchestra (*D*)

WOODIN, WILLIAM
Chinese Suite: On the Yangtze River: Orchestra—G. Shackley (*C*)

ZEMACHSON, ARNOLD
Chorale and Fugue in D Minor, Op. 4: Minneapolis Symphony Orchestra—E. Ormandy (*V*)

ZIMBALIST, EFREM
String Quartet in E Minor: Gordon String Quartet (*S*)

LIST OF COMPOSERS BY STATES IN WHICH THEY WERE BORN

ALABAMA
W. C. Handy
William Levi Dawson

ARIZONA
Robert McBride

CALIFORNIA
Henry Cowell
Albert Elkus
Frederick Jacobi
Quinto Maganini

COLORADO
Harl McDonald
Frederick Preston Search

CONNECTICUT
Dudley Buck
Richard Donovan
Charles E. Ives
Quincy Porter
Harold J. Rome
Frances Terry
Donald Tweedy

DISTRICT OF COLUMBIA
Duke Ellington

FLORIDA
J. Rosamond Johnson

GEORGIA
Wallingford Riegger
Beryl Rubinstein

IDAHO
Arthur Shepherd

ILLINOIS
Milton Ager
Ernst Bacon
John Alden Carpenter
Edward E. ("Zez") Confrey
Henry Eichheim
Arthur Fickenscher
Florence Grandland Galajikian
Gardner Read
Robert L. Sanders
Albert Spalding
Max Wald
Allan A. Wilman

INDIANA
Hoagy Carmichael
Joseph W. Clokey
Carl Eppert
Cole Porter
David Van Vactor

IOWA
Thurlow Lieurance
Mortimer Wilson

KENTUCKY
John J. Becker
Carl Bricken

LOUISIANA
Louis Moreau Gottschalk
James G. Heller

MAINE
Frank E. Churchill
Carl McKinley

APPENDIX

John Knowles Paine
Walter Piston
Paul White

MARYLAND
Franz Carl Bornschein
Mortimer Browning
Robert Mills Delaney
John Woods Duke
Adolph Weiss

MASSACHUSETTS
Paul Hastings Allen
William Ames
George W. Chadwick
Philip Greeley Clapp
Frederick Shepherd Converse
Mabel W. Daniels
Blair Fairchild
Arthur Foote
Henry F. Gilbert
Elliot Griffis
Henry Hadley
Walter Helfer
Edward Burlingame Hill
William J. Hill
David Holden
Horace Johnson
Daniel Gregory Mason
George W. Meyer
Horatio Parker
Edward Royce
Carl Ruggles
Charles Sanford Skilton
Alexander Steinert

MICHIGAN
Rosseter Gleason Cole
Eric Delamarter

Leo Sowerby
Mark Wessel

MINNESOTA
Herbert Elwell
Arthur Farwell
Ross Lee Finney
Wesley La Violette

MISSISSIPPI
A. Lehman Engel
William Grant Still

MISSOURI
Robert Russell Bennett
Ray Green
Albert Stoessel
Dana Suesse
Virgil Thomson

MONTANA
Herbert Inch

NEBRASKA
Howard Hanson
Burrill Phillips

NEW HAMPSHIRE
Mrs. H. H. A. Beach
Avery Claflin

NEW JERSEY
George Antheil
Seth Bingham
Henry Holden Huss
Ernest Schelling
Harry Tierney

NEW YORK
Frederick Ayres (Johnson)
Samuel L. M. Barlow
David Barnett
John Beach

Anton Bilotti
Paul Frederick Bowles
Howard Brockway
Mark Brunswick
Cecil Burleigh
Norman Cazden
Abram Chasins
Ulric Cole
Aaron Copland
Paul Creston
David Diamond
Walter Donaldson
James Philip Dunn
Dante Fiorillo
Rudolf Forst
Harvey Gaul
George Gershwin
Rubin Goldmark
Morton Gould
Charles T. Griffes
Ferde Grofé
Ray Henderson
Bernard Herrmann
Philip James
Werner Janssen
Jerome Kern
A. Walter Kramer
Eastwood Lane
Normand Lockwood
Harvey Worthington Loomis
Edward MacDowell
Mana-Zucca
Douglas Moore
Jerome Moross
Ralph Rainger
Richard Rodgers
Bernard Rogers
William Schuman

Arthur Schwartz
Roger Sessions
Elie Siegmeister
Timothy Mather Spelman
George Templeton Strong
Deems Taylor
Randall Thompson
Burnet C. Tuthill
Harry Warren
Mabel Wayne
Frederick Woltmann
Vincent Youmans

NORTH CAROLINA
Eugene MacDonald Bonner
Hunter Johnson
Lamar Stringfield

NORTH DAKOTA
Clarence Loomis

OHIO
Edward Ballantine
Wayne Barlow
Robert Braine
Ruth Crawford
C. Hugo Grimm
Charles Haubiel
Ethel Glenn Hier
Arne Oldberg
David Stanley Smith
Emerson Whithorne

OKLAHOMA
Roy Harris
Gail Kubik

PENNSYLVANIA
Samuel Barber
Evelyn Berckman
Marc Blitzstein

Henry Thacker Burleigh
Charles Wakefield Cadman
Theodore Cella
Arthur Cohn
Eleanor Everest Freer
Vittorio Giannini
William Clifford Heilman
Oscar Levant
Frances McCollin
Irvine McHose
Arthur Nevin
Ethelbert Nevin
Paul Nordoff

RHODE ISLAND
Theodore Ward Chanler
George M. Cohan

TENNESSEE
Mary Carr Moore
Clarence Cameron White

TEXAS
Radie Britain

Annabel Morris Buchanan
David Wendell Fentress Guion
Harold Morris
Julia Smith

UTAH
LeRoy J. Robertson

VIRGINIA
Mary Howe
John Powell

WASHINGTON
Marion Bauer
Frederic Hart
George McKay
Earl Robinson

WISCONSIN
Kent Kennan
Otto Luening
Edgar Stillman Kelley
Edwin J. Stringham

ORCHESTRAL WORKS WHICH HAVE RECEIVED THE EASTMAN SCHOOL PUBLICATION AWARD

Wayne Barlow, *The Winter's Passed*
G. W. Chadwick, *Rip Van Winkle* overture
Eric DeLamarter, The 144th Psalm, for voice and orchestra
Herbert Elwell, *The Happy Hypocrite*, ballet suite for full orchestra
Howard Hanson, Symphony No. 2, "Romantic"
Kent Kennan, *Night Soliloquy*
Robert McBride, Mexican Rhapsody
Douglas Moore, *The Pageant of P. T. Barnum*, for full orchestra
Burrill Phillips, Concert Piece, for bassoon and string orchestra
Quincy Porter, Ukrainian Suite, for strings
Bernard Rogers, *Soliloquy*, for flute and strings
Edward Royce, *Far Ocean*, symphonic poem
Leo Sowerby, *Mediaeval Poem*, for organ and small orchestra
Leo Sowerby, Suite of *Four Ironics*, for full orchestra
William Grant Still, *Darker America*, for small orchestra
Randall Thompson, Symphony No. 1
Randall Thompson, Symphony No. 2
Charles Vardell, *Joe Clark Steps Out*
Bernard Wagenaar, Suite, Divertimento

ORCHESTRAL WORKS WHICH HAVE RECEIVED THE JUILLIARD PUBLICATION AWARD

NICOLAI BEREZOWSKY, *Sinfonietta*
DAVID DIAMOND, Psalm for orchestra
ALBERT ELKUS, *Impressions from a Greek Tragedy*
VITTORIO GIANNINI, String Quartet
LOUIS GRUENBERG, *Enchanted Isle*
SANDOR HARMATI, Prelude to a Melodrama
PHILIP JAMES, Suite for orchestra
WERNER JOSTEN, *Concerto Sacro*
WERNER JOSTEN, Symphony in F
CHARLES MARTIN LOEFFLER, *Evocation*
DANIEL GREGORY MASON, *Chanticleer*
HAROLD MORRIS, Concerto for piano and orchestra
GARDNER READ, *Sketches of the City*
BERNARD ROGERS, *Once Upon a Time*
ARTHUR SHEPHERD, *Horizons*
EMERSON WHITHORNE, Second Symphony
ELLIOT CARTER, Suite from *Pocahontas*

NATIONAL BROADCASTING COMPANY COMMISSIONS AND PRIZES

COMMISSIONED BY NBC

GIAN-CARLO MENOTTI, *The Old Maid and the Thief*, opera

TOM BENNETT, *Christmas Masquerade; He Runs on Scylla; Towers of Hate; Where the Cross is Made; The Cottingham's Last Banshee; Paul Bunyan; Back to Methuselah; The Fountain.* (All radio dramas.)

WELLS HIVELY, *The Courtship of Miles Standish; The Holy Grail; The Man Who Wed the Wind and Water; The Outcasts of Poker Flat; Rip van Winkle; Robin Hood; The Christmas Carol.* (All radio dramas.)

WINNERS OF NBC ORCHESTRAL AWARDS, 1931

NICOLAI T. BEREZOWSKY, Sinfonietta
CARL EPPERT, *Traffic*
FLORENCE G. GALAJIKIAN, Symphonic Intermezzo
PHILIP JAMES, *Station WGZBX*
MAX WALD, *The Dancer Dead*

WINNERS OF NBC MUSIC GUILD AWARDS, 1936

RUDOLF FORST, String Quartet
ALOIS REISER, String Quartet, Op. 18
MITYA STILLMAN, String Quartet No. 7

HONORABLE MENTION, NBC MUSIC GUILD AWARDS, 1936

JOHN R. BARROWS, Quintet in A minor, for wind instruments
DEZSO D'ANTALFFY, Quintet for piano and strings
DAVID HOLDEN, String Quartet in E major
GEORGE F. MCKAY, Quintet, Op. 11, for wind instruments
WILLY STAHL, String Quartet in E major

COLUMBIA BROADCASTING SYSTEM COMMISSIONS

IN 1936, the Columbia Broadcasting System issued its first Columbia Composers Commissions to six American composers who were asked to write pieces for radio in whatever form they chose. The works were to be for an orchestra of not more than a certain size (approximately that of a Beethoven Symphony) and were to be between eight and forty minutes in length. The composers were paid $500 each for sustaining broadcast rights on Columbia, and all other performing rights were theirs.

In 1936 Columbia commissioned the following works:

AARON COPLAND, *Music for Radio* (*The Saga of the Prairie*, sub-title later chosen from suggestions submitted by listeners)
HOWARD HANSON, *Third Symphony* (three movements)
WILLIAM GRANT STILL, *Lenox Avenue* (for narrator, chorus, and orchestra)
ROY HARRIS, *Time Suite*
WALTER PISTON, *Concertino* (for Piano and Chamber Orchestra)
LOUIS GRUENBERG, *Green Mansions* (radio opera based on W. H. Hudson's novel)

In 1938 Columbia commissioned the following works on the same basis:

QUINCY PORTER, *Two Dances for Radio*
JEROME MOROSS, *A Tall Story*
ROBERT RUSSELL BENNETT, *Eight Symphonic Etudes*
R. NATHANIEL DETT, *American Sampler*
LEO SOWERBY, *Theme in Yellow* (after poem by Carl Sandburg)
VITTORIO GIANNINI, *Beauty and the Beast* (half-hour radio-opera with libretto by Robert A. Simon)

In 1939 Columbia commissioned the following works:

VITTORIO GIANNINI, *Blennerhassett* (radio-opera based on an incident in American history)

Irving Graham, *The Taming of the Shrew* and *The Fish Story* (Columbia Workshop musico-dramatic productions, with librettos by Joseph Gottlieb)

Nicholas Nabokoff, *America Was Promises* (text by Archibald MacLeish)

In 1939–1940 Columbia commissioned the following works (each three to four minutes in length and based on American folk melodies) for Columbia's American School of the Air:

Henry Brant, *A Fisherman's Overture*
Frederick Converse, *Haul Away Joe*
Aaron Copland, *John Henry*
Ruth Crawford, *Rissolty-Rossolty*
William L. Dawson, *Stewball*
R. Nathaniel Dett, *No Mo' Peck o' Corn*
Amadeo di Filippi, *Arrangement of Western Melodies; The Boll Weevil; Georgia Boy; A Raftsman's Dance; Springfield Mountain*
Ross Lee Finney, *The Dark-Eyed Canaler*
David Guion, *The Little Brown Bulls*
Roy Harris, *Cowboy Songs*
Philip James, *Brennan on the Moor*
Quinto Maganini, *Old Joe Bowers of the Days of '49*
Jerome Moross, *Ramble on a Hobo Tune*
Charles Seeger, *John Hardy*
Julia Smith, *Liza Jane*
Hans Spialek, *No, Sir, No*
William Grant Still, *Caincha Line 'em?*
Lamar Stringfield, *Frogs*
Nathan Van Cleve, *Chilly Winds*
Bernard Wagenaar, *Fantasietta*

COMPOSERS WHO HAVE RECEIVED GUGGENHEIM FELLOWSHIPS

(WITH THE YEAR OF FIRST APPOINTMENT)

George Antheil, 1932
Ernst Bacon, 1939
Robert Russell Bennett, 1928
Marc Blitzstein, 1940
Carl Bricken, 1930
Juan José Castro (Argentina), 1933
Carlos Chávez (Mexico), 1938
Aaron Copland, 1925
Henry Cowell, 1931
Ruth Porter Crawford, 1930
Paul Creston, 1938
Robert Delaney, 1929
David Diamond, 1938
Alvin Etler, 1940
Ross Lee Finney, 1937
Dante Fiorillo, 1935
Anis Fuleihan, 1939
Roy Harris, 1927

Otto Luening, 1930
Quinto Maganini, 1928
Leopold Damrosch Mannes, 1926
Robert McBride, 1937
Carl McKinley, 1927
Douglas Stuart Moore, 1934
Paul Nordoff, 1935
Walter Hamor Piston, 1935
Quincy Porter, 1929
Earl Robinson, 1940
Bernard Rogers, 1927
William Schuman, 1939
Roger Sessions, 1926
Theodore Stearns, 1927
William Grant Still, 1934
Randall Thompson, 1929
Adolph Weiss, 1932
Mark Wessel, 1930

COMPOSERS WHO HAVE BEEN FELLOWS OF THE AMERICAN ACADEMY IN ROME

(WITH THE YEAR OF APPOINTMENT)

Samuel Barber, 1935
William D. Denny, 1939
George H. Elwell, 1924
Vittorio Giannini, 1932
Howard H. Hanson, 1921
Walter Helfer, 1925
Herbert R. Inch, 1931
Werner Janssen, 1930
Hunter Johnson, 1933
Kent W. Kennan, 1936
Arthur Kreutz, 1940
Normand Lockwood, 1929
Charles Naginsky, 1938
Robert L. Sanders, 1925
Roger Sessions, 1928
Leo Sowerby, 1921
Alexander L. Steinert, 1927
Randall Thompson, 1922
Frederick Woltmann, 1937

PULITZER TRAVELING SCHOLARS IN MUSIC

Ernst Bacon, 1932
Samuel Barber, 1935 and 1936
Carl Bricken, 1929
Lucile Crews, 1926
Robert Delaney, 1933
Ross Lee Finney, 1937
Dante Fiorillo, 1939
Samuel Gardner, 1918
Elliott Griffis, 1931
Foster Montgomery Hankins, 1921
Sandor Harmati, 1922
Quinto E. Maganini, 1927
Douglas Moore and Leopold Damrosch Mannes, 1925
Paul Nordoff, 1940
Percival Price, 1934
Bernard Rogers, 1920
Meyer I. Silver, 1917
Lamar Stringfield, 1928
Wintter Watts, 1923
Mark Wessel, 1930
No award in 1938

WORKS ISSUED BY SOCIETY FOR THE PUBLICATION OF AMERICAN MUSIC

1920—Daniel Gregory Mason: Sonata for Clarinet (or Violin) and Piano. Alois Reiser: Quartet for Strings
1921—Henry Holden Huss: Quartet for Strings. Leo Sowerby: Quartet for Strings—Serenade in G major
1922—David Stanley Smith: Quartet for Strings. Tadeuz Jarecki: Quartet for Strings
1923—Wm. Clifford Heilman: Piano Trio. Ch. M. Loeffler: Music for Four Stringed Instruments. Daniel Gregory Mason: Three Pieces for Quartet, Flute and Harp
1924—David Stanley Smith: Sonata for Piano and Violin. Albert Stoessel: Suite Antique for Two Violins and Piano
1925—Frederic Ayres: Piano Trio. Aurelio Giorni: Sonata for Piano and Violoncello. Carlos Salzedo: Sonata for Harp and Piano
1926—David Stanley Smith: Sonata for Piano and Oboe. Frederick Jacobi: Quartet for Strings
1927—Arthur Shepherd: Triptych for Soprano and String-Quartet. Edward Burlingame Hill: Sonata for Piano and Clarinet
1928—Bernard Wagenaar: Sonata for Violin and Piano
1929—James G. Heller: Three Aquatints for String-Quartet. Parker Bailey: Sonata for Flute and Piano
1930—Ulric Cole: Sonata for Violin and Piano. Daniel Gregory Mason: Quartet on Negro Themes, Op. 19 (for Strings)
1931—Leo Sowerby: Quintet for Flute, Oboe, Clarinet, Horn, and Bassoon. Frances Terry: Op. 15, Sonata for Violin and Piano
1932—Vittorio Giannini: Quintet for Piano and Strings—Complete
1933—Quincy Porter: Sonata No. 2 for Violin and Piano. Wallingford Riegger: Piano Trio in B minor
1934—Daniel Gregory Mason: Serenade for String Quartet. Frederick Preston Search: Sextet in F minor
1935—Frederick Jacobi: String Quartet No. 2. Arthur Shepherd: Quartet for Strings
1936—Quincy Porter: Third String Quartet. Leroy J. Robertson: Quintet in A minor for Piano and Strings

1937—David Stanley Smith: String Quartet No. 6 in C major
1938—Douglas Moore: Quartet for Strings. Edward Burlingame Hill: Op. 39, Sextet for Flute, Oboe, Clarinet, Horn, Bassoon, and Piano
1939—David Holden: Music for Piano and Strings
1940—Bernard Wagenaar: String Quartet No. 3

WORKS COMMISSIONED BY THE LEAGUE OF COMPOSERS

A. FOR PERFORMANCE BY THE LEAGUE

ANTHEIL, GEORGE, Chamber Concerto for Eight Instruments, 1932
BLITZSTEIN, MARC, *The Harpies*, one-act opera
COPLAND, AARON, *Music for the Theatre* (chamber orchestra), 1925; *Elegies for Violin and Viola*, 1933
WHITHORNE, EMERSON, *Saturday's Child* (soprano, tenor, and chamber orchestra), 1926

B. FOR PERFORMANCE BY OTHER ORGANIZATIONS

1934–1935

BEREZOWSKI, NICOLAI, String Quartet, Stradivarius Quartet
GRUENBERG, LOUIS, *Serenade to a Beauteous Lady*, Chicago Symphony Orchestra, Frederick Stock, Cond.
HARRIS, ROY, *Song for Occupations*, Westminster Choir, John Finley Williamson, Cond.
THOMSON, VIRGIL, Mass, for women's voices, Adesdi Choir, Margarete Dessoff, Cond.

1935–1936

ACHRON, JOSEPH, String Quartet, Pro Arte Quartet
COPLAND, AARON, *Statements*, Minneapolis Symphony Orchestra, Eugene Ormandy, Cond.
MCPHEE, COLIN, *From the Revelation of St. John, The Divine*, Princeton University Glee Club, James Gidding, Cond.
ORNSTEIN, LEO, *Nocturne and Dance of the Fates*, St. Louis Symphony Orchestra, Vladimir Golschmann, Cond.
PISTON, WALTER, *Symphonic Piece*, Cleveland Orchestra, Artur Rodzinski, Cond.

PORTER, QUINCY, String Quartet, Gordon String Quartet

SESSIONS, ROGER, Symphony, Philadelphia Orchestra, Leopold Stokowski, Cond.

STILL, WILLIAM GRANT, *Kaintuck*, for piano and orchestra, Cincinnati Orchestra, Eugene Goossens, Cond.

THOMPSON, RANDALL, *The Peaceable Kingdom*, Harvard University Glee Club, G. Wallace Woodworth, Cond.

1936–1937

BENNETT, ROBERT RUSSELL, *Hollywood*, NBC Symphony Orchestra, Frank Black, Cond.

MCBRIDE, ROBERT, *Go Choruses*, Philharmonic Chamber Orchestra, Hans Lange, Cond.

SAMINSKY, LAZARE, *Pueblo*, National Symphony Orchestra, Hans Kindler, Cond.

SHEPHERD, ARTHUR, String Quartet, Manhattan String Quartet

1937–1938

DIAMOND, DAVID, Quintet in B minor for flute, strings, and piano, Barrère Ensemble

NAGINSKI, CHARLES, *Sinfonietta*, WOR Orchestra, Alfred Wallenstein, Cond.

1938–1939

BEREZOWSKI, NICOLAI, String Quartet,
ETLER, ALVIN, *New Music for Brass*,
GERSCHEFSKI, EDWIN, Septet for brass instruments,
} for broadcasting over the Columbia Broadcasting System

1939–1940

SCHUMAN, WILLIAM, String Quartet, "Town Hall Award"

BAUER, MARION,
    Concerto for oboe, clarinet
        and string quartet,
CAZDEN, NORMAN,
    Quartet, Op. 23, for } for broadcasting over the Columbia Broadcasting System
        clarinet and strings,
THOMPSON, RANDALL,
    Four Pieces for oboe,
        clarinet and viola,

1940–1941

CHANLER, THEODORE WARD, *Five Rhymes from "Peacock Pie,"* "Town Hall Award" (for Dorothy Maynor)

WORKS HONORED BY THE NATIONAL FEDERATION OF MUSIC CLUBS (SINCE 1930*)

1931—Class I: *Excalibur,* Symphonic Poem, Louis Adolph Coerne (deceased)

Class II: *Spring in Heaven,* three-part chorus for women's voices, Frances McCollin

1933—Two composers were commissioned for works to be performed at the 1933 Biennial Convention: one was John Powell, for a symphonic work based on Anglo-Saxon folk themes, the commission to be $1,000; the second was Annabel Morris Buchanan, for a chorus for women's voices, also based upon folk themes, the commission to be $150. Mrs. Buchanan's work is *Come All Ye Fair and Tender Ladies.*

1939—Class I: Solo for medium voice with piano accompaniment (contest for federated club member who has heretofore had no compositions bought or published by music publishing houses): Tie between Mae Louise Nelson and Genevieve Davisson

Class II: Composition for piano, C. A. Prayer

Class III: Composition for violin and piano, H. M. Lewis. Honorable mention: Eitel Allen Nelson

Class IV: Division 1—Concerto for two pianos and orchestra, Arthur Farwell; Division 2—Concerto for violin and orchestra, Harold Morris

* The list of works so honored before 1930 will be found in the author's *Our American Music,* original edition (1931).

AMERICAN WORKS PERFORMED AT THE FESTIVALS OF THE INTERNATIONAL SOCIETY FOR CONTEMPORARY MUSIC

Salzburg, 1922—ERNEST BLOCH, Schelomo (with piano), Violin Sonata;
    LEO SOWERBY, Sonata for violin and piano.
Salzburg, 1923—EMERSON WHITHORNE, New York Nights and Days, for piano.
Prague, 1924—ERNEST BLOCH, Twenty-second Psalm.
Venice, 1925—HENRY EICHHEIM, Nocturnal Impressions of Peking, for chamber orchestra, Korean Sketch, for chamber orchestra.
    CARL RUGGLES, Angels, for six trumpets;
    LOUIS GRUENBERG, Daniel Jazz, for voice, string quartet, piano, and percussion.
Zürich, 1926—FREDERICK JACOBI, String Quartet.
Frankfurt, 1927—HENRY F. GILBERT, The Dance in Place Congo, symphonic poem;
    AARON COPLAND, Music for the Theatre, for chamber orchestra.
Siena, 1928—ERNEST BLOCH, Piano Quintet.
Geneva, 1929—ROGER SESSIONS, Symphony in E minor.
Oxford, 1931—ROGER SESSIONS, Piano Sonata;
    VLADIMIR DUKELSKY, Second Symphony;
    GEORGE GERSHWIN, An American in Paris.
Amsterdam, 1933—AARON COPLAND, Piano Variations;
    RUTH CRAWFORD, Three Songs (Carl Sandburg's three poems "Rat-Riddles").
Barcelona, 1936—MARK BRUNSWICK, Two Movements for String Quartet, Op. 1;
    WALTER PISTON, Five Sonnets of Elizabeth Browning, for soprano and string quartet;
    CARL RUGGLES, Sun-Treader.

Index

INDEX

(*The names of the chief composers appear in capitals; the pages on which appear the main discussions of them are set in italics.*)

Abbey Theater, 258
Abraham Lincoln (Grimm), 202
Abraham Lincoln, A Likeness in Symphonic Form (Bennett), 314
Abraham Lincoln Song (Damrosch), 17
Académie Tournefort, 179
Academy of Music (Philadelphia), 62, 179
Academy of Santa Cecilia, 121
ACHRON, ISIDOR (1892), *196*
   Piano Concerto, 196
ACHRON, JOSEPH (1886), *196*
   Children's Suite, 196
   Golem Suite, 196
   Sonatas, 196
   Violin Concertos, 196
Adagio Eroico (Bennett), 317
Adagio for Strings (Barber), 221
Adamowski, Joseph, 108
Adams, John, 237
Adding Machine, The (Rice), 34
Adirondack Sketches (Lane), 71
Adler, F. Charles, 51
Adonis (Rogers), 98
Adoration (Borowski), 68
Adventures in a Perambulator (Carpenter), 36
A.E.F. General Headquarters Band, 172
Aeolian Hall, 305
Africa (Still), 281
Afro-American Symphony (Still), 281
AGER, MILTON (1893), *300*
   Ain't She Sweet, 300
   Happy Days Are Here Again, 300
   I Wonder What's Become of Sally, 300
Ah, Love, but a Day (Mrs. Beach), 16

Aïda (Verdi), 68
Ain't She Sweet (Ager), 300
À la Chinoise (Ornstein), 204
Aladdin (Kelley), 15
Alba (S. Barlow), 93
Alcott, A. Bronson, 246
Alexander's Ragtime Band (Berlin), 299
Ali Baba and the Forty Thieves (Cesana), 318
Alice in Wonderland (Carroll), 35
Alice in Wonderland (Kelley), 15-16
Alice in Wonderland (Tweedy), 61
All About Jazz (Nelson), 307
Allah's Holiday (Friml), 285
All Alone (Berlin), 299
Allegro, L' (Tweedy), 61
Allen, Maud, 121
ALLEN, PAUL HASTINGS (1883), *196-197*
   Cleopatra, 197
   Ex Hocte, 197
   Filtro, Il, 197
   Last of the Mohicans, The, 197
   Milda, 197
   O Munasterio, 197
   Serenade, 197
   Symphony in D major, 197
ALESSANDRO, VICTOR, *218*
   Serenade, 218
   Sinfonietta, 218
Along the Columbia River (Saar), 20
Alpine Impressions (Cella), 107
Alta Notte (Casella), 254
ALTER, MARTHA, *218*
   Anthony Comstock, 218
   Orchestral Introduction and Song from *Bill George*, 218
   Suite, 218

Altschuler, Modest, 50
Alvin Theater, 309
Always (Berlin), 299
Amanda (S. Barlow), 94
Amelia al Ballo (Menotti), 222, 223
America (Bloch), 122-123, 308, 314
Americana (Luening), 187
Americana (Strube), 52
Americana (Thompson), 111
American Academy in Rome, 31, 61, 75, 81, 96, 110, 170, 200, 202, 208, 213, 216, 220, 229, 325, 382. *See also* American Prix de Rome
American Academy of Arts and Letters, 26, 31, 53
American Academy of Arts and Sciences, 119
Americana Suite (Gould), 319
American Ballet Company, 259
American Book Company, 107
American Composers' Alliance, 341-342
American Composers' Concerts, 74, 75, 87, 106, 169, 202, 205, 206, 211, 216, 217, 218, 324
American Composers of Today (ed. Reis), 328
American Composers on American Music (Cowell), 240, 241, 248, 250
American Conservatory of Music, 81, 184, 232, 279
American Creed (Harris), 144
American Federation of Music Clubs, 276
American Festival Overture (Schuman), 225
American Festivals of Contemporary Music, 148
American Folksongs and Ballads (Lomax & Crawford), 240
American Guild of Organists, 46, 268
American Indian Melodies (Farwell), 131
American in Paris, An (Gershwin), 308, 328
American Jazz Music (Hobson), 290
American Jubilee (Schwartz), 303
American Life (Weiss), 248
American Lyric Theater, 71, 88
American Mercury, 111
American Music Center, 341

American Musicological Society, 119
American Opera Company, 49, 70, 186
American Opera Society, 73
American Piece (Howe), 193
American Prix de Rome, 220, 229, 232, 234. *See also* American Academy in Rome
American Quartet (Dvořák), 6
American Revolution, 4
American School of the Air, 211
American Sketches (Converse), 55
American Sketches (Strong), 22
American Society of Composers, Authors and Publishers, 31, 124, 169, 173-174, 302, 335-341, 342, 344
American Songbag, The (Sandburg), 55
American Suite (Cadman), 51
American Symphony (Antheil), 259
American Symphony (Cesana), 318
America the Beautiful (Hier), 202
Amériques (Varèse), 256
Ames, Elizabeth, 333
AMES, WILLIAM (1901), 62
Ames, Winthrop, 172
Amphitryon (Giraudeux), 93
Ampico Recording Laboratories, 178
Andante and Scherzo (Galajikian), 230
Andersen, Arthur Olaf, 184, 226
Anderson, Marian, 278
Andreieff, Leonid, 170, 183
And They Lynched Him on a Tree (Still), 281-282
Angelo's Letter (J. Beach), 129
Animal Pictures (Ganz), 112
Ann Arbor Festival, 77
ANTHEIL, GEORGE (1900), 257-259, 261
  American Symphony, 259
  Archipelago, 259
  Ballet Mécanique, 257
  Capriccio, 259
  Dreams, 259
  Fighting the Waves, 258
  Helen Retires, 258
  Piano Concerto, 258
  String Quartet, 258
  Symphony in F, 258
  Transatlantic, 258-259
  Zingareska, 258

INDEX

Anthony Comstock (Alter), 218
Antony and Cleopatra (Shakespeare), 263
Aquatints (Heller), 106
Arcana (Varèse), 256
Archipelago (Antheil), 259
Argonauts, The (Eppert), 194
Argonauts, The (Maganini), 103
Arise, Arise!, 43
Aristophanes, 212, 236
Arizona (Nevin), 66
Arizona, University of, 186, 222
Arkansas Traveler (Guion), 274, 277
Armstrong, Louis, 291-292, 293, 295
Arthur Jordan Conservatory of Music, 71
Asolani (J. Beach), 129
Astarte (Johnson), 99
At Dawning (Cadman), 49
Atkinson, Brooks, 310
Atonement of Pan, The (Hadley), 25
At the Fair (Powell), 272
Auer, Leopold, 52
Auf Wiedersehn (Romberg), 285
Augusteo (Rome), 94
Ausonia (Saminsky), 166
Authors' League, 341
Ave atque Vale (Converse), 54
Ave Rota (Jacobi), 169
Awakening of the Woods, The (Ballantine), 60
Ayres, Frederick, see Johnson, Frederick Ayres
Azora (Hadley), 24

Baal Shem (Bloch), 120
Babar (S. Barlow), 94
Babbitt (Lewis), 88
Bach, Johann Sebastian, 12, 92, 104, 178, 188, 242, 244, 275, 286, 287, 295
Bach Cantata Club, 163
Bach Goes to Town (Templeton), 303
BACON, ERNEST (1898), 187-188
  Black and White Songs, 188
  Coal Scuttle Blues, 188
  Country Roads, 187
  First Symphony, 187
  Kankakee River, 188
  Midnight Special, 188
  My River, 188

Postponeless Creature, The, 188
Prelude and Fugue, 187
Second Symphony, 187
Suite to the Children, 188
Wastin' Time, 188
Whispers of Heavenly Death, 188
Bailey, James Montgomery, 245
Balakovic, Zlatko, 40
Balendonck, Armand, 66
Bali (Eichheim), 199
Bali (McPhee), 190
Balinese Ceremonial Music (McPhee), 190
Ballade (Weiss), 248
Ballade Hongroise (Terry), 74
Ballade of the Night (Wilman), 233
Ballad for Americans (Robinson), 319
Ballad of Trees and the Master (Chadwick), 11
BALLANTINE, EDWARD (1886), 59, 60
  Awakening of the Woods, The, 60
  Eve of St. Agnes, The, 60
  From the Garden of Hellas, 60
  Overture to the Piper, 60
  Prelude to The Delectable Forest, 60
  Variations on Mary Had a Little Lamb, 60
Ballet Caravan, 226
Ballet Mécanique (Antheil), 257
Ballet Suite (Nelson), 219
Baltimore Sun, 52
Baltimore Symphony Orchestra, 52, 62, 95, 198
Bamberger Little Symphony, 172
Bambolina (Youmans), 304
Bampton, Rose, 72, 79
Bandanna Sketches (C. C. White), 280
Band Wagon (Schwartz), 303
Bankhead, Tallulah, 263
Barbara Frietchie (Bonner), 198
Barbaresques (Spelman), 206
BARBER, SAMUEL (1910), 220-221
  Adagio for Strings, 221
  Dover Beach, 221
  Essay for Orchestra, 221
  God's Grandeur, 221
  Music for a Scene from Shelley, 220
  Overture to The School for Scandal, 220

BARBER, SAMUEL (*Continued*)
  Serenade, 221
  Sonata, 221
  String Quartet in B minor, 221
  Symphony in One Movement, 220-221
Barber of Seville, The (Rossini), 316, 317
Barber's Sixth Brother, The (Dunn), 21
Barbirolli, John, 43, 50, 92, 191, 197, 318
Barlow, Howard, 95, 342
BARLOW, SAMUEL L. M. (1892), 92-94
  Alba, 93
  Amanda, 94
  Babar, 94
  Biedermeyer Waltzes, 94
  Eugénie, 94
  For Strings, 94
  Mon Ami Pierrot, 94
  Piano Concerto, 93-94
BARLOW, WAYNE (1912), 217
  De Profundis, 217
  False Faces, 217
  Poem, 217
  Sonata, 217
  String Quartet, 217
  Three Moods for Dancing, 217
  Winter's Past, The, 217
  Zion in Exile, 217
BARNETT, DAVID (1907), 197
  Divertimento, 197
Barnum, Phineas Taylor, 87
Barrère, Georges, 46, 127, 174, 254
Barrie, Sir James M., 269
Barry Philip, 88
Barrymore, John, 32
Barrymore, Lionel, 32
BARTH, HANS (1897), 53, 62, 238-239
  Miragia, 239
  Pantomime Symphony, 239
  Piano Concertos, 239
  Piano Sonatas, 239
  Suite, 239
Bartók, Béla, 259, 293, 346
Basie, William ("Count"), 292, 293
Batouala (Josten), 178
Battle Cry of Freedom, The, 123

Baudelaire, Charles, 118
Bauer, Emilie Frances, 192
Bauer, Harold, 129, 200, 205
BAUER, MARION (1887), 192-193
  Dance Sonata, 192
  Fantasia quasi una Sonata, 192
  Pan, 192
  Prometheus Bound, 192
  String Quartet, 192
  Sun Splendor, 192
  Viola Sonata, 192
BAUM, RUSSELL, 218
  Passacaglia and Fugue, 218
  Variations on a Theme of Paganini, 218
BEACH, MRS. H. H. A. (1867), 10, 16-17
  Ah, Love, but a Day, 16
  Canticle of the Sun, 16
  Festival Jubilate, 16
  Gaelic Symphony, 16
  Panama Hymn, 16
  Piano Concerto, 16
  Song of Welcome, 16
  Theme and Variations, 16
  Year's at the Spring, The, 16
BEACH, JOHN (1877), 129
  Angelo's Letter, 129
  Asolani, 129
  Concert for Six Instruments, 129
  Enter Buffoon, 129
  Mardi Gras, 129
  Naïve Landscapes, 129
  Orleans Alley, 129
  Phantom Satyr, 129
  Pippa's Holliday, 129
  Poem, 129
Beale Street Blues (Handy), 293
Bearns Prize, 209, 220
Beauty and the Beast (Giannini), 208
BECKER, JOHN J. (1886), 183, 329
  Dance Figure, 183
  Life of Man, 183
  Marriage with Space, A, 183
  Obongo, Dance Primitive, 183
  Soundpieces, 183
Beckett, Henry, 173
Beebe, Carolyn, 31, 82
Beecham, Sir Thomas, 158
Beethoven, Ludwig van, 3, 28, 42, 175, 224, 246, 317

INDEX

Beethoven Association, 343
Before the Dawn (Hanson), 76
Beggar on Horseback (Connelly & Kaufman), 35
Begin the Beguine (C. Porter), 302
Beiderbecke, Leon Bismarck ("Bix"), 292, 295
Belle Dame sans Merci, La (Riegger), 249
Bellini, Vincenzo, 222
Belshazzar (Hadley), 25
Benét, Stephen Vincent, 88, 89, 90, 233
BENNETT, ROBERT RUSSELL (1894), 148, *313-317*
  Abraham Lincoln, A Likeness in Symphonic Form, 314
  Adagio Eroico, 317
  Charleston Rhapsody, 317
  Concerto Grosso, 317
  Endymion, 314
  Hour of Delusion, The, 314
  March, 317
  Maria Malibran, 315-317
  Paysage, 314
  Sights and Sounds, 314
  Symphony, 314
Bennington College, 186, 224, 225
BERCKMAN, EVELYN (1900), *197*
  County Fair, 197
  From the Odyssey, 197
BEREZOWSKY, NICOLAI (1900), 14, 47, *184-185*
  Concerto Lirico, 185
  Fantasia, 185
  Hebrew Suite, 185
  Piano Sonata, 185
  Sinfonietta, 184
  String Quartet, 185
  String Sextet, 185
  Toccata, Variations and Finale, 185
  Violin Concerto, 185
  Wood-Wind Quintet, 185
Berg, Alban, 202, 227
BERGSMA, WILLIAM, *218*
  Pioneer Saga, 218
Bériot, Charles de, 315
Berkshire Festival, 81, 144, 213
Berkshire Quartet, 81
Berlin, Ellen Mackay, 299
BERLIN, IRVING (1888), 202, 289, *298-299*, 319, 320, 340

Alexander's Ragtime Band, 299
All Alone, 299
Always, 299
Blue Skies, 299
Everybody Step, 299
Everybody's Doin' It, 299
God Bless America, 298, 319
He's a Devil, 299
Lady of the Evening, 299
Louisiana Purchase, 299
Marie from Sunny Italy, 298
My Wife's Gone to the Country, 299
Oh, How I Hate to Get Up in the Morning, 299
Pack Up Your Sins, 299
Pretty Girl Is Like a Melody, A, 299
Remember, 299
Russian Lullaby, 299
What'll I Do, 299
When My Baby Smiles at Me, 299
When that Midnight Choo-choo Leaves for Alabam, 299
Who, 299
Berlin Philharmonic Orchestra, 58, 63, 76, 179
Berlin State Theatre, 258
Berlioz, Hector, 266
Bethlehem (Tuthill), 206
Betrothal, The (Delamarter), 68
Bianca (Hadley), 24
Biddle, Francis, 281
Biedermeyer Waltzes (S. Barlow), 94
Bierlich, Bernhardt, 312
Bierlich, Elsa Johanna, 312
Bierlich, Julius, 312
Big Brown Bear, The (Mana-Zucca), 104
Biggs, E. Power, 82
Biguine (Moroso), 213
Billings, Josh, 107
BILOTTI, ANTON (1904), *235*
  Concerto, 235
BINDER, ABRAHAM W., *218*
  Valley of Dry Bones, 218
BINGHAM, SETH (1882), *90-91*
  Breton Cadence, The, 90
  Charelzenn, La, 90
  Harmonies of Florence, 90
  Memories of France, 90
  Mother of Men, 90
  Passacaglia, 90

BINGHAM, SETH (*Continued*)
  Pioneer America, 90
  Suite, 90
  Tame Animal Tunes, 90
  Wall Street Fantasy, 90
  Wilderness Stone, 90
Birchard, Clarence, 129
Birchard & Company, C. C., 344
Birds, The (Aristophanes), 212, 236
Birthday of the Infanta, The (Carpenter), 36-37
Bispham, David, 25, 126
Bispham medal, 184, 280
Bishop, Henry Rowley, 316
Black, Frank, 101
Black and White Songs (Bacon), 188
Black Maskers, The (Sessions), 170
Blake, William, 227
Blennerhasset (Giannini), 208
Bletheris, a Monody, from the Hamlet of Archibald MacLeish (Finney), 228
Bliss, Arthur, 327
BLITZSTEIN, MARC (1905), 264-266
  Cradle Will Rock, The, 265
  I've Got the Tune, 264-265
  No for an Answer, 265
  Triple-Sec, 264
BLOCH, ERNEST (1880), 86, 97, 110, *119-124*, 148, 162, 164, 170, 187, 198, 200, 201, 202, 205, 232, 235, 258, 308, 314, 327, 340, 344, 345
  America, 122-123, 308, 314
  Baal Shem, 120
  B minor String Quartet, 121
  Concerto Grosso, 121
  Evocations, 121
  From Jewish Life, 120
  Helvetia, 122
  Hiver, 120, 123
  Israel Symphony, 120
  Macbeth, 120, 121
  Méditation hébraïque, 120
  Piano Sonata, 121
  Printemps, 120, 123
  Psalms, 120
  Quintet, 121
  Sacred Service, 120
  Schelomo, 120, 121

  Sonata, 121
  Suite, 121
  Trois Poemes Juifs, 120, 121
  Violin Concerto, 121
  Voice in the Wilderness, 120
Blossom Time (Romberg), 285
Blue Skies (Berlin), 299
Blue Steel (Still), 281
Bodanzky, Artur, 121
Boepple, Paul, 215
Bohemian Club, 25
Boise, Otis Bardwell, 20, 53, 66, 197
Bok, Mary Louise Curtis, 325
Bolm, Adolf, 191
Bolshoi Theater, 185
Bolton, Guy, 309
Bonne Chanson, La (Loeffler), 118
BONNER, EUGENE MACDONALD (1889), *197-198*
  Barbara Frietchie, 198
  Celui qui epousa une femme muette, 198
  Gods of the Mountain, The, 198
  Venetian Glass Nephew, The, 198
  Whispers of Heavenly Death, 197-198
  White Nights, 197
  Young Alexander, The, 198
Bori, Lucrezia, 34
Boris Godunov (Moussorgsky), 79, 120
BORNSCHEIN, FRANZ CARL (1879), 72
  Cape Cod Impressions, 72
  Mission Road, The, 72
  Mystic Trumpeter, 72
  String Quartet, 72
  Three Persian Poems, 72
  Violin Concerto, 72
BOROWSKI, FELIX (1872), 68-69
  Adoration, 68
  Boudoir, 68
  Fernando del Nonsensico, 68
  First Symphony, 68
  Second Symphony, 68-69
Boston Evening Transcript, 99
Boston Music Company, 119
Bostonians, The, 312
Boston Opera Company, 53
Boston String Quartet, 59
Boston Symphony Orchestra, 13, 25,

39, 40, 42, 43, 46, 52, 53, 54,
55, 57, 58, 63, 76, 82, 99, 105,
107, 116, 117, 118, 121, 124, 127,
138, 148, 149, 150, 154, 157,
160, 177, 185, 195, 199, 203,
213, 218, 225, 233, 309, 343-344
Boudoir (Borowski), 68
Boulanger, Nadia, 62, 86, 97, 135, 147, 149, 160, 163, 178, 193, 196, 198, 200, 215, 226, 227, 232, 233, 234, 260, 264, 314, 346
Boult, Sir Adrian, 149
BOWLES, PAUL FREDERIC (1911), *226-227*
  Cantata, 227
  Denmark Vesey, 227
  Melodia, 227
  Suite, 226-227
  Trio, 227
  Yankee Clipper, 226
Boys' High School, 147
Bradford, William, 78
Brahms, Johannes, 13, 19, 42, 92, 93, 101, 287, 290
BRAINE, ROBERT (1896), *105-106*
  Choreographic Impressions, 105
  City of Dreams, 105
  Concerto in Jazz, 105
  Harlequin and Columbine, 105
  House of Usher, The, 105
  Rhapsody in E flat, 105
  Song of Hiawatha, The, 105
  S.O.S., 105
  Theater Sheet, 105-106
BRANSCOMBE, GENA (1881), *72-73*
  Festival Prelude, 73
  Pilgrims of Destiny, 73
  Quebec, 73
  Youth of the World, 73
BRANT, HENRY DREYFUSS (1913), *259-260*
  Concerto, 260
  Crying Jag, 260
  Entente cordiale, 260
  Lyric Cycle, 260
  Miss O'Grady, 260
  Quintet, 260
  Sonata Sacra, 260

Symphony in B flat minor, 260
Variations in Oblique Harmony, 260
Bree, Malwine, 187
Bret Harte (James), 172-173
Breton Cadence, The (Bingham), 90
BRICKEN, CARL ERNEST (1898), *103*
  Prelude, 103
  Suite, 103
  Symphony, 103
Bridge, Frank, 97
Bridge Builders, The (Search), 108
Brigham Young University, 205
Brisk Young Sailor, A, 43
BRITAIN, RADIE (1903), *232*
  Heroic Poem, 232
  Southern Symphony, 232
  Theme and Variations on the Old Gray Mare, 232
Britt, Horace, 174, 254
Broadcast Music, Inc., 339, 340
Broadway (Gardner), 105
BROCKWAY, HOWARD A. (1870), *52-53*, 178, 197, 277
  Symphony in D, 53
Broken Troth, The (R. Cole), 67
Brooke, Rupert, 182
Brooklyn Daily Eagle, 197
Brooklyn Symphony Orchestra, 26, 172
BROOKS, SHELTON (1886), *300-301*
  Darktown Strutters' Ball, 301
  Swing that Thing!, 301
BROWNING, MORTIMER (1891), *104*
  Concerto in F, 104
  Mary Poppins Suite, 104
  Sonatina, 104
Browning, Robert, 64, 100
Bruch, Max, 67
BRUNSWICK, MARK (1902), *232*
  Lysistrata, 232
  Symphony, 232
Buccaneer, The, 258
BUCHANAN, ANNABEL MORRIS (1889), *276*
Bucharest, University of, 285
Buck, Dudley, 4, 244, 268
Buck, Gene, 335, 342
Budapest Quartet, 293

Budapest Royal Academy, 235
Burkan, Nathan, 335
BURLEIGH, CECIL (1885), 52
　Concertos, 52
　Evangeline, 52
　Mountain Pictures, 52
BURLEIGH, HENRY THACKER (1866), 278-279
　Deep River, 109, 279
Burma (Eichheim), 199
Burmeister, Richard, 193
BUSCH, CARL (1862), 70, 314
　Chant from the Great Plains, 70
　Elegy, 70
　Four Indian Tribal Melodies, 70
　Minnehaha's Vision, 70
　Ozarka, 70
　Passing of Arthur, The, 70
　String Quartet, 70
Bush Conservatory, 229, 230
Busoni, Ferruccio, 102, 112, 152, 186, 235, 248, 255, 273
Bustini, Alessandro, 230
Bye Bye Blackbirds (Henderson), 302
By the Light of the Silvery Moon (Edwards), 301
By the Porta Catania (Heilman), 60
By the Rivers of Babylon (Loeffler), 118
By the Waters of Minnetonka (Lieurance), 270

Cabin in the Sky, 199
CADMAN, CHARLES WAKEFIELD (1881), 47-51, 282, 340
　American Suite, 51
　At Dawning, 49
　Dance of the Scarlet Sister Mary, 50
　Dark Dancers of the Mardi Gras, 50-51
　Far Horizon, The, 51
　From the Land of the Sky Blue Water, 48, 49
　Garden of Mystery, The, 49
　Hollywood Suite, 50
　Oriental Rhapsody, 49-50
　Piano Sonata, 49, 50
　Shanewis, 48, 49
　Sonata in G major, 50
　Sunset Trail, The, 49
　Thunderbird Suite, 49

To a Vanishing Race, 50
Trio in D major, 49
White Enchantment, 51
Willow Tree, The, 51
Witch of Salem, The, 49
Caliban (MacKaye), 131
California (Converse), 55
California, University of, 110, 131, 135, 170, 200, 232, 236, 252
Call of the Plains, The (Goldmark), 14
Calypso (Fuleihan), 192
Campbell, Tipton, Louis, 193
Can't Help Lovin' that Man of Mine (Kern), 300
Canticle of the Sun (Mrs. Beach), 16
Canticum Fratris Solis (Loeffler), 117-118
Cape Cod Impressions (Bornschein), 72
Capet, Lucien, 233
Capitals, Capitals (Thomson), 261
Capitol Theater (New York), 109
Caponsacchi (Hageman), 64-65
Capriccio (Antheil), 259
Captive, The (Strube), 52
Carl F. Lauber Music Award, 223
Carl Schurz Memorial Foundation, 75-76
Carmel Bach Festival, 187
Carmen (Bizet), 68
CARMICHAEL, HOAGY (1903), 301
　Come Easy Go Easy Love, 301
　In the Still of the Night, 301
　Lazy Bones, 301
　Stardust, 301
Carnegie Fellowship, 170
Carnegie Foundation, 110, 236
Carnegie Hall, 49, 51, 63, 71, 96, 211, 309, 312-313
Carnegie Steel Corporation, 48
Carnival (Cella), 107
CARPENTER, JOHN ALDEN (1876), 35-40, 104, 114, 306, 320, 340, 344
　Adventures in a Perambulator, 36
　Birthday of the Infanta, The, 36-37
　Concertino, 36, 37
　Concerto, 40
　Danza, 40

Green River, The, 36
Krazy Kat, 37, 306
Patterns, 39
Quintet, 39-40
Sea Drift, 39
Skyscrapers, 35, 37-38, 114
Song of Faith, 38-39
String Quartet, 38
Violin Sonata, 35, 36, 37
Carroll, Lewis, 31
Caruso, Enrico, 84
Casadesus, Robert, 63
Casa Mañana Revues, 313
Casanova (Giannini), 209
Casanova (Taylor), 35
Casella, Alfredo, 254
Castellana (Howe), 193
Castelnuovo-Tedesco, Mario, 346
Cat and the Fiddle, The (Kern), 300
Cat and the Mouse, The (Copland), 148
Cathedral Prelude (Smith), 46
Caturla, Alejandro, 328
Caussade, 61
CAZDEN, NORMAN (1914), 212, 213
    String Quartet, 213
CELLA, THEODORE (1897), 107
    Alpine Impressions, 107
    Carnival, 107
    Lido, The, 107
    On a Transatlantic Liner, 107
    Through the Pyrenees, 107
Celui qui épousa une femme muette (Bonner), 198
Central Park Suite (Lane), 71
CESANA, OTTO (1899), 317-318
    Ali Baba and the Forty Thieves, 318
    American Symphony, 318
    Concerto, 318
    Negro Heaven, 318
    Overture, 318
    Three Moods, 318
CHADWICK, GEORGE WHITEFIELD (1854-1931), 10, 11-12, 23, 24, 40, 55, 56, 59, 129, 130, 280
    Ballad of Trees and the Master, 11
    Judith, 11
    Sinfonietta, 11
    Symphonic Sketches, 11

Vagrom Ballad, 11
Chain Gang Song (Howe), 194
Chambered Nautilus, The (Taylor), 31
Chamber Music for Piano and Strings (Holden), 213
Chamlee, Mario, 64
CHANLER, THEODORE WARD (1902), 198
    Epitaphs, 198
    Five Short Colloquies, 198
    Mass, 198
    Sonata, 198
Chansonette (Friml), 285
Chansons Populaires (Harling), 202
Chant from the Great Plains (Busch), 70
Chanticleer (Mason), 42
Chapin, Katherine Garrison, 281, 282
Charelzenn, La (Bingham), 90
Charles I, King of England, 272
Charleston Rhapsody (Bennett), 317
Charpentier, Gustave, 124
    Louise, 124
CHASINS, ABRAM (1903), 91-92
    First Piano Concerto, 91
    Flirtation in a Chinese Garden, 91
    Preludes, 91
    Rush Hour in Hong Kong, 91
    Second Piano Concerto, 92
Chautauqua Institution, 84
Chavez, Carlos, 328
Cheerful Little Earful (Warren), 304
CHESLOCK, LOUIS (1899), 198
    French Horn Concerto, 198
    Sonata, 198
    String Quartet, 198
    Symphony, 198
    Tone-Poems, 198
    Violin Concerto, 198
    Violin Sonata, 198
Chicago, University of, 103, 187, 230
Chicago Civic Opera Company, 49, 149, 202
Chicago Civic Orchestra, 68, 230, 279
Chicago Conservatory of Music, 230
Chicago Musical College, 19, 69, 73, 112, 184, 199, 230, 233, 277, 301
Chicago Opera Company, 24, 36
Chicago Record-Herald, 68

OUR CONTEMPORARY COMPOSERS

Chicago Symphony Orchestra, 40, 42, 43, 46, 67, 68, 69, 81, 82, 98, 101, 103, 105, 144, 149, 154, 157, 169, 215, 232, 234, 343
Chicago *Tribune*, 68
Chicago World's Fair, 16, 124
Children's Suite (Naginski), 213
Children's Theatre of Greenwich House, 104
Child's Garden of Verses (Stevenson), 57
Chinese Legend (Eichheim), 199
Chiquita (Wayne), 304
Choeur de l'Université Populaire, 255
Chopin, François Frédéric, 28, 92, 113, 132
Chorale (Harris), 141
Chorale and Fugue in Jazz (Gould), 318
Chorale on a Theme by Hassler (Strong), 21
Choréographe (Hier), 202
Choreographic Impressions (Braine), 105
Christ and the Blind Man (Spelman), 206
CHURCHILL, FRANK E. (1901), 301
   Whistle While You Work, 301
   Who's Afraid of the Big Bad Wolf?, 301
Cincinnati College of Music, 19, 105
Cincinnati Conservatory of Music, 100, 106, 201, 206
Cincinnati Symphony Orchestra, 42, 93, 106, 158, 191, 194, 195, 196, 215, 235
Circus Days (Taylor), 34, 312
CITKOWITZ, ISRAEL (1909), 226, 227
   Lamb, The, 227
   Sonatine, 227
   Song Cycle to Words of Joyce, 227
   Songs of Protest, 227
   String Quartet, 227
City, The, 150
City College (New York), 20, 103
City in the Sea (Shepherd), 181
City of Brass, The (Herrmann), 211
City of Dreams (Braine), 105
Civil War, 272

CLAFLIN, AVERY (1898), *198*
   Fall of the House of Usher, The, 198
   Hester Prynne, 198
   Moby Dick Suite, 198
   Symphony, 198
CLAPP, PHILIP GREELEY (1888), *60-61*
   Dramatic Poem, 61
   In Summer, 61
   Norge, 61
   Song of Youth, A, 61
Clari, the Maid of Milan (Bishop & Payne), 316
Cleopatra (Allen), 197
Cleopatra's Night (Hadley), 24
Cleveland, Grover, 242
Cleveland Institute of Music, 101, 121, 162, 170, 215
Cleveland Orchestra, 42, 86, 118, 121, 182, 183, 200, 220, 232
Cleveland Plain Dealer, 200
Cleveland Press, 182
Clifton, Chalmers, 99
CLOKEY, JOSEPH WADDELL (1890), *106-107*
   Cocaine Lil, 107
   Frankie and Johnnie, 107
Clouds (Griffes), 128
Coal Scuttle Blues (Bacon & Luening), 188
Coates, Albert, 179, 306
Cocaine Lil (Clokey), 107
Cocteau, Jean, 261, 274
COHAN, GEORGE M. (1878), *297*, 339
   Forty-Five Minutes from Broadway, 297
   Give My Regards to Broadway, 297
   I'm a Yankee Doodle Dandy, 297
   Little Nellie Kelly, 297
   Mary Is a Grand Old Name, 297
   Over There, 297
   Rise of Rosie O'Reilly, The, 297
COHN, ARTHUR (1910), *212-213*
COLE, ROSSETTER GLEASON (1866), *66-67*
   Ballade, 67
   Broken Troth, The, 67
   Heroic Piece, A, 67
   Maypole Lovers, The, 67
   Passing of Summer, The, 67

Pioneer, 67
Rock of Liberty, The, 67
Sonata, 67
Symphonic Prelude, 67
COLE, ULRIC (1905), *196*
　Concerto, 196
　Divertimento, 196
　Fantasy Sonata, 196
　Piano Quintet, 196
　Sonatas, 196
　String Quartet, 196
　Suite, 196
　Suite for Trio, 196
Coleridge, Samuel Taylor, 127
Coleridge-Taylor, Samuel, 280
College Music (Thompson), 110
College of the Pacific, 75
Collegiana (La Violette), 184
Collier, Constance, 32
Collier's Weekly, 30
Colorado, University of, 196
Colors of War, The (Rogers), 98
Colossus (Griffis), 109
Columbia Broadcasting System, 76, 141, 146, 154, 160, 162, 208, 211, 213, 264, 279, 280, 281, 319, 328, 379-380
Columbia Phonograph Company, 101, 138, 256
Columbia University, 20, 41, 67, 86, 88, 90, 200, 209, 216, 220, 225, 241
Columbia Workshop, 211
Comedy Overture (Wald), 184
Comedy Overture on Negro Themes (Gilbert), 124-125, 126
Come Easy Go Easy Love (Carmichael), 301
Come Seven (Tuthill), 206
Comes Autumn Time (Sowerby), 81
Composers' Forums, 332
Composers in America (Reis), 328
Composers' Music Corporation, 163
Concert for Six Instruments (J. Beach), 129
Concerto da Camera (Hanson), 76
Concerto Grosso (Bennett), 317
Concerto Grosso (Stoessel), 83
Concerto in Jazz (Braine), 105
Concerto Lirico (Berezowsky), 185
Concerto Sacro (Josten), 177-178

Concerto Sinfonico (Steinert), 206
Concert Piece (Kinney), 219
Concert Piece (Phillips), 217
Concert Waltz Suite (Eppert), 194
Concord Sonata (Ives), 246-247
CONFREY, EDWARD E. ("ZEZ") (1895), *301*
　Kitten on the Keys, 301
　Poor Buttermilk, 301
　Stumbling, 301
Connecticut-Tercentenary (Hadley), 26
Connecticut Yankee, A (Rodgers & Hart), 302
Constanza e Fortezza (Fux), 177
CONVERSE, FREDERICK SHEPHERD (1871-1940), *53-56*, 162, 283
　American Sketches, 55
　Ave atque Vale, 54
　California, 55
　Concertino, 55
　Endymion's Narrative, 54
　Festival of Pan, 53
　Flivver Ten Million, 54-55, 283
　Job, 54
　Mystic Trumpeter, The, 54
　Ormazd, 54
　Pipe of Desire, The, 53
　Prophecy, 55
　Sacrifice, The, 53
　String Quartet, Opus 18, 54
　String Quartet in E minor, 55
　Symphony in C minor, 54
　Symphony in D minor, 53
　Symphony in E major, 54
　Youth, 53
Converse College, 187
Coolidge, Elizabeth Sprague, 59, 81, 118, 144, 199, 249, 254
Coolidge Festival, 39, 47, 59, 158, 171, 185
Coolidge Foundation, 88, 118, 119. *See also* Library of Congress
Coolidge Quartet, 171, 185
Coon, Oscar, 30
Cooper, James Fenimore, 197
Copenhagen, University, 70
COPLAND, AARON (1900), 14, *145-150,* 208, 226, 227, 283, 342

COPLAND, AARON (*Continued*)
  Cat and the Mouse, The, 148
  Cortège Macabre, 148
  Dance Symphony, 148
  First Symphony, 148-149
  Grohg, 148
  Hear Ye! Hear Ye!, 149
  Lento Molto, 149
  Music for Radio, 146-147
  Music for the Theatre, 149, 150
  Outdoor Overture, 149
  Piano Concerto, 146, 149, 150
  Rondino, 149
  Saga of the Prairie, 146
  Salón México, El, 149
  Second Hurricane, The, 146, 147, 283
  Statements, 149
  Symphonic Ode, 148, 149, 150
  Two Blues, 149
  Vitebsk, 145, 149
Copland-Sessions Concerts, 148, 190, 198, 264
Cornell, Katharine, 35, 210
Cornell University, 130, 269
Cornemuse, La (Loeffler), 118
Corona, Leonora, 79, 213
Corrigan, Douglas, 237
Cortège Macabre (Copland), 148
Cosmophony (Rudhyar), 253
Coulennes (Howe), 193
Country Gardens (Grainger), 273
Country Pictures (Mason), 42
Country Roads (Bacon), 187
County Fair (Berckman), 197
Course in Modern Harmony (Cesana), 317
Courthouse Square (Phillips), 217
COWELL, HENRY (1897), 183, 240, 241, 242, 243, 245-246, 250-251, 252, 253, 257, 328, 329
  Piano Concerto, 251
  Polyphonica, 251
  Rhythmicana, 251
  Suite, 251
  Synchrony, 251
Cradle Will Rock, The (Blitzstein), 265
CRAWFORD, RUTH (1901), 202, 240
  Diaphonic Suites, 240

String Quartet, 240
Three Movements, 240
Three Songs, 240
Two Movements, 240
Violin Sonata, 240
Creation, The (Gruenberg), 150, 153
CRESTON, PAUL (1906), 230-231
  Concertino, 231
  Partita, 231
  Prelude and Dance, 231
  Suite for Saxophone, 231
  Symphony, 231
  Two Choric Dances, 231
Crist, Bainbridge, 99
Cristobal Colon (Van Vactor), 232
Cromwell Fellowship, 214
Crying Jag (Brant), 260
Cuban Rhapsody (Maganini), 103
Cullen, Countee, 158
Culprit Fay, The (Hadley), 25
Currier and Ives Suite (Herrmann), 211
Curtis, Cyrus H. K., 325
Curtis Institute, 91, 110, 220, 222, 254, 264, 325
Cynthia Parker (Smith), 213
Cyrano de Bergerac (Damrosch), 17

Dalcroze Institute, 170, 227
Dame Libellule (Fairchild), 22
Damrosch, Leopold, 18
DAMROSCH, WALTER (1862), 17-19, 24, 29, 34, 102-103, 116, 149, 283, 307-308, 325, 340
  Abraham Lincoln Song, 17
  Cyrano de Bergerac, 17
  Man Without a Country, The, 17, 283
  Scarlet Letter, The, 17, 283
Damrosch Fellowship, Walter, 213
Danbury News, 245
Dance (Phillips), 217
Dance (Weiner), 219
Dance Episodes on an Exotic Theme (Shepherd), 182
Dance Figure (Becker), 183
Dance in the Place Congo (Gilbert), 125-126
Dance in Three-Time (Q. Porter), 162
Dance Music (Hammond), 164
Dance of Salome (Rogers), 98

INDEX

Dance of the Scarlet Sister Mary (Cadman), 50
Dancer Dead, The (Wald), 184
Dance Sonata (Bauer), 192
Dance Symphony (Copand), 148
Dancing in the Dark (Schwartz), 303
Daniel Jazz, The (Gruenberg), 150, 153
DANIELS, MABEL W. (1879), 72
   Deep Forest, 72
   Song of Jael, The, 72
   Villa of Dreams, 72
Dante Alighieri, 171
Danza (Carpenter), 40
Daphnis and Chloë (Zimbalist), 112
Dark Dancers of the Mardi Gras (Cadman), 50-51
Darker America (Still), 281
Darktown Strutters' Ball (Brooks), 301
Dartmouth College, 61, 96
Daughter of the Forest, A; see Twilight
Daughters of the American Revolution, 8
David (Weiss), 248
Davide Rizzio (M. Moore), 73
Davies, Walford, 303
Davison, Archibald T., 260
Dawn (Farwell), 131
Dawn in the Woods (Spelman), 206
DAWSON, WILLIAM LEVI (1899), 279
   Negro Folk Symphony No. 1, 279
   Scherzo, 279
   Sonata, 279
   Trio, 279
Day in the Peterborough Woods, A (Hier), 202
Day of Gayomair, The (Skilton), 269
Day of Judgment (Fickenscher), 240
Dearest Enemy (Rodgers & Hart), 302
Death, Mr. President (Horgan), 188
Debussy, Claude Achille, 28, 33, 36, 42, 65, 101, 155, 266
Dédicaces (Dukelsky), 199
Dedications (La Violette), 184
Deep Forest (Daniels), 72
Deep River (H. T. Burleigh), 109, 279
Deer Dance (Skilton), 268-269

De Koven, Reginald, 285, 300
DELAMARTER, ERIC (1880), 68
   Betrothal, The, 68
   Faun, The, 68
   Sonata in E flat, 68
DELANEY, ROBERT MILLS (1903), 233-234
   Don Quixote Symphony, 233
   John Brown's Song, 233, 234
   String Quartets, 234
   Symphonic Piece No. 1, 233
   Symphonic Piece No. 2, 234
   Violin Sonata, 234
   Work 22, 234
Delectable Forest, The (Hagedorn), 60
Delius, Frederick, 39
   Sea Drift, 39
Demoiselle Paysanne (Dukelsky), 199
Denby, Edwin, 146, 147
Denishawn Dancers, 191
Denmark Vesey (Bowles), 227
DENNY, WILLIAM D. (1910), 232-233
Density 21.5 (Varèse), 256
Denver Symphony Orchestra, 305
De Paul University, 184
De Paul University Press, 184
Depression (McBride), 225
De Profundis (W. Barlow), 217
Derain, André, 259
Derweis, Baron Paul von, 116
Dessoff Choirs, 227
De Sylva, Brown, and Henderson, 302
Déthier, Gaston Marie, 109, 231
Detroit Symphony Orchestra, 42, 176
DETT, R. NATHANIEL (1882), 279-280
   Juba Dance, 279
   Ordering of Moses, 279
Devil and Daniel Webster, The (D. Moore), 88-90
DIAMOND, DAVID (1915), 215-216
   Chamber Symphony, 216
   Concerto, 215
   Concert Piece, 215
   Divertimento, 216
   Elegy in Memory of Ravel, 215
   Heroic Piece, 215
   Piano Sonata, 215

DIAMOND, DAVID (*Continued*)
  Psalm for Orchestra, 215
  Quintet, 215
  Serenade, 215
  Sinfonietta, 215
  Sonata, 215
  Sonatina, 216
  Symphony, 215
  Trio, 215
  Variations on an Original Theme, 215
  Violin Concerto, 215
  Violin Sonatina, 215
Diaphonic Suites (Crawford), 240
Dichotomy (Riegger), 249
Dickinson, Emily, 188
Dillingham, Charles, 30
Dirge (Howe), 193
Disney, Walt, 35, 301
Ditson, James E., 56
Divertimento (Barnett), 197
Divertimento (U. Cole), 196
Divertimento (Loeffler), 117
Divertimento (Mason), 44-45
Divertimento (Strube), 52
Divertimento (Wagenaar), 176
Dobici, Cesare, 230
Doctor Faustus (Marlowe), 226
Dr. Joe (Tuthill), 206
Do, Do, Do (Gershwin), 306
Domain of Hurakan, The (Farwell), 131
DONALDSON, WALTER (1893), *301*
  How Ya Gonna Keep 'em Down on the Farm?, 301
  My Blue Heaven, 301
  My Mammy, 301
DONATO, ANTHONY, *218*
  Three Imitations, 218
Donizetti, Gaetano, 222
Donkey Serenade (Friml), 285
DONOVAN, RICHARD F. (1891), *162-163*, 214
  Four Songs, 163
  Serenade, 163
  Sextet, 163
  Smoke and Steel, 163
  Suite, 163
  Symphony, 163
  Trio, 163

Wood-Notes, 163
Don Quixote Symphony (Delaney), 233
Dorsey, Jimmy, 292
Dorsey, Tommy, 144, 292
Dover Beach (Barber), 221
Downes, Olin, 79, 125, 138, 150-151, 153-154, 174-175, 177, 191, 262-263, 280-281, 309
Downtown Glee Club, 173
Drake, Allison, 210
Drama of the Yellowstone (Lieurance), 270
Dramatic Poem (Clapp), 61
Dramatists' Guild, 341
Dream of McCorkle, The (Search), 108
Dream Pedlar, The (Whithorne), 155, 157
Dreams (Antheil), 259
Drum Taps (Hanson), 77
Drum Taps (Lockwood), 234
Dryden, John, 210
DUBENSKY, ARCADY (1890), *188-189*
  Fugue for Eighteen Violins, 188-189
  Raven, The, 189
  Russian Bells, 189
  Romance with Double Bass, 189
  Suite Anno 1600, 189
  Tom Sawyer Overture, 189
Dubin, Al, 304
Dukas, Paul, 26, 232, 233
  Sorcerer's Apprentice, The, 26
DUKE, JOHN WOODS (1899), *178*
  Fantasie in A minor, 178
  Overture in D minor, 178
  Suite, 178
  Trio, 178
Duke, Vernon; *see* Dukelsky, Vladimir
DUKELSKY, VLADIMIR (1903), *198-199*
  Dédicaces, 199
  Demoiselle Paysanne, 199
  End of St. Petersburg, The, 199
  Piano Concerti, 199
  Symphonies, 199
Du Maurier, George, 29
DUNN, JAMES PHILIP (1884–1936), *20-21*
  Barber's Sixth Brother, The, 21

INDEX

Galleon, The, 21
  Overture on Negro Themes, 21
  We, 21
Dunsany, Edward John Moreton Drax Plunkett, Baron, 131
Dupré, Marcel, 232
Durieux Ensemble, 229
Dvořák, Antonín, 5-6, 13, 204, 269, 278-279, 285
Dying Cowboy, The, 182
Dynamic Overture (Pimsleur), 204

Earl Carroll's Vanities, 280
East and West (Fairchild), 22
Eastman, George, 324
Eastman Festival, 39, 58, 63, 68, 98, 195, 216, 217, 233
Eastman School of Music, 61, 62, 68, 74, 75, 97, 186, 194, 195, 200, 202, 203, 214, 215, 216, 217, 218, 281, 324, 325
Eastman School Orchestra, 218
Eastman School Publication Award, 176, 376
Eberhart, Nelle Richmond, 51
Echo, The, 30
École Normale de Musique, 169, 233
École Polytechnique, 255
Edison, Thomas, 237
EDWARDS, GUS (1878), *301*
  By the Light of the Silvery Moon, 301
  Hello Melody, Goodbye Jazz, 301
  School Days, 301
  Tammany, 301
Edwards, Hilda, 69
EICHHEIM, HENRY (1870), *199*
  Bali, 199
  Burma, 199
  Chinese Legend, 199
  Japanese Nocturne, 199
  Java, 199
  Korean Sketch, 199
  Oriental Impressions, 199
Einstein, Alfred, 346
Electra (Sophocles), 269
Elegy (Busch), 70
Elegy (Heller), 106
Elegy in Memory of Ravel (Diamond), 215
Elfrida Whiteman Scholarship, 215

Elgar, Sir Edward, 35, 303, 305
Eliot, T. S., 212
ELKUS, ALBERT I. (1884), *199-200, 235*
  Impressions from a Greek Tragedy, 199
ELLINGTON, EDWARD K. ("DUKE") (1899), *292*
  Mood Indigo, 292
  Solitude, 292
Elman, Mischa, 113
Elschuco Trio, 105, 201
ELWELL, HERBERT (1898), *200*
  Happy Hypocrite, The, 200
  Quintet, 200
  Piano Sonata, 200
  Sonata, 200
  String Quartet, 200
Embraceable You (Gershwin), 306
Emerson, Ralph Waldo, 246
Emery, Stephen A., 11, 24
Emperor Jones, The (Gruenberg), 150-151, 153, 283
Emperor Jones, The (O'Neill), 190
Enchanted Isle, The (Gruenberg), 150, 153
Enchanted Isle, The (Salzedo), 253
Encyclopaedia Britannica, 30
End of St. Petersburg, The (Dukelsky), 199
Endymion (Bennett), 314
Endymion (Josten), 178
Endymion's Narrative (Converse), 54
ENGEL, A. LEHMAN (1910), *212*
  Introduction and Allegretto, 212
  Jungle Dance, 212
  Medea, 212
  Phobias, 212
  Piano Sonata, 212
  Pierrot of the Minute, 212
  Scientific Creation, 212
  String Quartet, 212
  Traditions, 212
ENGEL, CARL (1883), 11, *118-119*
  Triptych, 119
Entente cordiale (Brant), 260
Enter Buffoon (J. Beach), 129
Epitaphs (Chanler), 198
Epoch (McKay), 204
EPPERT, CARL (1882), *194*
  Argonauts, The, 194

EPPERT, CARL (*Continued*)
  Concert Waltz Suite, 194
  Escapade, 194
  Little Symphony, A, 194
  Pioneer, The, 194
  Speed, 194
  Symphony in C minor, 194
  Symphony of the City, A, 194
  Traffic, 194
  Vitamins, 194
Equatorial (Varèse), 256
Erewhon (Reiser), 205
Erotic Poem (Grimm), 201
Erskine, John, 102, 150, 153, 210, 258, 324
Escapade (Eppert), 194
Espace (Varèse), 256
Essay for Orchestra (Barber), 221
Étang, L' (Loeffler), 118
Ethical Culture School, 29, 167
ETLER, ALVIN, *218*
  Music for Chamber Orchestra, 218
Etude, 320
Eugene Onegin (Tschaikowsky), 19
Eugénie (S. Barlow), 94
Evangeline (C. Burleigh), 52
Evangeline (Luening), 187
Evans, Maurice, 226
Eve of St. Agnes, The (Ballantine), 60
Everybody's Doin' It (Berlin), 299
Everybody Step (Berlin), 299
Evocation (Loeffler), 118
Evocations (Bloch), 121
Ewen, David, 91-92, 169, 227
Exaltation (Hanson), 76
Excursion (Hammond), 164
Exhilaration (Search), 108
Ex Hocte (Allen), 197

FAIRCHILD, BLAIR (1877–1933), 22
  Dame Libellule, 22
  East and West, 22
  Psalms, 22
Faithful, The (Rogers), 97
Fall of the House of Usher, The (Claflin), 198
Fall of the House of Usher, The (Hill), 57

Fall of the House of Usher, The (C. Loomis), 71
Fall of the House of Usher, The (Poe), 57, 71
False Faces (W. Barlow), 217
Faltering Dusk, The (Kramer), 104
Famous Music, 313
Fandango (Whithorne), 158
Fanny Blair (Mason), 42
Fantasia, 35
Fantasia quasi una Sonata (Bauer), 192
Fantastic Concerto (Loeffler), 117
Fantasy in Delft (Gilbert), 126
Fantasy on a Western Folksong (McKay), 203-204
Farewell of Hiawatha, The (A. Foote), 13
Farewell to Pioneers (Harris), 141
Far Horizon, The (Cadman), 51
Far Ocean (Royce), 205
FARWELL, ARTHUR (1872), *129-132*, 135, 282
  American Indian Melodies, 131
  Dawn, 131
  Domain of Hurakan, The, 131
  Fugue Fantasia, 131
  Gods of the Mountain, 131
  Impressions of the Wa-Wan Ceremony, 131
  Mountain Song, 131
  Navajo War Dance, 131
  Pawnee Horses, 131
  Rudolph Gott, 132
  Symphonic Hymn on March! March!, 131
  Symphonic Song on Old Black Joe, 131
Fascinating Rhythm (Gershwin), 306
Fata Morgana (Whithorne), 157
Faun, The (Delamarter), 68
Federal Concert Band, 108
Federal Music Project, 68, 99, 108, 183, 187, 212, 226, 234, 240, 275, 330-332
Federal Symphony Orchestra (New York), 210
Federal Symphony Orchestra (San Francisco), 108, 187
Federal Theater Project, 187, 249, 265, 319

INDEX

Ferguson, Donald, 227
Ferguson, Ethel, 71
Fernando del Nonsensico (Borowski), 68
Festival Jubilate (Mrs. Beach), 16
Festival of American Music (New York), 344
Festival of Gauri, The (La Monaca), 219
Festival of Pan (Converse), 53
Festival of the Workers (McDonald), 181
Festival Overture (Mason), 42
Festival Overture (Search), 108
Festival Prelude (Branscombe), 73
Fête Galante (Smith), 46
Feuilles Symphoniques (White), 195
FICKENSCHER, ARTHUR (1871), 239-240
  Day of Judgment, 240
  Out of the Gay Nineties, 240
  Variations on a Theme in Medieval Style, 240
  Willowwave and Wellaway, 240
Fidgety Feet (Gershwin), 306
Fielitz, Alexander von, 183
Fiery Sonata (Pimsleur), 204
Fiesta (Fuleihan), 192
Fighting the Waves (Antheil), 258
FILIPPI, AMEDEO DE (1900), 200
  Concerto, 200
  Piano Quintet, 200
  Sonata, 200
  String Quartet, 200
  Suite, 200
  Symphony, 200
Filtro, Il (Allen), 197
FINNEY, ROSS LEE (1906), 227-228
  Bletheris, a Monody, from the Hamlet of Archibald MacLeish, 228
  John Brown, 228
  Masse Mensch, 228
  Piano Concerto, 228
  Piano Sonatas, 228
  Prelude for a Drama, 228
  Sonata, 228
  String Quartets, 228
  Trio, 228
  Violin Concerto, 228

FIORILLO, DANTE (1905), 228-229
  Concerti, 229
  Horn Quintet, 229
  Partitas, 228
  Piano Quintets, 229
  Sonatas, 229
  String Quartets, 229
  Symphonies, 228
  Trios, 229
Fire-Bringer, The (Royce), 205
Firefly, The (Friml), 285
Fischer, Carl, Inc., 344
Fischer & Brother, J., 344
Five American Dances (Lane), 71
Five Chinese Fairy Tales (Hammond), 164
Five Fairy Tales (Rogers), 98
Five Inhibitions (Mourant), 219
Five Miniatures (White), 195
Five Pieces (Schoenberg), 254
Five Pieces (Weiss), 248
Five Short Colloquies (Chanler), 198
Flem, Paul le, 190
Flirtation in a Chinese Garden (Chasins), 91
Flivver Ten Million (Converse), 54-55, 283
Flonzaley Quartet, 121
Flowers (Smith), 46
Flying Colors (Schwartz), 303
Folk Hymns of America (Buchanan), 276
Folk-Song Symphony (Harris), 144, 283
Folk Symphony from the Carolina Hills (Vardell), 219
Follow the Swallow (Henderson), 302
FOOTE, ARTHUR WILLIAM (1853-1937), 10, *12-13*, 16, 269
  Farewell of Hiawatha, The, 13
  Four Character Pieces after Omar Khayyam, 13
  Francesca da Rimini, 13
  Night-Piece, 13
  Skeleton in Armor, The, 13
  Suite in E, 13
  Wreck of the Hesperus, The, 13
FOOTE, GEORGE, *218*
  Variations on a Pious Theme, 218
Ford, Henry, 23, 54, 95, 237

Forever Is a Long Time (A. Von Tilzer), 297
For Me and My Gal (Meyer), 302
For One Who Fell in Battle (Loeffler), 118
FORST, RUDOLF (1900), *200*
   Sonata, 200
   Sonata da Camera, 200
   String Quartet, 200
   Symphonic Rhapsody, 200
   Symphonietta, 200
   Symphony, 200
For Strings (S. Barlow), 94
Fortune Teller, The (Herbert), 312
Fort Worth Exposition, 313
Forty-Five Minutes from Broadway (Cohan), 297
Foster, Stephen, 4, 5, 71, 72, 107, 122, 210, 318, 339, 340
Foster Gallery (Gould), 318
Foster Hall, 71
Fosteriana (Gaul), 72
Foster Suite (Janssen), 94
Fountain of the Acqua Paola, The (Griffes), 128
Four Character Pieces after Omar Khayyam (A. Foote), 13
Four Indian Tribal Melodies (Busch), 70
Four Indiscretions (Gruenberg), 150
Four Museum Pieces (D. Moore), 86
Four Saints in Three Acts (Stein & Thomson), 261-263
Four Seasons, The (Hadley), 25
Four Sketches (Heller), 106
Fourth of July (Lane), 71
Fox Studios, 205
Fragment from Orestes (Slonimsky), 257
Francesca da Rimini (A. Foote), 13
Francis, Saint, 117
Franck, César, 11, 12, 36, 42
Franco-American Musical Society, 254
Frank, Philip, 101
Frankie and Johnnie (Clokey), 107
Frederick the Great, 78
Free and Easy Five-Step (Mason), 45
FREED, ISADORE (1900), *201*
   Ballad, 201
   Jeux de Timbres, 201
   Pastorales, 201

Pygmalion, 201
String Quartets, 201
Symphony, 201
Triptyque, 201
Vibrations, 201
FREER, ELEANOR EVEREST (1864), 73
Free Variations (Landau), 219
Freund, John C., 104
Friedheim, Arthur, 190
Friends and Enemies of Modern Music, 198, 261
Friends of Music (New York), 121, 193
FRIML, RUDOLF (1881), *285, 286, 340*
   Allah's Holiday, 285
   Chansonette, 285
   Donkey Serenade, 285
   Firefly, The, 285
   High Jinks, 285
   Indian Love-Call, 285
   Katinka, 285
   Piano Concerto, 285
   Rose Marie, 285
   Vagabond King, The, 285
From a Lute of Jade (Read), 215
From Jewish Life (Bloch), 120
From Mt. Rainier (Reiser), 205
From My Youth (Wilson), 14
From Sea to Sea (Miller), 50
From the Canebrake (Gardner), 105
From the Garden of Hellas (Ballantine), 60
From the Great Smokies (Gaul), 72
From the Journal of a Wanderer (Still), 281
From the Land of Dreams (Still), 280-281
From the Land of the Sky Blue Water (Cadman), 48, 49
From the Mountain Kingdom of the Great North West (Saar), 20
From the Northland (Sowerby), 82
From the Odyssey (Berckman), 197
From the Plains (F. A. Johnson), 269
From the Revelation of St. John the Divine (McPhee), 190
From the Southern Mountains (Stringfield), 275

INDEX

Fuchs, Robert, 156
Fugato on a Well-Known Theme (McBride), 224
Fugue Fantasia (Farwell), 131
Fugue for Eighteen Violins (Dubensky), 188-189
Fugue with Chorale (Leidzen), 219
Fuji in the Sunset Glow (Rogers), 97
FULEIHAN, ANIS (1900), *190-192*
   Calypso, 192
   Fiesta, 192
   First Symphony, 191
   Mediterranean Suite, 191
   Piano Concertos, 191-192
   Preface to a Child's Storybook, 191
   Preludes, 192
   Symphonic Episode, 192
   Symphony Concertante, 192
Funny Face (Gershwin), 306
Fux, Johann Joseph, 177

Gabrilowitsch, Ossip, 42, 109, 176
Gade, Niels Wilhelm, 70
Gaelic Symphony (Mrs. Beach), 16
Gagliarda of the Merry Plague (Saminsky), 165, 166
GALAJIKIAN, FLORENCE GRANDLAND (1900), *230*
   Andante and Scherzo, 230
   Fantasie, 230
   Symphonic Intermezzo, 230
   Tragic Overture, 230
   Transitions, 230
Gala Night, 104
Galaxy Music Corporation, 104
Galimir String Quartet, 171
Galleon, The (Dunn), 21
Gallico, Paolo, 167
Gannett, Lewis, 77
GANZ, RUDOLPH (1877), 101, *111-112*
   Animal Pictures, 112
   Konzertstück, 112
   Suite, 112
   Symphony, 112
García, Manuel, 315
Garden of Mystery, The (Cadman), 49
Gardner, Mrs. Jack, 117
GARDNER, SAMUEL (1891), *105*
   Broadway, 105

From the Canebrake, 105
New Russia, 105
Prelude and Fugue, 105
String Quartet, 105
To the Fallen, 105
Violin Concerto, 105
Garrick, David, 84
Garrick (Stoessel), 83-84
Garrick Gaieties, 198, 264, 303
GAUL, HARVEY BARTLETT (1881), 72
Fosteriana, 72
From the Great Smokies, 7
Introduction to a Speaker, 72
New England Prelude, 72
Père Marquette, 72
Tennessee Devil Tunes, 72
Three Palestinian Pastels, 72
Three Pennsylvania Portraits, 72
Gaynor, William J., 130
Gebhard, Heinrich, 117, 260
Gédalge, André, 129, 193, 206
General William Booth Enters Heaven (James), 173
George White's Scandals (Gershwin), 306
Gericke, Wilhelm, 54
GERSHWIN, GEORGE (1898-1937), 14, 19, 27, 202, 289, 305, *306-311*, 328, 340
American in Paris, An, 308
Concerto in F, 19, 307-308
Do, Do, Do, 306
Embraceable You, 306
Fascinating Rhythm, 306
Fidgety Feet, 306
Funny Face, 306
George White's Scandals, 306
Girl Crazy, 306
Lady Be Good, 306
La La Lucille, 306
Let 'Em Eat Cake, 306
Man I Love, The, 306
Maybe, 306
My One and Only, 306
Of Thee I Sing, 306
Oh, Kay, 306
Porgy and Bess, 309-311
   I Got Plenty o' Nuttin', 310
   Oh, de Lawd Shake de Heaven, 310

GERSHWIN, GEORGE (*Continued*)
    There's a Boat that's Leavin' Soon for New York, 310
    Woman Is a Sometime Thing, A, 310
    Preludes, 311
    Rhapsody in Blue, 306-307, 308, 309, 312
    'S Wonderful, 306
    Second Rhapsody, 309
    Strike Up the Band, 306
    Swanee, 306
    Sweet and Lowdown, 306
    That Certain Feeling, 306
Gershwin, Ira, 309, 311
Get Out of Town (C. Porter), 302
Gettysburg Address (Lincoln), 14
Gettysburg Address, The (Goldmark), 283
Giannini, Dusolina, 209
GIANNINI, VITTORIO (1903), 14, *208-209*, 214
    Beauty and the Beast, 208
    Blennerhasset, 208
    Casanova, 209
    Concerti, 208, 209
    Lucedia, 208
    Madrigal, 209
    Piano Concerto, 209
    Piano Quintet, 208-209
    Quintet, 209
    Requiem, 208
    Scarlet Letter, The, 208, 209
    Sonatas, 208
    String Quartet, 208
    Suite, 208
    Symphony in Memoriam Theodore Roosevelt, 208
    Trios, 208
    Triptych, 209
Gieseking, Walter, 157
GILBERT, HENRY F. (1868–1928), 115, *124-126*, 129, 130, 282
    Comedy Overture on Negro Themes, 124-125, 126
    Dance in the Place Congo, 125-126
    Fantasy in Delft, 126
    Negro Rhapsody, 125
    Pirate Song, 126
    Symphonic Prelude to *Riders to the Sea*, 126

Gilbert, William Schwenk, 294
Gilman, Lawrence, 28-29, 32, 39, 44, 79, 85, 89, 102, 109-110, 120, 155, 162, 174, 178, 199, 222-223, 224-225, 243, 247, 254, 258, 262, 264, 310-311, 317
GIORNI, AURELIO (1895–1938), 201
    Orlando Furioso, 201
    Piano Quartet, 201
    Piano Quintet, 201
    Piano Trio, 201
    Sinfonia Concertante, 201
    Sonata, 201
    String Quartet, 201
    Symphony in D, 201
Girl Crazy (Gershwin), 306
Girl Friend, The (Rodgers & Hart), 302
Gitanjali (Tagore), 100
Giulietta e Romeo (Zingarelli), 316
Give My Regards to Broadway (Cohan), 297
GLEASON, HAROLD, *218*
    Prelude on a Gregorian Theme, 218
GLICK, HENRIETTA, *218-219*
    Paris, 219
Glière, Reinhold, 199, 203
Gluck, Christoph Willibald von, 175
Gobi (Reiser), 204
Go Choruses (McBride), 224
Godard, Benjamin Louis Paul, 70
God Bless America (Berlin), 298, 319
GODOWSKY, LEOPOLD (1870–1938), 71, *112-113*
    Metamorphoses, 113
    Triakontameron, 113
God's Grandeur (Barber), 221
Gods of the Mountain, The (Bonner), 198
Gods of the Mountain (Farwell), 131
Goetschius, Percy, 40, 61, 97, 105, 196, 202, 248
Gogol, Nikolai, 117
Gogorza, Emilio de, 220
Gold, Julius, 317
Goldberg, Isaac, 305
Goldmark, Carl, 13
GOLDMARK, RUBIN (1872–1936), *13-14*, 91, 109, 147, 167, 196,

INDEX

200, 208, 210, 212, 213, 226, 230, 232, 283
Call of the Plains, The, 14
Gettysburg Address, The, 283
Negro Rhapsody, 14
Requiem, 14
Goldoni, Carlo, 184
Goldwyn Follies, The, 311
Golem Suite (J. Achron), 196
Golschmann, Vladimir, 204, 258
Goodman, Benny, 292-293, 295
Goodrich, Arthur, 64
Goodrich, John Wallace, 260
Goossens, Eugene, 93, 158, 187, 194, 196
Gordon String Quartet, 88, 161, 225
Gottschalk, Louis Moreau, 4, 16
GOULD, MORTON (1913), *318-319*
  Americana Suite, 319
  Cantata, 319
  Chorale and Fugue in Jazz, 318
  Foster Gallery, 318
  Piano Concerto, 318
  Piano Sonatas, 318
  Swing Symphonettes, 319
  Symphony, 319
Graham, Martha, 218, 249, 250
Grainger, Ella Viola Strom, 274
GRAINGER, PERCY ALDRIDGE (1882), 42, *273-275*, 279, 340, 345
  Country Gardens, 273
  Irish Tune from County Derry, 273
  Mock Morris, 273
  Molly on the Shore, 273
  Shepherd's Hey, 273
  To a Nordic Princess, 274
  Tribute to Foster, 273
Grand Canyon Suite (Grofé), 312
Grand Street Follies, The, 303
Grand Street Playhouse, 146
Grant, Ulysses S., 244
GRANT, WILLIAM P., *219*
  Symphony in D minor, 219
Great Day (Youmans), 304
Greek Impressions (Whithorne), 156, 158
Greek Theatre (Los Angeles), 73
GREEN, RAY (1908), *235-236*
  Concertino, 236
  Prelude and Fugue, 236

Green Mansions (Gruenberg), 154-155
Green Mansions (Hudson), 154
Green River, The (Carpenter), 36
Greenwich House Music School, 228
Grieg, Edvard, 273
GRIFFES, CHARLES TOMLINSON (1884-1920), 115, *126-129*
  Lake at Evening, The, 126
  Old Song Re-Sung, An, 128
  Piano Sonata, 127
  Pleasure Dome of Kubla Khan, The, 127, 128
  Poem, 127-128
  Roman Sketches, 126, 128
    Clouds, 128
    Fountain of the Acqua Paola, The, 128
    Nightfall, 128
    White Peacock, The, 126-127, 128
  Sorrow of Mydah, 128
GRIFFIS, ELLIOT (1893), *108-109*
  Colossus, 109
  Persian Fable, A, 109
  Piano Sonata, 108
  String Quartet, 108
  Symphony, 108
  Variations, 109
GRIMM, CARL HUGO (1890), *201-202*
  Abraham Lincoln, 202
  Erotic Poem, 201
  Fantasia, 201
  Serenade, 201
  Song of Songs, 201-202
  String Quartet, 201
  Suites, 201
  Symphonic Poems, 201
Grim Troubadour, The (Whithorne), 158
Grofé, Emil von, 312
GROFÉ, FERDE (1892), 71, 305, 307, *311-313*, 332
  Grand Canyon Suite, 312
  Hollywood Suite, 312
  Knute Rockne, 312
  Mississippi Suite, 312
  Ode to the Star-Spangled Banner, 312
  Symphony in Steel, 312

GROFÉ, FERDE (*Continued*)
  Three Shades of Blue, 312
  Wheels, 312
Grohg (Copland), 148
Groningen Orchestra, 210
Grosser, Maurice, 261
Grotesque Dance from a Projected Ballet (Phillips), 217
Gruenberg, Eugene, 52
GRUENBERG, LOUIS (1884), 148, 150-155, 283, 327
  Creation, The, 150, 153
  Daniel Jazz, The, 150, 153
  Emperor Jones, The, 150-151, 153, 283
  Enchanted Isle, The, 150, 153
  First Symphony, 150, 154
  Four Indiscretions, 150
  Green Mansions, 154-155
  Hill of Dreams, 150
  Jack and the Beanstalk, 150, 153-154
  Jazettes, 150
  Jazz Suite, 150, 153
  Piano Concertos, 155
  Quintet, 155
  Second Symphony, 155
  Serenade to a Beauteous Lady, 154
  String Quartets, 155
Grünewald, Mathias, 177
Guggenheim Fellowship, 97, 103, 109, 110, 136, 147, 162, 170, 186, 188, 191, 195, 202, 208, 209, 215, 218, 224, 225, 228, 231, 233, 240, 248, 251, 259, 280, 314, 319, 381
Guiablesse, La (Still), 281
Guilmant, Alexandre, 68, 90
GUION, DAVID WENDELL FENTRESS (1895), 274, 277
  Arkansas Traveler, 274, 277
  Sheep and Goat Walkin' to Pasture, 277
  Shingandi, 277
  Turkey in the Straw, 271, 274, 277
Guiterman, Arthur, 17, 18
Guitry, Sascha, 94
Gunn, Glenn Dillard, 187, 226

Hába, Alois, 134
Hackley School, 128

HADLEY, HENRY KIMBALL (1871-1937), 23-27, 53, 342
  Atonement of Pan, The, 25
  Azora, 24
  Belshazzar, 25
  Bianca, 24
  Cleopatra's Night, 24
  Concertino, 26
  Connecticut-Tercentenary, 26
  Culprit Fay, The, 25
  Four Seasons, The, 25
  Hector and Andromache, 24
  In Bohemia, 25
  Legend of Hani, The, 25
  Lucifer, 25
  Night in Old Paris, A, 24
  North, East, South, and West, 25
  Ocean, The, 25
  Othello, 25
  Safie, 24
  Salome, 25
  Scherzo Diabolique, 26
  Streets of Pekin, The, 25
  Symphonic Fantasia, 25
  Third Symphony, 25
  Youth and Life, 25
Henry Hadley Foundation, 219
Henry Hadley Medal, 342
Henry Hadley Memorial Library, 342
Hagedorn, Herman, 60
HAGEMAN, RICHARD (1882), 64-65
  Caponsacchi, 64-65
HAINES, EDMUND, 219
  Symphony in Miniature, 219
Hale, Edward Everett, 17, 18
Hale, Philip, 11
Hallelujah (Youmans), 304
Hambitzer, Charles, 306
Hamilton College, 61, 187
Hamlet (Shakespeare), 263
Hammond, John Hays, 163
Hammond, John Hays, Jr., 163
HAMMOND, RICHARD (1896), 163-164
  Dance Music, 164
  Excursion, 164
  Five Chinese Fairy Tales, 164
  Sea of Heaven, The, 164
  Sinfonietta, 164
  Sonata, 164

INDEX

Suite after Reading "The Woman of Andros," 164
Voyage to the East, 164
West Indian Dances, 164
Hampton Choral Union, 280
Hampton Institute, 280
Handel, George Frideric, 177, 181, 242, 262, 290
HANDY, WILLIAM CHRISTOPHER (1873), 280, *293*, 296
   Beale Street Blues, 293
   Memphis Blues, 293
   St. Louis Blues, 267, 293
   Yellow Dog Blues, 293
Hanson, Hans, 75
HANSON, HOWARD (1896), 45, 66-67, 74-80, 106, 114, 148, 208, 214, 216, 249, 259, 324, 340
   Before the Dawn, 76
   Concerto da Camera, 76
   Concerto for organ and orch., 76
   Drum Taps, 77
   Exaltation, 76
   Heroic Elegy, 77
   Lament for Beowulf, The, 77
   Lux Aeterna, 76
   Merry Mount, 45, 66, 77-80
   Nordic Symphony, 76
   North and West, 76
   Pan and the Priest, 76
   Quintet in F minor, 76
   Romantic Symphony, 76
   String Quartet, 76
   Symphonic Legend, 76
   Symphonic Prelude, 76
   Symphonic Rhapsody, 76
   Third Symphony, 75, 76
   Three Poems from Walt Whitman, 77
Hanson, Wilma, 75
Happy Days Are Here Again (Ager), 300
Happy Hypocrite, The (Elwell), 200
Harbor Narrative (McKay), 204
Harlem House, 228
Harlequin and Columbine (Braine), 105
HARLING, WILLIAM FRANKE (1887), *202*
   Chanson Populaires, 202
   Deep River, 202
   Jazz Concerto, 202
   Light from St. Agnes, The, 202
   Venetian Fantasy, 202
Harmon Award, 280
Harmonies of Florence (Bingham), 90
Harms, T. B., 313
Harris, Joel Chandler, 125
HARRIS, ROY (1898), 47, *132-145*, 146, 208, 225, 256, 283, 340, 342, 344
   American Creed, 144
   Andante, 135, 136
   Chorale, 141
   Concerto, 135, 136-137
   Farewell to Pioneers, 141
   Folk-Song Symphony, 144, 283
   Fourth Symphony, 144
   1933, 137-138, 139, 140
   Piano Sonatas, 136, 137, 144
   Poem, 145
   Quintet, 143, 145
   Second Symphony, 141
   Song for Occupations, 140
   String Quartets, 136, 144
   String Sextet, 144
   Suite, 135
   Symphony for Voices, 140-141
   Third Symphony, 143-144
   Time Suite, 141-142, 146
   Trio, 144
   Variations on a Theme, 144
   Western Landscape, 144
   When Johnny Comes Marching Home, 138-140, 283
HART, FREDERIC (1898), *226*
   Concert Overture, 226
   Romance of Robot, 226
   String Quartet, 226
   Suite, 226
   Wheel of Fortune, The, 226
Hart, Lorenz, 302
Harte, Bret, 173
Hartley, Randolph, 65
Hartmann, Johann Peter Emilius, 70
Harvard Glee Club, 110
Harvard Musical Association, 12
Harvard University, 13, 35, 40, 55, 56, 57, 59, 60, 61, 62, 93, 109, 110, 159, 160, 170, 197, 205, 206, 227, 242, 260, 302
Haskell Institute, 268

Hasty Pudding Club, 40
HAUBIEL, CHARLES (1894), *101*, *225*, *229*
   Karma, 101
   Mars Ascending, 101
   Passacaglia in A minor, 101
   Pastoral, 101
   Ritratti, 101
   Solari, 101
   Suite Passecaille, 101
   Vox Cathedralis, 101
Hawkins, Coleman, 293
Hawthorne, Nathaniel, 49, 78, 246
Haydn, Franz Josef, 175, 290
Hayes, Helen, 226
Hayes, Patrick, 112
Hayes, Roland, 278
Headless Horseman, The (D. Moore), 88
Heads Up (Rodgers & Hart), 302
Hearn, Lafcadio, 286
Hear Ye! Hear Ye! (Copland), 149
Hebraic Poems (McDonald), 179
Hebrew Suite (Berezowsky), 185
Hector and Andromache (Hadley), 24
Heffley, Eugene, 193
Heifetz, Jascha, 113
HEILMAN, WILLIAM CLIFFORD (1877), *59-60*
   By the Porta Catania, 60
   Trio, 60
Hekking, André, 248
Helen Retires (Antheil), 258
HELFER, WALTER (1896), *61-62*
   Concert Overture in D major, 61
   Prelude, Intermezzo, and Fugue, 61
   Symphony on Canadian Airs, 61
   Water Idyl, 61
HELLER, JAMES G. (1892), *106*
   Aquatints, 106
   Elegy, 106
   Four Sketches, 106
   Four Solo Services for Friday Evening, 106
   Pastorale, 106
   Sonata, 106
   Trio, 106
   Watchman, What of the Night?, 106
Hello Melody, Goodbye Jazz (Edwards), 301

Helvetia (Bloch), 122
HENDERSON, ARTHUR, *219*
   Sonata, 219
Henderson, Fletcher, 293
Henderson, Horace, 293
HENDERSON, RAY (1896), *301-302*
   Bye Bye Blackbirds, 302
   Follow the Swallow, 302
   My Sin, 302
   Sonny Boy, 302
Henderson, William J., 53, 150
Henry, Patrick, 237
Herbert, Victor, 172, 262, 285, 300, 312, 332, 335, 340
Hero Chants (Rudhyar), 253
Heroic Elegy (Hanson), 77
Heroic Piece, A (R. Cole), 67
Heroic Piece (Diamond), 215
Heroic Poem (Britain), 232
Herriman, George, 37
HERRMANN, BERNARD (1911), *210-212*, *283*
   City of Brass, The, 211
   Concerto, 212
   Currier and Ives Suite, 211
   Johnny Appleseed, 212
   Moby Dick, 211-212, 283
   Nocturne and Scherzo, 211
   Orchestral Variations on Deep River and Water Boy, 211
   Sinfonietta, 211
   Skating Pond, The, 211
   String Quartet, 211
   Symphony, 212
   Violin Concerto, 211
He's a Devil (Berlin), 299
Hester Prynne (Claflin), 198
Heyward, Dorothy, 309
Heyward, Du Bose, 309
Hiawatha (Longfellow), 70
Hicks, Edward, 111
HIER, ETHEL GLENN (1889), *202*
   America the Beautiful, 202
   Choréographe, 202
   Day in the Peterborough Woods, A, 202
   Quartets, 202
   Sextet, 202
   Suite, 202
Higginson, Thomas Wentworth, 116

INDEX

Higher and Higher (Rodgers & Hart), 302
High Jinks (Friml), 285
Highwayman, The (Taylor), 31
HILL, EDWARD BURLINGAME (1872), 56-59, 110, 159, 227
  Concertino, 57-58
  Concertino, Opus 46, 59
  Concerto, 59
  Fall of the House of Usher, The, 57
  Jazz Studies, 57
  Lilacs, 57
  Quartet, Opus 42, 59
  Sextet, Opus 39, 59
  Sinfonietta, Opus 40A, 58
  Sinfonietta, Opus 57, 58
  Sonata for clarinet, 59
  Stevensoniana, No. 1, 56
  Stevensoniana, No. 2, 56-57
  String Quartet, Opus 40, 58, 59
  Third Symphony, 58-59
Hill, Thomas, 56
HILL, WILLIAM J. ("BILLY") (1899-1940), 302
  Last Roundup, The, 302
  Wagon Wheels, 302
Hill of Dreams (Gruenberg), 150
Hindemith, Paul, 159, 249, 259, 346
Hip-Hip Hooray for the NRA (Siegmeister), 213
Hit the Deck (Youmans), 304
Hiver (Bloch), 120, 123
Hobson, Wilder, 290, 291, 293
Hochschule für Musik, 167
Hoffman, Hildegarde, 20
Hofmann, Josef, 42, 91, 325
HOLDEN, DAVID (1912), 213
  Chamber Music for Piano and Strings, 213
Holiday (Wessel), 195
Holidays (Ives), 245-246
Hollywood Bowl, 39, 50, 69, 204, 216, 274
Holywood Suite (Cadman), 50
Hollywood Suite (Grofé), 312
Holm, Hanya, 250
Holmes, Oliver, 335, 336
Homer, 65
Homer, Louise, 220
Homer, Sidney, 12
Home, Sweet Home, 244, 316

Hora Mystica (Loeffler), 117
Hora Novissima (Parker), 11
Horgan, Paul, 188
Horizons (Shepherd), 182-183
Horner Institute, 279
Horse Eats Hat, 226
Hotchkiss School, 86
Hot Mikado, The, 294
Hound of Heaven, The (Lockwood), 234
Hour of Delusion, An (Bennett), 314
House of Usher, The (Braine), 105
Howard, Eunice, 26
Howard, Leslie, 263
Howard, Sidney, 61
HOWE, MARY (1882), 193-194
  American Piece, 193
  Castellana, 193
  Chain Gang Song, 194
  Coulennes, 193
  Dirge, 193
  Fugue, 194
  Poema, 193
  Sand, 193
  Sonata, 193
  Spring Pastoral, 193
  Stars, 193
  String Quartet, 193
  Whimsy, 193
How Music Grew (Bauer & Peyser), 193
How Ya Gonna Keep 'em Down on the Farm? (Donaldson), 301
Hřimaly, Ottokar, 189
HRUBY, FRANK, 219
  Satirical Suite, 219
H_2O (McPhee), 190
Huber, Hans, 62
Hudson, W. H., 154
Hughes, Langston, 281
Humoresque, 35
Humperdinck, Engelbert, 65, 66, 73, 126, 128, 130
Humphrey, Doris, 144, 250
Huneker, James Gibbons, 113
Hunter College, 62, 202
HUSS, HENRY HOLDEN (1862), 20, 193
  Concerto for piano and orchestra, 20
  Nocturne, 20
  Rhapsody, 20

HUSS, HENRY HOLDEN (*Cont.*)
   Ride of Paul Revere, The, 20
   String Quartet in B minor, 20
Huss, John, 20
Hutcheson, Ernest, 83, 91, 193, 226, 324-325
Hyperprism (Varèse), 254, 256

I Believe in Miracles (Meyer), 302
Idyls of an Inland Sea (Terry), 74
I Found a Million Dollar Baby (Warren), 304
I Got Plenty o' Nuttin' (Gershwin), 310
I'll Be with You in Apple-blossom Time (A. Von Tilzer), 297
Illinois State Centennial, 67
I Love Life (Mana-Zucca), 104
Ilyinsky, Alexander Alexandrovich, 189
Imagery (Johnson), 99
I'm a Yankee Doodle Dandy (Cohan), 297
Impetuous Sonata (Pimsleur), 204
Impetuous Toccata and Fugal Fantasia (Pimsleur), 204
Impressionistic Suite (Rudin), 219
Impressions (Smith), 46
Impressions from a Greek Tragedy (Elkus), 199
Impressions from an Artist's Life (Schelling), 63
Impressions of the Wa-Wan Ceremony (Farwell), 131
Impromptu Appassionato (Terry), 74
In a Little Spanish Town (Wayne), 304
In Bohemia (Hadley), 25
INCH, HERBERT (1904), 202-203
   Divertimento, 203
   Mediterranean Sketches, 203
   Piano Concerto, 202
   Piano Sonata, 203
   Quintet, 203
   Serenade, 203
   Sonata, 203
   String Quartet, 203
   Suite, 203
   Symphony, 202
   To Silvanus, 202
   Variations on a Modal Theme, 203

Incidental Music for a Satirical Play (Strang), 252
Incredible Flutist, The (Piston), 160
Indianapolis Symphony Orchestra, 230
Indian Dances (Jacobi), 167
Indian Legend (Stringfield), 275
Indian Love-Call (Friml), 285
Indian Love Lyrics, 92
Indian Suite (MacDowell), 10
Indian Summer Idyl (McKinley), 109
Indy, Vincent d', 40, 86, 90, 162, 201, 206, 255
Inferno (Dante), 171
Information Please, 233
Injunction Granted, 263
In Old Virginia (Powell), 272
In Praise of Johnny Appleseed (Kubik), 218
Inscriptions (Whitman), 140-141
Institute of Folk Music, 275
Institute of Musical Art, 19, 75, 103, 107, 162, 163, 174, 275, 302, 324, 325
In Summer (Clapp), 61
Intégrales (Varèse), 256
International Composers' Guild, 190, 243, 252, 254, 255, 280, 326, 32
International Music Congress, 276
International Society for Contemporary Music, 104, 119, 170, 176, 184, 196, 227, 240, 243, 327-328, 389
International Society of Musicology, 119
In the American Manner (Johnson), 99
In the Still of the Night (Carmichael), 301
In the Still of the Night (C. Porter), 302
Introduction and Allegretto (A. L. Engel), 212
Introduction to a Speaker (Gaul), 72
Ionisation (Varèse), 256
Iowa, University of, 61
Irene (Tierney), 303
Irish Tune from County Derry (Grainger), 273
Irish Washerwoman, The (Sowerby), 82
Israel Symphony (Bloch), 120

INDEX

Ithaca Conservatory, 205
I'se Gwine to Alabamy, Oh!, 125
I've Got the Tune (Blitzstein), 264-265
IVES, CHARLES E. (1874), 183, 241, 242, 243-247, 250, 256, 328
   Cantatas, 247
   Concord Sonata, 246-247
   Holidays, 245-246
   New England Scenes, 247
   Overtures, 247
   Piano Sonata, 247
   String Quartet, 247
   Suites, 247
   Symphonies, 247
   Violin Sonata, 247
Ives, George E., 244
Ives & Myrick, 245
I Want a Girl (H. Von Tilzer), 297
I Want to Be Happy (Youmans), 304
I Wonder What's Become of Sally (Ager), 300

Jack and the Beanstalk (Gruenberg), 150, 153-154
Jackson, George Pullen, 277
JACOBI, FREDERICK (1891), 14, 167-169, 208
   Ave Rota, 169
   Cello Concerto, 169
   Indian Dances, 167
   Piano Concerto, 169
   Sabbath Evening Service, 169
   String Quartet, 168
   String Quartet on Indian Themes, 167
   Violin Concerto, 169
Jacobi, Irene, 169
Jadassohn, Salomon, 11, 21
Jagel, Frederick, 79
JAMES, DOROTHY (1901), 219
   Paolo and Francesca, 219
   Three Orchestral Fragments, 219
JAMES, PHILIP (1890), 171-174
   Bret Harte, 172-173
   General William Booth Enters Heaven, 173
   Judith, 173
   Kammersymphonie, 172
   Overture on French Noëls, 173
   Piano Quintet, 173

   Sea-Symphony, 173
   Song of the Night, 172
   Station WGZBX, 172
   String Quartet, 173
   Suite, 172, 173
Janssen, August, 95, 96
JANSSEN, WERNER (1899), 39, 94-97, 220
   Foster Suite, 94
   Louisiana Suite, 94, 96
   Miniature Fantasy on Popular American Melodies, 96
   New Year's Eve in New York, 94, 96
   Second String Quartet, 96-97
Japanese Nocturne (Eichheim), 199
Jaques-Dalcroze, Emile, 120
Jarnach, Philipp, 187
Java (Eichheim), 199
Jazettes (Gruenberg), 150
Jazz Concerto (Harling), 202
Jazz Concerto (Suesse), 313
Jazz Hot and Hybrid (Sargeant), 289
Jazz Poem (Thompson), 110
Jazz Studies (Hill), 57
Jazz Suite (Gruenberg), 150, 153
Jeanne d'Arc (MacKaye), 54
Jepson, Helen, 64
Jeux d'eau (Ravel), 128
Jeux de Timbres (Freed), 201
Jingle Jangle (McBride), 224
Jiranek, Aloys, 285
Joachim, Joseph, 116
Job (Converse), 54
Joe Clark Steps Out (Vardell), 219
John Brown (Finney), 228
John Brown's Body (Benét), 90, 233
John Brown's Song (Delaney), 233, 234
Johnny Appleseed (Herrmann), 212
Johnson, Edward, 34, 79
JOHNSON, FREDERICK AYRES (1876), 268, 269
   From the Plains, 269
   Piano Trios, 269
   Seeonee Wolves, The, 269
   Sonata, 269
   String Quartet, 269
JOHNSON, HORACE (1893), 98-99
   Astarte, 99
   Imagery, 99
   In the American Manner, 99

JOHNSON, HORACE (*Continued*)
  Joyance, 99
  Pirate, The, 98
  Streets of Florence, 99
  Three Cherry Trees, The, 98
  Thy Dark Hair, 98
  When Pierrot Sings, 98
JOHNSON, HUNTER (1906), 217, 218
  Andante, 218
  Concerto, 218
  Letter to the World, 218
  Piano Sonata, 218
  Prelude, 218
  Symphony, 218
JOHNSON, J. ROSAMOND (1873), 296-297
  Lift Every Voice and Sing, 297
JOHNSON, JAMES WELDON (1871–1939), 296-297
Johnston, Alva, 95
Jolson, Al, 306
Jonàs, Alberto, 191
Jones, Vincent, 318
Joseffy, Rafael, 13
Joseph and His Brethren (Josten), 177
JOSTEN, WERNER (1888), 176-178
  Batouala, 178
  Concerto Sacro, 177-178
  Endymion, 178
  Joseph and His Brethren, 177
  Jungle, 178
  Serenade, 178
  Symphonies, 178
Joyance (Johnson), 99
Juba Dance (Dett), 279
Judith (Chadwick), 11
Judith (James), 173
Juilliard, Frederic A., 324
Juilliard Foundation, 42, 98, 100, 101, 118, 158, 182, 199, 215, 216, 325, 328
Juilliard Publication Award, 377
Juilliard School of Music, 14, 83, 84, 100, 101, 102, 107, 153, 167, 172, 174, 177, 200, 208, 209, 210, 212, 213, 254, 258, 259, 313, 315, 324-325
Julius Caesar (Shakespeare), 265
June in January (Rainger), 302

Jungle (Josten), 178
Jungle Dance (A. L. Engel), 212
Juniata College, 30-31
Juon, Paul, 167
Jurgen (Taylor), 34

Kaintuck (Still), 281
Kalopin (Skilton), 269
Kammersymphonie (James), 172
Kammersymphonie (Weiss), 248
Kankakee River (Bacon), 188
Kansas, University of, 66, 268
Karma (Haubiel), 101
Katinka (Friml), 285
KEENAN, GERALD, 219
  Andante, Interlude, and Finale, 219
KELLER, HOMER, 219
  Serenade, 219
  Symphony, 219
Keller, Walter, 184
KELLEY, EDGAR STILLMAN (1857), 14-16, 106, 130, 202, 248, 269
  Aladdin, 15
  Alice in Wonderland, 15-16
  Gulliver, 15
  New England Symphony, 15
  Pilgrim's Progress, The, 16
  Pit and the Pendulum, The, 15
  Quintet, 16
  String Quartet, 16
KENNAN, KENT (1913), 217, 218
  Night Soliloquy, 218
Kent School, 170
KERN, JEROME (1885), 202, 289, 299-300, 340
  Cat and the Fiddle, The, 300
  Oh Boy, 300
  Sally, 300
  Showboat, 299-300
    Can't Help Lovin' that Man of Mine, 300
    My Bill, 300
    Old Man River, 300
    Why Do I Love You, 300
  Sunny, 300
  Sweet Adeline, 300
Kerr, Harrison, 341
Kilenyi, Edward, 306
Kindler, Hans, 43, 231
King of Babylon, The (Wessel), 195

INDEX

King's Henchman, The (Taylor), 27, 30, 31-32
KINNEY, GORDON, *219*
   Concert Piece, 219
Kipling, Rudyard, 65
Kirkpatrick, John, 247
Kirkpatrick, Ralph, 229
Kitten on the Keys (Confrey), 301
Klengel, Julius, 108
Klindworth, Karl, 66
Knee-High to a Grasshopper (Lane), 71
Kneisel, Franz, 105, 116
Kneisel Quartet, 42, 54, 105
Knorr, Iwan, 120
Knute Rockne (Grofé), 312
Kodály, Zoltán, 235
Koechlin, Charles, 206
Konzertstück (Ganz), 112
Korean Sketch (Eichheim), 199
Koussevitzky, Serge, 54, 58, 59, 76, 99, 138, 144, 149, 160, 177, 309, 342, 343, 344
KOUTZEN, BORIS (1901), *203*, 254
   Concerto, 203
   Solitude, 203
   Sonata, 203
   String Quartets, 203
   Symphonic Movement, 203
   Symphony, 203
   Trio, 203
   Valley Forge, 203
KRAMER, A. WALTER (1890), *103-104*
   Faltering Dusk, The, 104
   Last Hour, The, 104
   Symphonic Rhapsody, 104
   Symphonic Sketches, 104
Krazy Kat (Carpenter), 37, 306
Kreisler, Fritz, 63, 280
Křenek, Ernst, 346
Kreutzer, Rodolphe, 116
KROEGER, A. C., *219*
   Symphony in E flat, 219
Krupa, Gene, 293-294
Kubelik, Jan, 285
KUBIK, GAIL (1914), *218*
   In Praise of Johnny Appleseed, 218
Kummer, Frederic Arnold, 52
Kunitz, Luigi von, 48

KURTZ, EDWARD, *219*
   Scherzo, 219
Kwast, James, 273

Labor Stage, 303
Lady, Be Good (Gershwin), 306
Lady of the Evening (Berlin), 299
La Flesche, Francis, 48
La Guardia, Fiorello, 333
Lake at Evening, The (Griffes), 126
Lake Placid Club, 155
La La Lucille (Gershwin), 306
Lamb, The (Citkowitz), 227
Lambert, Alexander, 101-102
Lambert, Constant, 307, 308, 320
Lament for Beowulf, The (Hanson), 77
Lament for the Stolen (McDonald), 181
LA MONACA, JOSEPH, *219*
   Festival of Gauri, The, 219
LANDAU, IRVING, *219*
   Free Variations, 219
   Sinfonietta, 219
Landon Conservatory, 276
LANE, EASTWOOD, *71-72*
   Adirondack Sketches, 71
   Central Park Suite, 71
   Five American Dances, 71
   Fourth of July, 71
   Knee-High to a Grasshopper, 71
   Persimmon Pucker, 71
   Sea Burial, 71
   Sleepy Hollow, 71
Lang, Andrew, 98
Lang, Benjamin Johnson, 13
Lange, Hans, 69
Lanier, Nicholas, 271-272
Lanier, Sidney, 11
Last Hope (Gottschalk), 16
Last Hour, The (Kramer), 104
Last of the Mohicans (Allen), 197
Last Roundup, The (Billy Hill), 302
La Touche, John, 319
Laura Schirmer-Mapleson Opera Company, 24
Laurentia (Tuthill), 206
Laurent String Quartet, 59
LA VIOLETTE, WESLEY (1894), *184*
   Chorale, 184

LA VIOLETTE, WESLEY (*Cont.*)
  Collegiana, 184
  Concerto, 184
  Dedications, 184
  Nocturne, 184
  Octet, 184
  Osiris, 184
  Penetrella, 184
  Piano Concerto, 184
  Piano Quintet, 184
  Requiem, 184
  Shylock, 184
  String Quartets, 184
  Violin Sonatas, 184
Lazy Bones (Carmichael), 301
League of Composers, 87, 98, 104, 110, 119, 140, 149, 153, 154, 158, 160, 163, 168, 181, 185, 190, 197, 198, 204, 210, 215, 217, 224, 264, 281, 326-327, 385-387
Lefebvre, Channing, 173
Légende Symphonique (Schelling), 63
Legend of Hani, The (Hadley), 25
Legend of John Henry, The (Stringfield), 275-276
Leggenda Sinfonica (Steinert), 206
Lehar, Franz, 285
Leichtentritt, Hugo, 205
LEIDZEN, ERIK, 219
  Fugue with Chorale, 219
Leipzig Conservatory, 52, 312
Leipzig Symphony Orchestra, 76
Leland Stanford University, 252
Lenox Avenue (Still), 281
Lento Molto (Copland), 149
Leper, The (M. Moore), 73
Leschetizky, Theodor, 62, 69, 156, 272
Let 'Em Eat Cake (Gershwin), 306
Letter to the World (Johnson), 218
LEVANT, OSCAR (1906), 233
  Nocturne, 233
  Piano Concerto, 233
  String Quartet, 233
Lewis, Meade ("Lux"), 294
Lewis, Sinclair, 88
Lewisohn, Irene, 158
Lewisohn Stadium, 131, 197
Lhévinne, Josef, 91, 101, 196, 200
Libation Bearers (Weiss), 248
Library of Congress, 38, 39, 47, 96, 118, 119, 171, 185, 193, 211

See also Coolidge Foundation
Lido, The (Cella), 107
Liebling, Emil, 276
Liebling, Leonard, 231
LIEURANCE, THURLOW (1878), 269-270
  By the Waters of Minnetonka, 270
  Drama of the Yellowstone, 270
Life of Man (Becker), 183
Lift Every Voice and Sing (Johnson & Johnson), 297
Light from St. Agnes (Harling), 202
Lilacs (Hill), 57
Lilacs (Lowell), 57
Lilienthal, Abraham W., 235, 248
Liliom (Molnar), 34
Lilly, Josiah K., 71
Lincoln, Abraham, 14, 44, 67, 133, 244
Lincoln Symphony, A (Mason), 43-44, 283
Lindbergh, Charles E., 21, 181
Lindsay, Vachel, 88, 173, 218
List, Eugene, 192
Listemann, Bernhard, 116
Litchfield County Festival, 125
Little Nellie Kelly (Cohan), 297
Little Show, The, 303
Little Story (Weiner), 219
Little Symphony, A (Eppert), 194
Little Symphony in G (Sanders), 101, 229-230
Livery Stable Blues, 305
Living Newspaper, 263
Ljungberg, Goeta, 79
Loache, Benjamin de, 189
Locandiera, La (Goldoni), 184
LOCKWOOD, NORMAND (1906), 234
  Drum Taps, 234
  Hound of Heaven, The, 234
  Out of the Cradle Endlessly Rocking, 234
  Quintet, 234
  Requiem, 234
  Symphony, 234
Loeb Prize, 105
LOEFFLER, CHARLES MARTIN (1861-1935), 20, 107, 115-118, 129, 206, 344
  Bonne Chanson, La, 118
  By the Rivers of Babylon, 118

INDEX

Canticum Fratris Solis, 117-118
Cornemuse, La, 118
Divertimento, 117
Étang, L', 118
Evocation, 118
Fantastic Concerto, 117
For One Who Fell in Battle, 118
Hora Mystica, 117
Memories of My Childhood, 118
Mort de Tintagiles, La, 117
Music for Four String Instruments, 117
Pagan Poem, 117
Partita, 118
Symphonic Fantasy, 117
Veillées de l'Ukraine, Les, 117
Villanelle du Diable, La, 118
Lomax, Alan, 240, 277
Lomax, John, 240, 277
Longfellow, Henry Wadsworth, 70
LOOMIS, CLARENCE (1888), 70-71
Fall of the House of Usher, The, 71
Susannah, Don't You Cry, 71
Yolanda of Cyprus, 70-71
LOOMIS, HARVEY WORTHINGTON (1865-1930), 130, *269*
Lyrics of the Red Man, 269
Lorna Doone Suite (Nevin), 66
Los Angeles *Examiner,* 157
Los Angeles Symphony Orchestra, 138, 157, 312
Lotos Eaters, The (Read), 215
Louise (Charpentier), 124
Louisiana Purchase (Berlin), 299
Louisiana Suite (Janssen), 94, 96
Lover Come Back to Me (Romberg), 285
Lowell, Amy, 57
Luboschutz, Pierre, 209
Lucedia (Giannini), 208
Lucia di Lammermoor (Donizetti), 68
Lucifer (Hadley), 25
Lucky Lindy, 21
Lucrece (Taylor), 35
LUENING, OTTO (1900), *186-187*, 188, 225
Americana, 187
Concertino, 187
Dirge, 187
Divertimento, 187
Evangeline, 187

Piano Sonata, 187
Prelude to a Hymn-tune, 187
Quartets, 187
Sextet, 187
Suite, 187
Symphonic Interludes, 187
Symphonic Poems, 186-187
Symphonietta, 187
Luther College, 75
Lux Aeterna (Hanson), 76
Lyric Cycle (Brant), 260
Lyrics of the Red Man (H. W. Loomis), 269
Lysistrata (Brunswick), 232

Macbeth (Bloch), 120, 121
Macbeth (Shakespeare), 263
MacDOWELL, EDWARD (1861-1908), 4, *10-11,* 20, 21-22, 115, 124
Indian Suite, 10
Second Piano Concerto, 10
MacDowell, Mrs. Edward, 325-326
MacDowell Club, 202
MacDowell Colony, 325-326
MacDowell Festival, 31
MacDowell Memorial Association, 126
Machine Age Blues (McKay), 204
MacKaye, Percy, 54, 131
MacKOWN, MARJORIE T., *219*
Piano Quartet, 219
Theme and Variations, 219
MacLeod, Fiona, 128
Madrigal Singers, 212
Maeterlinck, Maurice, 117
MAGANINI, QUINTO (1897), *102-103*
Argonauts, The, 103
Cuban Rhapsody, 103
Ornithological Suite, 103
South Wind, 103
Sylvan Symphony, 103
Tuolumne, 103
Mahler, Gustav, 255
Malibran, Maria, 315-316
Malipiero, G. Francesco, 129, 202, 227
MANA-ZUCCA (1890), *104*
Big Brown Bear, The, 104
I Love Life, 104
Piano Concerto, 104

MANA-ZUCCA (*Continued*)
  Rachem, 104
  Sonata, 104
Mandyczewski, Eusebius, 24
Manhattan Symphony Orchestra, 24, 26, 88
Man I Love, The (Gershwin), 306
Mannes, David, 88, 131
Mannes (David) Music School, 53, 103, 121
Mannheim Conservatory, 52
Mannone, "Wingy," 294
Manual of Harmonic Technic, Based on the Practice of J. S. Bach (Tweedy), 61
Manuscript Society of New York, 24
Man Without a Country, The (Damrosch), 17, 283
March (Bennett), 317
March of Time, 261
Marco's Millions (O'Neill), 158-159
Mardi Gras (J. Beach), 129
Maria Malibran (Bennett), 315-317
Marie from Sunny Italy (Berlin), 298
Marlowe, Christopher, 226
Marriage of Aude, The (Rogers), 98
Marriage with Space, A (Becker), 183
Mars Ascending (Haubiel), 101
Mary Is a Grand Old Name (Cohan), 297
Mary Poppins Suite (Browning), 104
Mary Rose (Barrie), 269
Mask of the Red Death (Poe), 165
MASON, DANIEL GREGORY (1873), 40-45, 46, 86, 200, 283, 340
  Chanticleer, 42
  Country Pictures, 42
  Divertimento, 44-45
  Fanny Blair, 42
  Festival Overture, 42
  Free and Easy Five-Step, 45
  Lincoln Symphony, A, 43-44, 283
  Prelude and Fugue, 42-43
  Russians, 42
  Sentimental Sketches, 45
  Serenade, 45
  String Quartet on Negro Themes, 42
  Suite after English Folk-Songs, 43
  Variations on a Theme by John Powell, 42

Mason, Henry, 40
Mason, Lowell, 40
Mason, Stuart, 61, 108
Mason, William, 40
Mason & Hamlin, 40
Masque of the Red Death (Van Vactor), 232
Masquerade (McKinley), 109
Massachusetts Institute of Technology, 130
Massachusetts School of Art, 160
Massart, Joseph Lambert, 116
Masse Mensch (Finney), 228
Massenet, Jules, 28, 65
Mathematical Basis of the Arts, The (Schillinger), 240
Mathias, Georges Amadée St. Claire, 62
Mattfeld, Julius, 328
Maybe (Gershwin), 306
May Day (Siegmeister), 213
Maynor, Dorothy, 198, 278
Maypole Lovers, The (R. Cole), 67
Maytime (Romberg), 285
McBRIDE, ROBERT GUYN (1911), 224-225
  Depression, 225
  Fugato on a Well-Known Theme, 224
  Go Choruses, 224
  Jingle Jangle, 224
  Mexican Rhapsody, 225
  Prelude and Fugue, 225
  Prelude to a Tragedy, 224-225
  Show Piece, 225
  Swing Stuff, 224
  Wise-Apple Five, 225
  Workout, 224
McCOLL, HUGH, 219
  Romantic Suite in Form of Variations, 219
McCOLLIN, FRANCES (1892), 74
  Adagio, 74
  Piano Quintet, 74
  Scherzo, 74
  Spring in Heaven, 74
  String Quartet, 74
  Trio, 74
McCormack, John, 49
McCoy, Bessie, 30

INDEX

McDONALD, HARL (1899), 179-181
  Concerto, 181
  Festival of the Workers, 181
  Fourth Symphony, 180-181
  Hebraic Poems, 179
  Lament for the Stolen, 181
  Miniature Suite, 181
  Mojave, 179
  Piano Concerto, 179
  Rhumba Symphony, 180
  San Juan Capistrano, 181
  Santa Fe Trail, 180
  Songs of Conquest, 179, 181
  String Quartets, 179, 181
  Third Symphony, 180
  Tragic Cycle, 181
  Trios, 181
McGill University, 259
McHOSE, IRVINE, 218
  Concerto, 218
McKAY, GEORGE (1899), 203-204
  Epoch, 204
  Fantasy on a Western Folksong, 203-204
  Harbor Narrative, 204
  Machine Age Blues, 204
  Sinfoniettas, 204
  Symphonic Prelude in American Idiom, 204
McKINLEY, CARL (1895), 109
  Indian Summer Idyl, 109
  Masquerade, 109
McPHEE, COLIN (1901), 189-190, 328
  Bali, 190
  Balinese Ceremonial Music, 190
  Concerto, 190
  From the Revelation of St. John the Divine, 190
  H_2O, 190
  Mechanical Principles, 190
  Sarabande, 190
  Sonatina, 190
  Symphony, 190
Mechanical Principles (McPhee), 190
Medea (A. L. Engel), 212
Medieval Poem (Sowerby), 82
Méditation hébraïque (Bloch), 120
Mediterranean Sketches (Inch), 203
Mediterranean Suite (Fuleihan), 191

Meistersinger, Die (Wagner), 295
Melodia (Bowles), 227
Memories of France (Bingham), 90
Memories of My Childhood (Loeffler), 118
Memphis Blues (Handy), 293
Memphis College of Music, 206
Men and Mountains (Ruggles), 243
Mencken, Henry Louis, 111
Mendel, Arthur, 134, 143, 145
Mendelssohn-Bartholdy, Felix, 245
Mendelssohn Club, 181
Mendelssohn Mows 'em Down (Templeton), 303
Mengelberg, Willem, 63, 105, 175, 176
MENOTTI, GIAN-CARLO (1911), 220, 221-223
  Amelia al Ballo, 222, 223
  Old Maid and the Thief, The, 223
  Pastorale, 223
  Variations on a Theme of Robert Schumann, 223
Mercury Theater, 265
Merry Mount (Hanson), 45, 66, 77-80
Merry Mount (Smith), 45-46
Metamorphoses (Godowsky), 113
Metropolitan Opera Company, 11, 17, 24, 30, 32, 66, 77, 216
Metropolitan Opera House, 17, 19, 31, 34, 37, 48, 53, 64, 79, 125, 150, 167, 222, 252
Metropolitan Opera Orchestra, 102, 312
Mexican Rhapsody (McBride), 225
MEYER, GEORGE (1884), 302
  For Me and My Gal, 302
  I Believe in Miracles, 302
Michigan, University of, 218, 234
Michigan State College, 131
Middelschulte, Wilhelm, 67, 68, 183
Middlebury College, 205
Midnight Special (Bacon), 188
Milda (Allen), 197
Milhaud, Darius, 235, 346
Millay, Edna St. Vincent, 31
Miller, Gilbert, 35
Miller, Joaquin, 50
Mills Music, 344
Milwaukee Civic Orchestra, 194

Milwaukee Symphony Orchestra, 194
Miniature Fantasy on Popular American Melodies (Janssen), 96
Miniature Suite (McDonald), 181
Miniature Suite (Nevin), 66
Minneapolis Symphony Orchestra, 210, 216
Minnehaha's Vision (Busch), 70
Minnesota, University of, 129
Minotaur, The (Naginski), 213
Miragia (Barth), 239
Mirandolina (Wald), 184
Mirrorrorrim (Strang), 252
Mission Road, The (Bornschein), 72
Mississippi Suite (Grofé), 312
Miss O'Grady (Brant), 260
Mitropoulos, Dimitri, 121, 216
Moanin' Low (Rainger), 302
Moby Dick (Herrmann), 211-212, 283
Moby Dick (D. Moore), 87
Moby Dick Suite (Claflin), 198
Mock Morris (Grainger), 273
Modern Music, 143, 164, 263, 314, 327
Moeller, Philip, 155
Moiseivitsch, Benno, 91
Mojave (McDonald), 179
Mole, Milfred, 294
Molly on the Shore (Grainger), 273
Mona (Parker), 11
Mon Ami Pierrot (S. Barlow), 94
Money Musk (Sowerby), 82
Monte Carlo Quartet, 94
Monteux, Pierre, 158, 235, 248, 343-344
Monteverdi, Claudio, 175, 177
Mood Indigo (Ellington), 292
Moods of the Moonshiner (Stringfield), 275
Moon Trail, The (Whithorne), 156, 157
MOORE, DOUGLAS (1893), 41, 85-90, 283
 Devil and Daniel Webster, The, 88-90
 Four Museum Pieces, 86
 Headless Horseman, The, 88
 Moby Dick, 87
 Overture on an American Theme, 88
 Pageant of P. T. Barnum, The, 86-87, 283
 Quartet, 88
 Simon Legree, 88
 Symphony of Autumn, 85, 87
 Violin and Piano Sonata, 87
 White Wings, 88
MOORE, MARY CARR (1873), 73
 Davide Rizzio, 73
 Leper, The, 73
 Narcissa, 73
 Oracle, The, 73
 Rubios, Los, 73
More than You Know (Youmans), 304
Morocco (Schelling), 63
MOROSO, JEROME (1913), 213
 Paean's Biguine, 213
 Symphony, 213
 Tall Story, 213
MORRIS, HAROLD (1890), 99-101
 Piano Concerto, 99-100
 Piano Sonata, 100
 Quartet for violin, piano, cello, and flute, 100
 Quintet, 100
 String Quartets, 100
 Symphonic Poem after Tagore's *Gitanjali*, 100
 Symphony after Browning's *Prospice*, 100
 Violin and Piano Sonata, 100
 Violin Concerto, 100-101
Mort de Tintagiles, La (Loeffler), 117
Morton, Thomas, 77, 78, 79
Moscow Conservatory, 165
Moscow Imperial Opera Orchestra, 189
Moszkowski, Moritz, 62
Mother of Men (Bingham), 90
Mountain Pictures (C. Burleigh), 52
Mountain Song (Farwell), 131
MOURANT, WALTER, 219
 Five Inhibitions, 219
 Three Dances, 219
Moussorgsky, Modest, 28, 79, 120
Moyse, Marcel, 232
Mozart, Wolfgang Amadeus, 175, 222, 286
Mozart Clarinet Quintet, 293
Mozarteum Academy, 225
Mozart Sinfonietta, 51
Muck, Karl, 63, 121, 255
Munich Opera House, 177
Municipal Theatre (Freiburg), 64

INDEX

Murder in the Cathedral (Eliot), 212
Musical America, 30, 43, 55, 58-59, 67, 69, 73, 97, 104, 108, 118, 123, 154, 159, 166, 173, 182, 220, 262, 314
Musical Courier, 57, 78, 99, 166, 257, 258
Musical Leader, 193
Musical Quarterly, The, 119, 132
Music for a Scene from Shelley (Barber), 220
Music for Chamber Orchestra (Etler), 218
Music for Four String Instruments (Loeffler), 117
Music for Radio (Copland), 146-147
Music for the Theatre (Copland), 149, 150
Musicians' Emergency Fund, 93
Music of Our Day (Saminsky), 167
Music of the Ghetto and the Bible (Saminsky), 167
Music Publishers' Protective Association, 342
Music School Settlement, 131
Music School Settlement for Colored People, 296
Music Since 1900 (Slonimsky), 257
Music Through the Ages (Bauer & Peyser), 193
My Bill (Kern), 300
My Blue Heaven (Donaldson), 301
My Country (Wilson), 14
My Mammy (Donaldson), 301
My One and Only (Gershwin), 306
My River (Bacon), 188
My Sin (Henderson), 302
Mystic Trumpeter (Bornschein), 72
Mystic Trumpeter, The (Converse), 54
My Wife's Gone to the Country (Berlin), 299

Nacht, Die (Strong), 21
NAGINSKI, CHARLES (1909-1940), *213-214*
  Children's Suite, 213
  Minotaur, The, 213
  Sinfonietta, 213-214
Naïve Landscapes (J. Beach), 129
Naples Conservatory, 235

Narcissa (M. Moore), 73
Natchez on the Hill (Powell), 271
Nation, The, 134
National Association for American Composers and Conductors, 23, 26, 342
National Association for the Advancement of Colored People, 296
National Association of Broadcasters, 337
National Broadcasting Company, 21, 24, 51, 90, 101, 105, 149, 155, 158, 172, 184, 194, 200, 203, 204, 221, 223, 235, 269, 318, 328, 378
National Committee for Music Appreciation, 144
National Conservatory of Music, 13, 19, 278
National Federation of Music Clubs, 20, 25, 31, 72, 74, 100, 182, 201, 313, 388
National Institute of Arts and Letters, 174
National Music Camp, 214
National Orchestral Association, 191-192, 203, 209, 235
National Symphony Orchestra of Washington, 172, 193, 231
Naumburg Fellowship, 109
Navajo War Dance (Farwell), 131
Navrátil, Karl, 272
NBC
  —See National Broadcasting Company
Negro Folk Symphony No. 1 (Dawson), 279
Negro Heaven (Cesana), 318
Negro Parade (Stringfield), 276
Negro Rhapsody (Gilbert), 125
Negro Rhapsody (Goldmark), 14
Negro Rhapsody (C. C. White), 280
Neighborhood Playhouse, 158, 191
NELSON, ROBERT, *219*
  Ballet Suite, 219
Nelson, Stanley R., 306-307
Nelson's Loose-Leaf Encyclopaedia, 30
Nemenoff, Genia, 209
NEVIN, ARTHUR (1871), *65-66*
  Arizona, 66
  Lorna Doone Suite, 66

NEVIN, ARTHUR (*Continued*)
  Miniature Suite, 66
  Poia, 65
  Springs of Saratoga, 66
  String Quartet in D minor, 66
  Symphonic Poem, 66
  Twilight, 66
Nevin, Ethelbert, 4, 40, 48, 65
New Amsterdam Theatre, 222
New Chamber Music Orchestra, 211
New England Conservatory of Music, 11, 12, 22, 24, 25, 56, 65, 108, 109, 124, 129, 162, 182, 194, 205
New England Prelude (Gaul), 72
New England Scenes (Ives), 247
New England Symphony (Kelley), 15
New Freeman, 242
New Jersey Orchestra, 172
New Moon (Romberg), 285
New Music, 163, 190, 213, 215, 236, 329
New Musical Resources (Cowell), 250
New Music Publications, 249, 250, 252, 260
New Music Quarterly Recordings, 249, 329
New Music School, 215
New Music Society, 251, 252, 329
New Music Workshops, 251
New Russia (Gardner), 105
New School for Social Research, 147, 229, 241, 250
New Singers, 227
New Symphony Orchestra, 255
New World Symphony (Dvořák), 6, 278-279
New Year's Eve in New York (Janssen), 94, 96
New York Board of Education, 93
New York Chamber Music Society, 31, 82
New York City Symphony Orchestra, 234
New York Civic Orchestra, 66, 229
New York College of Music, 200
New York Community Chorus, 93
New York Days and Nights (Whithorne), 156
New Yorker, The, 95, 315

New York Herald Tribune, 30, 32, 51, 59, 77, 85, 96, 102, 222, 224, 247, 264, 343
New York High School of Music and Art, 215, 333-334
New York Männergesangverein, 18
New York Oratorio Society, 18
New York Orchestra, 50
New York Philharmonic-Symphony Chamber Orchestra, 229
New York Philharmonic-Symphony Society, 18, 19, 21, 24, 27, 39, 42, 43, 50, 51, 62, 63, 92, 95, 97, 98, 101, 103, 105, 107, 109, 112, 135, 148, 157, 162, 166, 172, 173, 175, 176, 185, 189, 191, 192, 195, 196, 197, 211, 214, 216, 220, 221, 224, 226, 229, 230, 231, 248, 271, 281, 318, 343, 344
New York State Theodore Roosevelt Committee, 208
New York Symphony Society, 81, 102, 103, 149, 189, 285, 307
New York Telegraph, 255
New York Times, 65, 122, 229, 255, 282, 310
New York University, 29, 30, 84, 172, 193, 273, 318, 346
New York Women's Symphony Orchestra, 172
New York World, 30
New York World's Fair, 280, 294, 317
New York World-Telegram, 66
Nichols, Loring ("Red"), 294
Nicholson, N., 298
Niedermayr, Otto, 232
Nigger Mike's, 298
Night and Day (C. Porter), 302
Night Clouds (Wynn), 219
Nightfall (Griffes), 128
Night in Old Paris, A (Hadley), 24
Night-Piece (A. Foote), 13
Night Soliloquy (Kennan), 218
Nikisch, Artur, 108
Niles, John Jacob, 276-277
1929—A Satire (Smith), 46
Nobody Knows the Trouble I've Seen (C. C. White), 280
Nocturne (Huss), 20
Nocturne (Stringham), 107

INDEX

Nocturne and Dance of the Fates (Ornstein), 204
Noelte, Albert, 230, 232
No for an Answer (Blitzstein), 265
No, No, Nanette (Youmans), 304
Nordic Symphony (Hanson), 76
NORDOFF, PAUL (1909), 14, 209-210
    Concerto, 210
    Piano Concerto, 210
    Piano Quintet, 210
    Prelude and Three Fugues, 210
    Prelude and Variations, 209
    Secular Mass, 209-210
    Sonata, 210
    String Quartets, 210
    Triptych, 210
Norfolk Festival, 25, 46
Norge (Clapp), 61
North and West (Hanson), 76
North Carolina, University of, 275
North Carolina Symphony Orchestra, 275
North, East, South, and West (Hadley), 25
North Shore Festival, 281
Northwestern Conservatory, 129
Northwestern University, 69, 75, 187, 195, 196, 214, 227, 230, 232
Notre Dame University, 183
Notturno (Stringham), 107
Novelty Piano Playing (Confrey), 301
Noyes, Alfred, 63
Nuit Méridionale (Steinert), 206

Oberlaender Trust, 75
Oberlin Conservatory, 234, 280
Obongo, Dance Primitive (Becker), 183
O Captain, My Captain (Whitman), 17
O'Casey, Sean, 212
Ocean, The (Hadley), 25
Octandre (Varèse), 256
Ode to the Star-Spangled Banner (Grofé), 312
Oedipus Rex (Sophocles), 258
Oehmler, Leo, 48
Offrandes (Varèse), 254, 256
Of Men and Music (Taylor), 30
Of Mice and Men (Steinbeck), 150

Of Thee I Sing (Gershwin), 306
Oh Boy (Kern), 300
Oh, de Lawd Shake de Heaven (Gershwin), 310
Oh, How I Hate to Get Up in the Morning (Berlin), 299
Oh, Kay (Gershwin), 306
OLDBERG, ARNE (1874), 69-70
    First Piano Concerto, 70
    Piano Sonata, 70
    Sea, The, 69-70
    Second Piano Concerto, 69
    String Quartet, 70
Old Black Joe (Foster), 267
Old Chisholm Trail, The, 182
Old Hundred, 122
Old Maid and the Thief, The (Menotti), 223
Old Man River (Kern), 300
Old Ship of Zion, 125
Old Song Re-Sung, An (Griffes), 128
Oliver, Joe ("King"), 293, 294
O Munasterio (Allen), 197
On a Transatlantic Liner (Cella), 107
Once in a Blue Moon, 258
One Big Union for Two (Rome), 303
O'Neill, Eugene, 151, 190
One Tenth of a Nation, 144-145
O No, John, 43
On Your Toes (Rodgers & Hart), 302
Opéra-Comique (Paris), 22, 94
Oracle, The (M. Moore), 73
Oratorio Society of New York, 84, 279
Orchestral Variations on *Deep River* and *Water Boy* (Herrmann), 211
Ordering of Moses (Dett), 279
Oriental Impressions (Eichheim), 199
Oriental Rhapsody (Cadman), 49-50
Orlando Furioso (Giorni), 201
Orleans Alley (J. Beach), 129
Ormandy, Eugene, 181, 209, 210
Ormazd (Converse), 54
Ornithological Suite (Maganini), 103
ORNSTEIN, LEO (1895), 91, 204, 327
    À la Chinoise, 204
    Cello Sonata, 204
    Nocturne and Dance of the Fates, 204
    Piano Concerto, 204
    Piano Sonata, 204

ORNSTEIN, LEO (*Continued*)
  Quartet, 204
  Quintet, 204
  Sonata, 204
  Wild Men's Dance, The, 204
Osiris (La Violette), 184
Othello (Hadley), 25
Ouanga (C. C. White), 280
Our American Music (Howard), 300
Ouranos (Rudhyar), 253
Our Town, 150
Outdoor Overture (Copland), 149
Outline of Piano Pedagogy (Rubinstein), 102
Outlook, The, 197
Out of the Cradle Endlessly Rocking (Lockwood), 234
Out of the Gay Nineties (Fickenscher), 240
Ouverture Joyeuse (Shepherd), 182
Over There (Cohan), 297
Overture "1849" (Wilson), 14
Overture on an American Theme (D. Moore), 88
Overture on French Noëls (James), 173
Overture on Negro Themes (Dunn), 21
Overture to a Comedy (Van Vactor), 232
Overture to the Piper (Ballantine), 60
Overture to *The School for Scandal* (Barber), 220
Ozarka (Busch), 70

Pachmann, Vladimir de, 235
Pack Up Your Sins (Berlin), 299
Paderewski, Ignace Jan, 62, 63
Paderewski Prize, 25, 182, 196, 233, 249
Paeans (Moroso), 213
Paean to the Great Thunder (Rudhyar), 253
Pagan Festival (White), 195
Pagan Poem (Loeffler), 117
Pageant of Autumn (Sowerby), 82
Pageant of P. T. Barnum, The (D. Moore), 86-87, 283
Pageant Play (Parker), 130
Paging Danger, 104

Paine, John Knowles, 4, 11, 13, 35, 40, 55, 56
Painted Desert, The (Read), 215
Palestrina, Giovanni Pierluigi da, 175
Pall Mall Gazette, 156
PALMER, ROBERT, 219
  Poem, 219
Palmgren, Selim, 203
Pan (Bauer), 192
Panama Hattie (C. Porter), 302
Panama Hymn (Mrs. Beach), 16
Panama-Pacific Exposition, 16
Pan American Association of Composers, 190, 249, 250, 254, 255, 257, 259, 328-329
Pan and the Priest (Hanson), 76
Pantomime Symphony (Barth), 239
Paoli, Domenico de, 164, 166
Paolo and Francesca (James), 219
Paramount Studios, 202, 213
Paris (Glick), 219
Paris Conservatoire, 62, 253, 255
Parker, Henry Taylor, 99-100, 138
PARKER, HORATIO (1863-1919), 10-11, 12, 45, 86, 90, 108, 162, 170, 244, 325
  Hora Novissima, 11
  Mona, 11
Parker, Louis, 130
Park Theatre, 315
Parsifal (Wagner), 19
Partita (Loeffler), 118
Pasadena Music and Arts Association, 136
Pasdeloup Orchestra, 116
Passacaglia and Fugue (Baum), 218
Passacaglia, Interlude and Fugue (Sowerby), 82
Passepied (Rubinstein), 102
Passing of Arthur, The (Busch), 70
Passing of Summer, The (R. Cole), 67
Passing Show (Romberg), 285
Pastoral (Haubiel), 101
Pastorale (Heller), 106
Pastorale (Menotti), 223
Pastorale (Rogers), 98
Pastorales (Freed), 201
Patterns (Carpenter), 39
Pawnee Horses (Farwell), 131
Payne, John Knowles, 316
Paysage (Bennett), 314

INDEX

Peabody Conservatory of Music, 52, 53, 72, 178, 197, 198
Peaceable Kingdom, The (Thompson), 110-111
Pelléas et Mélisande (Debussy), 28, 155, 262
Penetrella (La Violette), 184
Penn, William, 111
Pennsylvania, University of, 179, 201, 264
Pentacle (Salzedo), 253
People's Philharmonic Choral Society, 226
People, Yes, The (Robinson), 319
Père Marquette (Gaul), 72
Perkins, Francis D., 51, 59, 171, 185, 209, 210, 211-212, 221, 222, 223, 231, 234, 343
Persian Fable, A (Griffis), 109
Persimmon Pucker (Lane), 71
Persin, 225
Pervigilium Veneris (Spelman), 206
Peter Ibbetson (Taylor), 28, 29, 30, 32-34
Pettis, Ashley, 332
Peyser, Ethel R., 193
Peyser, Herbert, 65
Pfitzner, Hans Erich, 130
Phantom Satyr (J. Beach), 129
Philadelphia Chamber String Sinfonietta, 223, 229
Philadelphia Conservatory of Music, 201, 203, 210
Philadelphia Orchestra, 21, 42, 43, 54, 91, 92, 94, 107, 109, 112, 148, 155, 160, 172, 174, 177, 179, 180, 181, 188, 189, 195, 199, 203, 210, 217, 226, 235, 249, 279, 281, 318
Philadelphia String Sinfonietta, 189
Philipp, Isidor, 93, 190
PHILLIPS, BURRILL (1907), 216-217
  Concert Piece, 217
  Courthouse Square, 217
  Dance, 217
  Grotesque Dance from a Projected Ballet, 217
  Piano Concerto, 217
  Play Ball, 217
  Princess and Puppet, 217
  Selections from McGuffey's Reader, 216-217
  String Quartet, 217
  Symphony Concertante, 217
Phobias (A. L. Engel), 212
Piatigorsky, Gregor, 185
Pierrot and Cothurnus (Thompson), 110
Pierrot of the Minute (A. L. Engel), 212
Pilgrims of Destiny (Branscombe), 73
Pilgrim's Progress, The (Kelley), 16
PIMSLEUR, SOLOMON (1900), 204
  Dynamic Overture, 204
  Fiery Sonata, 204
  Impetuous Sonata, 204
  Impetuous Toccata and Fugal Fantasia, 204
  Symphonic Ballade, 204
Pins and Needles, 303
Pioneer (R. Cole), 67
Pioneer, The (Eppert), 194
Pioneer America (Bingham), 90
Pioneer Saga (Bergsma), 218
Pipe of Desire, The (Converse), 53
Piper at the Gates of Dawn, The (Thompson), 110
Pippa's Holliday (J. Beach), 129
Pirate, The (Johnson), 98
Pirate Song (Gilbert), 126
PISTON, WALTER (1894), 159-161
  Concertino, 160
  Concerto, 159, 160
  First Symphony, 160
  Incredible Flutist, The, 160
  Prelude and Fugue, 160
  Sonata, 161
  String Quartet, 160
  Suite, 159-160
  Symphonic Piece, 160
  Three Pieces, 160-161
  Trio, 161
Pit and the Pendulum, The (Kelley), 15
Pittsfield Festival, 199
Plainsman, The, 258
Play Ball (Phillips), 217
Play of Words, The (Van Vactor), 232
Pleasure Dome of Kubla Khan, The (Griffes), 127, 128

Plow That Broke the Plains, The, 263
Poe, Edgar Allan, 57, 71, 118, 165, 166, 189
Poem (J. Beach), 129
Poem (Griffes), 127-128
Poem (Harris), 145
Poem (Palmer), 219
Poem (Whithorne), 157
Poem (Woltmann), 216
Poema (Howe), 193
Poem and Dance (Q. Porter), 161
Poèmes Ironiques (Rudhyar), 252
Poia (Nevin), 65
Polyphonica (Cowell), 251
Pomp and Circumstance (Elgar), 305
Pons, Lily, 63
Pool of Pegasus, The (Woltmann), 216
Poor Buttermilk (Confrey), 301
Pop Goes the Weasel, 122
Porgy and Bess (Gershwin), 309-311
Portals (Ruggles), 243
PORTER, COLE (1892), 302
   Begin the Beguine, 302
   Get Out of Town, 302
   In the Still of the Night, 302
   Night and Day, 302
   Panama Hattie, 302
   Rosalie, 302
   What Is This Thing Called Love?, 302
PORTER, QUINCY (1897), 39, 56, *161-162*
   Dance in Three-Time, 162
   First Symphony, 161-162
   Poem and Dance, 161
   Sonatas, 161
   String Quartets, 161
   Suite in C minor, 161
   Two Dances for Radio, 162
   Ukrainian Suite, 161
Portrait of a Lady, The (Taylor), 31, 34
Posselt, Ruth, 59, 160
Postponeless Creature, The (Bacon), 188
POWELL, JOHN (1882), 42, 125, 270-272, 276, 340
   At the Fair, 272
   In Old Virginia, 272
   Piano Concerto, 272

Rhapsodie Nègre, 125, 272
Set of Three, A, 270-271
Sonata Noble, 272
Sonate Virginianesque, 272
Symphony in A, 272
Powell, John Henry, 271
Prague Conservatory, 204
Prairie (Sowerby), 80-81
Préambule et Jeux (Salzedo), 253-254
Preface to a Child's Storybook (Fuleihan), 191
Prelude (Weiner), 219
Prelude and Fugue (Mason), 42-43
Prelude and Three Fugues (Nordoff), 210
Prelude for a Drama (Finney), 228
Prelude on a Gregorian Theme (Gleason), 218
Prelude to a Hymn-tune (Luening), 187
Prelude to a Tragedy (McBride), 224-225
Prelude to Hamlet (Rogers), 98
Pretty Girl Is Like a Melody, A (Berlin), 299
Prince Hal (Smith), 46
Princess and Puppet (Phillips), 217
Princeton Glee Club, 88, 190
Princeton University, 170
Principles of Harmonic Analysis (Piston), 161
Printemps (Bloch), 120, 123
Private Life of Helen of Troy, The (Erskine), 102
Pro Arte Quartet, 168
Proem Press, 216
Prometheus Bound (Bauer), 192
Prometheus Unbound (Shelley), 220
Pro Musica, 254
Prophecy (Converse), 55
Prospice (Browning), 100
Pruckner, Dionys, 62
Psalm for Orchestra (Diamond), 215
Psalms (Bloch), 120
Public Works Administration, 331
Puccini, Giacomo, 32, 33, 65, 222, 258
Pueblo—A Moon Rhapsody (Saminsky), 166
Pugno, Raoul, 193
Pulitzer Scholarship, 86, 97, 103, 105,

INDEX

108, 188, 195, 208, 210, 220, 228, 233, 275, 382
Purcell, Henry, 93
Pygmalion (Freed), 201

Quaboag Quickstep, 44
Quaile, Elizabeth, 226
Quebec (Branscombe), 73
Queens College, 107
Queen's Hall (London), 25

Raab, Alexander, 187
Rachem (Mana-Zucca), 104
Radcliffe Choral Society, 110
Radio City Music Hall, 275, 318
Raff, Joseph Joachim, 12
RAINGER, RALPH (1901), *302*
   June in January, 302
   Moanin' Low, 302
   Thanks for the Memory, 302
Rain or Shine, 280
Raising of Lazarus, The (Rogers), 98
Rambling Sailor, The, 43
Ramona (Wayne), 304
Ramuntcho (Taylor), 30
Ranck, Carty, 67
Randegger, Giuseppe Aldo, 231
Randolph, Harold, 193
Rappaccini's Daughter (Hawthorne), 49
Rasse, François, 120
Ravel, Maurice, 85, 93, 128, 148, 249, 326
Raven, The (Dubensky), 189
Razz's Band, 286
RCA–Victor Company, 138, 148, 149, 150, 224
READ, GARDNER (1913), *214-215*
   Fantasy, 215
   From a Lute of Jade, 215
   Lotos Eaters, The, 215
   Painted Desert, The, 215
   Passacaglia and Fugue, 215
   Piano Sonata, 215
   Prelude and Toccata, 215
   Sketches of the City, 215
   Symphony, 214, 215
REED, OWEN, *219*
   Symphony, 219
Reger, Max, 14, 108
Reiner, Fritz, 42, 93, 220, 222, 318

Reis, Claire, 328
REISER, ALOIS (1887), *204-205*
   Cello Concerto, 204
   Erewhon, 205
   From Mt. Rainier, 205
   Gobi, 204
   Slavic Rhapsody, 205
   Sonata, 205
   String Quartets, 204, 205
   Summer Evening, A, 204
   Trios, 205
Remember (Berlin), 299
Remick & Company, J. H., 306
Republican National Convention, 319
Requiem (Giannini), 208
Requiem (Goldmark), 14
Requiem (La Violette), 184
Requiem (Lockwood), 234
Resettlement Administration, 240
Resnikoff, Vera, 180
Respighi, Ottorino, 61, 93, 230, 234
Retrospectives (Wald), 184
Revenge with Music (Schwartz), 303
Rhapsodie Nègre (Powell), 125, 272
Rhapsody in Blue (Gershwin), 306-307, 308, 309, 312
Rhapsody of St. Bernard (Smith), 46
Rheinberger, Joseph Gabriel, 11, 19, 20, 56, 69
Rhumba Symphony (McDonald), 180
Rhythmicana (Cowell), 251
Rice Institute, 100
Rickaby, Franz, 277
Ride of Paul Revere, The (Huss), 20
Riders to the Sea (Synge), 126
RIEGGER, WALLINGFORD (1885), 190, *248-250*, 254, 328, 329
   Belle Dame sans Merci, La, 249
   Dichotomy, 249
   Fantasy and Fugue, 249
   Prelude and Fugue, 249
   Scherzo, 249
   Study in Sonority, 249
   Three Canons, 249
   Trio in B minor, 249
Rimsky-Korsakoff, Nikolai, 92, 124
Ring and the Book, The (Browning), 64
Rio Rita (Tierney), 303

Rise of Rosie O'Reilly, The (Cohan), 297
Rita Coventry, 35
Ritratti (Haubiel), 101
River, The, 263
ROBERTSON, LE ROY J., 205
  Quintet, 205
Robeson, Paul, 190, 278, 319
Robin Hood (De Koven), 312
Robin Hood Dell, 25
Robinson, Bill, 294
ROBINSON, EARL (1910), 319
  Ballad for Americans, 319
  People, Yes, The, 319
Robinson, Edwin Arlington, 166
Robinson, Franklin, 93
Rochester Civic Orchestra, 195
Rochester Philharmonic Orchestra, 93, 98, 187, 195, 215, 249
Rockefeller Foundation, 145
Rock of Liberty, The (R. Cole), 67
Rococo Suite (Saar), 20
RODGERS, RICHARD (1902), 302
  Connecticut Yankee, A, 302
  Dearest Enemy, 302
  Girl Friend, The, 302
  Heads Up, 302
  Higher and Higher, 302
  On Your Toes, 302
Rodzinski, Artur, 148, 220, 221, 281
ROGERS, BERNARD (1893), 97-98, 214, 216
  Adonis, 98
  Colors of War, The, 98
  Dance of Salome, 98
  Faithful, The, 97
  Five Fairy Tales, 98
  Fuji in the Sunset Glow, 97
  Marriage of Aude, The, 98
  Pastorale, 98
  Prelude to Hamlet, 98
  Raising of Lazarus, The, 98
  Second Symphony, 98
  Soliloquy, 98
  String Quartet, 98
  Supper at Emmaus, The, 98
  Third Symphony, 98
  To the Fallen, 97
  Two American Frescoes, 98
Rogers, James H., 156
Roi Arthur, Le (Strong), 22

Roldan, Amadeo, 328
Rollinat, 117
Roman Sketches (Griffes), 126, 128
Romance of Robot (Hart), 226
Romance with Double Bass (Dubensky), 189
Romantic Suite in Form of Variations (McColl), 219
Romantic Symphony (Hanson), 76
ROMBERG, SIGMUND (1887), 285, 286
  Auf Wiedersehn, 285
  Blossom Time, 285
  Lover Come Back to Me, 285
  Maytime, 285
  New Moon, 285
  Passing Show, 285
  Rosalie, 285
  Student Prince, The, 285
  Will You Remember?, 285
ROME, HAROLD J. (1908), 303
  One Big Union for Two, 303
  Sing Me a Song of Social Significance, 303
  Sunday in the Park, 303
Rome String Quartet, 96
Romeo and Juliet (Shakespeare), 210
Rondino (Copland), 149
Rondo Appassionato (Smith), 46
Roosevelt, Theodore, 65, 297
Rosalie (C. Porter), 302
Rosalie (Romberg), 285
Rosary, The (Nevin), 48, 65
Rose, Billy, 313
Rose Marie (Friml), 285
Rosemary (Thompson), 111
Rosen, Lucie Bigelow, 104
Rosenfeld, Paul, 115, 116, 136-137, 151
Rosenwald Fellowship, 280
Rossetti, Dante Gabriel, 118
Rossini, Gioacchino, 222, 244, 262, 316
Roth Quartet, 88
Rothwell, Walter Henry, 109, 193
Roussel, Albert, 255
Royal Academy of Music (London), 303
Royal Academy of Music (Munich), 19, 56, 240
Royal Conservatory (Vienna), 277

# INDEX

Royal Opera (Berlin), 65
ROYCE, EDWARD (1886), 205, 208, 214
  Far Ocean, 205
  Fire-Bringer, The, 205
  Piano Variations, 205
Royce, Josiah, 205
Rubinstein, Anton Gregorovich, 12
RUBINSTEIN, BERYL (1898), 101-102
  Passepied, 102
  Scherzo, 102
  Second Piano Concerto, 101, 102
  Sleeping Beauty, The, 101, 102
  Suite, 102
Rubios, Los (M. Moore), 73
RUDHYAR, DANE (1895), 252-253, 326
  Cosmophony, 253
  Hero Chants, 253
  Ouranos, 253
  Paean to the Great Thunder, 253
  Poèmes Ironiques, 252
  Sinfonietta, 253
  Surge of Fire, The, 253
  Symphony, 253
  To the Real, 253
  Vision Végétale, 252
RUDIN, HERMAN, 219
  Impressionistic Suite, 219
  Quartet, 219
  Suite, 219
  Symphonic Fragments, 219
Rudolph Gott (Farwell), 132
Rüfer, Philippe Bartholomé, 126
RUGGLES, CARL (1876), 241-243, 256, 326, 328
  Men and Mountains, 243
  Portals, 243
  Sun Treader, 243
Rush Hour in Hong Kong (Chasins), 91
Russell, "Pee Wee," 294
Russian Bells (Dubensky), 189
Russian Lullaby (Berlin), 299
Russians (Mason), 42
Russian Symphony Orchestra, 126
Rybner, Cornelius, 20, 248, 276

SAAR, LOUIS VICTOR (1868-1937), 19-20

Along the Columbia River, 20
From the Mountain Kingdom of the Great North West, 20
Rococo Suite, 20
Sabbath Evening Service (Jacobi), 169
Sachs, Curt, 346
Sacre du Printemps, Le (Stravinsky), 151, 252
Sacred Service (Bloch), 120
Sacrifice, The (Converse), 53
Safie (Hadley), 24
Saga of the Prairie (Copland), 146
Sahdji (Still), 281
St. Joan (Shaw), 210
St. Louis Blues (Handy), 267, 293
St. Louis Chamber Orchestra, 162
St. Louis Exposition (1904), 131
St. Louis Orchestra, 84, 204
St. Paul's School, 24
St. Petersburg Conservatory, 240
Saint-Saëns, Charles Camille, 19
St. Scholastica, College of, 183
Saints' Days (Spelman), 206
Salammbô's Invocation to Tanith (Gilbert), 126
Sally (Kern), 300
Salome (Hadley), 25
Salón México, El (Copland), 149
Salzburg Chamber Music Festival, 156
SALZEDO, CARLOS (1885), 174, 253-254, 326, 328
  Concerto, 253
  Enchanted Isle, The, 253
  Pentacle, 253
  Préambule et Jeux, 253-254
  Sonata, 254
Samaroff, Olga, 210
SAMINSKY, LAZARE (1882), 143, 164-167, 326, 327
  Ausonia, 166
  Gagliarda of the Merry Plague, 165, 166
  Pueblo—A Moon Rhapsody, 166
  Stilled Pageant, 166
  Three Shadows, 166
  To a Young World, 166
Samson and Delilah (Saint-Saëns), 19
Sand (Howe), 193
Sandburg, Carl, 55, 319
Sandby, Hermann, 273

SANDERS, ROBERT L. (1906), 101, 229-230
   Cello and Piano Sonata, 230
   Little Symphony in G, 229-230
   Saturday Night, 230
   Scenes of Poverty and Toil, 230
   String Quartet, 230
   Suite for Large Orchestra, 230
   Trio, 230
   Violin and Piano Sonata, 230
   Violin Concerto, 230
San Francisco Conservatory of Music, 121, 235
San Francisco People's Symphony Orchestra, 305
San Francisco Symphony Orchestra, 24, 102, 179, 248, 343
Sanjuan, Pedro, 328
San Juan Capistrano (McDonald), 181
Sanromá, Jesús María, 57, 58, 59
Santa Barbara School, 233
Santa Fe Trail (McDonald), 180
Sarabande (McPhee), 190
Sarah Lawrence College, 225, 226
Saratoga Spa Music Festival, 191, 223
Sargeant, Winthrop, 289-290, 296
Satie, Erik, 261
Satirical Suite (Hruby), 219
Saturday Evening Post, The, 325
Saturday Night (Sanders), 230
Saturday's Child (Whithorne), 158
Scalero, Rosario, 101, 103, 220, 222, 260, 264
Scarecrow, The (MacKaye), 54
Scarlet Letter, The (Damrosch), 17, 283
Scarlet Letter, The (Giannini), 208, 209
Scenes of Poverty and Toil (Sanders), 230
Schalk, Franz, 200
Scharwenka, Franz Xaver, 74
Schaun, George, 52
Scheel, Fritz, 54
Scheherazade (Rimsky-Korsakov), 15
SCHELLING, ERNEST (1876–1939), 62-63, 95, 112
   Impressions from an Artist's Life, 63
   Légende Symphonique, 63
   Morocco, 63
   Suite Fantastique, 63

   Suite Varié, 63
   Symphony in C minor, 63
   Victory Ball, A, 63
   Violin Concerto, 63
Schelomo (Bloch), 120, 121
Scherzo (Riegger), 249
Scherzo (Woltmann), 216
Scherzo Diabolique (Hadley), 26
SCHILLINGER, JOSEPH (1895), 240-241
   Symphonic Rhapsody, 241
Schillings, Max von, 61
Schirmer, Rudolph, 344
Schirmer, Inc., G., 119, 130, 191, 234, 344
Schmidt, Johann Christoph, 181
Schmitz, E. Robert, 254
Schnabel, Artur, 178
Schoenberg, Arnold, 127, 134, 165, 195, 202, 217, 233, 242, 244, 248, 252, 254, 259, 264, 346
Schola Cantorum (New York), 22, 90, 199
Schola Cantorum (Paris), 255, 302
School Days (Edwards), 301
School of Modern Art, 185
Schreker, Franz, 71
Schubert, Franz Peter, 19
Schubert Centennial Contest, 101
SCHUMAN, WILLIAM (1910), 225-226
   American Festival Overture, 225
   First Symphony, 225
   Prelude and Fugue, 225
   Second Symphony, 225
   String Quartets, 225
   This Is Our Time, 225-226
Schumann, Robert, 42, 132, 287
Schumann-Heink, Ernestine, 54
SCHWARTZ, ARTHUR (1900), 303
   American Jubilee, 303
   Band Wagon, 303
   Dancing in the Dark, 303
   Flying Colors, 303
   Revenge with Music, 303
   Something to Remember You By, 303
   You and the Night and the Music, 303
Scientific Creation (A. L. Engel), 212
Scott, Cyril, 273

INDEX

Scriabin, Alexander, 42
Sea, The (Oldberg), 69-70
Sea Burial (Lane), 71
Sea Drift (Carpenter), 39
Sea Drift (Delius), 39
Sea-drift (Whitman), 140
Sea of Heaven, The (Hammond), 164
SEARCH, FREDERICK PRESTON (1889), *107-108*
  Bridge Builders, The, 108
  Cello Concerto, 108
  Cello Sonatas, 108
  Dream of McCorkle, The, 108
  Exhilaration, 108
  Festival Overture, 108
  Piano Quintet, 108
  Piano Septet, 108
  Rhapsody, 108
  Sextet in F minor, 108
  String Quartets, 108
Sea Rovers, The (Spelman), 206
Sea-Symphony (James), 173
Sea Symphony (Vaughan Williams), 39
Seattle Symphony Orchestra, 24
Second Hurricane, The (Copland), 146, 147, 283
Secular Mass (Nordoff), 209-210
Seeger, Charles, 240, 241, 250
Seeonee Wolves, The (F. A. Johnson), 269
Selections from McGuffey's Reader (Phillips), 216-217
Sennett, Mack, 301
Sentimental Promenades (Wald), 184
Sentimental Sketches (Mason), 45
Serafin, Tullio, 79
Serenade (Alessandro), 218
Serenade (Donovan), 163
Serenade (Josten), 178
Serenade (Keller), 219
Serenade (Mason), 45
Serenade (Sowerby), 81
Serenade to a Beauteous Lady (Gruenberg), 154
SERLY, TIBOR (1900), *234-235*
  String Quartet, 235
  Symphonic Movements, 235
  Symphony, 235
  Viola Concerto, 235
  Violin Sonata, 235

SESSIONS, ROGER (1896), 147-148, *169-171*, 208, 213, 215, 227, 232, 340
  Black Maskers, The, 170
  Choral Preludes, 170
  Dirges, 171
  First Symphony, 170
  Piano Sonata, 170
  Second Symphony, 171
  String Quartet, 171
  Third Symphony, 171
  Violin Concerto, 171
Set of Four, A (Sowerby), 81
Set of Three, A (Powell), 270-271
Set of Three Pastels (Stringham), 107
Sevitzky, Fabien, 58
Shakespeare, William, 188
Shanewis (Cadman), 48, 49
Sharp, Cecil, 277
Sheep and Goat Walkin' to Pasture (Guion), 277
Shelley, Harry Rowe, 268
SHEPHERD, ARTHUR (1880), *181-183*
  City in the Sea, 181
  Dance Episodes on an Exotic Theme, 182
  Horizons, 182-183
  Ouverture Joyeuse, 182
  Piano Sonata, 181
  Song of the Pilgrims, The, 181-182
  String Quartet, 181
  Symphony No. 2, 183
  Triptych, 181
Shepherd's Hey (Grainger), 273
Shingandi (Guion), 277
Ship of the Desert, The (Miller), 50
Showboat (Kern), 299-300, 314
Show Is On, The, 198
Show Piece (McBride), 225
Shrine Civic Auditorium, 73
Shuffle Along, 280
Shylock (La Violette), 184
Sibelius, Jean, 12, 94, 96, 346
Siegel, Rudolf, 177
SIEGMEISTER, ELIE (1909), *213*
  Hip-Hip Hooray for the NRA, 213
  May Day, 213
Sierra Morena (Whithorne), 158
Sights and Sounds (Bennett), 314
Siloti, Alexander, 264

Silva, Giulio, 235
Simon, Robert A., 83, 84, 209, 315
Simon Legree (D. Moore), 88
Sinbad the Sailor, 306
Sinding, Christian, 203
Sinfonia Concertante (Giorni), 201
Sinfonietta (Berezowsky), 184
Sinfonietta (Chadwick), 11
Sinfonietta (Rudhyar), 253
Sinfonietta (Wagenaar), 176. See also Symphonietta
Sing for Your Supper, 319
Sing Me a Song of Social Significance (Rome), 303
Siren Song, The (Taylor), 31
Skating Pond, The (Herrmann), 211
Skeleton in Armor, The (A. Foote), 13
Sketches of the City (Read), 215
SKILTON, CHARLES SANFORD (1868), 268-269, 332
　Communion Service in G, 268
　Day of Gayomair, The, 269
　Deer Dance, 268-269
　Kalopin, 269
　Suite Primeval, 269
　Sun Bride, The, 269
　War Dance, 268-269
Skyscrapers (Carpenter), 35, 37-38, 114
Slavic Rhapsody (Reiser), 205
Sleeping Beauty, The (Rubinstein), 101, 102
Sleepy Hollow (Lane), 71
SLONIMSKY, NICOLAS (1895), 138, 159-160, 169-170, 256-257, 328, 329
　Fragment from Orestes, 257
　Suite in Black and White, 256
Smallens, Alexander, 226
Smith, Alfred E., 298
Smith, Bessie, 294-295
SMITH, DAVID STANLEY (1877), 45-47, 86, 162
　Cathedral Prelude, 46
　Fête Galante, 46
　First Symphony, 46
　Flowers, 46
　Fourth Symphony, 46
　Impressions, 46
　Merry Mount, 45-46
　1929—A Satire, 46

Prince Hal, 46
Rhapsody of St. Bernard, 46
Rondo Appassionato, 46
Second Symphony, 46
Sinfonietta, 46
Sonatas, 46
Sonatina, 46
String Quartets, 46-47
Third Symphony, 46
Tomorrow, 46
Vision of Isaiah, 46
Smith, George Henry Lovett, 143-144
SMITH, JULIA (1911), 213
　Cynthia Parker, 213
Smith College, 163, 170, 177, 178, 201, 227, 228, 269, 346
Smoke and Steel (Donovan), 163
Société française de musicologie, 119
Society for the Publication of American Music, 20, 42, 46, 47, 59, 60, 104, 106, 107-108, 161, 168, 176, 181, 196, 201, 205, 206, 209, 213, 254, 383-384
Society of American Singers, 24
SODERLUND, GUSTAVE, 219
　Symphonic Interlude, 219
Sokoloff, Nikolai, 42
Solari (Haubiel), 101
Soliloquy (Rogers), 98
Solitude (Ellington), 292
Solitude (Koutzen), 203
Solitude (Wilman), 233
Something to Remember You By (Schwartz), 303
Sonata da Camera (Forst), 200
Sonata da Chiesa (Thomson), 260
Sonata Noble (Powell), 272
Sonata Sacra (Brant), 260
Sonate Virginianesque (Powell), 272
Sonatine (Citkowitz), 227
Song and Dance (Wessel), 195
Song Cycle to Words of Joyce (Citkowitz), 227
Song for Occupations (Harris), 140
Song of Faith (Carpenter), 38-39
Song of Hiawatha, The (Braine), 105
Song of Jael, The (Daniels), 72
Song of Songs (Grimm), 201-202
Song of the Night (James), 172
Song of the Pilgrims, The (Shepherd), 181-182

INDEX

Song of Welcome (Mrs. Beach), 16
Song of Youth, A (Clapp), 61
Songs for Autumn (Woltmann), 216
Songs of Conquest (McDonald), 179, 181
Songs of Protest (Citkowitz), 227
Song Writers' Protective Association, 342
Sonneck, Oscar George, 119
Sonny Boy (Henderson), 302
Sonzogno, Edoardo, 197
Sooner and Later (Whithorne), 158
Sophocles, 258, 269
Sorcerer's Apprentice, The (Dukas), 26
Sorrow of Mydah (Griffes), 128
S.O.S. (Braine), 105
Soundpieces (Becker), 183
Sousa, John Philip, 287, 332, 333, 335
Southern California, University of, 252
Southern Symphony (Britain), 232
South Wind (Maganini), 103
SOWERBY, LEO (1895), 80-82, 327, 340
  Ballad, 82
  Comes Autumn Time, 81
  Concerto, 82
  First Piano Concerto, 82
  Fourth String Quartet, 82
  From the Northland, 82
  Irish Washerwoman, The, 82
  Medieval Poem, 82
  Money Musk, 82
  Pageant of Autumn, 82
  Passacaglia, Interlude and Fugue, 82
  Prairie, 80-81
  Quintet, 80, 82
  Second Piano Concerto, 82
  Serenade, 81
  Set of Four, A, 81
  Sinfonietta, 82
  Sonata, 82
  Suite for violin and piano, 81-82
  Symphony in G, 82
  Trio, 81
  Vision of Sir Launfal, The, 82
SPALDING, ALBERT (1888), 53, 112, 169, 280
  String Quartet, 112
  Suite, 112
  Violin Concertos, 112

  Violin Sonata, 112
Spalding, Walter Raymond, 110
Spanish-American War, 5
Spanish Earth, 265
Speed (Eppert), 194
SPELMAN, TIMOTHY MATHER (1891), 205-206
  Barbaresques, 206
  Christ and the Blind Man, 206
  Dawn in the Woods, 206
  Pervigilium Veneris, 206
  Saints' Days, 206
  Sea Rovers, The, 206
  Symphony in G minor, 206
Spiering, Theodore, 67
Spring in Heaven (McCollin), 74
Spring Pastoral (Howe), 193
Springs of Saratoga (Nevin), 66
Stadium Concerts (N.Y. Philharmonic-Symphony Orchestra), 21, 135, 281
Stardust (Carmichael), 301
Stars (Howe), 193
Statements (Copland), 149
State of Music, The (Thomson), 263-264
Station WGZBX (James), 172
Stein, Gertrude, 261, 263
STEINERT, ALEXANDER LANG (1900), 206
  Concerto Sinfonico, 206
  Leggenda Sinfonica, 206
  Nuit Méridionale, 206
  Sonata, 206
  Three Poems by Shelley, 206
  Trio, 206
Sternberg, Constantin von, 258
Stevenson, Robert Louis, 57, 126
Stevensoniana, No. 1 (Hill), 56
Stevensoniana, No. 2 (Hill), 56-57
STILL, WILLIAM GRANT (1895), 280-282, 326
  Africa, 281
  Afro-American Symphony, 281
  And They Lynched Him on a Tree, 281-282
  Blue Steel, 281
  Darker America, 281
  From the Journal of a Wanderer, 281
  From the Land of Dreams, 280-281

STILL, WILLIAM GRANT (Cont.)
   Guiablesse, La, 281
   Kaintuck, 281
   Lenox Avenue, 281
   Sahdji, 281
   Symphony in G minor, 281
   Troubled Island, 281
Stilled Pageant (Saminsky), 166
Stock, Frederick, 46, 63, 67, 68, 69, 279, 281, 343
Stoeckel, Mrs. Carl, 26
STOESSEL, ALBERT (1894), 72, 82-84, 114, 176
   Concerto Grosso, 83
   Garrick, 83-84
   Suite Antique, 82
Stojowski, Sigismond, 233
Stokes, Richard L., 77, 78, 254, 256
Stokowski, Leopold, 42, 63, 92, 94, 112, 148, 160, 177, 188, 193, 195, 210, 217, 249, 279, 281, 318, 343
STRANG, GERALD (1908), 251-252
   Incidental Music for a Satirical Play, 252
   Mirrorrorrim, 252
   Passacaglia, 252
   Percussion Music, 252
   Quintet, 252
   String Quartets, 252
   Suite, 252
   Vanzetti in the Death House, 252
Strasbourg, University of, 19
Straus, Oskar, 285
Strauss, Richard, 65, 154, 159, 244, 255, 258
Stravinsky, Igor, 39, 42, 85, 134, 148, 151, 154, 177, 244, 252, 259, 261, 326, 346
Streets of Florence (Johnson), 99
Streets of Pekin, The (Hadley), 25
Strike Up the Band (Gershwin), 306
STRINGFIELD, LAMAR (1897), 275-276
   From the Southern Mountains, 275
   Indian Legend, 275
   Legend of John Henry, The, 275-276
   Moods of the Moonshiner, 275
   Negro Parade, 276
   Thirty and One Folk-Songs from the Southern Mountains, 276
STRINGHAM, EDWIN JOHN (1890), 107
   Concert Overture, 107
   Nocturne, 107
   Notturno, 107
   Quartet, 107
   Set of Three Pastels, 107
   Symphonic Poems, 107
   Symphony, 107
String Quartet on Indian Themes (Jacobi), 167
String Quartet on Negro Themes (Mason), 42
STRONG, GEORGE TEMPLETON (1856), 21-22
   American Sketches, 22
   Chorale on a Theme by Hassler, 21
   Nacht, Die, 21
   Roi Arthur, Le, 22
STRUBE, GUSTAV (1867), 51-52, 189, 193
   Americana, 52
   Captive, The, 52
   Divertimento, 52
   Sinfonietta, 52
   Sylvan Suite, 52
   Symphonic Prologue, 52
   Symphony in G, 52
   Violin Concertos, 52
Student Prince, The (Romberg), 285
Study in Sonority (Riegger), 249
Stumbling (Confrey), 301
Stuttgart Symphony Orchestra, 76
SUESSE, DANA (1911), 313
   Concerto in E minor, 313
   Jazz Concerto, 313
   Symphonic Waltzes, 313
   Two Irish Fairy Tales, 313
Suite after English Folk-Songs (Mason), 43
Suite after Reading "The Woman of Andros" (Hammond), 164
Suite Anno 1600 (Dubensky), 189
Suite Antique (Stoessel), 82
Suite Fantastique (Schelling), 63
Suite in Black and White (Slonimsky), 256
Suite Passecaille (Haubiel), 101
Suite Primeval (Skilton), 269

INDEX

Suite to the Children (Bacon), 188
Suite Varié (Schelling), 63
Sullivan, Arthur, 262, 294
Sullivan, Joe, 295
Summer Evening, A (Reiser), 204
Sun Bride, The (Skilton), 269
Sunday in the Park (Rome), 303
Sunny (Kern), 300
Sunset Trail, The (Cadman), 49
Sun Splendor (Bauer), 192
Sun Treader (Ruggles), 243
Supper at Emmaus, The (Rogers), 98
Surge of Fire, The (Rudhyar), 253
Susannah, Don't You Cry (C. Loomis), 71
Swanee (Gershwin), 306
Swanee River (Foster), 92
Swarthout, Gladys, 79
Sweet Adeline (Kern), 300
Sweet and Lowdown (Gershwin), 306
Sweethearts (Herbert), 335
Sweet Little Alice Blue Gown (Tierney), 303
Swift & Company, 101, 232, 234
Swing, Raymond Gram, 321
Swing Stuff (McBride), 224
Swing Symphonettes (Gould), 319
Swing that Thing! (Brooks), 301
'S Wonderful (Gershwin), 306
Swords (Howard), 61
Sylvan Suite (Strube), 52
Sylvan Symphony (Maganin), 103
Symphonic Ballade (Pimsleur), 204
Symphonic Episode (Fuleihan), 192
Symphonic Fantasia (Hadley), 25
Symphonic Fragments (Rudin), 219
Symphonic Hymn on March! March! (Farwell), 131
Symphonic Interlude (Soderlund), 219
Symphonic Intermezzo (Galajikian), 230
Symphonic Ode (Copland), 148, 149, 150
Symphonic Piece (Piston), 160
Symphonic Prelude (R. Cole), 67
Symphonic Prelude in American Idiom (McKay), 204
Symphonic Prologue (Strube), 52
Symphonic Rhapsody (Schillinger), 241
Symphonic Sketches (Chadwick), 11

Symphonic Sketches (Kramer), 104
Symphonic Song on Old Black Joe (Farwell), 131
Symphonic Waltzes (Suesse), 313
Symphonietta (Forst), 200
    See also Sinfonietta
Symphonischer Chor, 255
Symphony 1933 (Harris), 137-138, 139, 140
Symphony Concertante (Fuleihan), 192
Symphony Concertante (Phillips), 217
Symphony Concertante (Wessel), 195
Symphony for Voices (Harris), 140-141
Symphony in Memoriam Theodore Roosevelt (Giannini), 208
Symphony in Miniature (Haines), 219
Symphony in One Movement (Barber), 220-221
Symphony in Steel (Grofé), 312
Symphony of Autumn (D. Moore), 85, 87
Symphony of the City, A (Eppert), 194
Symphony on a Hymn Tune (Thomson), 263
Symphony on Canadian Airs (Helfer), 61
Symphony Society of New York, 18, 19, 34
Synchrony (Cowell), 251
Synge, John Millington, 126
Syracuse University, 72
Szigeti, Joseph, 121, 293

Taft School, 163
Taggard, Genevieve, 225
Tagore, Rabindranath, 99, 100
Take Me Down Where the Würzburger Flows (H. von Tilzer), 297
Take Your Choice, 187
Tall Story (Moross), 213
Tame Animal Tunes (Bingham), 90
Tamiris, 250
Tammany (Edwards), 301
Tanglewood School, 148
Tapper, Mrs. Thomas, 91
Taubman, Howard, 214, 282

TAYLOR, DEEMS (1885), 27-35, 47, 312, 340
  Casanova, 35
  Chambered Nautilus, The, 31
  Circus Days, 34, 312
  Highwayman, The, 31
  Jurgen, 34
  King's Henchman, The, 27, 30, 31-32
  Lucrece, 35
  Peter Ibbetson, 28, 29, 30, 32-34
  Portrait of a Lady, The, 31, 34
  Ramuntcho, 30
  Siren Song, The, 31
  Through the Looking Glass, 27, 30, 31
Tea for Two (Youmans), 304
Teagarden, Jack, 295
Tempest, The (Shakespeare), 188
TEMPLETON, ALEC (1910), 303
  Bach Goes to Town, 303
  Mendelssohn Mows 'em Down, 303
  Tennessee Devil Tunes (Gaul), 72
TERRY, FRANCES, 73-74
  Ballade Hongroise, 74
  Idyls of an Inland Sea, 74
  Impromptu Appassionato, 74
  Sonata, 73-74
Texas, University of, 100
Thanks for the Memory (Rainger), 302
That Certain Feeling (Gershwin), 306
Theater Guild, 34, 93, 158, 309
Theater Sheet (Braine), 105-106
Theme and Variations (Mrs. Beach), 16
Theme and Variations on the Old Gray Mare (Britain), 232
Theremin, Leon, 251
There's a Boat that's Leavin' Soon for New York (Gershwin), 310
Thirty and One Folk-Songs from the Southern Mountains (Stringfield), 276
This Is Our Time (Schuman), 225-226
Thomas, John Charles, 25, 79
Thomas, Theodore, 19, 116, 199
Thompson, Oscar, 89-90, 316-317
THOMPSON, RANDALL (1899), 109-111, 325
  Americana, 111
  Jazz Poem, 110
  Peaceable Kingdom, The, 110-111
  Pierrot and Cothurnus, 110
  Piper at the Gates of Dawn, The, 110
  Rosemary, 111
  Second Symphony, 109-110
  Suite, 111
THOMSON, VIRGIL (1896), 145, 226, 260-264, 265, 291-292
  Capitals, Capitals, 261
  Four Saints in Three Acts, 261-263
  Sonata da Chiesa, 260
  Symphony, 263
  Symphony on a Hymn Tune, 263
Thoreau, Henry David, 246
Three Cherry Trees, The (Johnson), 98
Three Dances (Mourant), 219
Three Imitations (Donato), 218
Three Moods (Cesana), 318
Three Moods for Dancing (W. Barlow), 217
Three Movements (Crawford), 240
Three Orchestral Fragments (James), 219
Three Palestinian Pastels (Gaul), 72
Three Pennsylvania Portraits (Gaul), 72
Three Persian Poems (Bornschein), 72
Three Poems by Shelley (Steinert), 206
Three Poems from Walt Whitman (Hanson), 77
Three's a Crowd, 199, 303
Three Shades of Blue (Grofé), 312
Three Shadows (Saminsky), 166
Three Songs (Crawford), 240
Through the Looking Glass (Taylor), 27, 30, 31
Through the Pyrenees (Cella), 107
Thuille, Ludwig, 120
Thunderbird Suite (Cadman), 49
Thy Dark Hair (Johnson), 98
Tibbett, Lawrence, 34, 64, 79
TIERNEY, HARRY (1890), 303
  Irene, 303
  Rio Rita, 303
  Sweet Little Alice Blue Gown, 303
Time Suite (Harris), 141-142, 146
To a Nordic Princess (Grainger), 274

INDEX

To a Vanishing Race (Cadman), 50
To a Young World (Saminsky), 166
Toccata, Variations and Finale (Berezowsky), 185
Tomorrow (Smith), 46
Tom Sawyer Overture (Dubensky), 189
Toscanini, Arturo, 21, 176, 203, 221
To Silvanus (Inch), 202
To the Fallen (Gardner), 105
To the Fallen (Rogers), 97
To the Real (Rudhyar), 253
Tovey, Donald Francis, 272
Town Hall (New York), 22, 104, 198, 247
To Youth (White), 195
Traditions (A. L. Engel), 212
Traffic (Eppert), 194
Tragic Cycle (McDonald), 181
Tragic Overture (Galajikian), 230
Tragödie in Arezzo; see Caponsacchi
Tramp, Tramp, Tramp, 123
Transatlantic (Antheil), 258-259
Transitions (Galajikian), 230
Trans-Mississippi Exposition, 16
Trask, Spencer, 333
Triakontameron (Godowsky), 113
Tribute to Foster (Grainger), 273
Triple-Sec (Blitzstein), 264
Triptych (C. Engel), 119
Triptych (Giannini), 209
Triptych (Nordoff), 210
Triptych (Shepherd), 181
Triptyque (Freed), 201
Tristan und Isolde (Wagner), 15, 28, 31
Triumph of St. Patrick, The (Yon), 112
Trois Poèmes Juifs (Bloch), 120, 121
Troubled Island (Still), 281
Tschaikowsky, Peter Ilyich, 19
Tufts College, 26
Tuolumne (Maganini), 103
Tureck, Rosalyn, 209
Turkey in the Straw (Guion), 271, 274, 277
Tuskegee Institute, 279
TUTHILL, BURNET C. (1888), 206
  Bethlehem, 206
  Come Seven, 206
  Dr. Joe, 206
  Laurentia, 206
  Sextet, 206
  Sonata, 206
  Symphonic Overture, 206
Twain, Mark, 189
TWEEDY, DONALD (1890), 61
  Alice in Wonderland, 61
  Allegro, L', 61
  Dances, 61
Twelfth Night (Shakespeare), 226
Twentieth Century Club, 126
Twentieth Century Music (Bauer), 193
Twilight (Nevin), 66
Two American Frescoes (Rogers), 98
Two Blues (Copland), 149
Two Choric Dances (Creston), 231
Two Dances for Radio (Q. Porter), 162
Two Impressions of Rome (Woltmann), 216
Two Irish Fairy Tales (Suesse), 313
Two Magicians, The, 43
Two Movements (Crawford), 240

Ukrainian Suite (Q. Porter), 161
Uncle Remus (Harris), 125
Union Theological Seminary, 107
United States George Washington Bicentennial Commission, 38

Vagabond King, The (Friml), 285
Vagrom Ballad (Chadwick), 11
Valley Forge (Koutzen), 203
Valley of Dry Bones (Binder), 218
Van der Stucken, Frank, 201
Vanity Fair, 263
VAN VACTOR, DAVID (1906), 231-232
  Chaconne, 232
  Concerto, 232
  Concerto Grosso, 232
  Cristobal Colon, 232
  Masque of the Red Death, 232
  Overture to a Comedy, 232
  Passacaglia and Fugue in D minor, 232
  Play of Words, The, 232
  Symphony in D, 231-232
Van Vechten, Carl, 262

Vanzetti in the Death House (Strang), 252
VARDELL, CHARLES, 219
  Folk Symphony from the Carolina Hills, 219
  Joe Clark Steps Out, 219
VARÈSE, EDGAR (1885), 190, 243, 254-256, 280, 281, 326, 328, 329
  Amériques, 256
  Arcana, 256
  Density 21.5, 256
  Equatorial, 256
  Espace, 256
  Hyperprism, 254, 256
  Intégrales, 256
  Ionisation, 256
  Octandre, 256
  Offrandes, 254, 256
Variations in Oblique Harmony (Brant), 260
Variations on a Modal Theme (Inch), 203
Variations on an Old English Folk-tune (Woltmann), 216
Variations on an Original Theme (Diamond), 216
Variations on a Pious Theme (G. Foote), 218
Variations on a Theme by John Powell (Mason), 42
Variations on a Theme in Medieval Style (Fickenscher), 240
Variations on a Theme of Paganini (Baum), 218
Variations on a Theme of Robert Schumann (Menotti), 223
Variations on Mary Had a Little Lamb (Ballantine), 60
Variety, 340
Vassar College, 61, 162
Vaughan Williams, Ralph, 39
Veillées de l'Ukraine, Les (Loeffler), 117
Venetian Fantasy (Harling), 202
Venetian Glass Nephew, The (Bonner), 198
Vengerova, Isabella, 257
Venice Festival, 196
Verdi, Giuseppe, 222
Verlaine, Paul, 118
Vibrations (Freed), 201

Victor Record Review, 144
Victory Ball, A (Schelling), 63
Vienna Conservatory, 13
Vienna Gesellschaft der Musikfreunde, 208
Villa-Lobos, Hector, 249
Villanelle du Diable, La (Loeffler), 118
Villa of Dreams (Daniels), 72
Virgil (Publius Virgilius Maro), 117
Virginia, University of, 239
Virginia State Choral Festival, 270, 276
Vision of Isaiah (Smith), 46
Vision of Sir Launfal, The (Sowerby), 82
Vision Végétale (Rudhyar), 252
Vitamins (Eppert), 194
Vitebsk (Copland), 145, 149
Voice in the Wilderness (Bloch), 120
VON TILZER, ALBERT (1878), 297
  Forever Is a Long Time, 297
  I'll Be with You in Apple-blossom Time, 297
VON TILZER, HARRY (1872), 297
  I Want a Girl, 297
  Take Me Down Where the Würzburger Flows, 297
  Wait Till the Sun Shines, Nellie, 297
Voorhees, Don, 280
Vox Cathedralis (Haubiel), 101
Voyage of the Mayflower, The (White), 195
Voyage to the East (Hammond), 164

WAGENAAR, BERNARD (1894), 14, 174-176, 254
  Divertimento, 176
  First Symphony, 175-176
  Second Symphony, 175-176
  Sinfonietta, 176
  Sonata, 176
  Sonatina, 176
  String Quartets, 176
  Third Symphony, 176
  Triple Concerto, 174-175
Wagner, Oscar, 325
Wagner, Wilhelm Richard, 3, 12, 19, 28, 30, 32, 33, 52, 65, 92, 175, 222, 254, 266

INDEX

Wagon Wheels (Billy Hill), 302
Wait Till the Sun Shines, Nellie (H. Von Tilzer), 297
WALD, MAX (1889), *183-184*
   Comedy Overture, 184
   Dancer Dead, The, 184
   Mirandolina, 184
   Retrospectives, 184
   Sentimental Promenades, 184
Waller, Thomas ("Fats"), 295
Wall Street Fantasy (Bingham), 90
Walter, Bruno, 43
Wanamaker, Rodman, 279
War Dance (Skilton), 268-269
Warner Brothers Studios, 204
WARREN, HARRY (1893), *304*
   Cheerful Little Earful, 304
   I Found a Million Dollar Baby, 304
   Where Do You Work-a John?, 304
   Would You Like to Take a Walk?, 304
Washburn College, 279
Washington, Chas., 286
Washington, George, 87
Washington, University of, 203, 319
Wastin' Time (Bacon), 188
Watchman, What of the Night? (Heller), 106
Water Idyl (Helfer), 61
Wa-Wan Press, 124, 129-130, 269
WAYNE, MABEL (1898), *304*
   Chiquita, 304
   In a Little Spanish Town, 304
   Ramona, 304
We (Dunn), 21
Weber, Carl Maria von, 28
Webster, Daniel, 89
Wedge, George A., 325
Weidig, Adolf, 240, 248
Weidman, Charles, 250
Weigl, Karl, 187
Weill, Kurt, 346
WEINER, LAZAR, *219*
   Dance, 219
   Little Story, 219
   Prelude, 219
WEISS, ADOLPH (1891), *248*, 328
   American Life, 248
   Ballade, 248
   David, 248
   Five Pieces, 248

   Kammersymphonie, 248
   Libation Bearers, 248
   String Quartets, 248
   Theme and Variations, 248
Welles, Orson, 265
Wellesley College, 110
Wellesz, Egon, 202
Werrenrath, Reinald, 42
WESSEL, MARK (1894), *195-196*
   Concertino, 195
   Holiday, 195
   King of Babylon, The, 195
   Quintet, 195
   Sextet, 195
   Song and Dance, 195
   String Quartet, 195
   Symphonic Poem, 195
   Symphony, 195
   Symphony Concertante, 195
Western College, 15
Western Landscape (Harris), 144
Western Reserve University, 102, 182
West Indian Dances (Hammond), 164
Westminster Choir, 140
Westminster Choir School, 136
Westminster Festival, 104, 200, 213, 221, 231
What Is This Thing Called Love? (C. Porter), 302
What'll I Do (Berlin), 299
Wheel of Fortune, The (Hart), 226
Wheels (Grofé), 312
When Johnny Comes Marching Home (Harris), 138-140, 283
When My Baby Smiles at Me (Berlin), 299
When Pierrot Sings (Johnson), 98
When that Midnight Choo-choo Leaves for Alabam (Berlin), 299
Where Do You Work-a John? (Warren), 304
Whimsy (Howe), 193
Whispers of Heavenly Death (Bacon), 188
Whispers of Heavenly Death (Bonner), 197-198
Whistle While You Work (Churchill), 301
WHITE, CLARENCE CAMERON (1880), *280*
   Bandanna Sketches, 280

WHITE, CLARENCE C. (*Cont.*)
  Negro Rhapsody, 280
  Nobody Knows the Trouble I've Seen, 280
  Ouanga, 280
  String Quartet, 280
White, George, 298
WHITE, PAUL (1895), *194-195*, 214
  Feuilles Symphoniques, 195
  Five Miniatures, 195
  Pagan Festival, 195
  Sinfonietta, 195
  Sonata, 195
  Symphony in E minor, 195
  To Youth, 195
  Voyage of the Mayflower, The, 195
White Enchantment (Cadman), 51
WHITEMAN, PAUL (1891), 71, 81, 105, 280, 292, 295, 305-306, 307, 312, 313
White Nights (Bonner), 197
White Peacock, The (Griffes), 126-127, 128
Whiteside, Abby, 318
White Top Folk Trails (Buchanan), 276
White Top Mountain Folk Music Festival, 270, 276
White Wings (Moore), 88
WHITHORNE, EMERSON (1884), *155-159*, 163, 327
  Dream Pedlar, The, 155, 157
  Fandango, 158
  Fata Morgana, 157
  Greek Impressions, 156, 158
  Grim Troubadour, The, 158
  Moon Trail, The, 156, 157
  New York Days and Nights, 156
  Piano Quintet, 158
  Poem, 157
  Saturday's Child, 158
  Sierra Morena, 158
  Sooner and Later, 158
  String Quartet, 158
  Symphonies, 157-158
  Violin Sonata, 158
Whiting, Arthur, 12
Whitman, Walt, 17, 39, 140, 188, 197
Who (Berlin), 29

Who's Afraid of the Big Bad Wolf? (Churchill), 301
Who's Who in America, 30
Why Do I Love You (Kern), 300
Widor, Charles Marie Jean Albert, 56, 68, 90, 163, 255
Wilderness Stone (Bingham), 90
Wild Men's Dance, The (Ornstein), 204
William Tell (Rossini), 244
Williams, Roger, 237
Willow Tree, The (Cadman), 51
Willowwave and Wellaway (Fickenscher), 240
Will Shakespeare (Dane), 35
Will You Remember? (Romberg), 285
WILSON, MORTIMER (1876-1932), *14*, 163, 226
  From My Youth, 14
  My Country, 14
  Overture "1849," 14
Wilson, Teddy, 295
WILMAN, ALLAN A. (1909), *233*
  Ballade of the Night, 233
  Piano Sonata, 233
  Solitude, 233
  Suite, 233
  Symphonic Overture, 233
Winter's Past, The (W. Barlow), 217
Wisconsin, University of, 52, 103
Wise-Apple Five (McBride), 225
Witch of Salem, The (Cadman), 49
Witek, Anton, 52
Within the Gates (O'Casey), 212
WNYC, 342-343
Woffington, Peg, 84
Wolff, Albert, 197
WOLTMANN, FREDERICK (1908), *216*
  Piano Concerto, 216
  Poem, 216
  Pool of Pegasus, The, 216
  Rhapsody, 216
  Scherzo, 216
  Songs for Autumn, 216
  Two Impressions of Rome, 216
  Variations on an Old English Folktune, 216
Woman Is a Sometime Thing, A (Gershwin), 310

INDEX

Wood-Notes (Donavan), 163
WOR, Radio Station, 318
Worcester Festival, 16, 43, 54, 72, 77, 83, 84, 181, 194, 279
Workout (McBride), 224
Works Progress Administration, 99, 212, 234, 240, 263, 265, 275, 319, 330-332
Work 22 (Delaney), 234
World War, 4, 10, 63, 86, 129, 135, 163, 167, 172, 197, 255, 297, 314, 321, 322-323, 335, 345
Would You Like to Take a Walk? (Warren), 304
WPA—*See* Works Progress Administration
Wreck of the Hesperus, The (A. Foote), 13
Wyman, Loraine, 53, 277
WYNN, YORK, 219
  Night Clouds, 219

Yaddo, 197, 227, 229, 231, 234, 249, 259, 264, 332-333
Yale Symphony Orchestra, 103
Yale University, 45, 86, 90, 103, 108, 162, 163, 170, 244, 245, 268, 346
Yankee Clipper (Bowles), 226
Yasser, Joseph (1893), 239
Year's at the Spring, The (Mrs. Beach), 16
Yeats, William Butler, 118, 258
Yellow Dog Blues (Handy), 293

Yolanda of Cyprus (C. Loomis), 70-71
YON, PIETRO (1886), *112*, 231
  Triumph of St. Patrick, The, 112
You and the Night and the Music (Schwartz), 303
YOUMANS, VINCENT (1898), *304*
  Bambolina, 304
  Great Day, 304
  Hallelujah, 304
  Hit the Deck, 304
  I Want to Be Happy, 304
  More than You Know, 304
  No, No, Nanette, 304
  Tea for Two, 304
Young Alexander, The (Bonner), 198
Young People's Concerts, 62, 112
Youth (Converse), 53
Youth and Life (Hadley), 25
Youth of the World (Branscombe), 73
Ysaÿe, Eugène, 120, 194

Zacharewitsch, Michael, 280
Zeitschrift für Musikwissenschaft, 346
Ziegfeld Follies, 198, 303
Ziehn, Bernhard, 35
ZIMBALIST, EFREM (1889), *112*
  Daphnis and Chloë, 112
  Sonata, 112
  String Quartet, 112
Zingarelli, Niccolò Antonio, 316
Zingareska (Antheil), 258
Zion in Exile (W. Barlow), 217

780.973 Howard.
H 84 ou Our
Contemporary
Composers.